SPACES OF CULTURE

Theory, Culture & Society

Theory, Culture & Society caters for the resurgence of interest in culture within contemporary social science and the humanities. Building on the heritage of classical social theory, the book series examines ways in which this tradition has been reshaped by a new generation of theorists. It also publishes theoretically informed analyses of everyday life, popular culture and new intellectual movements.

EDITOR: Mike Featherstone, *Nottingham Trent University*

SERIES EDITORIAL BOARD
Roy Boyne, *University of Durham*
Mike Hepworth, *University of Aberdeen*
Scott Lash, *Goldsmiths College, University of London*
Roland Robertson, *University of Pittsburgh*
Bryan S. Turner, *University of Cambridge*

THE TCS CENTRE
The Theory, Culture & Society book series, the journals *Theory, Culture & Society* and *Body & Society*, and related conference, seminar and postgraduate programmes operate from the TCS Centre at Nottingham Trent University. For further details of the TCS Centre's activities please contact:

Centre Administrator
The TCS Centre, Room 175
Faculty of Humanities
Nottingham Trent University
Clifton Lane, Nottingham, NG11 8NS, UK
e-mail: tcs@ntu.ac.uk
web: http://tcs@ntu.ac.uk

Recent volumes include:

Simmel on Culture: Selected Writings
edited by David Frisby and Mike Featherstone

Nation Formation
Towards a Theory of Abstract Community
Paul James

Contested Natures
Phil Macnaghten and John Urry

The Consumer Society
Myths and Structures
Jean Baudrillard

Georges Bataille – Essential Writings
edited by Michael Richardson

Digital Aesthetics
Sean Cubitt

Facing Modernity
Ambivalence, Reflexivity and Morality
Barry Smart

SPACES OF CULTURE

City, Nation, World

edited by

Mike Featherstone and Scott Lash

SAGE Publications Ltd
London • Thousand Oaks • New Delhi

Published in association with *Theory, Culture & Society*,
Nottingham Trent University

First published 1999

SAGE Publications Ltd
6 Bonhill Street
London EC2A 4PU

SAGE Publications Inc.
2455 Teller Road
Thousand Oaks, California 91320

SAGE Publications India Pvt Ltd
32, M-Block Market
Greater Kailash – I
New Delhi 110 048

British Library Cataloguing in Publication data

A catalogue record for this book is available
from the British Library

ISBN 0 7619 6121 6
ISBN 0 7619 6122 4 (pbk)

Library of Congress catalog card number 98–61590

Typeset by Mayhew Typesetting, Rhayader, Powys
Printed in Great Britain

CONTENTS

CONTRIBUTORS

Barbara Adam is Reader in Social Theory at Cardiff University. She has published extensively on socio-environmental time and is the founding editor of *Time and Society*. Her first two books were awarded book prizes. Her latest monograph *Timescapes of Modernity. The Environment and Invisible Hazards* (1998) arises from research conducted during a two-year Fellowship under the British (ESRC) Global Environmental Change Research Programme.

Göran Dahl is Professor in Sociology at Lund University. His latest books are *Psykoanalys och kulturkritik* (*Psychoanalysis and Cultural Criticism*, 1992) and *Radical Conservatism and the Future of Politics* (1999). His recent research area is the New Right, fascism and radical conservatism in Europe and the USA. This project is funded by the Bank of Sweden Tercentenary I Foundation.

Michael Dear is Director of the Southern California Studies Center and Professor of Geography at the University of Southern California. He has been a Guggenheim Fellow and a fellow at Stanford's Center for Advanced Study in the Behavioral Sciences, and has won awards for creativity in research from the Association of American Geographers and the University of Southern California.

Ron Eyerman is Professor of Sociology at Uppsala University and at the Center for Cultural Research, Växjö University. His latest books include *Music and Social Movements* (1998) and *Between Culture and Politics* (1994)

Mike Featherstone is Director of the *Theory, Culture & Society Centre* and Professor of Sociology and Communications at Nottingham Trent University, UK. He is founding editor of *Theory, Culture & Society* and the *TCS Book Series*. He is co-editor of the journal *Body & Society*. He is author of *Consumer Culture and Postmodernism* (1991) and *Undoing Culture* (1995). His edited and co-edited books include: *Global Culture* (1990), *The Body* (1991), *Global Modernities* (1995), *Cyberspace/Cyberbodies/Cyberpunk* (1995), *Images of Ageing* (1995), *Simmel on Culture* (1997) and *Love and Eroticism* (1999).

Steven Flusty is a doctoral student at the Department of Geography, University of Southern California, where he utilizes narrative commodity chains to investigate quotidian globalization. He has worked as consultant to numerous architects and public agencies, and his study of exclusionary urban design has been published by the Los Angeles Forum for Architecture and Urban Design under the title 'Building paranoia: the proliferation of interdictory space and the erosion of spatial justice'.

Jonathan Friedman is Director d'Etudes at the Ecole des Hautes Etudes en Sciences Sociales in Paris and Professor of Social Anthropology at the University of Lund, Sweden. He has written on structuralism and Marxism, theories of social transformation, the imaginary, and more recently on global processes, cultural formations and the practice of identity. His books include, *Modernity and Identity* with S. Lash (eds) (1992), *Cultural Identity and Global Process* (1994), *Consumption and Identity* (ed.) (1994), *System Structure and Contradiction in the Evolution of 'Asiatic' Social Formations* (1998).

Heidrun Friese, Berlin and Warwick, has published widely on social constructions of time and history, the anthropology of science and on social imagination. Her publications include *Lampedusa. Historische Anthropologie einer Insel* (1996), *Der Raum des Gelehrten. Eine Topographie akademischer Praxis* (with Peter Wagner, 1993), and *Identitäten* (ed. with Aleida Assmanu, 1998).

Scott Lash is Professor of Sociology at Goldsmiths College, University of London. He is the author of *Sociology of Postmodernism* (1990), and co-author of *The End of Organized Capitalism* (1987), *Economies of Signs and Space* (1993) and *Reflexive Modernization* (1994). He is co-editor of *Risk, Environment and Modernity* (1996).

Timothy W. Luke is Professor of Political Science at Virginia Polytechnic Institute and State University in Blacksburg, Virginia. His most recent books are *The Politics of Cyberspace* (co-edited with Chris Toulouse, 1998) and *Ecocritique: Contesting the Politics of Nature, Economy and Culture* (1997).

Hilary Radner is Associate Professor in the Department of Film, Television and Theater at the University of Notre Dame, USA. She is the author of *Shopping Around: Feminine Culture and the Pursuit of Pleasure* (1995), and co-editor of *Film Theory Goes to the Movies* (with Jim Collins and Ava Preacher Collins, 1993), *Constructing the New Consumer Society* (with Pekka Sulkenen, John Holmwood and Gerhard Schulze, 1997) and *Swinging Single: Representing Sexuality, the 1960s* (with Moya Luckett, 1999).

Saskia Sassen is Professor of Sociology, University of Chicago and Visiting Centennial Professor, London School of Economics. Her most recent books are *Globalization and its Discontents: Selected Essays 1984–1998.* (1998) and *Losing Control? Sovereignty in an Age of Globalization* (1996). Her books have been translated into several languages. She has just completed *Immigration Policy in the Global Economy: From National Crisis* *to Multilateral Management.* She continues work on two projects, 'Cities and their Crossborder Networks' and 'Governance and Accountability in a Global Economy.' She is a member of the Council on Foreign Relations and a Fellow of the American Bar Foundation.

Richard Sennett is Visiting Centennial Professor in the Department of Sociology at the London School of Economics and Political Science. He is author of *Flesh and Stone: The Conscience of the Eye* and *The Fall of Public Man.*

Michael J. Shapiro is Professor of Political Science at the University of Hawaii. Among his recent publications are: *Reading 'Adam Smith': Desire, History and Value* (1993), *Violent Cartographies: Mapping Cultures of War* (1997) and *Cinematic Political Thought: Narratives of Race, Nation and Gender* (1999).

Boaventura de Sousa Santos is Professor of Sociology at the School of Economics at the University of Coimbra, Portugal, Director of the Center for Social Studies at the University of Coimbra, and Visiting Professor at the University of Wisconsin-Madison, USA. His research interests include political sociology and sociology of law, epistemology, sociology of culture, counter-hegemonic globalization and participatory democracy. His publications include *O Pulsar da Revolução: Cronologia da Revolução de 25 de Abril 1973–1976* (1997), *Macau: O Pequeníssimo Dragão* (with Conceição Gomes, 1998) and *La Globalización del Derecho: Los Nuevos Caminos de la Regulación y la Emancipación* (1998).

Couze Venn teaches cultural studies and postcolonial theory at the University of East London and is a member of the editorial board of *Theory, Culture & Society.* His current research interests include the critique of modernity and postcoloniality, the theorization of subjectivity and the development of a critical phenomenology. He was a founder member of the influential journal *Ideology & Consciousness.* He is the co-author of *Changing the Subject* (1984 and 1998), and has written on various aspects of postcoloniality and on Foucault. His forthcoming work is *Occidentalism. Essays on Modernity and Subjectivity.*

Peter Wagner, Florence and Warwick, works on themes of a sociology and history of modernity in terms of both social and political institutions and intellectual discourses. His publications include *A Sociology of Modernity* (1994), *Der Raum des Gelehrten* (with Heidrun Friese, 1993), *Le travail et la nation* (co-editor, 1998), *Discourses on Society* (co-editor, 1991).

Wolfgang Welsch is Professor of Philosophy at the Friedrich-Schiller University of Jena. Visiting Professorships include the University of Erlangen-Nürnberg (1987), the Free University of Berlin (1987–1988), Humboldt University of Berlin (1992–1993), Stanford University (1994–1995) and Emory University (1998). He received the Max Planck Research Award in 1992. His research interests include philosophy of culture, epistemology, aesthetics and philosophy of the twentieth century. He is the author of *Aisthesis. Grundzüge und Perspektiven der Aristotelischen Sinneslehre* (1987), *Unsere postmoderne Moderne* (1987, 5th ed. 1997), *Ästhetisches Denken* (1990, 5th ed. 1998), *Vernunft. Die zeitgenössische Vernunftkritik und das Konzept der transversalen Vernunft* (1995), *Grenzgänge der Ästhetik* (1996), *Undoing Aesthetics* (1997). He has edited the volumes *Wege aus der Moderne. Schlüsseltexte der Postmoderne-Diskussion* (1989), *Ästhetik im Widerstreit. Interventionen zum Werk von Jean-François Lyotard* (1991), *Die Aktualität des Ästhetischen* (1993), *Medien – Welten – Wirklichkeiten* (1998).

PREFACE

The chapters in this volume are revised versions of papers initially presented at the second *Theory, Culture & Society* Conference on Culture and Identity: City/Nation/World, held at the Berlin Hilton in August 1995. We are very much aware that the conference could not have taken place without the organizational skills, patience and good humour of Hermann Schwengel. We would also like especially to thank: Barbara Cox, Lisa Gollogly and Ana Zahira Bassit, who worked non-stop on the conference desk to cope with double the number of people we anticipated attending. At the University of Teesside, Victoria Cave, Roy Boyne and other colleagues in the Centre for the Study of Adult Life were also very supportive. After the relocation of *Theory, Culture & Society* at Nottingham Trent University in May 1996, Wendy Patterson, Caroline Potter, Justin Reeson and Neal Curtis helped in various ways with the preparation of the volume. Other colleagues at the centre, especially Chris Rojek, Roger Bromley, John Tomlinson and Joost van Loon have also been very supportive. The next *Theory, Culture & Society* conference on Technological Culture is planned for Amsterdam in August 2000. Details of this and other *TCS* Network activities are available on the *TCS* homepage: http://tcs@ntu.ac.uk. Finally, we would like to thank our colleagues on the *Theory, Culture & Society* editorial board and associate editors list for all their help and support.

Mike Featherstone
Scott Lash

INTRODUCTION

Mike Featherstone and Scott Lash

If we seek to understand culture today, it is clear that we face a growing range of complexities. Culture which was assumed to possess a coherence and order, to enable it to act as the grounds for the formation of stable identities, no longer seems to be able to perform this task adequately. The linkages between culture and identity have become more problematic as the sources of cultural production and dissemination increase, and the possibilities of inhabiting a shared cultural world in which cultural meanings function in a common sense taken-for-granted manner recedes. In effect, both inside and outside the academy, we are all asked to do more cultural work today.

This can be linked to the process of globalization which, as has been pointed out many times, does not result in the homogenization and unification of culture, but rather in the provision of new spaces for the clashing of cultures (Robertson, 1992, 1995; Lash and Urry, 1993; Featherstone, 1995). The clashing and mixing of culture occurs not only across the boundaries of nation-state societies, but within them too. More voices demand to be heard and the assumed uniformity of national cultures begins to be seen as a myth. In one sense it can be argued that there have never been national cultures: it is a myth of comparable import to the myth Latour (1993) speaks about when he says 'we have never been modern'. For Latour, modernity has not been a realized or 'realizable' entity, but should be seen as a project, or better still as a projection.

The theorization of culture within sociology has been caught up in this process. As Heidrun Friese and Peter Wagner argue in their chapter in this collection, the tendency within sociology has been to move from an understanding of social life through structures and systems to a growing appreciation of the role of contingencies and uncertainties, coupled with a growing sense of cultural diversity. It is no longer adequate to conceptualize culture as an integrated whole. Rather, we are asked to focus upon the diverse and often incompatible range of cultural practices people engage in. Hence the linkages between culture and social structure and culture and action are perceived as weaker and more complex. Terms such as 'structure' and 'culture' were formerly used to point to the stability and coherence of social life: now they no longer perform the theoretical work asked of them. One of the implications here may well be to ask us to rethink the boundaries of sociology and other social science disciplines, especially if we take into account Friese and Wagner's argument that we need to develop a greater understanding of the impact of globalization on social life.

This perspective is developed further by Barbara Adam in her contribution 'Radiated Identities'. Adam argues that the attempt to understand a global event such as the Chernobyl nuclear explosion and spread of radiation challenges our classical theoretical framework. To make sense of this event necessitates going beyond the traditional separation of disciplines, and the traditional focus upon intra-societal processes. To understand Chernobyl through separate disciplines becomes impossible when we are looking at globally networked processes which transcend national boundaries and which intermesh cultural and natural processes. Radiation disregards the boundaries of bodies, locality, nation and species. Adam suggests this makes us aware of networked global connectedness: something which is demonstrated when 'the actions of workers in the Ukraine can threaten the livelihood of farmers in North Wales and when, in turn, their milking of cows radiates babies in Malaysia'. This unsettles our traditional concepts of identity, and points to the limits of traditional scientific practices with their reductionism, analytical separation and assumptions of linear temporality. Instead, if we are to understand global processes, we need to develop a greater appreciation of chaos, complexity, temporality, disorder, context and connectivity.

A further discussion of some of the implications of global complexity is taken up in Richard Sennett's chapter 'Growth and failure: the new political economy and its culture'. Sennett argues that the transformations accompanying the new global economy exposes people to the consequences of the marketplace and erodes their self-worth. Instead of capitalism becoming ossified and bureaucratized along the lines of Max Weber's 'iron cage', we are now entering a period of instability in which loyalties to institutions diminish. Whereas strong stable institutions and bureaucratized work regimes favoured the values of purposiveness and responsibility, the basis for a coherent life narrative, today career pathways are replaced by jobs as we move towards a society without institutional shelters, a society in which individuals must bear the responsibility for their own survival. In this context of uncertainty the need to belong to a particular place becomes increasingly valued. At the same time, Sennett argues, there is potential for an 'active edge' – a productive interchange between the economic and place zones – yet the danger is that place does not act on the economy, but only reacts to it in a defensive way. The problem with globalization is that capital is mobile and place has little to bargain with against multinational corporations which can easily find another node in the global network for their operations.

The role of cities is important here, for they offer the potential of an open public life built around the values of diversity, urbanity and experience. Here the urban crowd, as described by Baudelaire, Aragon and Benjamin, offers some antidote to the predominant survivalist ethic of self-responsibility. There have, of course, been a series of debates about the gendered nature of urban public space and whether the *flâneuse* was visible or invisible in the nineteenth-century city (Wolff, 1985; Wilson, 1992; Ryan, 1994; Nava, 1997). This aspect of cities, the freedom to wander the street, to immerse oneself in the crowd, as Hilary Radner notes in her chapter 'Roaming the City', migrated into fashion photography in the second half of the twentieth century. The 'street look' became a powerful new image of urban femininity. But, as Radner points out, rather than the invisible *flâneuse* who is lost in the crowd, fashion photography picks out and makes the fashion model highly visible in the street. The photographic images which became successful in the fashion magazines were images of active woman, whose dress code no longer became associated with authority, but with the defiantly youthful adolescent body, which adopted strong movements and a highly visible active image.

The representations of fashionable women which appeared in fashion magazines derive a particular set of the images of the city as entailing the cultural mixing of people and signs, of exciting, crowded, diverse street life. Hence the city was treated as a site for representation, masquerade and sociability, a theme which we find central to Richard Sennett's (1976) depiction of urban public space, which he takes up again in his piece in this book. For Sennett, if the city can retain the public spaces which harbour the cosmopolitan life, it can offer the possibility for people to develop forms of sociability based upon tolerance and self-distance, qualities which form the basis for an active public. Yet this means that cities need to find some way to become more open. How far can the contemporary cities achieve this?

The difficulties here are apparent if we seek to look at what some regard as the prototypical contemporary city: Los Angeles. This is the city notably described by Mike Davis (1990) with its freeways, fortified architecture, high-technology surveillance, private policing, panopticon malls, social diversions and exclusions. A city marked by its absence of public space. A city which, as Michael Dear and Steven Flusty remind us in their contribution to this volume, is more of a 'large dynamic urban region' than the traditional concentric zone model based on Chicago. This is the city that can be seen as part of 'the third wave of urbanization', which entails the domination of the car, the expansion of new communications technology and the increasing participation of women in the labour market. As Dear and Flusty remind us, it is now assumed that every city in the USA is growing in the fashion of Los Angeles; indeed, it is argued that in many ways it is the paradigmatic form for global cities. In this respect Los Angeles is seen as post-Fordist, tied into the new global circuits of capital. This results in a mosaic of monocultures, a fragmented pastiche of land-use, driven by the spatial logic of 'flexism' and global capital's capacity to evade any long-term commitment to place.

Dear and Flusty see flexism as leading to a balkanized divided city with a bifurcated social structure. At the top we have the 'cybergoisie' who live in 'cyburbia' on the urban edges, habitats which are teleintegrated through state-of-the-art data transmission to form interactive virtual communities. Some of the inhabitants of cyburbia work in high-rise towers which form the business citadels, which are also linked into global electronic networks. At the bottom we have the 'protosurps' who live in the 'cyberias', the mulches of cheap on-call labour, along with the various groups of the excluded: the homeless, vagrants and criminalized, who are confined to the state of 'surpdom', and are left to inhabit the electronic outlands restricted to basic telephone services.

The mobility of capital and electronic information flows, according to Dear and Flusty, makes the discussion of *the* city, the city as a generic type, obsolete. Rather, urbanization should be understood as a quasi-random field of opportunities. The new spatial logic points to the emergence of the 'citistat', the net of megalopoles which form a single integrated urban system. Dear and Flusty's term 'citistat' resonates with the collective world city referred to by Virilio (1993: 72; see discussion in Featherstone, 1996a) which, he argues, has emerged with the synchronization of world time made possible through the globalization of information technology. The informational city (Castells, 1989) becomes a key component of globalization. It is further argued that the network of global cities bound together through electronic communication creates a new social form: 'the network society' (Castells, 1996, 1997). The global cities are the physical locations, which are the key nodal points in the communications networks (see also Sassen, 1994). The expanding set of global cities become paralleled by the construction of another city, the city of bits (Featherstone, 1999a). This data city is a virtual city built in electronic space. According to Tim Luke in his chapter in this volume, we are now witnessing its formation into a totally new sphere of human endeavour: the cybersphere.

For Luke, technology should be seen as a part of a process of the alteration of human beings' relation to nature, a process whereby humans create additional natures which act as delimiting worlds for human activity which structure the possibilities for social life. The first nature is the original nature, the ecological biosphere which surrounds yet resists us. Here nature is seen as 'that which cannot be produced'. The second nature is the technosphere, the anthropogenetic domain of the built environment and material urban landscape which human beings have collectively created and inhabit. The third nature is the cybersphere/telesphere, a second anthropogenetic domain, but in this case the structure is built from 'bits', not atoms, to produce the digitalized information world (the Internet, cyberspace, virtual reality). We can also speculate that this third nature could even give rise to a fourth nature, the sphere of artificial life, a post-anthropogenetic domain, a domain in which the genetic structures of life-forms are reduced to an information code which can be replicated, manipulated and engineered to reproduce and make new life. The development of these new life-forms would introduce complexities into the three previous domains of nature with the emergence of new plants, animals, eventually humans, and computer-generated electronic organisms. The new systems have the potential to become self-replicating and self-mutating post-cyborg systems, in which the originating traces of the human species, which initiated the process, could become covered over and forgotten as new life-forms rapidly evolve in ways we cannot yet begin to foresee (De Landa, 1991, 1992; see discussion in Featherstone, 1996b).

For our present purposes we need to focus on the third nature, the cybersphere. According to Luke, the worlds of first and second nature were organized by state power so that the global and local were two ends of a geographical continuum defined by the nation-state. With the shift to the cybersphere we move to a postperspectival view of space and a new sense of time. There is a pluralization of subjects and objects of communication along with a proliferation of networks of information which renders the old unilinear view of the world and history impossible. In cyberspace we move beyond the old realist divisions of space/time, sender/receiver, medium/message. Through the extension of the Internet we are moving into the domain of 'dromoeconomics': where production is organized around the speed of flows of capital, labour, information and resources controlled through a network of virtual offices and virtual corporations. Manufacture gives way to 'digifacture', mass consumption gives way to mass customization. Cyberspace, then, offers the prospect of great changes in the ways in which wealth is produced, which point to major shifts in the structure of social interdependencies, power balances and modes of cultural reproduction.

As Saskia Sassen argues in her contribution, we have only just begun to move beyond the celebratory rhetoric of the Internet as a new form of democratic decentralization and are just starting to theorize the distri-bution of power in electronic space. She argues that the growing profit-ability of the Internet since business 'discovered' it in 1993, and the potential of the growing multimedia sector, will increase inequalities. It is not just that there will be slow lanes and fast lanes on the superhighway, depending on the ability to pay, but the fact that the Internet is being accompanied by a massive growth in intranets. Large corporations are able to use fire-walled nets at relatively low cost, hence, according to Sassen, we face a future of cyber-segmentation. One of Sassen's main intentions is to go beyond the usual analyses of the characteristics of the new electronic spaces which emphasize the speed, simultaneity and interconnectivity of the Internet, to focus on the embedding, the geography of the infrastructure. Electronic networks may well maximize the potential for geographical dispersal with globalization a consequence of following the economic logic of dispersal. Here we see the potential for a new form of centrality, the formation of a virtual, or transterrestrial centre, which binds together the global financial centres.

At the same time the coordination of dispersal points to a new terrestrial logic of agglomeration. Global cities are not only nodes in the flows across the financial networks, they are regional centres for the coordination of the various manufacturing, design and financial aspects of this process. Global cities become hyperconcentrations of the infrastructure to house the corporate headquarters, financial management and variety of specialist business services which spring up. They also develop a significant cultural sector with entertainment districts and cultural tourist sites to provide the meeting places with the necessary ambience for deals to be enacted. Rather than the eclipse of face-to-face relations through globalization, in global cities we see an upsurge of the 'face-work' necessary to establish trust (see Thrift, 1996). Yet while we see an expansion in members of the new middle classes, alongside the high-waged professional occupations there is a whole infrastructure of low-waged jobs, with women forming the bulk of this labour force of clerical workers, cleaners, restaurant, bar and hotel workers (Sassen, 1994: 123).

While global cities provide the hyperconcentrations of infrastructure which make the electronic networks possible, within them there are great differences in the distribution of this infrastructure. New York City, for example, has the highest concentration of fibre optic cable in the world – yet Harlem has only one building wired up. The cost of bringing up to standard the communications networks in East Europe and Third World countries is massive, yet the growing economic profitability of communications has meant a wave of deregulation and privatization. Investment by communications multinational corporations is, therefore, likely to follow the logic of the market rather than socially determined need. Sassen ends her chapter with the question: are we to see cyberspace dominated by multinational corporations to the detriment of health, education and other public applications? One problem is that national governments still largely operate in a predigital era; they do not have the capacity to regulate multinational corporations and the flows of capital across the global markets.

While there are some transocietal institutions developing (the United Nations and other non-governmental organizations (NGOs) along with international courts, foundations and associations), we are still a long way from the monopolization of the means of violence and taxation, which could lead to the formation of a world state. Proposals such as the Tobin tax designed to regulate international financial flows, along with the various calls for global citizenship, as still seen as highly speculative (see Featherstone, 1996b).[1] As Boaventura de Sousa Santos argues in his chapter on the multicultural conception of human rights, we still see a struggle between those who seek to maintain the state as the guarantor of human rights and those who look forward to its replacement through the emergence of a global civil society and some form of global government. In opposition to those who favour the extension of human rights from above, along the lines of the Western model (a form of what Santos calls 'globalized localism'), we have proposals for a more cosmopolitan multicultural dialogical, or diatopical, form of human rights emerging from below. These are complex issues to which we will return shortly in the context of a more sustained discussion of global culture. For our present purposes it is evident that to speak of the possibility of global citizenship and multicultural human rights is to raise a whole range of questions about the nature of the cultural spaces in which these new forms can develop. This takes us into questions about the changing nature of the public sphere, of the fate of public space in cities, and the possibility of a virtual or electronic public sphere.

Habermas's (1989) theory of the public sphere assumes that in eighteenth-century Europe various spaces (e.g., coffee houses, salons, table societies) developed, along with newspapers, journals, periodicals and reviews, which encouraged new forms of reasoned argumentation in public. For Habermas, this dialogical potential of the public sphere becomes eclipsed in the twentieth century with the expansion of the mass media, which he sees as essentially monological and instrumental, a means for the manipulation and closing down of public opinion. There is no sense that the mass media could be anything other than manipulative, or that new technologies such as the Internet and multimedia forms could increase interactivity and new forms of sociability and dialogue between distant others.

Contra Habermas, for whom technology is unavoidably tainted with instrumentality and is seen as part of the extension of system rationality which is closing off communicative interaction, it can be argued that the new forms of electronic communication could well provide a range of new quasi-public spaces, which encourage debate and active citizenship. In addition, as critics have pointed out against Habermas, the possibility of a unitary public sphere may not only be historically suspect, but also an unrealizable goal. Instead, it is possible to conceive a series of separate, yet overlapping, counter-public spheres which involve the working class, women, blacks and various social movements (see Calhoun, 1992). In addition, it may likewise not only be difficult to separate the public sphere from the literary public sphere (Hohendahl, 1982), but also be difficult to disentangle the public sphere from the broader cultural sphere (Featherstone, 1995: ch. 2). If this is the case, then, it may well be productive to explore not only questions of active citizenship and public participation, but also questions of cultural citizenship: the access to resources to participate in cultural production. The 'right' to access electronic networks and participate in virtual spaces, along with the means to explore the new blurred genres of multimedia communication, are emergent issues which threaten to bracket some of the long-held assumptions about the public sphere.

It can, therefore, be argued that the proliferation of these new cultural spaces provides one important reason to rethink the notion of the public sphere and citizenship. Likewise, a similar shift seems to be taking place in the related area of social movements. As Ron Eyerman points out in his contribution to this volume, the dominant resource mobilization and rational choice models of social movements have more recently been challenged by perspectives which emphasize cultural praxis. Eyerman argues against the usual way in which social movements are contrasted to tradition and points to the ways in which traditions can be reflexively constituted by social movements. Hence collective memories which are reinforced through ritual practices, along with art and music, become important emotional resources for sustaining allegiance to social movements. The way in which social movements seek to use cultural resources reflexively to create traditions suggests that the distinction between cultural movements and social movements may be more difficult to sustain than previously envisaged. Eyerman discusses the example of the role of the Harlem Renaissance in New York City in the 1920s in the formation of the black public sphere. The Harlem Renaissance was a cultural movement which drew on modernism to produce a great upsurge of Afro-American creativity in the arts and popular culture. While under existing definitions it should be seen as a cultural movement, because it lacked an expressed political aim, which is one of the defining characteristics of social movements, it was also a youth movement which contested the Uncle Tom stereotypes and respectability aspirations of previous black community leaders. Hence it suggests the line between social and cultural movements is not always easy to sustain.

There are, of course, those who prefer to have their traditions undiluted by reflexivity and who see the public sphere as having become a medium for the projection of private matters, the concern with celebrity and the lifestyles of the rich and famous, which preoccupy the mass media. Sacredness is seen as having become reduced to a quality of the marketplace, designed into the products of consumer culture, the identity industries, new social and religious movements. As Göran Dahl reminds us in his contribution to this volume, what is interesting is that this type of anti-bourgeois critique with its attack on reflexivity, individualization and the alleged homogenization and massification of culture, does not now come from the left, but increasingly from the radical right.

The new culturalism, as we find in the writings of de Benoist in France, seeks to stop what is seen as the reduction of all cultures to a single world civilization. Such rhetoric is strengthened by the perceived visibility of immigrants in Europe and the demands for increasing multiculturalism. We find similar arguments among technocratic conservatives such as Gehlen, Shelsky and Freyer in Germany. Gehlen, for example, argues that human beings need strong institutions which minimize the reflexivity and subjectivism which overburden the lives of ordinary people. We need to lower our horizons and accept that we now live in a 'post-history' in which genuine new developments and the possibility of utopian thought have become impossible. This was also the position of Carl Schmitt, who developed a strong critique of liberalism and universalism for their denial of cultural particularism, whose protection should be the duty of the state. At the same time, Dahl argues that the radical conservatives should be seen as modernists, for while they say 'no' to reflexivity, they say 'yes' to modern technology and the drive for efficiency. Yet this must be combined with the preservation of the longing for the sacred and the need for sacrifice. Hence this perspective is used to develop a strong critique of not only the dangers of reflexivity, but with it the dangers of its carriers: the cosmopolitan middle-class. The latter are seen as completely against sacrifice; they do not seek to belong to any community or nation, only to themselves.

This opposition between the new culturalism, with its emphasis upon the sacred, the community and the nation, and the cosmopolitan middle-class ideal of empathy and tolerance raises a series of issues about contemporary cultural processes and the dominant modes of conceptualizing culture we have become accustomed to using. In the first place it points to the globalization of not only assumed universal processes following on from marketization, but also to the reactive focus upon ethnicity, regional culture and the nation, in which culture can be represented as having an immediacy and pre-reflexive communal quality. Both processes are central to the struggles we see taking place on the global stage. As Boaventura de Sousa Santos reminds us in his chapter, this suggests that there is not a single globalization, but rather globalizations in the plural, or in his words: 'Globalization . . . is the process by which a given local condition or entity succeeds in extending its reach over the globe, and by doing so, develops the capacity to designate a rival social condition or entity as local' (p. 216). This leads him to argue that there are four forms of globalization. First, global-ized localism: the globalization of transnational corporations, McDonald-ization, Americanization and the extension of English as the lingua franca. Secondly, localized globalism: the effects of globalism imposed upon the peripheral countries such as deforestation, heritage tourism, free trade enclaves. Thirdly, cosmopolitanism: the development of global alliances through NGOs, environmental groups, world federation of trade unions, the north–south dialogues. Fourthly, the common heritage of humankind: the ozone layer, the Amazon, Antarctica, biodiversity, outer space are seen as global questions which unite us all.

In terms of human rights, Santos tells us that the assumed universal form of human rights is in fact a form of globalized localism, that is Western human rights 'imposed' from above. Yet there is a further possibility, that of multicultural human rights issues as part of a cosmo-politan counter-hegemonic form of globalization emerging from below.[2] This second approach tends to see universality as a particular Western question, and contests the assumption that there is a universal human nature which we can know by rational means. Santos argues that our central task is to transform the conception and practice of human rights from globalized localism into a cosmopolitan project. We need a diatopical hermeneutics, a cross-cultural dialogue between different local traditions which are acknowledged as incomplete.

The multicultural notion of human rights developed by Santos is built upon a mestiza or hybrid view of culture: cultures are incomplete mixtures. This perspective is taken further by Wolfgang Welsch in his chapter on transculturality. Welsch argues that we need to move beyond the view which originates with Herder of cultures as homogeneous, linguistically unified, autonomous 'islands'. This premise of culture as forming separate islands or spheres has been enormously influential and is still the basis for many conceptions of culture today. It is central to interculturalism, where cultures are seen as clashing or in dialogue, and multiculturalism, where societies are seen as being composed of a set of multiple cultures. Welsch argues that it is no longer realistic today to conceive cultures as either homogeneous or separate. Today cultures are internally differentiated and complex; externally they are entangled in complex networks with other cultures, and hence it is not easy to ascertain their boundaries. We have a process of mixing and hybridization in which all other cultures become the inner content of one's own culture. Transculturality, according to Welsch, alters the nature of the mode of diversity in the world for diversity in the form of single cultures will increasingly disappear. This means a movement from the perspective that differences are to be conceived in terms of the juxtaposition of delimited cultures, as we find in a mosaic format, to differences seen as the result of transcultural networks which have some things in common while differing in others. Hence the mode of differentiation has become more complex and we have overlaps and distinctions at the same time.

There are a number of points in common between this transcultural perspective and the argument developed by Couze Venn in his chapter 'Narrating the Postcolonial'. Postcolonialism recognizes the hybridity of all cultures as something which is a product of the encounter between cultures. Hybridity points to the situation of being neither inside nor outside a culture, but in a third space on the borderline, where one is inside and outside at the same time. Here we think of the 'double consciousness' described by Gilroy (1993) in relation to blacks in the West, along with the writings of Bhabha, Spivak, hooks, Hall and others. For Venn, postcolonial theory provides an opportunity to recover the capacity to pluralize modernity, to address the ethical project involved in recognizing the counter culture of modernity as addressed by Bauman and others. An analysis of the relationship between modernity, capitalism and colonialism has the potential for a recovery of the marginalized counter-discourses of modernity of those who do not fit in with the dominant rational masculine white subject – the exiles, Jews, slaves, women, homosexuals and colonized. The counter-discourse of modernity seeks to challenge the totalizing logocentric subject of modernity with its displacement of ontological questions and privileging of epistemology and equation of the progress of humanity with the progress of reason. This is also a theme taken up in Michael Shapiro's chapter on 'Triumphalist Geographies', in which he examines the ways in which modern European cartographies have sought to dehistoricize maps and impose a particular model of space on the rest of the planet. For Couze Venn, the relative displacement of the West through the rise of East Asia provides us with the possibility of thematizing multiple modernities, and recovering the traces of the memories of the victims of oppression which became forgotten in the construction of the history of modernity as a collective singular with its emphasis upon one time, one humanity and one history.

These assumptions about hybridity and globalization are vigorously contested in Jonathan Friedman's contribution on 'The Hybridization of Roots and the Abhorrence of the Bush'. Friedman argues that we should take a long-term view of the current changes which we refer to as globalization. The current phase of globalization should not be understood as a part of a general evolutionary process. Rather, it is a temporary delimited phase which should be understood in relation to the break-up of hegemonies. It is part of a period of hegemonic decline characterized by increasing competition and the shift of capital to East Asia. The growth of transnational corporations should also be understood in terms of this process of decentralization of wealth. Hybridity should be seen as the cultural corollary to economic globalization. Friedman raises the question whether there is actually more mixing now than in the past when we had blues, jazz, pasta, etc. If today there is a greater consciousness of mixing, this may have more to do with the formation of a particular type of gaze on the part of upper-class and middle-class Westerners who are consumers of cultural objects and images. Hybridization is the ideology of the intellectuals drawn from these groups; for Friedman it is a labelling device, 'an attempt to define the cultural state of the world, a reading for the more sophisticated cosmopolitans'. But for Friedman, this cosmopolitan celebration of rootlessness and anti-ethnic orientation, should be seen as part of the logic of modern experience. Unlike previous groups of cultural specialists, the cosmopolitans do not have a civilizing mission or high culture; rather, they engage in the accumulation of differences.

According to Friedman there is a clear connection between intellectual decline and hegemonic decline. This is manifest in the decline of the public sphere. As the public sphere becomes weakened, the principle of rational argumentation along with notions of falsification and an ethical code, suffers and other modes take over. We get the formation of various groupings and clientships aiming to colonize the public sphere, which do not seek to legitimate themselves via any standards of intellectual practice. Intellectual life becomes subordinated to the logic of accumulating social power and status: they are new groups striving to become cultural elites who take it on themselves to become self-appointed representatives of the non-white poor of the world. The postcolonial critics engage in a rhetoric of the flowing and mixing of cultures, something which is only surprising if one expected to find a prior ordered and highly classified world.

The problem is that cultural products may well seem mixed to outsiders, but if one looks closely there may be little evidence of cultural hybridization in the activities and discourses of actual groups of people. If we say all cultures are hybrid and mixed, this is merely a trivial truism, which denies any operational significance to the term 'hybridization'. Rather, according to Friedman, we need to focus on how cultures are experienced.

Hybridity may well be a form of identity which is on the increase, but largely among certain groups such as cultural specialists. Cultures may well travel and move around the world, but ethnicity is still about the maintenance of social boundaries, something which remains a powerful force in the current phase of globalization. What appears as a new stage of mixing and flows should be understood in terms of the decline of Western hegemony. The fragmentation of nation-states and multiculturalism in the West are expressions of this process. In the global circuits of intellectual and high culture, along with the media and diplomatic elites, a cosmopolitan identity of a multicultural world has developed. From the perspective of the self-identified hybrid inhabiting the world cities, local identities seem backward.

These are important issues which go to the heart of the questions we raised at the beginning of this introduction: how are we to understand social structures and culture today in a world which is becoming rapidly globalized? Is it still possible to relate particular perspectives on culture such as hybridization and postcolonialism to the projects of social groups and class fractions, or is the speed and complexity of cultural production and dissemination pushing us beyond traditional modes of analysis? Around a decade ago these questions preoccupied us in the journal *Theory, Culture & Society* in terms of the debates surrounding postmodernism (see Featherstone, 1988, 1991; Lash, 1990). We face them again today in terms of the need to understand the development of globalization and technological culture. These questions are not only important, from the theoretical perspective, in terms of our need to make sense of the world, but also in terms of the practical interest we retain in the question: how are we to live in the world? Likewise we have an interest in the questions of the future of public space, the possibilities for closing off, or opening up, the public sphere in global cities, along with the possibilities for an electronic virtual public sphere and global citizenship. It, therefore, can be argued that from both the theoretical and practical points of view, we have a continuing interest in the spaces of culture.

Notes

1 In 1994 the daily flow through the world's foreign exchange markets exceeded $1 trillion a day. The proposal for a small percentage tax on these flows was first outlined by James Tobin. It has been estimated that around 80 per cent of this daily flow of this volatile 'global casino' is speculative or linked to money laundering. A tax on international transfers of money at the rate of 0.003 per cent (the Walker tax proposal) would finance all UN operations and a tax of 0.5 per cent (the Tobin proposal) would yield around $1,500 billion a year. This could be collected by nation-states taxing the flows across their borders and used to finance welfare and other state-led reconstruction programmes.

2 Boaventura de Sousa Santos also makes the connection between cosmopolitanism and citizenship, taking us in the direction of global citizenship, in his book *Towards a New Common Sense* (1995). He argues that citizenship must be deterritorialized, decanonized and

socially reconstructable (more dual or even triple citizenship). In effect we need to work to construct broader, more flexible conceptions of membership than one tied exclusively to the nation-state.

References

Calhoun, C. (ed.) (1992) *Habermas and the Public Sphere*. Cambridge, MA: MIT Press.
Castells, M. (1989) *The Informational City*. Oxford: Blackwell.
Castells, M. (1996) *The Information Age, Volume 1: The Rise of the Network Society*. Oxford: Blackwell.
Castells, M. (1997) *The Information Age, Volume 2: The Power of Identity*. Oxford: Blackwell.
Davis, M. (1990) *City of Quartz*. London: Verso.
De Landa, M. (1991) *War in the Age of Intelligent Machines*. New York: Zone Books.
De Landa, M. (1992) 'Non-organic life', in J. Crary and S. Kwinter (eds), *Incorporations*. New York: Zone Books.
Featherstone, M. (ed.) (1988) *Postmodernism*. London: Sage. (*Theory, Culture & Society* special issue 5 (2–3).)
Featherstone, M. (1991) *Consumer Culture and Postmodernism*. London: Sage.
Featherstone, M. (1995) *Undoing Culture: Globalization, Postmodernism and Identity*. London: Sage.
Featherstone, M. (1996a) 'The global city, information technology and public life'. Paper presented at City Cultures conference, University of Campinas, São Paulo, December 1996. Published in German as 'Die globale Stadt: Informationstechnologie und öffenthcher Leben', in C. Rademacher, M. Schroer and P. Weichens (eds), *Spiel ohne Grenze? Ambivalenzen der Globalisierung*. Westdeutscher Verlag, 1999.
Featherstone, M. (1996b) 'Beyond the postmodern? Technologies of post-human development and the question of citizenship', Global Futures Series public lecture, Institute of Social Studies, The Hague, June 1996.
Gilroy, P. (1993) *The Black Atlantic*. London: Verso.
Habermas, J. (1989) *The Structural Transformation of the Public Sphere*. Cambridge: Polity Press.
Hohendahl, P. (1982) *The Institution of Criticism*. Ithaca, NY: Cornell University Press.
Lash, S. (1990) *Sociology and Postmodernism*. London: Routledge.
Lash, S. and Urry, J. (1993) *Economies of Signs and Space*. London: Sage.
Latour, B. (1993) *We Have Never Been Modern*. Hemel Hempstead: Harvester Wheatsheaf.
Nava, M. (1997) 'Women, modernity and the city', in P. Falk and C. Campbell (eds), *The Shopping Experience*. London: Sage.
Robertson, R. (1992) *Globalization*. London: Sage.
Robertson, R. (1995) 'Globalization: time–space and homogeneity–heterogeneity', in M. Featherstone, S. Lash and R. Robertson (eds), *Global Modernities*. London: Sage.
Ryan, J. (1994) 'Women, modernity and the city', *Theory, Culture & Society*, 11 (4): 35–63.
Santos, Boaventura de Sousa (1995) *Towards a New Common Sense*. London: Routledge.
Sassen, S. (1994) *Cities in a World Economy*. Thousand Oaks, CA: Sage.
Sennett, R. (1976) *The Fall of Public Man*. Cambridge: Cambridge University Press.
Thrift, N. (1996) *Spatial Formations*. London: Sage.
Virilio, P. (1993) 'Marginal groups', *Daidalos*, 50 (December): 72–81.
Wilson, E. (1992) 'The invisible *flâneur*', *New Left Review*, 191: 90–116.
Wolff, J. (1985) 'The invisible *flâneuse*', *Theory, Culture & Society*, 2 (3): 37–46.

Part I

TECHNOLOGICAL SPACE

1

GROWTH AND FAILURE: THE NEW POLITICAL ECONOMY AND ITS CULTURE

Richard Sennett

I'd like to begin by referring to two experiences which are being rapidly transformed in the modern world: work and place. Both are changing in ways which, a mere 20 years ago, seemed unimaginable.

Then, the great corporate bureaucracies and government hierarchies of the developed world seemed securely entrenched, the products of centuries of economic development and nation-building. Commentators spoke of 'late capitalism' or 'mature capitalism' as though earlier forces of growth had now entered an end-game phase. Now, a new chapter has opened: the economy is global, and makes use of new technology; ways of working have altered, as short-term jobs replace stable careers; mammoth government and corporate bureaucracies are changing form, becoming both more flexible and less secure institutions.

Place has a different meaning now as well, in large part thanks to these economic changes. An earlier generation believed nations, and within nations cities, were places that could control their own fortunes; now, the emerging economic network is less susceptible to the controls of geography. A divide has thus opened between polity and economy.

I want to discuss how human beings experience these institutional changes in work and place – discuss, that is, the culture of the new political economy. Culture holds a dialogue with material life in which it speaks with its own voice but always addresses its more brutal and frequently taciturn partner. I'd like to put forward two propositions which seem to be emerging from this difficult discussion.

The first is that as the material world grows, ordinary people are experiencing failure in new forms. The new order erodes people's sense of self-worth in the marketplace while also eroding traditional institutions which protected people against the market.

The second proposition is that the value of place has thereby increased. The sense of place is based on the need to belong not to 'society' in the abstract, but to somewhere in particular; in satisfying that need, people develop commitment and loyalty. As the shifting institutions of the economy diminish the experience of belonging somewhere special at work, people's commitments increase to geographic places like nations, cities and localities. The question is, commitments of what sort? Is place merely an icon for needs which cannot otherwise be satisfied? Or again, are actual places condemned to become defensive refuges against a hostile world?

These two themes might suggest an unrelievedly bleak view of our present condition. But this is not my view. Failure itself is not an unrelievedly bleak condition, for people often learn by failing at something – learn their limits, learn to pay attention to those who before they used merely as instruments of their own will. Most of all people may learn to put some distance between their sense of self and their troubled fortunes. Growth and failure thus stand in a different relationship from each other than do success and failure.

My hope is that, out of the troubled fortunes people are now experiencing in work, they might put some distance between self and work. Place could play a role in the experience of learning to separate one's sense of self from one's personal condition; one could have a place in the world on other terms. I am not invoking an abstract condition; this is what we mean by 'urbanity', it is the promise of urban life.

Impoverished Experience

To make sense of the culture of the emerging political economy, we might begin by defining its key word, 'growth'. The word can be divided, most simply, into four categories. The first is sheer increase in number. Growth of this sort appears in economic thinking among writers like Jean Baptiste Say, whose *loi des débouchés* postulated that 'increased supply creates its own demand'.[1] Increased number and size can of course lead to alteration of structure, which is how Adam Smith conceived growth in *The Wealth of Nations*. Larger markets trigger, he said, the division of labour in work. A third form of growth is metamorphosis; a body changes shape without necessarily increasing in number. Finally, a system can grow by becoming more open; its boundaries become febrile, its forms become mixed, it contracts or expands in parts without overall coordination.

The first sort of growth is the most familiar to us, because it is how we reckon profit and loss. The second, in which size begets complexity, is familiar to us in government bureaucracy as well as traditional corporations. Metamorphosis belongs most readily to our understanding of narratives, appearing for instance in the growth of a character in a novel. And communications networks such as the Internet are obvious examples of how open systems grow; less obviously, subjectivity grows through open systems.

The age of High Capitalism, for convenience's sake, can be said to span the two centuries following the publication of *The Wealth of Nations* in 1776. It was an era which lusted for sheer quantitative growth, but it had trouble dealing with the structural changes size inaugurated by its lust for more. Few of Smith's contemporaries in London or elsewhere in Europe wished to be cast on the uncharted seas of unregulated commerce; they wished the government to stand behind them, as it had in the past. In their magisterial study of the evolution of the American corporation, Oscar and Mary Handlin similarly depict uncertainty and fear among the very privatizing innovators divorcing corporation from commonwealth.[2]

Growth in this new capitalism entailed an inherent structural problem: the inverse relationship between quantitative increase and complexity on the one hand, and qualitative impoverishment on the other. Adam Smith believed that, rather than market exchange alone, the division of labour promoted by free markets would make for a more complex society. Society, he said, would become a honeycomb of tasks.[3] Yet individual experience becomes simpler as social structures grow more complex. Take his famous example of manufacturing nails: breaking down the task involved in making nails into its component parts condemned individual nail makers, like later workers on the Ford assembly lines, to a numbingly boring day, hour after hour spent doing one small job.

In the nineteenth century, critics of High Capitalism could see no easy way to end this trade-off of qualitative, experiential impoverishment for structural increase and complexity. In Marx's view, no reform could divorce numeric growth from the experiential impoverishment of labour; only a revolution could. Durkheim's advocacy of 'organic solidarity' as a solution to the human problems of the division of labour is, in the end, I believe, a religious solution. He was much influenced, for instance, by the views of Emmanuel Lammenais, the Christian socialist who believed only the cooperative, contemplative values of the monastic spirit could temper the boredom of industrial routine.

The paradox of experiential regression and structural development has both ended and become more acute in the emerging political economy. Modern technology promises to banish routine work to the innards of new machines, and does so. It could therefore be argued, from a strictly technological point of view, that the division of labour is coming to an end. But in the world using these machines, that argument doesn't hold. The division of labour now concerns those who get to work, and those who don't; large numbers of people are set free of routine tasks only to find themselves useless or under-used economically, especially in the context of the global labour supply.

The conditions of that labour market have been aptly and brutally summarized by the social commentator Garrick Utley as follows: '. . .

industry in the developed world today employs approximately 350 million people at an average hourly wage of $18.00, while in the past ten years international acceptance and expansion of the market economy has reached a potential labor force in developing countries of some 1.2 billion people working at an average cost of $2.00 an hour.'[4] The divide between the two is no longer simply between the skilled and the unskilled; computer code is written efficiently, for instance, in Bombay for one-third its cost in IBM home offices.

Unemployment and under-employment of the educated young give one picture of uselessness: too many qualified engineers, programmers, systems-analysts, not to speak of too many lawyers, MBAs, securities salespeople. But uselessness is a more ambiguous phenomenon, particularly among those with specialized training. Instead of the institutionally impoverished experience of the assembly line, poverty lies within the worker who hasn't made him or herself of value and so could simply disappear from view.

Glints of how the economic order arouses this fear of uselessness appear in popular classics about modern corporations like *Reengineering the Corporation* (1994). The authors, Michael Hammer and James Champy, defend 'reengineering' against the charge that it is a mere cover for firing people in saying, 'downsizing and restructuring only mean doing less with less. Reengineering, by contrast means doing *more* with less.'[5] The 'less' in the last sentence reverberates with the denials of an older Social Darwinism – that those who are not fit will somehow disappear.

The undertow connotation of uselessness is a dispensable self. Useless skills have a particular meaning in a skills-based economy. What Michael Young feared in his prophetic essay, *Meritocracy*, has come to pass: as the economy needs ever fewer highly educated people to run it, the 'moral distance' between mass and elite widens.[6] The Smithian paradox of experiential impoverishment in the course of structural development thus continues on new terms.

Unemployment and under-employment are of course long-standing economic ills, though some tough-minded economists argue that the new order has made these ills incurable, since the economy indeed profits from doing 'more with less'. What I wish to emphasize is that the classical model of growth offers no solution to its experiential deficits; neither sheer material increase nor the division of labour create richer human experience. Put abstractly, Number does not define the Good. Experiential impoverishment as a problem requires another model of development.

We might come closer to the qualitative dimensions of growth by exploring a form which seems far removed from the economic realm: metamorphosis.

Change from Within

'My purpose is to tell of bodies which have been transformed into shapes of a different kind', Ovid declared at the outset of the *Metamorphoses*.[7] You will recall he believed that the world came into being when a god first sorted into distinct forms a primal 'shapeless, uncoordinated mass . . . whose ill-assorted elements were indiscriminately heaped together in one place'.[8] Subsequently, change in form became the law of life: Darwin enjoyed Ovid for good reason. But Ovid thought his own era – an age of iron – was reverting to the sheer impurity of the world's beginning. Perhaps therefore, in a godlike spirit, he sought to edify it by telling stories of how the gods and humans who change shape grow in stature in each new guise.

This, more broadly, is what narrative does to character – events changing character so that at the end of a narrative its personages are different from those they were at the beginning. And again broadly, narrative transformations occur in two dimensions: one is disruptive, the other is accumulative. In Kafka, as in Ovid, nothing quite prepares us for a man suddenly turning into a cockroach. Kafka's *Metamorphosis* (1916) would be a far less compelling story, however, if Gregor Samsa had suddenly become a golden retriever; at the end, we hardly think of his cockroach condition as a mere disruption of sense. By the end of the story its changes remain in our memory as a gradual silting up of sediments of his tragedy as a man, each shift in the story seeming to prefigure what came next – which is the retrospective logic of narrative. Almost all good writers of fiction work in both dimensions of metamorphosis, disrupting sense while accumulating meaning through change.

To translate this artistic work into social terms, we could say that here is a model of change from within, of internal evolution, of what one modern school of social thought calls rather grandly 'auto-poesis'. All institutions experience such metamorphoses of this sort, making sudden, lurching alterations which are later rationalized into a narrative logic. Moreover, metamorphosis can serve a critical purpose. Sudden shifts of form can confront what came before.

When Durkheim studied the division of labour, he focused on differentiation, that is, how one category of work is logically as well as functionally distinct from another; the categories make room for each other and respect each other's boundaries. What we call today the 'difference principle' addresses the illogic of such distinctions. The difference principle does not respect boundaries, say of gender or of class, but it seeks to test them, and so change their forms. Kafka made this test with the category human, Ovid with the category god; even modern computers test boundary distinctions and are increasingly capable of self-metamorphosis.

Yet take alone, metamorphosis in its social versions as change from within or as the difference principle is insufficient as a model of social experience, and especially when sheer alteration of form is emphasized. For this slights the other side of narrative time, its coherence. Basic social bonds like trust, loyalty and obligation are not instantly formed; they require a long time to develop; they require continuity rather than rupture. A system open to the growth of these social experiences must, that is, possess the qualities and the power of *duration*.

Up to this point, I've described rather schematically three versions of growth: simple numeric increase, as Say imagined it; numeric increase coupled to complexity of structure, as Smith portrayed it in the division of labour; self-changing form, as writers and critics traditionally practised it and now, evidently, also practised by machines. To speak about the qualities of an open social system of growth, I want to be more historically specific.

Duration

Durability was a contested condition of time in the old order. The progress of capitalism was anything but steady and linear, instead lurching from disaster to disaster. Disaster occurred not only in the stock markets, but also in irrational capital investment, which squandered millions of pounds, francs and dollars in failed canal, railway and factory construction. Numeric growth and waste on a vast scale were, as the historian Oliver Zunz points out, inseparable companions.[9]

A certain kind of character type flourished under these conditions, a personage appearing in the pages of Balzac but also in the more mundane annals of finance: people feeding on crises, thriving on disorder, most of all marked by a capacity for disloyalty. For every responsible capitalist like Andrew Carnegie, there were hundreds of Jay Goulds, adept at walking away from their own disasters. They were adepts of metamorphosis of a sort, but, like Balzac's Vautrin, they seldom grew in stature. Less powerful, or more responsible, human beings could hardly flourish under these conditions.

Max Weber's famous image of modern life confined in an 'iron cage' does not, therefore, do justice to stability as an achievement, an achievement for ordinary people in the age of High Capitalism. The service ethic of steady, self-denying, life-long effort Weber evoked in *The Protestant Ethic and the Spirit of Capitalism* (1904) aided his less favoured contemporaries in purchasing a home, for instance; home ownership was one of the few bulwarks of stability in the nineteenth century against the capitalist storm, as well as a source of personal and family honour. Again, national bureaucracies and corporations made use of the service ethic, gaining the loyalty of those whom they made secure. Weber doubted that loyal servants make objectively minded citizens. Yet petty bureaucrats, time-servers and assorted 'little people' derived a sense of status and public honour from their stations in the bureaucracies.

Citizenship depends on some durable sense of self-worth. The rigid, large-scale bureaucracies which developed at the end of the nineteenth century provided an institutional architecture in which dependance became honourable, to which the worker could become loyal. Static institutions provide, unfortunately, a framework of daily trust, a reality which has to be acknowledged in thinking about efforts in our own time to take these institutions apart.

Take, for instance, the issue of loyalty. In the emerging political economy, as people increasingly do shifting, task-centred jobs rather than pursue stable careers guaranteed by bureaucracies, loyalties to institutions diminish. This generalization of course needs all sorts of qualification; for instance, one study of dismissed IBM programmers found the people with more than 20 years of service remain enthusiastic about the company, while accepting their firing as a matter of fate. A more diminished sense of loyalty appears among younger workers, who have more brutal dealings with the new economic order; many of these younger workers view the places where they work mostly as sites to make contacts with people who can get them better, or simply other, jobs.

In this, the young have not failed to do their duty, since new economic institutions make no guarantees in return, replacing permanent workers whenever possible with temporary workers, for instance, or 'offshoring' work. Loyalty requires that personal experience accumulate in an institution; the emerging political economy represses that experience, because it puts a low premium on institutional duration.

Most of the current discussions of the welfare state obscure this general truth, because they narrow the range of people who legitimately seem to need bureaucratic support to those who are failures or failing; questions about loyalty and honourable dependence are thus marginalized. Again, in current legal debates about rights, much is made of obligation, at the expense of entitlement. But obligations form and grow stronger in time, a time which requires socially durable institutions.

If a system is open to the growth of loyalty, trust and obligation, it must provision longevity and a certain structural immobility – the very vices, today, of the 'iron cage'. However, I do not mean to speak as a blind apologist. The defects of how our society has organized duration lie, as do its virtues, in the specific history we have had of capitalism. These actual vices arose in the way duration became a personal, subjective ethic of responsibility, an ethic formed in the past which becomes self-destructive when practised in the present.

Bureaucratic shelter meant, psychologically, that the patterns of subjective time became linear. A career is a lifetime project with clearly graded steps; as such, it is hardly a modern or a Western invention; the ancient Chinese and Egyptians followed rational career paths. Weber explored more modern forms, by tracing the ways in which careers became 'open to talent' rather than through purchase or inheritance, and talent became measured as performance on the job.

The long-term, linear accumulation of experience as is organized into a career has a subjective side. As subjective experience, such linear time devalues immediacy. In particular, for Victorians, 'right now' was a frightening dimension of time, for it belonged to the time frame of capitalism's upheavals and disasters, to the metamorphoses of the Vautrins and Jay Goulds. The Victorian values of purpose and will, Lionel Trilling observes, implicated a future yet to be experienced; will was divorced from immediate sensation. The school manuals of the Victorian age counselling the young to work hard for the sake of the future had little to do with doctrines of the will's immediacy as preached by Schopenhauer and Nietzsche.

This future-oriented devaluation of the present also inflated the value of the past, in subjective experience of time. In *Thus Spake Zarathustra* Nietzsche wrote, 'powerless against what has been done, he is an angry spectator of all that is past. The will cannot will backwards.'[10] But it can so bend, and it did.

The Victorian notion of responsibility lay exactly in bending the self backwards to compose, out of the dislocations, accidental changes of direction, or unused capacities of a life, a record of personal responsibility, even though these events might be beyond the actual control of the people who experienced them. As elements in a coherent narrative, the life history came to fit the model of the bureaucratic career. Freud's early case histories, like his study of the 'Wolf-Man', revolve around costs of organizing time in this cohering fashion – particularly the act of taking responsibility, and with its consequent feelings of guilt, for past events beyond one's control. Freud remarks in one of his letters to his colleague Fliess that such feelings of responsibility are modern sentiments, in contrast to earlier ages where people felt their life histories were in the hands of the gods, God or blind fortune. The poet Senancour combined the subjective time of future and past in declaring that 'I live to become, but I carry the unshakeable burden of what I have been.'

This modern subjective time is very different from earlier eras' sense of the past. For instance, the ancient Roman imperialists imagined the towns of their ever-expanding empire, and repeated the plan and mores of Rome at its founding; they filled the world with their origins. Similarly, later medieval traders sought to remove their increasing wealth from taint by arguing that trade helped fulfil a divine plan designed by God at the very moment of creation. But in these cases, there was neither a personal creation of the past nor institutional responsibility for it.

Placing such values of time in their institutional context helps us understand what happens when the values of personal responsibility survive, as they have, but the institutional context changes. Most dramatically this appears in the changed climate of the welfare state; the state apparatus shrinks, invoking the traditional ethic of people taking responsibility for themselves. Less obviously, the shrinking of institutional supports in work leaves individuals alone with their sense of responsibility, which now becomes a negative, a self-accusation in confronting such tangled personal experiences as uselessness. The ethic of personal responsibility creates a cultural dialectics of failure in the midst of material growth.

For instance, 25 years ago I interviewed workers in Boston who knew work was beyond their control, like Nietzsche's 'angry spectators', yet they took responsibility for what happened to them.[11] In that generation, what roused this double persona of being an angry spectator and a responsible agent were catastrophes in the economy which caused a worker, say, to lose his or her home. Today, exactly the processes that expand the economy put workers in this double bind.

Take what happens when career paths are replaced by jobs – an effort compounded in its force because 'lean and mean' corporations want raw, unprejudiced energy in their workers; the optimal age curve of workers is shifting from the late 20s–middle 50s to the early 20s–early 40s, even though adults are living longer and more vigorously.[12] Personal duration, as job experience and length of service, becomes an economic negative. A study of 'outsourcing', the polite name for politely sending dismissed workers out into the world, finds older workers both obsessed and puzzled by the liabilities of age. Rather than believing themselves faded and over the hill, they feel they know what to do, that they are more organized and purposeful than young workers. Yet they blame themselves for not having made the right moves, for not having prepared; both the past and the 'new' become their responsibility. Similarly, a study of temporary workers finds them with a dual consciousness of their work, knowing such work suits obligation-resistant companies, yet none the less believing that if only they had themselves managed their lives differently, they would have made a career out of their skills, permanently employed and advancing up the corporate ladder.

Nothing is more distressing, in this regard, than the rhetoric of modern management which attempts to disguise power in the new economy by making the worker believe he or she is a self-directing agent. Here is a typical example:

> When a process is reengineered . . . assembly-line work disappears. Functional departments lose their reasons for being. Managers stop acting like supervisors and behave more like coaches.[13]

It is not false consciousness that makes such statements credible to those who are likely to suffer from them, but rather, a twisting of moral agency.

In his *Oration on the Dignity of Man*, the Renaissance philosopher Pico della Mirandola declared '. . . man is an animal of diverse, multiform, and destructible nature'; in this pliant condition '. . . it is given to him to have that which he chooses and to be that which he wills'.[14] Man is his own maker; the chief of his works is his self-worth. In modernity, people take responsibility for their lives by bending the will backwards in time, for their past seems also of their own making. But when the ethical culture of modernity, with its codes of personal responsibility and life purpose, is carried into a society without institutional shelters, there appears not pride of self, but a dialectic of failure in the midst of growth. Growth in the new economy depends on gutting corporate size, ending bureaucratic guarantees, profiting from the flux and extensions of economic networks. Such dislocations people come to know as their own lack of direction. The ethics of responsibility becomes a subjective yardstick to measure the failure of experience to cohere.

Because of this specific history of bureaucratic and subjective time, to envision a truly open social system, then, requires thinking about the polity in ways that address the convoluted relations of failure and growth. Is there some way this subjective burden of modernity could be lightened? One way to explore that possibility is to think about where it could be lightened.

Place

I began this chapter by saying that having a place in the world is what makes the human animal a social being. And I suppose, because I am an urbanist, I want to believe physical places such as cities could play a role in creating that social sense of place. A city might ideally provide what the modern corporation denies: a site for forming loyalties and responsibilities, a site for shaping life purposes, a site that offers relief from the burdens of subjective life.

But this ideal city lies far from the realities that shape urban places today. People are indeed trying to compensate for their dislocations and impoverished experience in the economy by celebrating place – but on exclusionary terms. This compensatory, exclusionary mechanism operates as much at the local urban level as at the national level. To possess turf means to exclude difference: most obviously, the poor who are segregated in the centres of American cities, the poor and the ethnic outsiders who are segregated on the peripheries of European cities. Less obviously but as powerfully, modern place-making involves a search for the comforts of sameness in terms of shared identity, uniform building context and reduction of density. Such comforts of sameness appear, for instance, in the cute small towns designed by the American planners Elizabeth Platter-Zyberg and Andreas Duwany (among the architects in the UK working for the Prince of Wales to re-produce 'native' English architecture) and in the neighbourhood renovation work on the Continent undertaken by Leon Krier. All these place-makers are artists of claustrophobia, whose communities, however, promise stability, mutual trust and durability.

My worry is that, as people suffer more failure and injury in the economy, they will seek the comforts of place on these terms – which are those of place as a closed system.

There are planning strategies that can counter claustrophobia and open places up. For instance, new building can be directed to the edges between separate communities and away from local centres. This makes the edge a febrile zone of interaction and exchange, a zone where differences are activated. Planning work by Hugo Hinsley and others in East London is based on this principle of the active edge. Or within central spaces, dissimilar uses can be introduced: many planners in the USA are, for instance, seeking ways to put clinics, government offices and old-age centres into shopping malls which have been formerly devoted solely to consumption activities; planners in Germany are similarly exploring how pedestrian zones in the centres of cities can become civic as well as commercial sites.

Such urban strategies are not based on pre-determining the results; they are open strategies for growth, a planner's version of metamorphosis. They do make assumptions about the process of change – in the case of the active-edge planners, that the more people interact, the more they will become involved with those unlike themselves; in the case of the central-zone planners, that the value of place will increase when it is of more than commercial value. These are open systems, then, that try to develop, through place-making, mutual engagement, and so mutual obligation and loyalty.

But, as always in planning work, if strategies create opportunities, they cannot ensure people will participate. And people will not participate civically if these places, as polities, do not in some way act on the economy, rather than defensively react to it.

At present, places – by they a factory in Mexico, an office in Bombay or the multimedia centre in lower Manhattan – are nodes in a global network. Places exercise weak, or no, sovereignty over the network, fearing that, if the network is taxed or regulated locally, another node can as easily be found, in Canada if not Mexico, in Boston if not Manhattan.

One Draconian proposal advanced to empower place and polity is that localities threaten to expropriate the local property of migrant corporations, in order to tie the corporations down. Such threats, unfortunately, would ensure no investment would ever occur in the places which make them. A more rational approach would be to test the fear of being abandoned. It may be as illusory to think the global economy can function anywhere as it is to believe that workers in it are self-directing agents.

Already we are seeing signs that the economy is not as locationally indifferent as has been assumed: you can buy any stock in Dubuque, Iowa, but not make a market in stocks in cornfields; the ivy cloisters of Harvard may furnish plenty of raw intellectual talent, yet lack the craziness, messiness and surprise that makes Manhattan a stimulating if unpleasant place to work. Similarly, in the developing world in Southeast Asia, it is becoming clear that location is anything but an indifferent matter; local social and cultural geographies indeed count for a great deal. This offers the possibility for making collective, local demands.

But the relation between place-making and the economy I have in mind is rather different, though a planner would hardly think it economic.

Failure, as I remarked at the opening of this chapter, can sometimes have a positive side, as when it yields a sense of personal limits or prompts recognition of others to whom one might previously have been indifferent. But even more, a person can emerge from failure, standing at a distance from the activity itself, believing that one's character cannot be wholly tested by one's acts. The psychoanalyst Heinz Hartmann called this capacity for standing apart from the tests to which one is subject in the world an 'ego strength'. Such distance serves a person when failure is relative, that is, when not doing a task well enough compared to others. Furthermore, this is a necessary strength, when a man or woman cannot cease doing the thing that is not done well enough, like work.

The heavy burden of subjective time, which took form in the modern era, repressed the ego strength of standing at a distance from oneself; the ethic of personal responsibility would not allow it. The self weighted itself with its insufficiencies. How is this burden to be lightened? More particularly, we might want to ask, could a place aid in lifting that burden of subjective time, especially today, when the self is tested more nakedly, without institutional supports?

One of the great clichés about city life is that its impersonality is a vice, cold and inhuman. But this cliché misses the virtues of crowd life. An impersonal milieu is a source of personal release. One great theme in the literature of the modern city, from Baudelaire to Aragon to Benjamin, portrays in crowds a peculiar antidote to self with all its burdens, finds in cosmopolitan life the possibility of realizing the ego strength of distance. And that theme has been realized in fact as well as theory; the waves and waves of young people who have swelled the population of modern cities have come in search of something beyond the known confines of the farm, the village or the suburb. The cultural magnet of the city is its urbanity, its diversity, its thick texture of experience.

Of course no one could crudely argue that an impersonal city life will serve contemporary society as a remedy for economic failure. But one outcome of the emerging political economy may well be that people who do not do well in it come to care less about their work. If they seek in the places where they live an alternative forum for experience, the qualities of place must help them achieve a sense of distance from work. And so it has occurred to me that experiments in impersonality, in making places denser, have to be incorporated into other strategies for making the city an open system, a place in which truly modern loyalties, mutual commitments and the exercise of sovereignty can develop.

However specific questions of place evolve in the emerging economy, the challenge of this new material order is clear. It requires new forms of polity. These forms cannot simply mirror the economic order, because that order is inimical to the growth of social experience; the economy does not 'grow' trust, loyalty and commitment. Sheer economic increase will not grow these social experiences, nor will the division of labour. They cannot be incubated instantly or quickly, as in a sudden metamorphosis of form. They require time, and so a system of growth that is both open and cohering. The new economic order has combined, in a malign fashion, with a durable cultural ethic, institutional nakedness combined with the ethic of responsibility for one's life. The forms of polity we need have somehow to help people transcend both elements of that combination. If the economy denies belonging, belonging based on exclusion, sameness or regret, will prove a poisonous medicine. We are in need of a polity that transcends economy. This was Hannah Arendt's dream; she thought she had found such a place in the ancient city. We may instead have to grow such a polity in a city which looks nothing like the places of the past.

Notes

For Carl Schorske

1 See Edmund S. Phelps (1985) *Political Economy*. New York: W.W. Norton. p. 482.

2 See Oscar and Mary Handlin, *Commonwealth*. Cambridge, MA: Harvard University Press.

3 Adam Smith (1776) *The Wealth of Nations*.

4 Garrick Utley.

5 Michael Hammer and James Champy (1994) *Reengineering the Corporation: a Manifesto for Business Revolution*. New York: HarperCollins. p. 48.

6 Michael Young, *Meritocracy*.

7 Ovid (1988) *Metamorphoses* (trans. Mary Innes). London: Penguin. p. 29.

8 Ibid.

9 See Oliver Zunz (1990) *Making America Corporate: 1870–1920*. Chicago: University of Chicago Press.

10 Friedrich Nietzsche, *Thus Spake Zarathustra*, 'On Redemption' (trans. Walter Kauffmann), in Kauffmann (1978) *The Portable Nietzsche*. New York: Viking. p. 251.

11 See Richard Sennett and Jonathan Cobb, *The Hidden Injuries of Class*.

12 See Bennett Harrison, *Lean and Mean*.

13 M. Hammer and J. Champy, *Reengineering the Corporation: A Manifesto for Business Revolution*. New York: HarperCollins. p. 65.

14 Pico della Mirandola (1965) *Oration on the Dignity of Man* (trans. Charles Gleen Wallis). Indianapolis: Bobbs-Merrill. pp. 5, 6.

2

SIMULATED SOVEREIGNTY, TELEMATIC TERRITORIALITY: THE POLITICAL ECONOMY OF CYBERSPACE

Timothy W. Luke

This chapter has two goals. First, it develops some provisional ideas about the political economy of cyberspace. Secondly, given the characteristics of cyberspace as a social structure, it considers what new, alternative types of individual and collective subjectivity become possible in these domains. The proliferation of bit-generated spaces and places opens new sites for cultural contestation and economic exploitation, which are transforming radically the everyday politics of human agency and social structure. Comprehending cyberspace, however, requires a new sensibility – perhaps 'postmodern' (Jameson, 1991), maybe 'amodern' (Latour, 1993). Cyber-netic emulations of space are generated and carried across networks of computer networks, and their operational architectures now set important limits on the use of this space, defining who is inside/outside, access-granted/access-denied, platform-compatible/platform-incompatible, operational/inoperable. Conditions of network connectivity, then, become a new locus for social conflict as the power of rule-making, rule-applying or rule-interpreting devolve to network managers, systems operators or software designers, slipping away from traditional political jurisdictions still believing that cyberspaces served on their territory adhere to their legalities. These contradictions between 'virtual life' (VL) and 'real life' (RL) are a central concern in the following analysis.

Cyberspace, or Nature: First, Second, Third

Cyberspace is not a notion about things to come; it is embedded within the material condition of things at work today. An accurate census of Internet users needs to be updated daily or weekly, not monthly or yearly, to keep track of its exponential growth. Already, many millions of main-frame and personal computers – some 50 million at this time – are linked into this network, directly or through other smaller networks. How many users, however, actually use the Internet from these points-of-entry is less clear. Numbers can be cited, but they become inaccurate even as they are reported. Most of the world's money, much of its communication, transportation and distribution systems, and many forms of data analysis now move by means of operations conducted in cyberspace.

Cyberspaces are best understood as another practical manifestation of Nature's pluralization. Human technical artifice has the capacity to reshape environmental settings through purposive-rational action, as illustrated traditionally by the second nature of technological artifice fabricated out of human industrial and agricultural activity (Attali, 1991). Informationalization goes one more iteration beyond the technical artifice of second nature, creating the hyperreal domain of digitalized third nature. The physical environment of first nature, as well as the artificial environments of second nature, is supplemented by digital environments in a new third nature.

Stories defining space and place unfold within variously historicized readings of Nature (Blackburn, 1990). Power acts, boundaries get fixed, and space can be created on terrains with particular natural properties (Luke, 1993: 229–58). Nature's varying terrains are pluralized, and then differentiated in terms of 'firstness' and 'secondness' (Lukács, 1971: 8–149) as human presence gets located in the interplay of these two modes of nature's influence (Smith, 1984). Humanity's existence in 'first nature', which is seen as having some cosmogenic or theogenic origins, during human prehistory and antiquity traditionally has provided the key mythic point of origin and field of action for human communities. First nature, then, gains its identity from the varied terrains forming the bioscape/ecoscape/geoscape of *terrestriality*. Earth, water and sky provide the basic elements mapped in physical geographies of the biosphere/geosphere that, in turn, influence human life with natural forces. In this representation of nature as first nature, as Smith suggests, 'nature is generally seen as precisely that which cannot be produced; it is the antithesis of human productive activity . . . the natural landscape presents itself to us as the material substratum of daily life, the realm of use-values rather than exchange values' (Smith, 1984: 32).

Against these foundational fields, humanity's actions in first nature transform it. And, a new anthropogenic domain in the 'second nature' of artificial technospheres becomes more significant, particularly now in the more recent historical times of the modern/capitalist/industrial era (Agnew, 1987). That sense of human power, space, order, time, value and community, now considered 'normal', derives from human societies building their communities, as well as states forming their regimes, within the second nature manufactured out of modern science, capitalist exchange and industrial technology on a worldwide scale (Poggi, 1978: 1–3). In the expanses of second nature, 'this material sub-stratum is more and more the product of social production, and the dominant axes of differentiation are increasingly social in origin . . . the development of the material landscape presents itself as a process of the production of nature' (Smith, 1984: 32).

The nation-state, mass society and global geopolitics all are historical artifacts used for constructing, and then conquering, the built environments or social spaces of second nature. Second nature, therefore, finds expression on the technoscape/socioscape/ethnoscape of *territoriality* as atoms or matter get reordered to constitute its anthropogenic operations. The actions of people, cities, economies, states constitute the spaces and times of this elaborate technosphere, while human structures and agency acquire new characteristics beyond those possible in first nature alone (Corbridge et al., 1994).

Prevailing notions of power, subjectivity and community, however, cannot fully grasp many of the changes happening in both the industrial technosphere of second nature and ecological biosphere of first nature as these elaborate human constructions of Nature's qualities become overlaid, interpenetrated and reconstituted with the 'third nature' of an informational cybersphere/telesphere (Jones, 1995). As Vattimo argues, 'the society in which we live is a society of generalized communication. It is a society of the mass media' (1992: 1). Power shifts focus, speed overcomes space, orders become disordered, time moves standards, community loses centres, values change denomination as the settings of human agency are shaken completely. Third nature, at this juncture, assumes its forms in the cyberscape/infoscape/mediascape of *telemetricality*. It too is an anthropogenic domain, but its structure is built more from bits rather than atoms (Lyotard, 1984). If, as Smith contends, 'it is in the production of nature that use-value and exchange-value, and space and society, are fused together' (1984: 32), then third nature is now recombining society with space by producing new exchange-values in unprecedented ways from the use-values of the electromagnetic spectrum, the industrial era's telecommunication infrastructures and the contemporary restructuring of labour and leisure (Luke, 1989).

Even so, 'as a social product', the spatiality of third nature remains, like first and second nature, 'simultaneously the medium and outcome, presupposition and embodiment, of social action and relationship' (Soja, 1989: 129). Digitalization shifts human agency and structure to a register of informational bits from one of manufactured matter. With this change, the conflicts of humans against Nature, other humans, and themselves are recast as these cyberspaces twist and turn in new unforeseen directions (Featherstone et al., 1995). Most importantly, the setting of agency, the character of power, and the structure of order need more elaborate interpretations to mark the differences drawn by this emergent third nature, especially in its cyberspatial domains. State powers have organized the worlds of second and first nature in such a way that global and local are two ends of a geographic continuum divided by, but defined through, the national. The perspectival space and neutral time of political realism, however, are slipping away into many more postperspectival visions of place and new rhythmic markings of time (Toulmin, 1990). The oral, particular, local and timely agendas of extra-statist social forces, set loose in the informationalizing forces of third nature's hyperreality, are contesting the written, general, universal and timeless line of statist authorities. Pluralizing the subjects and objects of communication in the proliferating networks of information 'renders any unilinear view of the world and history impossible' (Vattimo, 1992: 6). And, as a result, it is becoming difficult, or even impossible, to continue abiding by the conceptual categories imposed by orthodox discourses of political realism (Luke, 1994).

The epistemological foundations of conventional reasoning in terms of political realism are grounded in the modernist laws of second nature. Beyond the outer or inner reaches of the industrial technosphere, do these epistemic visions of what is 'real' hold true? Perhaps not. Simulations of cyberspace in the global and local flow go far beyond the old realist divisions of space and time, sender and receiver, medium and message, expression and content as third nature's complex webs of electronic networks generate new 'glocalized' hyperspaces with 'no sense of place' (Robertson, 1992). Third nature, then, is a complex of simulacra, iterating agency and structure through which there are no stable originals. And, in these domains of cyberspace, many are constructing boundaries of bits, regimes on RAM, cultures from chips, dominions with disks, companies by code.

Cyberspatial Telemetricality

The fascination with cyberspace has evolved along with the development of networked computer systems over the past 25 years. However, its larger possibilities arguably were not appreciated fully until cyberpunk science-fiction writers, like William Gibson, set their futuristic stories in cyber-spatial locales, which more sharply underscored the impact of cyberspaces upon consciousness and action today. As Gibson's *Neuromancer* (1984) suggests, cyberspace gains definition as

> a consensual hallucination experienced daily by billions of legitimate operators, in every nation, by children being taught mathematical concepts. . . . A graphic representation of data abstracted from the banks of every computer in the human system. Unthinkable complexity. Lines of light ranged in the nonspace of the mind, clusters and constellations of data. Like city lights, receding. . . . (Gibson, 1984: 51)

Generated by the distributed interactive computing of innumerable networks, cyberspaces open new practical possibilities to human perception and manipulation at whatever terminal interface – textual, graphic, audio, visual – can disclose Gibson's nonspaces of the mind with their clusters and constellations of data.

All spaces are constructs, including cyberspace, but physical space constructs in first and second nature often are mistaken as having more materialized substance (Harvey, 1989). Humans, who construct and occupy them intellectually or materially, can gather in them to discuss their qualities (Anderson, 1991). Cyberspaces, however, seem to be even more like pure constructs, because they are generated out of telecommunication/ telecomputation network operations as the complex outcomes of programming function, data systematization and network interoperation used to gather, store, manage or interpret data. All spaces are produced by human subjects and non-human objects, but cyberspace, in particular, forces human beings to reconceptualize their spatial situation inasmuch as they experience their positionalizations in cyberspace only as simulations in some 'virtual life' form. As a subjectivity-emulating non-human object or a telepresent data point/terminal action/data packet on the Net, human agency flows through the objective domains of telecommunication/ computation systems by fusing an agent's commands with structures of software code in telematic simulations of human subjectivity. Here, third nature perhaps becomes populated by new kinds of digital being. By displacing human action into another domain, new sites of identity, community and sovereignty for human subjects emerge that are, on the one hand, linked to material realities, while working, on the other hand, quite differently because of the practical properties of such cyberspatial constructs, like speed or simultaneity (Der Derian, 1990: 295–310).

Cyberspace, at the same time, is more than a collective hallucination restricted to the symbolic domains of social superstructures. It has an immense material base underpinning its operations, which depend upon complex wired and wireless systems of transmission via microwave towers, communications satellites, fibreoptic networks and on-line services. Consequently, who designs, owns, manages or operates all of the hardware needed to generate cyberspace is a key question, and none of the answers given can be described as 'natural'. Instead, there is an elaborate and expensive political economy driving cyberspatial development, which is entirely 'artificial'. The historical/political/cultural/social forces currently imagining cyberspace as 'natural giveness' mostly stand to profit tremendously from every connection, line charge, network minute, computer terminal and CD-ROM sold to access its domains.

Few moments in history witness a material possibility for pluralizing Nature, so the apparent prospect for firms and individuals to create and own entire realms of hyperreal estate on-line has moved many to reimagine themselves and all computer literate users as possessing god-like attributes. Stewart Brand, for example, sees a clear direction in the work of MIT's Media Lab 'gods' and 'wizards', arguing that it is 'junior deities, we want to be. Reality is mostly given. Virtual reality is creatable' (Brand, 1987: 116). With an estimated potential for generating $3.5 trillion a year out of computer network activity in the USA alone (Slouka, 1995: 11), such god talk is perhaps to be expected. And, with the profits derived from such dollar turnover, cyberspatial theorists might well naturalize their net connections because money, at least for them, will be no object. Indeed, some of them even imagine a new kind of immortality on the Net for themselves after experiencing such power and profit. As John Barlow asserts, 'when the yearning for human flesh has come to an end, what will remain? Mind may continue, uploaded into the Net, suspended in an ecology of voltage as ambitiously capable of self-sustenance as was its carbon-based forebears' (cited in Slouka, 1995: 11–12).

Despite such cyberhype, cyberspace portends immense changes for how societies produce wealth, order institutions, enliven agency or reproduce culture (O'Brien, 1992). Cyberspace may well be a vast cloud of on-line code rising out of all of the fibreoptic lines and hard disks of the world, but without the material infrastructure carrying the wired and wireless signals of these symbolic infostructures, cyberspatialization itself is impossible. These material mediations of the mode of information through the productive means of information, then, must not be forgotten in the fascination with what cyberspace may become as a new psychosocial domain for human action.

Dromoeconomics: Real Profits through Virtual Speed

The open ranges of third nature, at this juncture, provide the material possibilities for organizing 'dromoeconomies', or modes of production organized around controlling the speeding flows of capital, labour, information, products, resources and techniques coursing through global modes of production as the output of 'virtual offices', 'virtual factories' and 'virtual corporations' (Davidow and Malone, 1992). Whatever can be produced as bits works very efficiently in the workings of the dromoeconomy. Atoms too can be tracked and targeted by cyberspatial virtual firms, although not as directly or constantly. So computer bar coding is being inscribed upon every possible existing commodity to track their lines of flight through the virtual offices, factories and stores of cyberspatialized commerce (Davidow and Malone, 1992: 50–72). The production of services and other informational commodities (legal contracts, product promotions, movie showings, scientific papers, etc.), however, can be conducted almost entirely on networks through shareware packages or on-line services. Acknowledging the existence of all these factors coming into motion from multiple points of supply and demand, corporate entities are virtualizing their operations, or 'hollowing out' their once solid company structures as bodies at rest engaged in shaping matter on site from start to finish, in order to generate value-added outputs by monitoring/controlling/managing information about these dromoeconomic flows (Reich, 1991). Instead of creating territories of exclusive domination, they are fabricating telemetries of additive benefit about these global flows of capital, technique, information in VL to control workers, products and resources in RL.

Virtualizing Capital: VL becomes M-C-M

Virtual firms, then, produce goods and services by creating knowledge about dromoeconomic flow-launch, flow-ballistics, flow-impact, which originates within or comes to their hollowed-out structures. Like the architectural structures that municipalities erect to attract the flows to their urban domains, virtual firms essentially are shell buildings that coordinate their enterprises outputs as *kanban* capitalism, or just-in-time commerce, in which their information about how and when to assemble distillations of globally sourced components for sale at local points-of-use equals their value-adding contribution to the process of production. As Davidow and Malone argue, virtual corporations in the dromoeconomy 'will appear almost edgeless, with permeable and continuously changing interfaces between company, supplier, and consumers' (1992: 5–6). Binary gas shells were invented by artillery and chemical warfare units to keep dangerous poisonous elements inert and stable until needed by mixing them in flight to activate particular chemical reactions. Today, many goods and services are becoming binary or polynomial shells in the *kanban* commerce of dromoeconomies, keeping their components less valuable or marketable until combined in transnational flight. Pre-assemblies for all goods and services exist as components in global flows, but they are unified only in flight from point-to-point by virtualized firms monitoring the flow of their respective products every business day. In the dromoeconomy, cyberspaces in VL interweave with material components in RL, flashing telemetries of surveillance information about territorially located factors of production. Knowledge about these energies-in-motion, as well as how to launch, steer and target their impact, now exceeds in profitability and importance control over bodies-at-rest, or models where firms still attempt to occupy markets by controlling resources and capital fixed in space.

Dromoeconomics will expect firms to 'quickly and globally deliver a high variety of customized products', and virtualizing its operations in cyberspace will transform it into 'a nobe in the complex networks or suppliers, customers, engineering, and other "service" functions' (Davidow and Malone, 1992: 6). Such mass customization through dromoeconomic organization increasingly eclipses mass standardization with conventional economic operations. These shifts away from rigid, fixed sites for 'manufacture' towards loosely articulated variable geometries of *kanban* assembly for 'digitafacture' are rational responses to dromoeconomics. Rather than controlling the hands used manually to factor resources into products, firms intent upon virtualizing their operations aim to interlace many fingers of digitized telemetry about production and consumption into goods or services. Bits of data about strings of matter and flows of energy, then, can be guided to and from the most profitable sites of extraction/production/ accumulation/circulation/consumption so that buyer/user gets what is needed at the time needed in the amount needed – no more, no less.

Therefore, if one reimagines flows in the dromoeconomy as turbulence, chaos, or phased dynamics, cyberspaces – with their inherent potential for imposing panoptic surveillance capabilities over these flows – permit economic enterprises to operate as singularities for decision-making, value-adding, profit-taking (Featherstone et al., 1995). The level of complexity in global trade, the number of internationally arrayed competent producers, the depth of mass world markets, and the degree of freedom afforded by these multiple flows all prompt many rational economic actors to virtualize their operations in these cyberspaces. Of course, not all segments of all industries or markets can support virtualization; many goods and services must be produced locally in traditional ways for familiar needs. But, many parts and pieces for even these products will undoubtedly incorporate outsourced elements supplied from the turnover of the dromoeconomy.

Virtual Capital in RL

Not surprisingly, *Time*'s special cyberspace issue reports that 'corporations . . . are scrambling to stake their claims in cyberspace. Every computer company, nearly every publisher, most communications firms, banks, insurance companies and hundreds of mail-order and retail firms are registering their Internet domains and setting up sites on the World Wide Web' (*Time*, 1995: 6). Thus, the connectivity and transparency of cyberspace already is slipping towards uses that extend the exclusive proprietary market logics of capitalistic corporate territoriality into the regions of action made accessible by the Internet. The enthusiasm that corporate enterprises display for cyberspatial projects is not difficult to understand. These domains increasingly provide an unprecedented opportunity for firms to exercise their commercially mediated authoritarian powers to determine who interacts with whom, when and how interactions occur, and why interactivity has what outcomes (Lash and Urry, 1993). Cyberspaces are not easily constructed by solitary individuals, even on a local area network basis, without considerable support for network connectivity from corporate and/or government telecom services. Consequently, the third nature of cyberspatial hyperreal estate gives private firms and/or public agencies an extraordinary capability to exercise a form of private tyranny or public authoritarianism in setting the conditions and costs of entering, using or traversing cyberspatial domains. These are the stakes typically celebrated in discussions of the 'information superhighway' with its mystified use of 'roads-and-bridges' infrastructure metaphors to discuss these communicative structures. This language fits only inasmuch as such systems often are monopolistic networks of tollways, tollbooths and tollrates that impede traffic as much as they facilitate it.

It is far more accurate to envision these undertakings as extraterritorial domains of telemetrical space, being turned into exclusive zones of service-provision, profit-generation, power-creation or goods-invention by their corporate vendors. As Davidow and Malone argue, virtual corporations in these dromoeconomic domains must be understood 'in terms of patterns of information and relationships. Building virtual products will require taking a sophisticated information network that gathers data on markets and customer needs . . . and then operating this system with an integrated network that includes not only highly skilled employees of the company but also suppliers, distributors, retailers, and even consumers' (Davidow and Malone, 1992: 6). Unable to dominate territorial jurisdictions exclusively in second nature, corporate enterprises are essentially free to control telemetrical zones of profitability in third nature as their own exhaustively encrypted hyperreal estate within which they fabricate infostructures with very little regulation, oversight or administration from without or above by state authorities. In an unusually apt phrase, then, cyberspace easily can operate, through MUDs – Multi-User Dungeons – in a literal sense as global corporate equivalents of CompuServe create 'CompuServants' or American On-Line keeps 'America in-line' with their own in-house, large bandwidth 'intranets'.

Virtual Labour in RL

Labour itself can be displaced into cyberspace by generating dedicated infostructures for work in groupware packages, or as the buzzwords go, 'virtual offices'. These infotectural projects essentially capture a workplace, a work process and a work project in code, enabling different workers or work teams to work independently or jointly from many RL sites on a common VL undertaking. The product of their labour can be stored on networks in its design, development, engineering and testing phases, and then archived there to interface with computer-controlled manufacturing, assembly and shipping systems. After spending over a trillion dollars on information technology in the 1980s, real productivity increases are being realized in the 1990s as virtualizing corporations recognize 'time' is now 'the critical commodity' in dromoeconomies (Rifkin, 1995: 91, 101). Networked groupware, then, virtualizes factory jobs as well as the enterprise capital, enabling the work process to develop at higher efficiencies by looping the best services into a shared system of labour at lower levels of cost.

Yet, these circuits of labour entirely change existing sociologies of work, which have assumed physical synchronous collocation in many instances to produce various goods and services. Once the work site becomes virtual, many work relations turn into virtualized ties that are much more tenuous than even prevailing industrial systems of labour. Increasingly, workers in such virtual enterprises may have to capitalize their own production by providing their own telecom links, computer work-stations or software capabilities. Or, if they do not supply their own tools, they still may have to provide their own workplace for temporary assignments of enterprise-provided work-stations. The product of one's labour no longer necessarily appears even temporarily as a physical presence or social interaction; instead, it is immediately embedded in a collective code system. Everyone's equally alienated labour product becomes an ephemeral electronic enterprise. Labour relations with superiors, co-workers, outside vendors and clients may be mediated entirely through network linkages, reducing each one to a telepresence dealing with other telepresences. As work becomes increasingly a system of temporary, outsourced, focused assignments, a new kind of global proletariat will emerge in rough constant competition among itself in continual bidding exchanges that rob many workers of effective control over their time, energy and skills. Access to work can be easily blocked in these virtual economies by denying workers' access to corporate groupware links, cutting network ties, or denying advanced software/hardware systems to troublesome elements. The flexible downsizing of a virtual office and factory simply provide capital new ways to externalize costs upon others, enhance control over the work process, and enlarge potential profits.

Fortune magazine's 'Quarterly Report on Information Technology' (15 May 1995: 73), for example, sees 'knowledge workers, selling their labor to new species of business that will flourish in the wired economy, may need to be ready to work at a moment's notice . . . such wired workers will form "overnight armies of intellectual mercenaries"'. Virtual firms will search global nets for talent, loop them into a task-oriented shareware space, combine labour, technology, capital and resources for a few days, weeks or months to produce the product, and then disband the work group as all push on into other projects. This vision may well be the perfect fantasy of certain corporate actors. Yet, this virtual mode of production in the dromoeconomy will obliterate many current conventions pertaining to state sovereignty, workplace regulation, labour protection, government taxation, intellectual property, and national production inasmuch as they remain conceptualized as activities contained within and sheltered by territorialized space where discrete national agents and sovereign structures operate away from this dromoeconomy.

Indeed, cyberspace work sites for the dromoeconomy use virtualization to take what they need when they need it from RL agents and structures, whose locally provided education, public utilities, civic security or technical skills now will be skimmed away globally without necessarily adding much value or profit back to non-dromoeconomic settings. State sovereignty with all of its presumed powers of labour protection, workplace regulation, technological licensing, business taxation, or market control over a discrete RL space faces major obstacles to exerting its authority over virtual firms/workplaces/management that may operate for only a few hours or days in assembling transnational goods and services as flexible polynomial shells. With dromoeconomic virtualization of production, more and more workers begin 'waiting for pink slips, being forced to work part-time at reduced pay, or being pushed into the welfare rolls. . . . They become expendable, then irrelevant, and finally invisible in the new high-tech world of global commerce and trade' (Rifkin, 1995: 197) formed in the dromoeconomy.

Unfortunately, most speculation thus far about such forms of work tends to be expressed by footloose journalists, who, more or less, envision it as being just like an ordinary job in terms of pay and benefits only without having to do compulsory seat time in one fixed point of work.

These myths of telecommuting, however, mystify the more problematic realities of dromoeconomics. Instead of these options providing tremendous choices for all workers as infomatic free agents, they mostly appear instead to become work-decomposing or value-reducing manoeuvres for virtual firms. Consequently, the cyberspatial resources of global computer nets permit virtual enterprises to employ thousands of poor women in Jamaica, Mauritius or the Philippines in low-paid, tedious data entry or word-processing jobs for firms in London, Paris or San Diego. Cyberspace permits dromoeconomic entrepreneurs to virtualize segments of a core workplace at these peripheral locations, while porting the telepresence of peripheral labourers into the productive systems of a core-based company. Even *Time* observes, 'in the virtual office, paper has disappeared – and so have most employees' (1995: 38).

Cyberspaces are both fascinating and problematic social sites. They are not truly 'atopian', because a nowhere is truly a nullity. They have a material origin location in the electronic systems which generate their dimensionality through physically networked telecomputation apparatuses. In some sense, then, they are 'ectopian', or outside of ordinary space, and open to multiple contradictory appropriations by those who create and then traverse their spatial properties. Like ordinary space, they generate value by allowing for varying levels of openness or closedness to be imposed upon them as well as fostering possibilities for intensive development with secondary structures, additional amenities or informatic improvements on/ in their sites. Once all or most of these sites are running, linked up together by networks as the shared site of VL, there are remarkable implications here for the conditions of identity, community and meaning prevailing still in RL as well as the operations of states, societies and cultures in all non-virtualized, non-cyberspatial settings. Indeed, VL begins to destabilize what agency is within cyberspaces as new digital beings begin evolving in the environments of third nature.

While computer savants, like Nicholas Negroponte, talk all about the exciting technological possibilities of 'being digital', neither he nor other hardware experts consider the social potentials of the 'digital being' that emerges in those cyberspatial domains where being digital gets put into digitized social practice (Negroponte, 1995: 11–20). Subjectivity typically denotes the qualities possessed by a conscious being with significant individuality, agency, personality. How are these factors becoming rearticulated through cybernetic systems? Negroponte's enthusiasm in his *Wired* writings for all the technical possibilities for 'being digital' prevents him from posing the much more interesting questions about 'digital being'. Save for his overdrawn exaltations – which were first noticed 15 years ago by the Tofflers (1980) in *The Third Wave* – over the shift from 'atoms' to 'bits' as the wave of the future, he too sticks with the usual interpretative conceit that these new (wo)man/machine interfaces in cyberspace will simply reposition existing material styles of social agency and structure in a new cybernetic register, making everything more or less the same there as it is here, only maybe more so, meaning essentially quicker, better, closer, sharper, etc. (Lucky, 1989). That is, most things will be as they are now in synchronous, material co-location, only they will happen on-line as we realize our net connections are simply creating newer, more flexible communities. These assumptions about cybernetic subjectivity, however, are questionable. It is *not* clear from the current computer interface of (wo)man/machine that digital being is the same, only more so, as material being in terms of personal agency/social community/cultural dynamics (Luke, 1996: 1–30). Ontologically, things are getting extremely complex, and quite rapidly.

Digital Beings Enter RL: A Cyber Ontology

Third nature brings with it new biota and fresh forms of being, usually called 'artificial life' by the cybertheorists, unseen on the terrains of first and second nature. The body as an organic site for defining subjectivity now can be contested in cyberspace as its substance and presence are digitized. Indeed, one also might anticipate an entirely new political economy emerging in the digital zones of telemetricality; one rooted in the production, circulation, consumption and reproduction of digital beings. The forms of these digital beings are still indistinct, but at least three definite varieties might be described somewhat speculatively here.

Digital Being: First Form

One form of digital being emerges when actual human beings begin experiencing the cybernetic agency of becoming a computer user, working on- and off-line with complex computational systems. The fusion, or (con)fusion, of (wo)man/machine in computer applications creates many new positionalizations of subjectivity – as hardware-based, calculator, reader, viewer, writer, composer, designer, communicator as well as software-driven worker, voter, debater, inventor, observer – to consider only a few. Without networked desktop video to visualize the actual operator's physical body, this form of digital being now uses existing interfaces to let anyone to assume their own virtual personae, hyperembodiments and agencies in various telematic contexts as either bursts of pure electronic writing or displays of playful graphics. The dromoeconomic labour performed in many virtual corporations essentially occurs within these roles and routines.

The telecommuter, the lurker, the hacker, the web surfer, the newbie, the flamer, the sysop, or the hot chatterer all constitute new posts for people to represent (or misrepresent) themselves and others as cybersubjects. These positionalizations of individual agency are more than minor variants of conventional tool usage; they provide new social roles to invent and/or evade a dramaturgy of collective cultural activity as telepresences or as cyberagents (Reingold, 1993: 145–96). The bandwidth constraining most network communications now more or less dictates that such digital beings represent themselves and deal with others through a textual interface. While some symbolic refunctioning of keyboard orthography into word-signs does happen, digital beings mostly exist now on-line through point-to-point, many-to-many exchanges of spare prose that rarely fills one entire VDT screen. Graphics, scanned photos, voice and desktop video can change this sociology of digital being, but most interactions still occur within bursts of electronic writing. These mediations of one's identity as a digital being, in turn, delimit how such telepresence of hyperembodiment is experienced as a meaningful variety of personal existence.

This kind of digital being in cyberspatial political economy veers back and forth between states of existence defined either by serious work roles or fantastic play roles. Highly mobile, symbolic-analyst workers, for example, envision telecommuting, usually in slick telecom or modem advertisements, as liberation from office politics, bureaucratic drudgery, or fixed careers, because their laptops and modems link them back into their physical workplaces as they perform new types of free, self-guided, pleasant labour at the beach or in the mountains. Digital being here is a liberated subjectivity able to go anywhere anytime anyway and still stay productive in efficient work relations. Telecommuting, however, also can assume the more common form of off-shore, low-wage sweatshops where female data-entry or wordprocessing specialists move raw data or text by the keystroke through satellite switches to major corporations in Los Angeles, London or Leipzig. On the other hand, cybersexual subjectivity can be thoroughly fantastic and playful. Because physical bodies do not appear in the interface, digital sexual beings can choose to be male, female, young, old, heterosexual, homosexual, transsexual, etc., even if they are not. Virtual identity varies widely in cybersex, allowing anyone to do anything anytime anyway with anyone or anything.

Telecommuting or cybersex can be linked back into real time and space, but the actual identity of the material beings actually acting most often is anonymous, disguised or fictional (Rushkoff, 1994). Digital being allows one to reinvent varying identities for work or play that can be adapted to different real or hyperreal contexts. Work contracts solicited over the Internet may be won by bidders who disguise their age/gender/race in virtual identities to compete more openly with bigger, different, richer competitors; sexual liaisons can occur between two digital beings – perhaps, for example, one male, one female – invented maybe, on the one hand, by a duo of bored junior female bankers and, on the other hand, a group of male transvestites, who all vicariously enjoy playing the virtual parlour games of these kinds of digital beings. The liberating possibilities of these activities, however, cut more than one way. As the current controversy over cyberporn on the Internet indicates, VL digital being also can be the mediation of dark violent urges from RL.

Digital being, as a positionalization of cybersubjectivity, is interesting morally, politically or socially. Many real ethical moves presume face-to-face contact, or materially embodied synchronous collocation, like politics

or sex. Yet, these digital beings create cybersubjective interactions that
apparently satisfy their initiators in screen-to-screen non-contact or
virtually disembodied asynchronous dis-location. Libertarians assert we
should be free to do anything in our own private sphere as long as it does
not harm others; yet, digital subjects may or may not inhabit personal
spheres that conform to such ordinary notions of privacy. Likewise, in
these realms of digital being, what is harmed and how is it harmed? What
new legal, political, cultural rules for VL should guide hyperreal behaviour? Digital beings of this sort might be encouraged, for example, to press
for teledemocracy in cybernetic referenda. Would voters approach it
somewhat seriously, like real embodied civic voting, or mostly as play, like
hyperreal on-line cybersex? Should digital beings, who indulge in imagining
acts of murder, rape, torture, dismemberment to other digital beings in
some kinky MUD be sanctioned somehow in VL or RL for their digital
acts of sociopathological being? Would only new digital VL laws pertain
here or would old RL laws need to be mapped over? Who would promul-
gate and enforce them? Telepresence is and is not like a material presence,
but might not digital beings expect some RL categorical imperatives to
operate in cyberspace? Or, because bodies are digitized and agency is
fictive, will the RL moralities of material being fit poorly the VL expectations of digital being in hyperreality.

Digital Being: Second Form

Secondly, and less prominent in most discussions, another variety of digital
being emerges out of software assemblies as computer designers push for
intelligent agency by designing new personal services into hardware and
code structures. Programming design has advanced significantly as new
bioemulations, or artificial life-forms, are being created to coevolve with
people. This sort of digital being has evolved with great rapidity alongside
computer machineries and networks. Looking at real computer systems,
for example, one finds thousands of artificially generated organisms, like
computer viruses, worms or bacteria, which essentially are digital parasites,
living off the ecological resources provided by computer hardware (Levy,
1992). Whether it is a diskette, a hard disk, a mainframe CPU, or network
server, these ecologies are colonized by digital beings, who survive as self-
reproducing pests, only in the cyberenvironments of real computers. At the
same time, artificial life designers create 'virtual computers' within real
computers, as a type of bioisolation lab, to generate new virtual organisms
that should occupy only the virtual environments emulated by these isolation chambers. Here digital being takes many forms as cellular automata,
pattern machines, game artifacts or genetic algorithms; their vitalistic
properties, in turn, can be controlled to prevent them from becoming viral
parasites in real computer systems (Emmeche, 1994: 39–42, 114–17; Kelly,
1994: 166–83).

Such digital beings are only being made out of computer code, but increasingly they have many conventional accepted signs of life – intelligence, sentience, agency, prudence, creativity. What are these digital beings who now are beginning to inhabit cyberspaces? The fusion, or (con)fusion, of labour/machine in software packages creates post-zoological agents with many new positionalizations of subjectivity – as receptionist, mail sorter, batman, personal assistant, chamberlain, travel planner, executive secretary as well as research assistant, data analyst, pattern detector, symbolic analyst, communications operator, calendar keeper, life master. Already a few crude intelligent agent systems, such as 'Bob' or 'Wildfire', occupy cyberspatial niches for their owners/users performing all or some of these tasks in virtual offices linked into the dromoeconomy. As these packages become individually customized by their users in particular cultural/ familial/historical practice, as well as more sapient in their intelligence or liberated in their agency, one must ask what these digital beings are *qua* beings in our time? Are they purely dead functional appliances or does their intelligent agency make them somehow alive?

Such personal digital assistants (PDAs) will be much more than a gizmo, like Apple's Newton, but maybe much less than a zoological life-form, like a seeing-eye dog. As they evolve, they could indeed become a very vital presence in many of our lives (Mazlish, 1993). In fact, as digital recorders with total omniscience, they can be the definitive chroniclers/ recorders/masters of our life inasmuch as their digital being mediates between us and other digital beings as well as between us and other living human and non-human beings. How will these digital beings be created? Who will introduce them into our existence? What protections will they have? Which ones will be empowered to do what for ends? And when will they be terminated? Particularly when one intelligent agent is directed to meet with, and negotiate with, another's intelligent agent with moral and legal force, in some sense as envoys/mediators/dealmakers/decisiontakers, how will their being be regarded: (1) as robotic extensions of their owners, like telephone 'answering' machines or audiotaped 'letters'; (2) as purely private property of their owners, like slaves or animals; (3) as subjects of employment by their owners, like bondsmen, or apprentices; or (4) as in-house chattel of computer networks, like Baby Bell voicemail systems or menu routines in Microsoft software packages? Are they virtual representatives with some modicum of their own pre-authorized discretion, actual representatives carrying only our direct brief, or physical representatives simply tracing telepresences from otherwise positioned human beings acting remotely from somewhere else? Empowered to protect and serve their users/owners in cyberspace, these intelligent agents in such forms of historicized being may be forced to give witness, endanger information, disclose secrets, reveal decisions, or provide access against their instructions. What rules would hold then? Are they truly conversant intelligent agents with some sort of legal protections? Or, are they essentially dumb dead boxes available for inspection at any time by anyone? If so, then what sort of respect or rights might be extended to them and why?

Musing about such cybernetic subjects may seem silly, because, after all, the intelligent agents being generated by computational biology can only be machinic slaves to or servants of their masters (Emmeche, 1994: 156–66). Yet, notwithstanding the issues raised by Hegel's master/slave dialectic, is this entirely fair? Some cybernetic visionaries foresee a human life beyond the body. And here they are not talking about some future biomechanical resurrection of a human being's zoological wetware from a cryogenic deep freeze. Instead, as Hans Moravec (1988) at Carnegie-Mellon University dreams, why not transfer all of a living human being's memories, intelligence, agency, knowledge, experience as sophisticated computer code on to chips or into software, bringing now perhaps even the living person's actual voice on a sound chip. Therefore, what if a living human being becomes another kind of PDA – a personified digital agency, a postbionic demonic avatar, or a previously embodied digital angel? What would these humanoid digital beings be: merely bizarre simulacra of once zoological forms or truly intelligent human agencies? Brain death in the body could be sublated by brain life on the Net, creating unbelievable dilemmas betwixt and between postzoological notions of life and death, agency and property, identity and power, being and time. Already one's home page on the Net carries ambiguous messages; what operates now as an on-line curriculum vitae can easily be reprogrammed as an interactive cybercenotaph.

While living beings cannot now migrate from carbon-based to silicon-based bodies, a king of *Jurassic Park*-like resurrection of the once dead from the still crypts of an analog grave occurs everyday as morphing magic pulls bits of code from the amber suspension of old celluloid film stock, plastic LP records or oxide audio tape. Mixed in morphing programs, simulated by sampling routines, colourized from chromatic computations, the crisp images of real bodies or rich echoes of actual voices long ago lost to real-time analog death return in Coca-Cola commercials or *Forest Gump*-eries as golems ground together out of gigabytes of digital dust. Now smart movies can cast living-dead digital actors in new supporting roles speaking in sampled voices and moving within morphed bodies alongside real actors. Smart recording studios already stage cyberspatial music jams, allowing us to listen to Hanks Williams, Sr. and Hank Williams, Jr. sing new kinds of digital ballads, hear Nat King Cole do duets with daughter Natalie Cole, and enjoy John Lennon rejoin the still living Beatles to sing on real-time records from cyberspace in hyperreal arrangements.

Digital Being: Third Form

These bizarre, but nonetheless real, possibilities return us to our taxonomy of digital being. Thirdly, and least prominent in many discussions, another kind of digital being is developing within 'smart machines' as engineers attempt to androidize hitherto dumb/mute machines, transforming them into smart/talking/expert digital beings. For this third form of digital being, computerized applications of intelligent agency are being substantively integrated into technical objects, giving many such artifacts most of the key classical traits of human life – consciousness, intelligence, personality, memory, speech, agency or experience (Negroponte, 1995: 206–18). The fusion, or (con)fusion, of living being/dead machine in a fabricated artifact generates another sort of parabionic agent with many new significant positionalizations of subjectivity – as talking car, smart house, electronic wallet, knobotic terminal, autopiloting boat, prudent drone, brilliant munition, aware apartment, surveillant store, intelligent toilet (Kelly, 1994: 166–202). There are only some of the virtual products that consumers seem to want from the mass customization machinery of virtual corporations.

Digital control plus digital speech synthesis and voice recognition are animating once dumb objects, permitting them to be voice-activated varieties of smart subjects. Unable to converse with most non-human beings in first nature, human beings are combining elements from second and third nature into a new kind of digital being with embodied/material/active/intelligent capabilities, including the powers of problem-solving or the facility of voice to permit them conversant interactions with humans. Entire new species of these digital beings can coevolve with human beings in quasi-objective/quasi-subjective networks, which essentially are the basic formative ecologies for a cyborg subjectivity (Stock, 1993).

Such beings are neither *Star Trek: Next Generation's* Data nor even *Star War's* C3PO with their Hollywood-styled forms of highly anthropomorphic digital being. Instead they are more like the Starship Enterprise in old *Star Trek* classic episodes in which the space vehicle itself with all of its on-board computer systems, human and non-human life supports, and sensing arrays was an intelligent digital being with distributed intelligence constructed into its own machinic structure. With enough conscious agency for its own baseline guidance, and a conversant consciousness with basic analytical problem-solving powers engineered into its own cybernetic systems, the Enterprise represents how complex a voice-activated digital being can be. Such forms of digital being are now beginning to coevolve as unique new species of beings anywhere humans attempt to androidize their tools. The closest approximation to this kind of intelligent technology today undoubtedly can be found in the decentralized, adaptive, flexible, collaborative, and distributed, systems evolving in the networks of networks looped into the Internet structure.

This form of digital being is not science fiction; precursors already exist in concrete prefigurations as intelligent materials, smart weapons, voice-activated mechanisms, fly-by-wire systems or robotic complexes. Even without contact with human cybernetic subjectivity of the first type, these beings would have qualities of digital life with their strong emulations of consciousness, sentience, prudence, agency or personality in each of their cybermechanical structures (De Landa, 1991: 179–231). Once they exist in greater numbers more widely, we might consider all of the implications of coexisting with such digital beings. And, when genetic algorithms are coupled with robotic factories to turn out new generations of conversant computers, intelligent materials, or expert tools, then truly new phyla of digital beings may well begin evolving separate and apart from any direct human intervention. The technological assumptions built into (semi)autonomous weapons systems, like PROWLER (Programmable Robot Observer with Logical Enemy Response) or Brilliant Pebbles (a Star Wars ABM system), plainly may make other forms of autonomous artifacts, expert systems or smart devices far more common inhabitants of our existing social spaces (De Landa, 1991: 160–78).

These distinctions between varieties of digital being have been analytical. As the evolution of different digital beings becomes more prevalent throughout many sectors of society, it is apparent that the second and third forms of digital being mostly are specialized derivations devised to cope with the shortcomings and downsides of the existing technical interfaces of (wo)man/machine for the first type of digital being. Being telepresent has its costs, including an open acceptance of other telepresent interactions that soon makes creating a cybernetic receptionist almost essential. More and more digital socialization by human beings as a digital impersonation invites a further and further elaboration of new digital networks of interaction, which, in turn, necessitate the creation of the second form of digital being to handle the traffic of the first form's digital existence. Intelligent agents evolve to cope with the human challenges of becoming and remaining a digital being; otherwise, much too much time is to be lost simply in sorting through blizzards of e-mail and returning them in kind as a first form of digital being.

The basic 'user unfriendliness' of the keyboard interface, even when its workings are massaged by the ministrations of an intelligent agent, invites further innovations in the domain of (wo)man/machine interfaces. Third-form digital beings that can be talked to, or ordered about, as part of normal patterns of ordinary speech create new types of humanity/technics interactivity by transcending crude, slow alphanumeric strings of electronic writing via QWERTY keyboards as the human being's mediation of his/her telepresence or cybersubstance. Turning hitherto mute and dumb objects into beings with native voice and intrinsic intelligence totally transforms the ecologies of digital being. All three forms certainly will evolve together as an existential ensemble of diverse repositionalizations of personal agency. At the same time, the second form enhances the operations of the first form just as the third form elaborates possibilities in the second and first forms by settling permanent cyberagencies of intelligence, memory, experience and perceptiveness into the material shape of software systems and hardware formations (Levy, 1992; Mazlish, 1993).

All of these digital beings are cyborg agents: hybrids of human and non-human, subject and object, (wo)man and machine, consciousness and corporeality in a new cybernetic register. Without the software/hardware/

network ensembles actually enabling the forms of digital being projected by telecommuting or cybersex, this sort of cybersubjective position could not be taken. Without routinized taskserving codes or network links, the digital being of intelligent agents would have no environment to adapt themselves as a new kind of existence in our forms of cybernetic subjectivity. And, without the command/control/communication packages being embedded into industrial artifacts to empower them with consciousness, voice and memory, the digital being of smart artifacts would have no agency to evince. Whether they are hybrids or not, these digital beings all are coexisting with us in our being and time, and our subjectivity is being enhanced and constrained by the qualities of many of our interactions with them. Essentially, digital beings invite us again to amend the ontological constitution we uphold with its various traditional articles for defining how human and non-human, agent and structure, subject and object might confederate in our Nature/Culture contracts (Latour, 1993: 136–45).

Once all of these digital beings are seen as existing *per se*, how will they be treated as beings? What legal status, political identity, economic agency, cultural structure, theological meaning will they have? Do they represent monstrous beings living on the margins, surviving at the edge, adapting to the infrastructures inside and outside of material and virtual reality? With digital gills and analog lungs, virtual fins and material legs, these amphibious agencies already are rapidly coevolving with humanity. New questions, however, arise with our coevolution in third nature (Stock, 1993). Will they reproduce as separate species? Or will even more fascinating hybrids emerge out of telemetricality as telepresent human beings (first form) couple with crews of expert systems (second form) on smart space probes (third form) to explore distant extraterrestrial sites, or, even more problematically, with weapons platforms to scan heavily defended territorial sites on Earth? Will material human beings nearing biological death in RL clone their personalities into software intelligent agents (second form) to take a hardline as VL immortals against real people in the material world? Or will they, as Moravec's software immortals (second form), really migrate into a smart house, talking car, or intelligent material (third form) to find new historical embodiments? Even more strangely, might any of these digital life-forms clone themselves, combine with viruses, or commingle as code-and-apparatus to create virtual reproductive lineages of VL artificial life in a purely postbionic RL zoology?

Infotectures for VL: A Conclusion

Cyberspaces are new realms of space – or a third nature – generated by digital computation and communication in flows of numerical data encrypted to represent video images, spoken language, musical performances, textual script, graphic displays or hardware instructions. Still, these domains of space even now rarely are apprehended in spatial terms as old interpretative registers of semiotics, cybernetics or even electronics still are used to appraise what has been traditionally called 'the man/machine' nexus of informatic activity. Software and networks do more than structure and present information; they also, more importantly, generate and sustain spaces, or hyperreal estates, which need to be rethought as spatial domains for human activity with their own unique properties of accessibility/inaccessibility, boundedness/unboundedness, underdevelopment/overdevelopment, security/insecurity, publicity/private, openness/ enclosure or commodification/collectivization for the various cybersubjectivies now beginning to inhabit them in groupware, thoughtware, mediaware formations as digital beings.

Ordinary language now speaks in terms of computer environments, office environments, telecommunications environments, software environments, etc. These metaphorical allusions disclose real shifts in how people/ systems interface/interact/interrelate, because 'environments' are, following the Old French origins of the English term, surrounded, encircled, beleaguered space. Who surrounds, encircles, beleaguers what, whom, when, why and how is a political question, moving far beyond naïve appraisals of cybernetics as mere machine performances or computing environments in simple systems applications. Cyberspaces, as environmental sites, are points of contestation where informational discourses seek to generate the identities or discipline behaviours of digital beings by stipulating what operating systems do, how software performs, why machines network, when database access occurs. Information design – its styling, assumptions, rhetoric, goals – expresses all of these tendencies in code by inventing new textual displays and graphic packages for interface design. Thus far, most of this has not been done very artfully.

Software and hardware ensembles need to be reappraised not as inert combinations of machine instructions and instructed machines but rather as sites of third nature's genesis, creating artificial environments for new social formations and digital beings out of their interactivities. Third nature will evolve its own inhabitants – digital beings will occupy cities of bits, biomes of bytes (Mitchell, 1995). Cyberspaces will be occupied by virtual im-personations of their users and/or avatars of machine functions; hence, informatic design needs to envision an evolution of cyborg lifeforms beyond today's simple artificial life, like existing computer viruses. In such cyberspaces, what shapes the digital being and time of such cyberpresence? How realistic or hyperrealistic will the im-personations of specific human subjects become? Are they repositionalizations of real agents in hyperreal spaces, reinventions of subjectivity for cyberspace, or recreations of life in another dimension that gives their encoder's theogenic powers? Whether or not such virtual built environments will feature other fauna or flora to coevolve/coexist in particular cyberecological niches now raises additional design issues for a very unique kind of bioengineering in/for/of cyberbiota and cyberbiomes.

What exists for human beings is mostly disclosed by words. Familiar words open only old worlds, but unfamiliar words might unlock new worlds that have yet to be clearly disclosed. Existing terms will gain new meanings, and now non-existent worlds will be discerned by bringing new languages of theory, culture and society into common currency (Featherstone, 1990). To comprehend the political economy of cyberspace, its worlds of cyberspatial hyperreality, or the realms of third nature, call for hyperreal words to capture the virtuality of the digital beings unfolding there. Power works insidiously enough now in ordinary institutional disciplines and expert discourses in RL: how might it work as these structural shifts become more widely realized for digital beings inside cyberspatial structures, enacting VL practices? Informatic communities or dromoeconomies must evaluate all of these questions in reinventing the rhetorics of their representation as the new subjectivities of digital being begin inhabiting the telematic territories of cyberspace.

References

Agnew, J. (1987) *Place and Politics: The Geographical Mediation of State and Society*. Boston: Allen & Unwin.

Anderson, B. (1991) *Imagined Communities* (rev. edn). London: Verso.

Attali, J. (1991) *Millenium: Winners and Losers in the Coming World Order*. New York: Random House.

Blackburn, R.J. (1990) *The Vampire of Reason: An Essay in the Philosophy of History*. London: Verso.

Brand, S. (1987) *The Media Lab: Inventing the Future at MIT*. New York: Viking.

Corbridge, S., Martin, R. and Thrift, N. (eds) (1994) *Money, Power and Space*. Oxford: Blackwell.

Davidow, W.H. and Malone, M.S. (1992) *The Virtual Corporation: Restructuring and Revitalizing the Corporation for the 21st Century*. New York: HarperCollins.

De Landa, M. (1991) *War in the Age of Intelligent Machines*. New York: Zone Books.

Der Derian, J. (1990) 'The (S)pace of international relations: simulation, surveillance, and speed', *International Studies Quarterly*, 34 (September): 295–310.

Emmeche, C. (1994) *The Garden in the Machine: The Emerging Science of Artificial Life*. Princeton, NJ: Princeton University Press.

Featherstone, M. (ed.) (1990) *Global Culture: Nationalism, Globalization and Modernity*. London: Sage.

Featherstone, M., Robertson, R. and Lash, S. (eds) (1995) *Global Modernities*. London: Sage.

Fortune (1995) 'Quarterly report on information technology', 131 (15 May): 73–88.

Gibson, W. (1984) *Neuromancer*. New York: Ace Books.

Harvey, D. (1989) *The Condition of Postmodernity*. Oxford: Blackwell.

Jameson, F. (1991) *Postmodernism, or the Cultural Logic of Late Capitalism*. Durham, NC: Duke University Press.

Jones, S.G. (ed.) (1995) *Cybersociety: Computer-mediated Communication and Community*. London: Sage.

Kelly, K. (1994) *Out of Control: The Rise of Neo-Biological Civilization*. Reading, MA: Addison-Wesley.

Lash, S. and Urry, J. (1993) *Economies of Signs and Space*. London: Sage.

Latour, B. (1993) *We Have Never Been Modern*. London: Harvester Wheatsheaf.

Levy, S. (1992) *Artificial Life*. New York: Pantheon.

Lucky, R.W. (1989) *Silicon Dreams: Information, Man and Machine.* New York: St Martin's Press.

Lukács, G. (1971) *History and Class Consciousness.* Cambridge, MA: MIT Press.

Luke, T.W. (1989) *Screens of Power: Ideology, Domination, and Resistance in Informational Society.* Urbana, IL: University of Illinois Press.

Luke, T.W. (1993) 'Discourses of disintegration, texts of transformation: re-reading realism', *Alternatives,* 18: 229–58.

Luke, T.W. (1994) 'Placing powers/siting spaces: the politics of global and local in the new world order', *Environment and Planning D: Society and Space,* 12: 613–28.

Luke, T.W. (1996) 'Liberal society and cyborg subjectivity: the politics of environments, bodies, and nature', *Alternatives,* 21: 1–30.

Lyotard, J.F. (1984) *The Postmodern Condition.* Minneapolis, MN: University of Minnesota Press.

Mazlish, B. (1993) *The Fourth Discontinuity: The Co-evolution of Humans and Machines.* New Haven, CT: Yale University Press.

Mitchell, W.J. (1995) *City of Bits: Space, Place and the Infobahn.* Cambridge, MA: MIT Press.

Moravec, H. (1988) *Mind Children.* Cambridge, MA: Harvard University Press.

Negroponte, N. (1995) *Being Digital.* New York: Knopf.

O'Brien, R. (1992) *Global Financial Integration: The End of Geography.* New York: Council on Foreign Relations Press.

Poggi, G. (1978) *The Development of the Modern State: A Sociological Introduction.* Stanford, CA: Stanford University Press.

Reich, R.B. (1991) *The Work of Nations: Preparing Ourselves for 21st-Century Capitalism.* New York: Knopf.

Reingold, H. (1993) *The Virtual Community: Homesteading on the Electric Frontier.* Reading, MA: Addison-Wesley.

Rifkin, J. (1995) *The End of Work: The Decline of the Global Labor Force and the Dawn of the Post-Market Era.* New York: G.P. Putnam's Sons.

Robertson, R. (1992) *Globalization: Social Theory and Global Culture.* London: Sage.

Rushkoff, D. (1994) *Cyberia: Life in the Trenches of Hyperspace.* San Francisco: HarperCollins.

Slouka, M. (1995) *War of the Worlds: Cyberspace and the High-Tech Assault on Reality.* New York: Basic Books.

Smith, N. (1984) *Uneven Development.* Oxford: Blackwell.

Soja, E. (1989) *Postmodern Geographies.* London: Verso.

Stock, G. (1993) *Metaman: The Merging of Humans and Machines into a Global Superorganism.* New York: Simon & Schuster.

Time (1995) 'Welcome to cyberspace: special issue', 145 (12) Spring.

Toffler, A. and Toffler, H. (1980) *The Third Wave.* New York: Bantam.

Toulmin, S. (1990) *Cosmopolis: The Hidden Agenda of Modernity.* New York: Free Press.

Vattimo, G. (1992) *The Transparent Society.* Baltimore, MD: Johns Hopkins University Press.

3

DIGITAL NETWORKS AND POWER

Saskia Sassen

This is a particular moment in the history of digital networks, one when powerful corporate actors and high-performance networks are strengthening the role of private electronic space and altering the structure of public electronic space. Electronic space has emerged not simply as a means for communicating, but as a major new theatre for capital accumulation and the operations of global actors.

Our thinking about electronic space and network power, however, has been shaped by the properties of the Internet. The Internet is a space of distributed power that limits the possibilities of authoritarian and monopoly control. It is by now well known that the particular features of the Internet are in part a function of the early computer hacker culture which designed software that strengthened the original design of the Net – openness and decentralization – and which sought to make it universally available at no cost. But it is becoming evident since the mid-1990s that it is also a space for contestation and segmentation. Now that business has discovered the Net, we are seeing attempts to commercialize it through the development of software that can capitalize on the Net's features and through the extension of copyrights – in other words, the opposite of the early hacker culture.

Further, it has become important to distinguish the Internet, or public space, and private electronic space. When it comes to the broader subject of network power, most computer networks are private. It might be worth repeating that even if we just consider Internet Protocol-compatible networks and we take the figures for the period preceding the explosion of business interest in the Net, also then most networks were private: just counting networks as opposed to traffic volume, in 1994 there were about 40,000 IP-compatible networks, but the Internet itself accounted for about 12,000 of these. Since then both figures have jumped enormously. The main point here is that a lot of network power may not necessarily have the attributes of the Internet. Indeed, much of this is concentrated power and reproduces hierarchy rather than distributed power. The financial markets, operating largely through private electronic networks, are a good instance of an alternative form of electronic network power. The three properties of electronic networks – speed, simultaneity and interconnectivity – have produced strikingly different outcomes in this case from those of the Internet.

In this regard, it seems to me that we need to re-theorize electronic space and uncouple it analytically from an exclusive focus on the properties of the Net which have so sharply shaped our understanding. For me, a political economist interested in space and power, this task is located at the intersection of a number of discourses and assumptions and at the intersection of the digital and the non-digital. This brief chapter is a mere beginning towards mapping the conditions for grounding a new type of theorization. The first section examines where we are at in terms of the analysis and theorization of the Internet – a sort of review of the state of the art. The second section examines what is different today in the actual conditions of electronic space compared to even a few years ago. The next two sections examine the internal segmentation of electronic space and the ways in which it is embedded in larger societal structures.

Narrating the Internet Today

The polarization between Internet romancers on the one hand, and the logic of business and markets on the other, is contributing to a parallell polarization in the discourse about electronic space: a utopian approach that emphasizes the decentralization and electronic democracy of the Net, and a dystopian approach that emphasizes the global power of the large corporations.

Neither account is adequate today. While corporate forces have immense power in the shaping of digital networks, it is also a moment when we are seeing the emergence of a fairly broad-based civil society – though as yet a minor share of world population – in electronic space, particularly in the Net, which signals the potential for further developing distributive forms of power. Further, each of these accounts rests on assumptions that limit the possibility of critical appraisals and future potentialities.

Two assumptions that run through much of the discourse of the Internet romancers veil the existence of new forms of concentrated power that may undermine the better features of the Internet; nor do these assumptions help us understand the limits of such new forms of concentrated power, an important political issue. One assumption is that it will always be the open, decentralized space it was designed to be. This is an ahistorical notion derived from the experience of what in my view can now be seen as a first era of the Internet. John Perry Barlow's 'A declaration of the independence of cyberspace' probably epitomizes this view (1997). Besides this political utopian vision there now is also an economic utopian view, especially strong in the USA, which sees the Net as offering the possibility of a whole new type of market economy, one truly open and democratic. The California-based *Wired* magazine is a key axis for this line of thought. The second assumption, tightly interlinked with the first, is that electronic space is a purely technological event, and in that sense an autonomous space to be read in technical terms. One implication of such a technological reading is the notion that it can escape existing structures of power and inequality.

The dystopian view of the Internet has its own limiting assumptions. Big capital will take over and the new high-income transnational class will also become a virtual class, with its spatial mobility further enhanced by digital mobility. The rest will be left out and at best reduced to passive consumers of Internet commerce. A different type of dystopian view is centred on questions of subjectivity: the transformation in the conditions through which our subjectivity is formed due to the overwhelming presence of technology-intermediated sociability. This is a cultural pessimism derived from a notion that the new digital technologies will replace all other technologies through which people connect: the telephone replaced by e-mail, work in office buildings by tele-work from home, social visits by on-line chat clubs, business travel replaced by video conferencing, actual experiences by virtual reality games. Strong examples of this view are found especially among European intellectuals, typically those who are not vigorous users, if users at all, of the Internet (see, for example, most of the presentations at the 1996 Frankfurt Römerberg Gesprache).

Both the utopian and the dystopian views rest on assumptions that limit our understanding of current conditions and developments, and in that sense are what I have elsewhere (Sassen, 1996b) described as narratives of eviction. The utopian view excludes the fact that electronic space is embedded in actual societal structures and is internally segmented. Both conditions produce new types of advantage and disadvantage and hence carry enormous implications for current and future developments as well as for the theorization of networked space and power. The dystopian view excludes the limitations and complementary dependencies of the new digital technologies – no technology is an absolute: it cannot replace all other technologies aimed at similar functions, in this case communication and interactivity. The dystopian view excludes the fact of growing contestation between powerful economic actors and civil society in public electronic space, a force for strengthening political activity.

My concern here is not to show fatal flaws. I am quite convinced that when we are dealing with issues of such complexity, which enter the realm of power and subjectivity, we need explorations that pursue a particular line to the end. To some extent both the utopian and dystopian views have done this. These explorations become analytic zones that we need to negotiate, rethinking their mutually exclusive narratives not as separated by dividing lines, but rather as being susceptible to unfolding into analytic zones in their own right – dividing lines become borderlands (see Sassen, 1996b for a more detailed account of the concept of analytic borderlands). Rather than lines that divide and therewith produce analytic silences, we need to construct borderlands that merit their own empirical and theoretical specification. I do think this is the point we are at in trying to theorize electronic space and power.

There is an incipient literature that enacts this negotiation. Among the more important is the ongoing work of the recently created collective *Nettime* (1997; Lovink, 1998), formed by people who are very knowledgeable about the Internet, many of whom are Net activists, but at the same time critical of the romancing of the Net I described above. Perhaps the most radical analysis and theorization about the Internet's power to inscribe lived experience and the mental categories through which we experience and understand can be found in the work of Arthur and Mari louise Kroker (e.g., 1996; see also their 'Cyberstories for the Road' presented at the Museum der Gestaltung in Zurich, 9 March 1996). I would also include in this incipient literature of negotiation, some of the work carried out by the Telepolis project of the Akademie des Jahres Drei Thausends in Munich (e.g., the on-line journal *Telepolis*); the work of the Interface project, of Hamburg, and the long-standing Ars Electronica of Linz (e.g., selections by such authors as Peter Weibel, Geert Lovink and Peter Druckrey in the 1995 volume). On a very different critical line is the work by such scholars as Calabrese and Borchert (1996) who are arguing that telecommunications policy cannot be reduced to deregulation in order to facilitate privatization and competition because communications media are deeply connected to basic rights of citizens in a democracy. Similarly, the Euricom group seeks to recast the role of the welfare state in terms of the expansion of basic citizen rights, including the right to access to communications media (see Euricom conference of October 1997, to be published in Calabrese and Burgelman, 1999; Münker and Roesler, 1997).

What much of this work does is to bring together knowledge about the Net (which many 'cultural pessimists' lack) and a deep awareness of the threats (which many utopians ignore) to the Internet as we have known it coming from the mass discovery by business of the Net. Some of these works also contain a deep and radical critique (again, by people who really know the Net, such as the Krokers) not so much of the Net but of a broader cultural condition which the Net can amplify. It used to be that most critiques came from those who did not know or use the medium and were deeply suspicious of it, all of it resulting in a total rejection.

Networks, Markets, Hierarchies

The Internet and private computer networks have coexisted for many years. But there is something different today, and it is this difference that drives my concern with the need to re-theorize the Net and the need to address the larger issue of electronic space or digital networks rather than just the Net, as well as the larger issue of network power rather than just the distributed form of power characterizing the Net. Suddenly, over the last few years, the two major actors in electronic space – the corporate sector and civil society – which until recently had little to do with one another in electronic space, are running into each other. Then as today, corporate actors largely operate in private computer networks and as recently as the early 1990s business had not yet discovered the Internet in any significant fashion.

But by the mid-1990s there were major new conditions. The World Wide Web – the multimedia portion of the Net – became available in 1993 with all its potentials for commercialization – and the digitalization of the entertainment industry and of business services exploded on the scene. We have seen a growing digitalization and globalization of leading economic sectors and a growing economic importance of electronic space. This has further contributed to the hyperconcentration of resources, infrastructure and central functions, with global cities as one strategic site in the new global economic order. Globalization and digitalization have furthered global alliances among firms and massive concentrations of capital and corporate power. They have also contributed to new forms of segmentation in electronic space, which has emerged as one of the sites for the operations of global capital and the formation of new power structures.

This is also the context within which we need to read the recent and sharp trends towards deregulation and privatization which have made it possible for the telecommunications industry to operate globally and in a growing number of economic sectors. Communication and information sectors are progressively being deregulated in an increasing number of countries all over the world: some governments, notably that of the USA, are reducing and even eliminating distinctions between local and international providers, between ownership of networks and production of software, and relaxing restrictions on ownership of television and radio stations. Perhaps one of the most far-reaching reforms in this regard is the recently approved new communications act of 8 February 1996 in the USA. Governments are under pressure to deregulate and privatize because the products are becoming increasingly global, the actors are global, and so are the major equipment manufacturers and the media companies. Most companies pursue this global project through international alliances and cooperations, which means that companies in many different countries are putting pressure on governments to deregulate and privatize the communications industry, a key part of the mix of industries usually referred to as the digital sector.

And yet, non-commercial uses still dominate the Internet. The race is on to invent ways of expanding electronic commerce and ensuring safety of payment transactions (e.g., Aspen Roundtable, 1998). But at the same time there has been a proliferation of non-commercial uses and users. Civil society, whether it be individuals or NGOs, is a very energetic presence in cyberspace. From struggles to support human rights, the environment and workers strikes around the world to genuinely trivial pursuits, the Net has emerged as a powerful medium for non-elites to communicate, support each other's struggles and create the equivalent of insider groups at scales going from the local to the global.

The political and civic potential of these trends is enormous. It offers the possibility for interested citizens to act in concert. Several authors have examined the possibility of enhancing democratic practices through the formation of communities on the Net and the possible role of governments in supporting them (Calabrese and Borchert, 1996). The possibility of doing so transnationally at a time when a growing set of issues are seen as escaping the bounds of nation-states makes this even more significant. We are also seeing a greater variety of subcultures on the Net in the last few years after being dominated by young white men, especially from the USA. The growth of global corporate actors has also profoundly altered the role of government in the digital era, and, as a consequence, has further raised the importance of civil society in electronic space as a force through which a multiplicity of public interests can, wittingly or not, resist the over-whelming influence of the new global corporate world.

Network Power

The power of networks is becoming evident on a whole range of planes. The Internet is probably the best known and most noted. Its particular attributes have engendered the notion of distributed power: decentralization, openness, possibility of expansion, no hierarchy, no centre, no conditions for authoritarian or monopoly control. In terms of global connectivity, there is nothing that compares with the Internet at this point, which is also why firms are intra-netting on the Net, as I discuss on pages 57–8. Other technologies and applications have been much slower to take off on a global basis because of lack of consistence in standards and the technology infrastructure. But we must recognize that digital networks are also making possible other forms of power.

The financial markets illustrate this well. The three properties of electronic networks – speed, simultaneity and interconnectivity – have produced orders of magnitude far surpassing anything we had ever seen in financial markets. The consequence has been that the global capital market now has the power to discipline national governments and destabilize national economies, as became evident with the Mexico 'crisis' of December 1994 and the current crisis in Asia. Further, these same properties of electronic networks have created elements of a crisis of control within the institutions of the financial industry itself. There are a number of instances that illustrate this: the stock market crash of 1987 brought on by program-trading and the collapse of Barings Bank brought on by a young trader who managed to mobilize enormous amounts of capital in several markets over a period of six weeks (Sassen, 1996a: Chapter 2).

That is to say, the power of these digital networks has produced conditions that cannot always be controlled by those who meant to profit the most from these new electronic capacities. Precisely because they are deeply embedded in telematics, advanced information industries also shed light on questions of control in the global economy that not only go beyond the state but also go beyond the notions of non-state-centred systems of coordination prevalent in the literature on governance. These are questions of control that have to do with the orders of magnitude that can be achieved in the financial markets thanks to the speed in transactions made possible by the new technologies. The best example is probably the foreign currency markets, which operate largely in electronic space and have achieved volumes that have left the central banks incapable of exercising the influence on exchange rates they are expected to have.

The form of network power exemplified by international finance can be seen as quite subversive in its own particular way in that it destabilizes existing hierarchies of control and power (such as central banks or other powerful institutions accustomed to far more control over the economy, as well as subordinating the logic of industrial capital to that of financial capital). Yet, it is very much a form of hierarchical power. It produces a vast concentration of capital and of profits and the capacity to mobilize this capital around the globe, often instantaneously.

Further, although in some ways the power of these financial electronic networks rests on a kind of distributed power, that is millions of investors and their millions of decisions, it ends up as concentrated power. The trajectory followed by what begins as a form of distributed power may assume many forms, in this case, one radically different from that of the Internet.

It signals the possibility that network power is not inherently distributive. Intervening mechanisms can re-shape its organization. To keep it as a form of distributed power requires that it be embedded in a particular kind of structure. In the case of the Internet, besides its feature as a network of networks and its openness – two crucial elements – it may well be the absence of commercialization that has allowed it to thrive the way it has.

What are the grounds on which commercialization can enter the Net? We can already detect several elements (see also Aspen Roundtable, 1998). One is the emergence of firms that sell services to speed up access. This is not an essential service to gain access, but it is a convenience, and an option for those with the income to pay for it. Another is the possibility of adding value (including commercial value) to Net features through the incorporation of voice and image, which consume enormous bandwidth and hence will eventually probably be more easily subjected to pricing mechanisms than is e-mail for instance. When we consider the enormous amount of software design effort that is right now going into producing programs that can ensure safe credit card processing, then we can see that commercialization on a vast scale may lie around the corner, even though today it appears as a non-factor. This could stimulate the creation of Web sites that incorporate the latest developments of voice and image and could charge for access. Indeed, I think of the growing use of voice and image for non-essential uses as a de-greening of the net. E-mail is a system of astounding efficiency and 'ecological soundness'. Voice and image, with their enormous consumption of bandwidth, are much less so. If they are used for the purposes of art it's one thing, for the purposes of advertising and profit-making it's another.

Because the Internet is such a special space and distributed power such a rare and important condition, it is essential that it be allowed to continue to thrive. I don't think we can take this for granted. The possibility of a poor person's e-mail (slow, at the end of the queue) and a rich person's e-mail (fast, prioritized) is real. Could we also wind up with the possibility of a poor person's net at the fringes and increasingly 'isolated' from a booming, increasingly commercialized or privatized, rich person's net?

The Net as a space of distributed power can thrive even against growing commercialization. But Net activists may have to reinvent its representation as a universal space. It may continue to be a space for *de facto* (i.e., not necessarily self-conscious) democratic practices. But it will be so partly as a form of resistance against overarching powers of the economy and of hierarchical power, rather than the space of unlimited freedom which is part of its representation today. The images we need to bring into this representation increasingly need to deal with contestation and resistance, rather than simply the romance of freedom and interconnectivity or the image of a 'new frontier' (though it needs to be said that the image of the historical frontier, that is the Far West in North America, has been subjected to a critical re-evaluation which rejects the notion that it was about freedom and escape from oppression and poverty). Further, one of the very important features of the Internet is that civil society has been an energetic user; but this also means that the full range of social forces will use it, from environmentalists to fundamentalist groups such as the Christian Coalition in the USA, from the Zapatistas in Chiapas to the new Russian maffias. It is a democratic space for many opposing views and drives.

Emergent Cyber-segmentations

There are at least three distinct forms of cyber-segmentation we can see today. One of these is the commercializing of access, a familiar subject. A second is the emergence of intermediaries to sort, choose and evaluate information for paying customers. A third, and the one I want to focus on in some detail, is the formation of privatized firewalled corporate networks and 'tunnels' on the Web.

Regarding commercialization of access, what matters for me here is not the current forms assumed by paid services, but what lies ahead. Current commercial forms of access are undergoing change. Microsoft, after being an Internet laggard, is now offering free Internet access and browser programs to lock in the market. And AT&T, the world's largest telephone company, recently launched a campaign to offer customers free access to the Internet. All this free access offered by giants in the industry is tactical.

There is right now an enormous battle among the major players to gain strategic advantages in what remains a fairly unknown, underspecified market. Microsoft's strategy in the past has been to set the standard, which it did for operating systems. The issue today, it seems, is once again to set standards, and to do this by providing the software for free in order eventually to control access and browsing standards and thus be able to charge. It is the copyright way to profits.

We cannot underestimate the extent of the search for ways to control, privatize, commercialize. Major global alliances are being formed to deliver a whole range of services to clients. While the solution to the problem of commercialization may not be available now, there is enormous effort to invent the appropriate billing systems (Aspen Roundtable, 1998). It is worth remembering that in the USA the telephone system started in the late 1800s as a decentralized, multiple-owner network of networks: there were farmers' telephone networks, mutual aid societies' telephone networks, etc. This went on for decades. But then in 1934 the Communications Act was passed defining the communication systems as a 'natural monopoly situation' and granting AT&T the monopoly. Before the 1996 deregulation, AT&T was up to 60 per cent a billing company: it invented and implemented billing systems. And much effort today is likely to be addressing the question of a billing system for access to and use of what is now public electronic space.

The approach towards gaining control is through strategic partnerships. Growth strategies and global alliances are not only geared to provide computer services and telephone calls, but also data transmission, video conferencing, home shopping, television, news, entertainment. Mergers and acquisitions have risen sharply in the global IT industries, as companies are seeking the size and technology to compete in global markets. In 1995 these transactions reached record numbers, with 2,913 deals, that is a 57 per cent increase over the 1,861 recorded in 1994. The total value of these deals was US$ 134 billion, which is a 47 per cent increase over the US$ 90.5 billion in 1994. Deregulation is a key step towards the expansion in service coverage and the formation of global alliances. But experts are forecasting that after a period of sharp global competition, a few major global players will monopolize the business. AT&T already has the nationwide infrastructure and a billing system in place to provide and charge for services.

Perhaps one of the most significant new developments is the use of the Web and firewalls by firms to set up their own internal computer networks. Rather than using costly computer systems that need expert staffing and employee training, firms can use the Web to do what those systems do at almost no cost and with little need for expert staffing. Firms save enormous amounts of money by using the Web for their own internal corporate purposes.

Around 1995, business discovered that the World Wide Web (WWW) is a great medium for communicating with customers, partners, investors. Now they are using the WWW to set up internal networks, surrounded by firewalls. Beyond very elementary uses, such as information about new developments or directories that can be updated easily, these intranets create access to a firm's various databases, and make these easy to use for everyone in the firm, no matter what computer systems, software or time zone they are in. Firms can avoid complicated, costly and time-consuming retrieval procedures which have often meant that these databases were *de facto* of little use in decision-making. Lotus Notes, long the leading internal computer network technology, has far more complexity than is often necessary; and it is expensive and requires expert staffing.

Private intranets use the infrastructure and standards of the Internet and WWW. This is cheap and astoundingly efficient compared to other forms of internal communication systems. Because Web browsers run on any type of computer, the same electronic information can be viewed by any employee. Intranets using the Web can pull all the computers, software and databases of a corporation into a single system that enables employees to find information wherever it is in the system. Most recently, firms have developed firewalled 'tunnels' that use the Internet to establish a 'private' network between two or more firms that do a lot of business with each other.

Is this a private appropriation of a public good? It seems to me there are definite elements of this here, especially in view of the millions of dollars firms can save. Are the firewalled intranets the citadels of electronic space? The formation of private intranets and tunnels on the Net is probably one of the sharper instances of cyber-segmentation.

The Embeddedness of Electronic Space

The central point I want to underline in this particular issue is that in so far as electronic space is embedded we cannot read it as a purely technological event and in terms merely of its technical capacities. It is inscribed by the structures and dynamics within which it is embedded: the Internet is a different type of space than the private networks of the financial industry; and the firewalled corporate sites on the Web are different from the public portion of the Web. Beyond this question of intentionality and use, lies the question of infrastructure: electronic space is going to be far more present in highly industrialized countries than in the less developed world; and far more present for middle-class households in developed countries than for poor households in those same countries.

There is no purely digital economy and no completely virtual corporation. This means that power, contestation, inequality, in brief, hierarchy, inscribe electronic space. And although the digitalized portions of these industries, particularly finance, have the capacity to subvert the established hierarchies, new hierarchies are being formed, borne out of the existing material conditions underlying power and the new conditions created by electronic space.

Let me illustrate some of these issues with what we could call the topography of private electronic space, which has received less attention than the Internet.

The Topi of E-Space: Global Cities and Global Value Chains

The vast new economic topography that is being implemented through electronic space is one moment, one fragment, of an even vaster economic chain that is in good part embedded in non-electronic spaces. There is no fully dematerialized firm or industry. Even the most advanced information industries, such as finance, are installed only partly in electronic space. And so are industries that produce digital products, such as software designers. The growing digitalization of economic activities has not eliminated the need for major international business and financial centres and all the material resources they concentrate, from state-of-the-art telematics infrastructure to brain talent (Castells, 1989; Sassen, 1994; Graham and Marvin, 1996).

Nonetheless, telematics and globalization have emerged as fundamental forces reshaping the organization of economic space. This reshaping ranges from the spatial virtualization of a growing number of economic activities to the reconfiguration of the geography of the built environment for economic activity. Whether in electronic space or in the geography of the built environment, this reshaping involves organizational and structural changes. Telematics maximizes the potential for geographic dispersal and globalization entails an economic logic that maximizes the attractions/ profitability of such dispersal.

One outcome of these transformations has been captured in images of geographic dispersal at the global scale and the neutralization of place and distance through telematics in a growing number of economic activities. Yet it is precisely the combination of the spatial dispersal of numerous economic activities and telematic global integration which has contributed to a strategic role for major cities in the current phase of the world economy. Beyond their sometimes long history as centres for world trade and banking, these cities now function as command points in the organization of the world economy; as key locations and marketplaces for the leading industries of this period (finance and specialized services for firms); and as sites for the production of innovations in those industries. The continued and often growing concentration and specialization of financial and corporate service functions in major cities in highly developed countries is, in good part, a strategic development. It is precisely because of the territorial dispersal facilitated by telecommunication advances that agglomeration of centralizing activities has expanded immensely. This is not a mere continuation of old patterns of agglomeration but, one could posit, a new logic for agglomeration. A majority of firms and economic activities do not inhabit these major centres.

Centrality remains a key property of the economic system but the spatial correlates of centrality have been profoundly altered by the new technologies and by globalization. This engenders a whole new problematic around the definition of what constitutes centrality today in an economic system where (i) a share of transactions occur through technologies that neutralize distance and place, and do so on a global scale; and (ii) centrality has historically been embodied in certain types of built environment and urban form. Economic globalization and the new information technologies have not only reconfigured centrality and its spatial correlates, they have also created new spaces for centrality. The pronounced orientation to the world markets evident in such cities raises questions about the articulation with their nation-states, their regions, and the larger economic and social structure in such cities. Cities have typically been deeply embedded in the economies of their region, indeed often reflecting the characteristics of the latter; and they still do. But cities that are strategic sites in the global economy tend, in part, to disconnect from their region. This conflicts with a key proposition in traditional scholarship about urban systems, namely, that these systems promote the territorial integration of regional and national economies.

As a political economist interested in the spatial organization of the economy and in the spatial correlates of economic power, it seems to me that a focus on place and infrastructure in the new global information economy creates a conceptual and practical opening for questions about the embeddedness of electronic space. It allows us to elaborate that point where the materiality of place/infrastructure intersects with those technologies and organizational forms that neutralize place and materiality. And it entails a conceptual elaboration of electronic space: this space is not simply about transmission capacities but also a space where new structures for economic activity and for economic power are being constituted.

A New Geography of Centrality

We are seeing a spatialization of inequality which is evident both in the geography of the communications infrastructure and in the emergent geographies in electronic space itself. Global cities are hyperconcentrations of infrastructure and the attendant resources while vast areas in less developed regions are poorly served. But also within global cities we see a geography of centrality and one of marginality. For instance, New York has the largest concentration of fibreoptic cable-served buildings in the world, but they are mostly in the centre of the city, while Harlem, the black ghetto, has only one such building, and South Central Los Angeles, the site of the 1993 uprisings, has none.

There are many instantiations of this new unequal geography of access. Infrastructure requires enormous amounts of money. For example, it is estimated that it will cost US$ 120 billion for the next 10 years just to bring the Central and East European countries communication networks up to date. The European Union will spend US$ 25 billion a year to develop a broadband telecommunications infrastructure. The levels of technical development to be achieved by different regions and countries, and indeed, whole continents, depend on the public and private resources available and on the logic guiding the development. This is evident even with very basic technologies such as telephone and fax: in very rich countries there are 50 telephone lines per person; in poor countries, fewer than 10. By 1994, the USA had 4.5 million fax machines and Japan, 4.3 million, but there were only 90,000 in Brazil, 30,000 each in Turkey and Portugal, and 40,000 in Greece (Garcia, 1995).

And then there are the finer points. The worldwide deployment of integrated services digital networks (ISDNs) depends on interoperability and on a technology base. Both of these conditions severely restrict where it will actually be available. For example, even in Europe where there is a common communications policy calling for harmonization, ISDN deployment varies greatly: in France it has reached 100 per cent; in Greece it is virtually non-existent. Another instance, the establishment of the General European Network which provided eight channels of two megabits per second each by 1995, did so only among nodes in Frankfurt, Paris, London, Madrid and Rome – a select geography. The availability of leased two Mbps circuits in Europe is highly uneven – from 40,000 circuits in Great Britain to 17 in Ireland (as of the early 1990s).

The growing economic value and hence potential profitability of communications are creating enormous pressures towards deregulation and privatization. The fact that the top players need state-of-the-art communication systems further creates pressure for immense amounts of capital and high-level expertise. This has meant that public telecoms all over the world are finding themselves between the pressure to privatize, coming from the private sector, and the insufficiency of public funds to develop state-of-the-art systems – systems which may well largely benefit top players. Even in countries such as France and Germany, with long-held preferences for state control, we are now seeing partial privatization. Similar developments are taking place in countries as diverse as Japan, Australia, New Zealand, Singapore, Indonesia, Malaysia. The notion, particularly in less developed countries, is that privatization will help them gain access to the foreign capital and expertise they need to develop their national infrastructure. Thus Mexico, Argentina, Venezuela, India and even China are considering such initiatives.

Deregulation and privatization are facilitating the formation of megafirms and global alliances. Further, new technological developments are facilitating convergence between telecommunications, computers and television, leading to the formation of a mega-multimedia sector. Globalization is a key feature of the new multimedia sector. And all developments signal that this will only grow. These global players and the state-of-the-art infrastructure and technologies they will have access to, can only increase the distance between the technological 'haves' and 'have nots' among firms and among consumers. Finally, once in cyberspace, users will also encounter an unequal geography of access. Those who can pay for it will have fast-speed servicing, and those who cannot will increasingly find themselves in very slow lanes.

* * *

In concluding, it is for these reasons that it becomes so important to take seriously the threats to the distributed power, the absence of hierarchy, of the Internet. Yes, it is a space of freedom; but it is also increasingly a space of resistance, and that means a contested space. The engagement is with some of the most powerful and innovative global actors we have yet seen. Further, electronic space, whether private or public, is partly embedded in actual societal structures and power dynamics: its topography weaves in and out of non-electronic space. This feature carries enormous implications for theory, for the results of the digitalization of economic activity, and for the conditions through which governments and citizens can act on this new electronic world of the economy and power.

Bibliography

ADILKNO (1998) *The Media Archive: World Edition*. New York: Autonomedia; Amsterdam: ADILKNO.
Aspen Roundtable (1998) *The Global Advance of Electronic Commerce: Reinventing Markets, Management and National Sovereignty*. A report of the sixth Annual Aspen Institute Roundtable on Information Technology, Aspen, Colorado, 21–3 August, 1997. Washington, DC: Aspen Institute, Communication and Society Program.
Barlow, John Perry (1997) 'A declaration of independence of cyberspace', in Edeltraud Stiftinger and Edward Strasser (eds), *Binary Myths: Cyberspace – the Renaissance of Lost Emotions*. Vienna: Zukunfts- und Kulturwerkstätte (in English and German).
Bauche, Gilles (1996) *Tout savoir sur Internet*. Paris: Arlea.
Calabrese, Andrew and Borchert, Mark (1996) 'Prospects for electronic democracy in the United States: rethinking communication and social policy', *Media, Culture and Society*, 18: 249–68.
Calabrese, Andrew and Burgelman, Jean-Claude (1999) *Communication, Citizenship and Social Policy: Re-thinking the Limits of the Welfare State*. Lanham, MD: Rowman & Littlefield.
Castells, Manuel (1989) *The Informational City*. Oxford: Blackwell.
Dencker, Klaus Peter (ed.) (1997) *Labile Ordnungen: Netze Denken*. Hamburg: Verlag Hans Bredow.
Garcia, Linda (1995) 'The globalization of telecommunications and information', in William J. Drake (ed.), *The New Information Infrastructure: Strategies for US Policy*. New York: Twentieth Century Fund Press. pp. 75–92.
Graham, Stephen and Marvin, Simon (1996) *Telecommunications and the City: Electronic Spaces, Urban Places*. London and New York: Routledge.
Kroker, Arthur and Marilouise (1996) *Hacking the Future: Stories for the Flesh-eating 90s*. New York: St Martin's Press.
Lovink, Geert (1998) 'Grundrisse einer Netzkritik', in K.P. Dencker (ed.), *Labile Ordnungen: Netze Denken*. Hamburg: Verlag Hans Bredow. pp. 234–45.
Münker, Stefan and Roesler, Alexander (eds) (1997) *Mythos Internet*. Frankfurt: Suhrkamp.

Nettime (1997) *Net Critique.* Compiled by Geert Lovink and Pit Schultz. Berlin: Edition ID-ARchiv.

Rapp, L. (1995) 'Toward French electronic highways. The new legal status of data transmissions in France', in L. Rapp (ed.), *Telecommunications and Space Journal*, Vol. 2 (Annual Edition). pp. 231–46.

Rotzer, Florian (1995) *Die Telepolis: Urbanitat im digitalen Zeitalter.* Mannheim: Bollmann.

Salomon, Ilan (1996) 'Telecommunications, cities and technological opportunism', *The Annals of Regional Science*, 30: 75–90.

Sassen, Saskia (1994) *Cities in a World Economy.* Thousand Oaks, CA: Pine Forge/Sage.

Sassen, Saskia (1996a) *Losing Control? Sovereignty in an Age of Globalization.* The 1995 Columbia University Leonard Hastings Schoff Memorial Lectures. New York: Columbia University Press.

Sassen, Saskia (1996b) 'Analytic borderlands: race and gender in the city', in A.D. King (ed.), *Representing the City. Ethnicity, Capital and Culture in the 21st Century.* New York: New York University Press.

Scherer, J. (1995) 'Regulatory reform in Germany: privatizing and regulating Deutsche Bundespost Telekom', in L. Rapp (ed.), *Telecommunications and Space Journal*, Vol. 2 (Annual Edition). pp. 207–30.

Part II

CULTURAL MAPPING

4

THE POSTMODERN URBAN CONDITION

Michael Dear and Steven Flusty

> This latest mutation in space – postmodern hyperspace – has finally succeeded in transcending the capacities of the human body to locate itself, to organize its immediate surroundings perceptually, and cognitively to map its position in a mappable external world. (Fredric Jameson, 1991: 44)

Los Angeles Urbanisms

Most world cities have an instantly identifiable signature: think of the boulevards of Paris, the skyscrapers of New York, or the churches of Rome. But Los Angeles appears to be a city without a common narrative, except perhaps the freeways or a more generic iconography of the bizarre. Twenty-five years ago, Rayner Banham (1973) provided an enduring map of the Los Angeles landscape. To this day, it remains powerful, evocative, and instantly recognizable. He identified four basic ecologies: *surfurbia* (the beach cities: 'The beaches are what other metropolises should envy in Los Angeles. . . . Los Angeles is the greatest City-on-the-shore in the world', 1973: 37); *the foothills* (the privileged enclaves of Beverly Hills, Bel Air, etc., where the financial and topographical contours correspond almost exactly); *the plains of Id* (the central flatlands: 'An endless plain endlessly gridded with endless streets, peppered endlessly with ticky-tacky houses clustered in distinguishable neighborhoods, slashed across by endless freeways that have destroyed any community spirit that may have once existed, and so on . . . endlessly', 1973: 161); and *autopia* ('[The] freeway system in its totality is now a single comprehensible place, a coherent state of mind, a complete way of life', 1973: 213).

For Douglas Suisman (1989), it is not the freeways but the boulevards that determine the city's overall physical structure. A boulevard is a surface street that: '(1) makes arterial connections on a metropolitan scale; (2)

provides a framework for civic and commercial destination; and (3) acts as a filter to adjacent residential neighborhoods.' Suisman argues that boulevards do more than establish an organizational pattern; they constitute 'the irreducible armature of the city's *public space*', and are charged with social and political significance that cannot be ignored. Usually sited along the edges of former *ranchos*, these vertebral connectors today form an integral link among the regions' municipalities (Suisman, 1989: 6–7).

For Ed Soja (1989), Los Angeles is a decentred, decentralized metropolis powered by the insistent fragmentation of post-Fordism, that is an increasingly flexible, disorganized regime of capitalist accumulation. Accompanying this shift is a postmodern consciousness, a cultural and ideological reconfiguration altering how we experience social being. The centre holds, however, because it functions as the urban panopticon, that is the strategic surveillance point for the state's exercise of social control. Out from the centre extend a melange of 'wedges' and 'citadels', interspersed between corridors formed by the boulevards. The consequent urban structure is a complicated quilt, fragmented yet bound to an underlying economic rationality: 'With exquisite irony, contemporary Los Angeles has come to resemble more than ever before a gigantic agglomeration of theme parks, a lifespace composed of Disneyworlds' (Soja, 1989: 246).

These three sketches provide differing insights into LA's landscapes. Banham considers the city's overall torso, and identifies three basic components (surfurbia, plains and foothills), as well as connecting arteries (freeways). Suisman shifts our gaze away from principal arteries to the veins that channel everyday life (the boulevards). Soja considers the body-in-context, articulating the links between political economy and postmodern culture to explain fragmentation and social differentiation in Los Angeles. All three writers maintain a studied detachment from the city, as though a voyeuristic, top-down perspective is needed to discover the rationality inherent in the cityscape. Yet a postmodern sensibility would relinquish the modernism inherent in such detached representations of the urban text. What would a postmodernism from below reveal?

One of the most prescient visions anticipating a postmodern cognitive mapping of the urban is Jonathan Raban's *Soft City* (1974), a reading of London' cityscapes. Raban divides the city into *hard* and *soft* elements. The former refers to the material fabric of the built environment – the streets and buildings that frame the lives of city dwellers. The latter, by contrast, is an individualized interpretation of the city, a perceptual orientation created in the mind of every urbanite.[1] The relationship between the two is complex and even indeterminate. The newcomer to a city first confronts the hard city, but soon:

> the city goes soft; it awaits the imprint of an identity. For better or worse, it invites you to remake it, to consolidate it into a shape you can live in. You, too. Decide who you are, and the city will again assume a fixed form around you. Decide what it is, and your own identity will be revealed. (Raban, 1974: 11)

Raban makes no claims to a postmodern consciousness, yet his invocation of the relationship between the cognitive and the real leads to insights that are unmistakably postmodern in their sensitivities.

Ted Relph (1987) was one of the first geographers to catalogue the material forms that comprise the places of postmodernity. He describes postmodern urbanism as a self-conscious and selective revival of elements of older styles, though he cautions that postmodernism is not simply a style but also a frame of mind (Relph, 1987: 213). He observes how the confluence of many trends – gentrification, heritage conservation, architectural fashion, urban design and participatory planning – caused the collapse of the modernist vision of a future city filled with skyscrapers and other austere icons of scientific rationalism. The new urbanism is principally distinguishable from the old by its *eclecticism*. Relph's periodization of twentieth-century urbanism involves a pre-modern transitional period (up to 1940), an era of modernist cityscapes (after 1945), and a period of postmodern townscapes (since 1970). The distinction between *cityscape* and *townscape* is crucial to his diagnosis. Modernist cityscapes, he claims, are characterized by five elements:

(1) Megastructural bigness (few street entrances to buildings, little architectural detailing, etc.);
(2) Straight-space/Prairie space (city center canyons, endless suburban vistas);
(3) Rational order and flexibility (the landscapes of total order, verging on boredom);
(4) Hardness and opacity (including freeways, and the displacement of nature); and
(5) Discontinuous serial vision (deriving from the dominance of the automobile). (Relph, 1987: 242–50)

Conversely, postmodern townscapes are more detailed, handcrafted and intricate. They celebrate difference, polyculturalism, variety and stylishness. Their elements are:

(6) Quaintspace (a deliberate cuteness);
(7) Textured façades (for pedestrians, rich in detail, often with an 'aged' appearance);
(8) Stylishness (appealing to the fashionable, chic and affluent);
(9) Reconnection with the local (involving deliberate historical/geographical reconstruction); and
(10) Pedestrian-automobile split (to redress the modernist bias toward the car). (Relph, 1987: 252–8)

Raban's emphasis on the cognitive and Relph's on the concrete underscore the importance of both dimensions in understanding socio-spatial urban process. The palette of urbanisms that arises from merging the two is thick and multidimensional. We turn now to the task of constructing that palette by examining empirical evidence of recent urban developments in Southern California. In this review, we take our lead from what exists, rather than what we consider to be a comprehensive urban research agenda.[2] From this, we move quickly to a synthesis that is prefigurative of a proto-postmodern urbanism which we hope will serve as an invitation to a more broadly based comparative urban analysis.

Edge Cities

Joel Garreau (1991) noted the central significance of Los Angeles in understanding contemporary metropolitan growth in the USA. He asserts that 'Every single American city that *is* growing, is growing in the fashion of Los Angeles', and refers to LA as the 'great-grandaddy' of edge cities (Garreau, 1991: 3). (He claims there are 26 of them within a five-county area in Southern California.) For Garreau, edge cities represent the crucible of America's urban future. The classic location for contemporary edge cities is at the intersection of an urban beltway and a hub-and-spoke lateral road. The central conditions that have propelled such development are the dominance of the automobile and the associated need for parking, the communications revolution, and the entry of women in large numbers into the labour market. Although Garreau agrees with Robert Fishman that '[a]ll new city forms appear in their early stages to be chaotic' (1991: 9), he is able to identify three basic types of edge city. These are: *uptowns* (peripheral pre-automobile settlements that have subsequently been absorbed by urban sprawl); *boomers* (the classic edge cities, located at freeway intersections); and *greenfields* (the current state of the art, 'occurring at the intersection of several thousand acres of farmland and one developer's monumental ego', 1991: 116).

One essential feature of the edge city is that politics is not yet established there. Into the political vacuum moves a 'shadow government' – a privatized protogovernment that is essentially a plutocratic alternative to normal politics. Shadow governments can tax, legislate for, and police their communities, but they are rarely accountable, are responsive primarily to wealth (as opposed to numbers of voters), and subject to few constitutional constraints (1991: 187). Jennifer Wolch (1990) has described the rise of the shadow state as part of a society-wide trend towards privatization. In edge cities, 'community' is scarce, occurring not through propinquity but via telephone, fax and private mail service. The walls that typically surround such neighbourhoods are social boundaries, but they act as community 'recognizers', not community 'organizers' (Wolch, 1990: 275–81). In the edge city era, Garreau notes, the term 'master-planned' community is little more than a marketing device (Garreau, 1991: 301). Other studies of suburbanization in LA, most notably by Hise (1997) and Waldie (1996), provide a basis for comparing past practices of planned community marketing in Southern California.

Privatopia

Privatopia, perhaps the quintessential edge city residential form, is a private housing development based in common-interest developments (CIDs) and administered by homeowners associations. There were fewer than 500 such associations in 1964; by 1992 there were 150,000 associations privately governing approximately 32 million Americans. In 1990, the 11.6 million CID units constituted over 11 per cent of the nation's housing stock (McKenzie, 1994: 11). Sustained by an expanding catalogue of covenants, conditions and restrictions (or CC&Rs, the proscriptive constitutions formalizing CID behavioural and aesthetic norms), privatopia has been fuelled by a large dose of privatization, and promoted by an ideology of 'hostile privatism' (1994: 19). It has provoked a culture of non-participation.

McKenzie warns that far from being a benign or inconsequential trend, CIDs already define a new norm for the mass production of housing in the USA. Equally importantly, their organizations are now allied through something called the Community Associations Institute, 'whose purposes include the standardizing and professionalizing of CID governance' (1994: 184). McKenzie notes how this 'secession of the successful' (the phrase is Robert Reich's) has altered concepts of citizenship, in which 'one's duties consist of satisfying one's obligations to private property' (1994: 196). In her futuristic novel of LA wars between walled-community dwellers and those beyond the walls (*Parable of the Sower*, 1993), Octavia Butler has envisioned a dystopian privatopian future. It includes a balkanized nation of defended neighbourhoods at odds with one another, where entire communities are wiped out for a handful of fresh lemons or a few cups of potable water, where torture and murder of one's enemies is common, and where company-town slavery is attractive to those who are fortunate enough to sell their services to the hyper-defended enclaves of the very rich.

Cultures of Heteropolis

One of the most prominent socio-cultural tendencies in contemporary Southern California is the rise of minority populations (Ong et al., 1994; Roseman et al., 1996; Waldinger and Bozorgmehr, 1996). Provoked to comprehend the causes and implications of the 1992 civil disturbances in Los Angeles, Charles Jencks (1993) zeroes in on the city's *diversity* as the key to LA's emergent urbanism: 'Los Angeles is a combination of enclaves with high identity, and multienclaves with mixed identity, and, taken as a whole, it is perhaps the most heterogeneous city in the world' (Jencks, 1993: 32). Such ethnic pluralism has given rise to what Jencks calls a *hetero-architecture*, which had demonstrated that: 'there is a great virtue, and pleasure, to be had in mixing categories, transgressing boundaries, inverting customs and adopting the marginal usage' (1993: 123). The vigour and imagination underlying these intense cultural dynamics is everywhere evident in the region, from the diversity of ethnic adaptations (Park, 1996) through the concentration of cultural producers in the region (Molotch, 1996), to the hybrid complexities of emerging cultural forms (Boyd, 1996, 1997).

The consequent built environment is characterized by transience, energy and unplanned vulgarity, in which Hollywood is never far away. Jencks views this improvisational quality as a hopeful sign: 'The main point of hetero-architecture is to accept the different voices that create a city, suppress none of them, and make from their interaction some kind of greater dialogue' (Jencks, 1993: 75). This is especially important in a city where *minoritization*, 'the typical postmodern phenomenon where most of the population forms the "other"', is the order of the day, and where most city dwellers feel distanced from the power structure (1993: 84). Despite Jencks's optimism, other analysts have observed that the same Southern California heteropolis has to contend with more than its share of socio-economic polarization, racism, inequality, homelessness, and social unrest (Gooding-Williams, 1993; Wolch and Dear, 1993; Baldassare, 1994; Bullard et al., 1994; Anderson, 1996; Rocco, 1996). Yet these charac-teristics are part of a socio-cultural dynamic that is also provoking the search for innovative solutions in labour and community organizing (e.g., Pulido, 1996), as well as in inter-ethnic relations (e.g., Martínez, 1992; Abelmann and Lie, 1995; Yoon, 1997).

City as Theme Park

California in general, and Los Angeles in particular, have often been promoted as places where the American (suburban) Dream is most easily realized. Its oft-noted qualities of optimism and tolerance, coupled with a balmy climate, have given rise to an architecture and society fostered by a spirit of experimentation, risk-taking and hope. Architectural dreamscapes are readily convertible into marketable commodities, that is saleable pre-packaged landscapes engineered to satisfy fantasies of suburban living.[3] Many writers have used the 'theme park' metaphor to describe the emergence of such variegated cityscapes. For instance, Michael Sorkin, in a collection of essays appropriately entitled *Variations on a Theme Park* (1992), describes theme parks as places of simulation without end, charac-terized by aspatiality plus technological and physical surveillance and control. The precedents for this model can be traced back to the World's Fairs, but Sorkin insists that something 'wholly new' is now emerging. This is because 'the 800 telephone number and the piece of plastic have made time and space obsolete', and these instruments of 'artificial adjacency' have eviscerated the traditional politics of propinquity (Sorkin, 1992: xi). Sorkin observes that the social order has always been legible in urban form; for example, traditional cities have adjudicated conflicts via the relations of public places such as the agora or piazza. However, in today's 'recombinant city', he contends that conventional legibilities have been obscured and/or deliberately mutilated. The telephone and modem have rendered the street irrelevant, and the new city threatens an 'unimagined sameness' characterized by the loosening of ties to any specific space, rising levels of surveillance, manipulation and segregation, and the city as a theme park. Of this last, Disneyland is the archetype – described by Sorkin as a place of 'Taylorized fun', the 'Holy See of Creative Geography' (1992:

227). What is missing in this new cybernetic suburbia is not a particular building or place, but the spaces between, that is the connections that make sense of forms (1992: xii). What is missing, then, is connectivity and community.

In extremis, California dreamscapes become simulacra. Ed Soja (1992), in a catalogue of Southern California's urban eccentricities, identified Orange County as a massive simulation of what a city should be. He describes Orange County as: 'a structural fake, and enormous advertisement, yet functionally the finest multipurpose facility of its kind in the country' (Soja, 1992: 111). Calling this assemblage 'exopolis', or the city without, Soja asserts that 'something new is being born here' based on the hyperrealities of more conventional theme parks such as Disneyland (1992: 101). The exopolis is a simulacrum, an exact copy of an original that never existed, within which image and reality are spectacularly confused. In this 'politically numbed' society, conventional politics is dysfunctional. Orange County has become a 'scamscape', notable principally as home of massive mail fraud operations, savings and loan failures, and county government bankruptcy (1992: 120).

Fortified City

The downside of the Southern Californian dream has, of course, been the subject of countless dystopian visions in histories, movies and novels.[4] In one powerful account, Mike Davis noted how Southern Californians' obsession with security has transformed the region into a fortress. This shift is accurately manifested in the physical form of the city, which is divided into fortified cells of affluence and places of terror where police battle the criminalized poor. These urban phenomena, according to Davis, have placed Los Angeles 'on the hard edge of postmodernity' (Davis, 1992a: 155). The dynamics of fortification involve the omnipresent application of high-tech policing methods to the 'high-rent security of gated residential developments' and 'panopticon malls'. It extends to 'space policing', including a proposed satellite observation capacity that would create an invisible Haussmannization of Los Angeles. In the consequent 'carceral city', the working poor and destitute are spatially sequestered on the 'mean streets', and excluded from the affluent 'forbidden cities' through 'security by design'.

Interdictory Space

Elaborating upon Davis's fortress urbanism, Steven Flusty observed how various types of fortification have extended a canopy of suppression and surveillance across the entire city. His taxonomy of interdictory spaces (Flusty, 1994: 16–17) identifies how spaces are designed to exclude by a combination of their function and cognitive sensibilities. Some spaces are passively aggressive: space concealed by intervening objects or grade changes is 'stealthy', and spaces that may be reached only by means of interrupted or obfuscated approaches are 'slippery'. Other spatial configurations are more assertively confrontational: deliberately obstructed 'crusty' space surrounded by walls and checkpoints; inhospitable 'prickly' spaces featuring unsittable benches in areas devoid of shade; or 'jittery' space ostentatiously saturated with surveillance devices. Flusty notes how combinations of interdictory spaces are being introduced 'into every facet of the urban environment, generating distinctly unfriendly mutant typologies' (1994: 21–33). Some are indicative of the pervasive infiltration of fear into the home, including the bunker-style 'blockhome', affluent palisaded 'luxury laager' communities, or low-income residential areas converted into 'pocket ghettos' by military-style occupation. Other typological forms betray a fear of the public realm, as with the fortification of commercial facilities into 'strongpoints of sale', or the self-contained 'world citadel' clusters of defensible office towers.

One consequence of the socio-spatial differentiation described by Davis and Flusty is an acute fragmentation of the urban landscape. Commentators who remark upon the strict division of residential neighbourhoods along race and class lines miss the fact that LA's micro-geography is incredibly volatile and varied. In many neighbourhoods, simply turning a street corner will lead the pedestrian/driver into totally different social and physical configurations. One very important feature of local neighbourhood dynamics in the fortified culture of Southern California cities is, of course, the presence of street gangs (Vigil, 1988; Klein, 1995).

Historical Geographies of Restructuring

Historical geographies of Southern California are relatively rare, especially when compared with the number of published accounts of Chicago and New York. For reasons that are unclear, Los Angeles remains, in our judgement, the least-studied major city in the USA. Until Mike Davis's *City of Quartz* (1990) brought the urban record up to the present, students of Southern California tended to rely principally on Carey McWilliams's (1973) seminal general history and Folgelson's *The Fragmented Metropolis* (1967), an urban history of LA up to 1930. Other chronicles of the urban evolution of Southern California have focused on transportation (Bottles, 1987; Wachs, 1996), the Mexican/Chicano experience (del Castillo, 1979), real-estate development and planning (Weiss, 1987; Hise, 1997; Erie, forthcoming) and oil (Tygiel, 1994). The political geography of the region is only now being written (Sonenshein, 1993; Fulton, 1997), but several more broadly based treatments of Californian politics exist, including excellent studies on art, poetry and politics (Cándida Smith, 1995), railways (Deverell, 1994) and the rise of suburbia (Fishman, 1987). In his history of Los Angeles between 1965 and 1992, Soja (1996) attempts to link the emergent patterns of urban form with underlying social processes. He identified six kinds of *restructuring*, which together define the region's contemporary urban process. In addition to *Exopolis* (noted above), Soja lists: *Flexcities*, associated with the transition to post-Fordism, especially deindustrialization and the rise of the information economy; and *Cosmopolis*, referring to the globalization of Los Angeles both in terms of its emergent world city status and its internal multicultural diversification. According to Soja, peripheralization, post-Fordism and globalization together define the experience of urban restructuring in Los Angeles. Three specific geographies are consequent upon these dynamics: *Splintered labyrinth*, which describes the extreme forms of social, economic and political polarization characteristic of the postmodern city; *Carceral city*, referring to the new 'incendiary urban geography' brought about by the amalgam of violence and police surveillance; and *Simcities*, the term Soja uses to describe the new ways of seeing the city that are emerging from the study of Los Angeles – a kind of epistemological restructuring that foregrounds a postmodern perspective.

Fordist versus Post-Fordist Regimes of Accumulation and Regulation

Many observers agree that one of the most important underlying shifts in the contemporary political economy is from a Fordist to a post-Fordist industrial organization. In a series of important books, Allen Scott and Michael Storper have portrayed the burgeoning urbanism of Southern California as a consequence of this deep-seated structural change in the capitalist political economy (Scott, 1988a, 1988b, 1993; Storper and Walker, 1989). For instance, Scott's basic argument is that there have been two major phases of urbanization in the USA. The first related to an era of Fordist mass production, during which the paradigmatic cities of industrial capitalism (Detroit, Chicago, Pittsburgh, etc.) coalesced around industries that were themselves based upon ideas of mass production. The second phase is associated with the decline of the Fordist era and the rise of a post-Fordist 'flexible production'. This is a form of industrial activity based on small-size, small-batch units of (typically subcontracted) production that are nevertheless integrated into clusters of economic activity. Such clusters have been observed in two manifestations: labour-intensive craft forms (in Los Angeles, typically garments and jewellery); and high technology (especially the defence and aerospace industries). According to Scott, these so-called 'technopoles' until recently constituted the principal geographical loci of contemporary (sub)urbanization in Southern California (a development prefigured in Fishman's description of the 'technoburb'; see Fishman, 1987; also Castells and Hall, 1994).

Post-Fordist regimes of accumulation are associated with analogous regimes of regulation or social control. Perhaps the most prominent manifestation of changes in the regime of regulation has been the retreat from the welfare state. The rise of neo-conservatism and the privatization ethos have coincided with a period of economic recession and retrenchment that has led many to the brink of poverty just at the time when the social welfare 'safety net' is being withdrawn. In Los Angeles, as in many other cities, an acute socio-economic polarization has resulted. In 1984, the city was dubbed the 'homeless capital' of the USA because of the concentration of homeless people there (see Wolch, 1990; Wolch and Dear, 1993; Wolch and Sommer, 1997).

Globalization

Needless to say, any consideration of the changing nature of industrial production sooner or later must encompass the globalization question (see Knox and Taylor, 1995). In his reference to the global context of LA's localisms, Mike Davis (1992b) claims that if LA is in any sense paradigmatic, it is because the city condenses the intended and unintended spatial consequences of post-Fordism. He insists that there is no simple master-logic of restructuring, focusing instead on two key localized macroprocesses: the overaccumulation in Southern California of bank and real-estate capital, principally from the East Asian trade surplus; and the reflux of low-wage manufacturing and labour-intensive service industries following upon immigration from Mexico and Central America. For instance, Davis notes how the City of Los Angeles used tax dollars gleaned from international capital investments to subsidize its downtown (Bunker Hill) urban renewal, a process he refers to as 'municipalized land speculation' (Davis, 1992b: 26). Through such connections, what happens today in Asia and Central America will tomorrow have an effect in Los Angeles. This global/local dialectic has already become an important (if somewhat imprecise) leitmotif of contemporary urban theory.

Politics of Nature

The natural environment of Southern California has been under constant assault since the first colonial settlements. Human habitation on a metropolitan scale has only been possible through a widespread manipulation of nature, especially the control of water resources in the American West (Gottlieb and FitzSimmons, 1991; M.L. Davis, 1993; Reisner, 1993). On one hand, Southern Californians tend to hold a grudging respect for nature, living as they do adjacent to one of the earth's major geological hazards, and in a desert environment that is prone to flood, landslide and fire (see, for instance, McPhee, 1989; Darlington, 1996). On the other hand, its inhabitants have been energetically, ceaselessly and sometimes carelessly unrolling the carpet of urbanization over the natural landscape for more than a century. This uninhibited occupation has engendered its own range of environmental problems, most notoriously air pollution, but also issues related to habitat loss and dangerous encounters between humans and other animals.

The force of nature in Southern California has spawned a literature that attempts to incorporate environmental issues into the urban problematic. The politics of environmental regulation have long been studied in many places, including Los Angeles (e.g., FitzSimmons and Gottlieb, 1996). However, the particular combination of circumstances in Southern California has stimulated an especially political view of nature, focusing both on its emasculation through human intervention (Davis, 1996) and on its potential for political mobilization by grass-roots movements (Pulido, 1996). In addition, Jennifer Wolch's Southern California-based research has led her to outline an alternative vision of biogeography's problematic (Wolch, 1996).

Synthesis: Proto-postmodern Urbanism

If these observers of the Southern California scene could talk with each other to resolve their differences and reconcile their terminologies, how might they synthesize their visions? At the risk of misrepresenting their work, we suggest a schematic that is powerful yet inevitably incomplete. It suggests a 'proto-postmodern' urban process, driven by a global restructuring that is permeated and balkanized by a series of interdictory networks; whose populations are socially and culturally heterogeneous, but politically and economically polarized; whose residents are educated and persuaded to the consumption of dreamscapes even as the poorest are consigned to carceral cities; whose built environment, reflective of these processes, consists of edge cities, privatopias and the like; and whose natural environment, also reflective of these processes, is being erased to the point of unlivability while at the same time providing a focus for political action.

The Postmodern Urban Condition

Recognizing that we may have caused some offence by characterizing others' work in this way, let us move swiftly to reconstruct their evidence into a postmodern urban problematic. We anchor this problematic in the straightforward need to account for the evolution of society over time and space. Such evolution occurs as a combination of deep-time (long-term) and present-time (short-term) processes; and it develops over several different scales of human activity (which we may represent summarily as micro-, meso- and macro-scales) (Dear, 1988). The structuring of the time–space fabric is the result of the interaction among ecologically situated human agents in relations of production, consumption and coercion. We do not intend any primacy in this ordering of categories, but instead emphasize their *interdependencies* – all are essential in explaining postmodern human geographies.

Our promiscuous use of neologisms in what follows is quite deliberate.[5] This technique has been used historically to good effect in many instances and disciplines (e.g., Knox and Taylor, 1995). Neologisms have been used here in circumstances where there were no existing terms to describe adequately the conditions we sought to identify; when neologisms served as metaphors to suggest new insights; when a single term more conveniently substituted for a complex phrase or string of ideas; and when neologistic novelty aided our avowed efforts to rehearse the break with modernism. The juxtaposing of postmodern and more traditional categories of modernist urbanism is also an essential piece of our analytical strategy. That there is an overlap between modernist and postmodern categories should surprise no one; we are, inevitably, building on existing urbanisms and epistemologies. The consequent neologistic pastiche may be properly regarded as a tactic of postmodern analysis; others could regard this strategy as analogous to hypothesis-generation or the practice of dialectics.

We begin with the assumption that urbanism is made possible by the exercise of instrumental control over both human and non-human ecologies. The very occupation and utilization of space, as well as the production and distribution of commodities, depends upon an anthropocentric reconfiguration of natural processes and their products. As the scope and scale of, and dependency upon, globally integrated consumption increases, institutional action converts complex ecologies into monocultured factors of production by simplifying nature into a *global latifundia*. This process includes both homogenizing interventions, as in California agriculture's reliance upon vast expanses of single crops, and forceful interdiction to sustain that intervention against natural feedbacks as in the aerial spraying of pesticides to eradicate fruit-flies attracted to these vast expanses of single crops. Being part of nature, humanity is subjected to analogous dynamics. *Holsteinization* is the process of monoculturing people as consumers so as to facilitate the harvesting of desires, including the decomposition of communities into isolated family units and individuals in order to supplant social networks of mutual support with consumersheds of dependent customers. Resistance is discouraged by means of *praedatorianism*, that is the forceful interdiction by a praedatorian guard with varying degrees of legitimacy.

The global latifundia, holsteinization, and praedatorianism are, in one form or another, as old as the global political economy; but the overarching dynamic signalling a break with previous manifestations is *flexism*, a pattern of econo-cultural production and consumption characterized by near-instantaneous delivery and rapid redirectability of resource flows. Flexism's fluidity results from cheaper and faster systems of transportation and telecommunications, globalization of capital markets, and concomitant flexibly specialized, just-in-time production processes enabling short product- and production-cycles. These result in highly mobile capital and commodity flows able to outmanoeuvre geographically fixed labour markets, communities and bounded nation-states. Globalization and rapidity permit capital to evade long-term commitment to place-based socio-economies, thus enabling a crucial social dynamic of flexism: whereas, under Fordism, exploitation is exercised through the alienation of labour in the place of production, flexism may require little or no labour at all from a given locale. Simultaneously, local down-waging and capital concentration operate synergistically to supplant locally owned enterprises with national and supranational chains, thereby transferring consumer capital and inventory selection ever further away from direct local control.

From these exchange asymmetries emerges a *new world bi-polar disorder*. This is a globally bifurcated social order, many times more complicated than conventional class structures, in which those overseeing the global latifundia enjoy concentrated power. Those who are dependent upon their command-and-control decisions find themselves in progressively weaker positions, pitted against each other globally, and forced to accept shrinking compensation for their efforts (assuming that compensation is offered in the first place). Of the two groups, the *cybergeoisie* reside in the 'big house' of the global latifundia, providing indispensable, presently unautomatable command-and-control functions. They are predominantly stockholders, the core employees of thinned-down corporations and write-your-own-ticket freelancers (e.g., CEOs, subcontract entrepreneurs and celebrities). They may also shelter members of marginal creative professions, who comprise a kind of paracybergeoisie. The cybergeoisie enjoy perceived socio-economic security and comparatively long-term horizons in decision-making; consequently, their anxieties tend towards unforeseen social disruptions such as market fluctuations and crime. Commanding, controlling and prodigiously enjoying the fruits of a shared global exchange of goods and information, the cybergeoisie exercise global coordination functions that predispose them to a similar ideology and, thus, they are relatively heavily holsteinized.

Protosurps, on the other hand, are the sharecroppers of the global latifundia. They are increasingly marginalized 'surplus' labour providing just-in-time services when called upon by flexist production processes, but otherwise alienated from global systems of production (though not of consumption). Protosurps include temporary or day labourers, fire-at-will service workers, and a burgeoning class of intra- and inter-national itinerant labourers specializing in pursuing the migrations of fluid investment. True surpdom is a state of superfluity beyond peonage – a vagrancy that is increasingly criminalized through anti-homeless ordinances, welfare-state erosion and widespread community intolerance (of, for instance, all forms of panhandling). Protosurps are called upon to provide as yet unautomated service functions designed so as to be performed by anyone. Subjected to high degrees of uncertainty by the omnipresent threat of instant unemployment, protosurps are prone to clustering into affinity groups for support in the face of adversity. These affinity groups, however, are not exclusive, overlapping in both membership and space, resulting in a class of marginalized indigenous populations and peripheral immigrants who are relatively less holsteinized.

The socio-cultural collisions and intermeshings of protosurp affinity groups, generated by flexist-induced immigration and severe social differentiation, serves to produce wild *memetic contagion*.[6] This is a process by which cultural elements of one individual or group exert cross-over influences upon the culture of another previously unexposed individual or group. Memetic contagion is evidenced in Los Angeles by such hybridized agents and intercultural conflicts as Mexican and Central American practitioners of Afro-Caribbean religion (McGuire and Scrymgeour, forthcoming), blue-bandanna'd Thai Crips or the adjustments prompted by poor African-Americans' offence at Korean merchants' disinclination to smile casually.[7] Memetic contagion should not be taken for a mere epiphenomenon of an underlying political economic order, generating colourfully chaotic ornamentation for a flexist regime. Rather, it entails the assemblage of novel ways of seeing and being, from whence new identities, cultures and political alignments emerge. These new social configurations, in turn, may act to force change in existing institutions and structures, and to spawn cognitive conceptions that are incommensurable with, though not necessarily any less valid than, existing models. The inevitable tensions between the anarchic diversification born of memetic contagion and the manipulations of the holsteinization process may yet prove to be the central cultural contradiction of flexism.

With the flexist imposition of global imperatives on local economies and cultures, the spatial logic of Fordism has given way to a new, more dissonant international geographical order. In the absence of conventional communication and transportation imperatives mandating propinquity, the once-standard Chicago School logic has given way to a seemingly haphazard juxtaposition of land uses scattered over the landscape. Worldwide, agricultural lands sprout monocultures of exportable strawberry or broccoli in lieu of diverse staple crops grown for local consumption. Sitting amidst these fields, identical assembly lines produce the same brand of automobile, supplied with parts and managed from distant continents. Expensive condominiums appear among squatter slums, indistinguishable in form and occupancy from (and often in direct communication with) luxury housing built atop homeless encampments elsewhere in the world. Yet what in close-up appears to be a fragmentary, collaged polyculture is, from a longer perspective, a geographically disjoint but hyperspatially integrated monoculture, that is, shuffled sames set amidst adaptive and persistent local variations. The result is a landscape not unlike that formed by a keno gamecard. The card itself appears as a numbered grid, with some squares being marked during the course of the game and others not, according to some random draw. The process governing this marking ultimately determines which player will achieve a jackpot-winning pattern; it is, however, determined by a rationalized set of procedures beyond the territory of the card itself. Similarly, the apparently random development and redevelopment of urban land may be regarded as the outcome of exogenous investment processes inherent to flexism, thus creating the landscapes of *keno capitalism*.

Keno capitalism's contingent mosaic of variegated monocultures renders discussion of 'the city' increasingly reductionist. More holistically, the dispersed net of megalopoles may be viewed as a single integrated urban system, or *Citistāt*. Citistāt, the collective world city, has emerged from competing urban webs of colonial and postcolonial eras to become a geographically diffuse hub of an omnipresent periphery, drawing labour and materials from readily substitutable locations throughout that periphery. Citistāt is both geographically corporeal, in the sense that urban places exist, and yet ageographically ethereal in the sense that communication systems create a virtual space permitting coordination across physical space. Both realms reinforce each another while (re)producing the new world bi-polar disorder.

Materially, Citistāt consists of commudities (centres of command and control) and the in-beyond (internal peripheries simultaneously undergoing but resisting instrumentalization in myriad ways). Virtually, Citistāt consists of cyburbia, the collection of state-of-the-art data-transmission, premium pay-per-use, and interactive services generally reliant upon costly and technologically complex interfaces; and cyberia, an electronic outland of rudimentary communications including basic telephone service and telegraphy, interwoven with, and preceptorally conditioned by, the disinformation superhighway (DSH).

Commudities are commodified communities created expressly to satisfy (and profit from) the habitat preferences of the well-recompensed cybergeoisie. They commonly consist of carefully manicured residential and commercial ecologies managed through privatopian self-administration, and maintained against internal and external outlaws by a repertoire of interdictory prohibitions. Increasingly, these pre-packaged environments jockey with one another for clientele on the basis of recreational, cultural, security and educational amenities. Commonly located on difficult-to-access sites like hilltops or urban edges, far from restless populations undergoing conversion to protosurpdom, individual commudities are increasingly teleintegrated to form *cyburbia* (Dewey, 1994), the interactive tollways comprising the high-rent district of Citistāt's hyperspatial electronic shadow. (This process may soon find a geographical analog in the conversion of automotive freeways linking commudities via exclusive tollways.) Teleintegration is already complete (and *de rigueur*) for the *citidels*, which are commercial commudities consisting of highrise corporate towers from which the control and coordination of production and distribution in the global latifundia are exercised.

Citistāt's internal periphery and repository of cheap on-call labour lies at the *in-beyond*, comprising a shifting matrix of protosurp affinity clusters. The in-beyond may be envisioned as a patchwork quilt of variously defined interest groups (with differing levels of economic, cultural and street influence), none of which possess the wherewithal to achieve hegemonic status or to secede. Secession may occur locally to some degree, as in the cases of the publicly subsidized reconfiguration of LA's Little Tokyo, and the consolidation of Koreatown through the import, adjacent extraction and community recirculation of capital. The piecemeal diversity of the in-beyond makes it a hotbed of wild memetic contagion. The global connectivity of the in-beyond is considerably less glamorous than that of the cybergeoisie's commudities, but it is no less extensive. Intermittent telephone contact and wire-service remittances occur throughout *cyberia* (Rushkoff, 1995; also see Knox and Taylor, 1995). The pot-holed public streets of Citistät's virtual twin are augmented by extensive networks of snail mail, personal migration and the hand-to-hand passage of mediated communications (e.g., cassette tapes). Such contacts occasionally diffuse into commudities.

Political relations in Citistät tend towards polyanarchy, a politics of grudging tolerance of *difference* that emerges from interactions and accommodations within the in-beyond and between commudities, and less frequently, between in-beyond and commudity. Its more pervasive form is *pollyannarchy*, an exaggerated, manufactured optimism that promotes a self-congratulatory awareness and respect for difference and the asymmetries of power. Pollyannarchy is thus a pathological form of polyanarchy, disempowering those who would challenge the controlling beneficiaries of the new world bi-polar disorder. Pollyannarchy is evident in the continuing spectacle of electoral politics, or in the citywide unity campaign run by corporate sponsors following the 1992 uprising in Los Angeles.

Wired throughout the body of the Citistät is the *disinformation super-highway* (or DSH), a mass info-tain-mercial media owned by roughly two dozen cybergeoisie institutions. The DSH disseminates holsteinizing ideologies and incentives, creates wants and dreams, and inflates the symbolic value of commodities. At the same time, it serves as the highly filtered sensory organ through which commudities and the in-beyond perceive the world outside their unmediated daily experiences. The DSH is Citistät's 'consent factory' (Chomsky and Herman, 1988), engineering memetic contagion to encourage participation in a global latifundia that is represented as both inevitable and desirable. However, since the DSH is a broad-band distributor of information designed primarily to attract and deliver consumers to advertisers, the ultimate reception of messages carried by the DSH is difficult to target and predetermine. Thus, the DSH also serves inadvertently as a vector for memetic contagion, for example, the conversion of cybergeoisie youth to wannabe gangstas via the dissemination of hip-hop culture over commudity boundaries. The DSH serves as a network of preceptoral control, and is thus distinct from the coercive mechanisms of the praedatorian guard. Overlap between the two is increasingly common, however, as in the case of televised disinfotainment programmes such as *America's Most Wanted*, in which crimes are dramatically re-enacted and viewers are invited to call in and betray alleged perpetrators.

As the cybergeoisie increasingly withdraw from the Fordist redistributive triad of big government, big business and big labour to establish their own micro-nations, the social support functions of the state disintegrate, along with the survivability of less-affluent citizens. The global migrations of work to the lowest-wage locations of the in-beyond, and of consumer capital to the citidels, result in power asymmetries that become so pronounced that even the DSH is at times incapable of obscuring them, leaving protosurps increasingly disinclined to adhere to the remnants of a tattered social contract. This instability in turn creates the potential for violence, pitting Citistät and cybergeoisie against the protosurp in-beyond, and leading inevitably to a demand for the suppression of protosurp intractability. The *praedatorian guard* thus emerges as the principal remaining vestige of the police powers of the state. This increasingly privatized public/private partnership of mercenary sentries, police expeditionary forces and their technological extensions (e.g., video cameras, helicopters, criminological data uplinks, etc.) watches over the commudities and minimizes disruptiveness by acting as a force of occupation within the in-beyond. The praedatorian guard achieves control through coercion, even at the international level where asymmetrical trade relations are reinforced by the military and its clientele. It may only be a matter of time before the local and national praedatorians are administratively and functionally merged, as exemplified by proposals to deploy military units for policing inner-city streets of the USA–Mexico border.

Invitation to a Postmodern Urbanism

We have begun the process of interrogating prior models of urban structure with an alternative model based upon the recent experiences of Los Angeles. We do not pretend to have completed this project, nor claim that the Southern Californian experience is necessarily typical of other metropolitan regions in the USA or the world. Still less would we advocate replacing the old models with a new hegemony. But discourse has to start somewhere, and by now it is clear that the most influential of existing urban models is no longer tenable as a guide to contemporary urbanism. In this first sense, our investigation has uncovered an *epistemological radical break* with past practices, which in itself is sufficient justification for something called a Los Angeles School. The concentric ring structure of the Chicago School was essentially a concept of the city as an organic accretion around a central, organizing core. Instead, we have identified a postmodern urban process in which the urban periphery organizes the centre within the context of a globalizing capitalism.

The postmodern urban process remains resolutely capitalist, but the nature of that enterprise is changing in very significant ways, especially through (for instance) the telecommunications revolution, the changing nature of work, and globalization. Thus, in this second sense also we understand that a *radical break* is occurring, this time in the conditions of our *material world*. Contemporary urbanism is a consequence of how local and inter-local flows of material and information (including symbols) intersect in a rapidly converging and globally integrated economy driven by the imperatives of flexism. Landscapes and peoples are homogenized to facilitate large-scale production and consumption. Highly mobile capital and commodity flows outmanoeuvre geographically fixed labour markets, communities and nation-states, and cause a globally bifurcated polarization. The beneficiaries of this system are the cybergeoisie, even as the numbers of permanently marginalized protosurps grow. In the new global order, socio-economic polarization and massive, sudden population migrations spawn cultural hybrids through the process of memetic contagion. Cities no longer develop as concentrated loci of population and economic activity, but as fragmented parcels within Citistät, the collective world city. Materially, Citistät consists of commudities (commodified communities) and the in-beyond (the permanently marginalized). Virtually, Citistät is composed of cyburbia (those hooked into the electronic world) and cyberia (those who are not). Social order is maintained by the ideological apparatus of the DSH, Citistät's consent factory, and by the praedatorian guard, the privatized vestiges of the nation-state's police powers.

Keno capitalism is the synoptic term that we have adopted to describe the spatial manifestations of the postmodern urban condition. Urbanization is occurring on a quasi-random field of opportunities. Capital touches down as if by chance on a parcel of land, ignoring the opportunities on intervening lots, thus sparking the development process. The relationship between development of one parcel and non-development of another is a disjointed, seemingly unrelated affair. While not truly a random process, it is evident that the traditional, centre-driven agglomeration economies that have guided urban development in the past no longer apply. Conventional city form, Chicago-style, is sacrificed in favour of a non-contiguous collage of parcelized, consumption-oriented landscapes devoid of conventional centres yet wired into electronic propinquity and nominally unified by the mythologies of the disinformation superhighway. Los Angeles may be a mature form of this postmodern metropolis; Las Vegas comes to mind as a youthful example. The consequent urban aggregate is characterized by acute fragmentation and specialization – a partitioned gaming board subject to perverse laws and peculiarly discrete, disjointed urban outcomes. Given the pervasive presence of crime, corruption and violence in the global city (not to mention geopolitical transitions, as nation-states give way to micro-nationalisms and transnational mafias), the city as gaming board seems an especially appropriate twenty-first-century successor to the concentrically ringed city of the early twentieth century.

We intend this chapter as an invitation to examine the concept of a postmodern urbanism. We recognize that we have only begun to sketch its potential, that its validity will only be properly assessed if researchers elsewhere in the world are willing to examine its precepts. We urge others to share in this enterprise because, even though our vision is tentative, we are convinced that we have glimpsed a new way of understanding cities.[8]

Acknowledgements

Versions of this chapter have been presented at a *Theory, Culture & Society* conference in Berlin; the University of Turku on behalf of the Finnish Academy of Science; the Howell Lecture in the School of Architecture at the University of Nebraska-Lincoln; the University of Oxford's Department of Geography; the School of Architecture, Building and Planning at the University of Melbourne; the annual meetings of the Association of Collegiate Schools of Architecture and the Association of American Geographers; and the Center for Advanced Study in the Behavioral Sciences at Stanford, CA. We are grateful to Scott Lash and Mike Featherstone, Harri Anderson and Jouni Haakli, Ross King and Ruth Fincher, Sharon Lord Gaber, Gordon Clark and Robert Harris for invitations to present on these occasions. Thanks also to the many conference participants who provided constructive criticism. Kim Dovey, Ruth Fincher, Robert Harris, John Kaliski, Carol and John Levy, Jan Nijman, Kevin Robins, Michael Webber and Jennifer Wolch were supportive of the enterprise and offered helpful comments. None of these people should be blamed for anything in this essay. This chapter was first written while Dear was a fellow at the Center for Advanced Study in the Behavioral Sciences at Stanford. The support of the Center and the National Science Foundation SES–9022192 is gratefully acknowledged.

Notes

A version of this essay was published as M. Dear and S. Flusty (1998) 'Postmodern urbanism', in the *Annals of the Association of American Geographers*, 88 (1): 50–72.

1 Raban's view finds echoes in the seminal work of de Certeau (1984).

2 It is worth emphasizing that in the overview we focus solely on the concatenation of urban events that are occurring in contemporary Southern California. This is not to suggest that such trends are absent in other cities, nor that a larger literature on these topics and cities is missing. A complete review of these other places and literatures is simply beyond the scope of this chapter.

3 Such sentiments find echoes in Neil Smith's assessment of the new urban frontier, where expansion is powered by two industries: real-estate developers (who package and define value) and the manufacturers of culture (who define taste and consumption preferences) (Smith, 1992: 75).

4 The list of LA novels and movies is endless. Typical of the dystopian cinematic vision are *Blade Runner* (Ridley Scott, 1986) and *Chinatown* (Roman Polanski, 1974); and of silly optimism, *LA Story* (Mick Jackson, 1991).

5 One critic accused us (quite cleverly) of 'neologorrhea'.

6 This term is a combination of René Girard's 'mimetic contagion' and animal ethologist Richard Dawkin's hypothesis that cultural informations are gene-type units, or 'memes', transmitted virus-like from head to head.

7 We here employ the term 'hybridized' in recognition of the recency and novelty of the combination, not to assert some prior purity to the component elements forming the hybrid.

8 The collection of essays assembled in Benko and Strohmayer (1997) is an excellent overview of the relationship between space and postmodernism, including the urban question. Kevin Robins's valuable work on media, visual cultures and representational issues also deserves wide audience (e.g., Morley and Robins, 1995; Robins, 1996).

References

Abelmann, N. and Lie, J. (1995) *Blue Dreams: Korean Americans and the Los Angeles Riots.* Cambridge, MA: Harvard University Press.

Anderson, S. (1996) 'A city called heaven: black enchantment and despair in Los Angeles', in A.J. Scott and E. Soja (eds), *The City: Los Angeles and Urban Theory at the End of the Twentieth Century.* Los Angeles, CA: University of California Press. pp. 336–64.

Baldassare, M. (ed.) (1994) *The Los Angeles Riots.* Boulder, CO: Westview Press.

Banham, R. (1973) *Los Angeles: The Architecture of Four Ecologies.* London: Penguin.

Benko, C. and Strohmayer, U. (eds) (1997) *Space and Social Theory: Interpreting Modernity and Postmodernity.* Oxford: Blackwell.

Bottles, S. (1987) *Los Angeles and the Automobile: The Making of the Modern City.* Los Angeles, CA: University of California Press.

Boyd, T. (1996) 'A small introduction to the "G" Funk era: gangsta rap and black masculinity in contemporary Los Angeles', in M. Dear, H.E. Schockman and G. Hise (eds), *Rethinking Los Angeles.* Thousand Oaks, CA: Sage. pp. 127–46.

Boyd, T. (1997) *Am I Black Enough for You?* Indianapolis, IN: University of Indiana Press.

Bullard, R.D., Grigsby, J.E. and Lee, C. (1994) *Residential Apartheid.* Los Angeles, CA: UCLA Center for Afro-American Studies.

Butler, O.E. (1993) *Parable of the Sower.* New York: Four Walls Eight Windows.

Cándida Smith, R. (1995) *Utopia and Dissent: Art, Poetry, and Politics in California.* Los Angeles: University of California Press.

Castells, M. and Hall, P. (1994) *Technopoles of the World: The Making of the 21st Century Industrial Complexes.* New York: Routledge.

del Castillo, R. (1979) *The Los Angeles Barrio, 1850–1890: A Social History.* Los Angeles, CA: University of California Press.

de Certeau, M. (1984) *The Practice of Everyday Life.* Berkeley, CA: University of California Press.

Chomsky, N. and Herman, E. (1988) *Manufacturing Consent.* New York: Pantheon Books.

Darlington, D. (1996) *The Mojave: Portrait of the Definitive American Desert.* New York: Henry Holt.

Davis, M. (1990) *City of Quartz: Excavating the Future in Los Angeles.* New York: Verso.

Davis, M. (1992a) 'Fortress Los Angeles: the militarization of urban space', in M. Sorkin (ed.), *Variations on a Theme Park.* New York: Noonday Press. pp. 154–80.

Davis, M. (1992b) 'Chinatown revisited? The internationalization of downtown Los Angeles', in D. Reid (ed.), *Sex, Death and God in LA.* New York: Pantheon Books.

Davis, M. (1996) 'How Eden lost its garden: a political history of the Los Angeles landscape', in A.J. Scott and E. Soja (eds), *The City: Los Angeles and Urban Theory at the End of the Twentieth Century.* Los Angeles, CA: University of California Press. pp. 160–85.

Davis, M.L. (1993) *Rivers in the Desert: William Mulholland and the Inventing of Los Angeles.* New York: HarperCollins.

Dear, M. (1988) 'The postmodern challenge: reconstructing human geography', *Transactions, Institute of British Geographers,* 13: 262–74.

Deverell, W. (1994) *Railroad Crossing: Californians and the Railroad 1850–1910.* Los Angeles, CA: University of California Press.

Dewey, F. (1994) 'Cyburbia: Los Angeles as the new frontier, or grave?', *Los Angeles Forum for Architecture and Urban Design Newsletter,* May: 6–7.

Erie, S.P. (forthcoming) *Global Los Angeles: Growth and Crisis of a Developmental City-State.* Stanford, CA: Stanford University Press.

Fishman, R. (1987) *Bourgeois Utopias: The Rise and Fall of Suburbia*. New York: Basic Books.

FitzSimmons, M. and Gottlieb, Robert (1996) 'Bounding and binding metropolitan space: the ambiguous politics of nature in Los Angeles', in A.J. Scott and E. Soja (eds), *The City: Los Angeles and Urban Theory at the End of the Twentieth Century*. Los Angeles, CA: University of California Press. pp. 186–224.

Flusty, S. (1994) *Building Paranoia: The Proliferation of Interdictory Space and the Erosion of Spatial Justice*. West Hollywood, CA: Los Angeles Forum for Architecture and Urban Design.

Folgelson, R.M. (1967) *The Fragmented Metropolis: Los Angeles 1850–1970*. Berkeley, CA: University of California Press.

Fulton, W. (1997) *The Reluctant Metropolis: The Politics of Urban Growth in Los Angeles*. Point Arena, CA: Solano Press Books.

Garreau, J. (1991) *Edge City: Life on the New Frontier*. New York: Doubleday.

Gooding-Williams, R. (ed.) (1993) *Reading Rodney King, Reading Urban Uprising*. New York: Routledge.

Gottlieb, R. and FitzSimmons, M. (1991) *Thirst for Growth: Water Agencies and Hidden Government in California*. Tucson, AZ: University of Arizona Press.

Hise, G. (1997) *Magnetic Los Angeles: Planning the Twentieth-century Metropolis*. Baltimore, MD: John Hopkins University Press.

Jameson, F. (1991) *Postmodernism, or, the Cultural Logic of Late Capitalism*. Durham, NC: Duke University Press.

Jencks, C. (1993) *Heteropolis: Los Angeles, the Riots and the Strange Beauty of Hetero-Architecture*. London: Academy Editions; Berlin: Ernst & Sohn; New York: St Martin's Press.

Klein, M. (1995) *The American Street Gang: Its Nature, Prevalence, and Control*. New York: Oxford University Press.

Knox, P. and Taylor, P.J. (eds) (1995) *World Cities in a World System*. Cambridge: Cambridge University Press.

Martínez, R. (1992) *The Other Side: Notes from the New LA Mexico City, and Beyond*. New York: Vintage Books.

McGuire, B. and Scrymgeour, D. (forthcoming) 'Santeria and Curanderismo in Los Angeles', in Peter Clarke (ed.), *New Trends and Developments in African Religion*. Westport, CT: Greenwood Publishing. pp. 211–22.

McKenzie, E. (1994) *Privatopia: Homeowner Associations and the Rise of Residential Private Government*. New Haven, CT: Yale University Press.

McPhee, J. (1989) *The Control of Nature*. New York: The Noonday Press.

McWilliams, C. (1973) *Southern California: An Island on the Land*. Salt Lake City, UT: Peregrine Smith Books.

Molotch, H. (1996) 'LA as Design Product: How Art Works in a Regional Economy', in A.J. Scott and E. Soja (eds), *The City: Los Angeles and Urban Theory at the End of the Twentieth Century*. Los Angeles, CA: University of California Press. pp. 225–75.

Morley, D. and Robins, K. (1995) *Spaces of Identity: Global Media, Electronic Landscapes, and Cultural Boundaries*. New York: Routledge.

Ong, P., Bonacich, E. and Cheng, L. (eds) (1994) *The New Asian Immigration in Los Angeles and Global Restructuring*. Philadelphia: Temple University Press.

Park, E. (1996) 'Our LA? Korean Americans in Los Angeles after the Civil Unrest', in M. Dear, H.E. Schockman and G. Hise (eds), *Rethinking Los Angeles*. Thousand Oaks, CA: Sage. pp. 153–68.

Pulido, L. (1996) 'Multiracial Organizing among Environmental Justice Activists in Los Angeles', in M. Dear, H.E. Schockman and G. Hise (eds), *Rethinking Los Angeles*. Thousand Oaks, CA: Sage.

Raban, J. (1974) *Soft City*. New York: E.P. Dutton.

Reisner, M. (1993) *Cadillac Desert: The American West and its Disappearing Water*. New York: Penguin.

Relph, E.C. (1987) *The Modern Urban Landscape*. Baltimore, MD: Johns Hopkins University Press.

Robins, K. (1996) *Into the Image: Culture and Politics in the Field of Vision.* New York: Routledge.

Rocco, R. (1996) 'Latino Los Angeles: Reframing Boundaries/Borders', in A.J. Scott and E. Soja (eds), *The City: Los Angeles and Urban Theory at the End of the Twentieth Century.* Los Angeles, CA: University of California Press. pp. 365–89.

Roseman, C., Laux, H.D. and Thieme, G. (eds) (1996) *EthniCity.* Lanham, MD: Rowman & Littlefield.

Rushkoff, D. (1995) *Cyberia: Life in the Trenches of Hyperspace.* New York: HarperCollins.

Scott, A.J. (1988a) *New Industrial Spaces: Flexible Production Organization and Regional Development in North America and Western Europe.* London: Pion.

Scott, A.J. (1988b) *Metropolis: From the Division of Labor to Urban Form.* Berkeley, CA: University of California Press.

Scott, A.J. (1993) *Technopolis: High-technology Industry and Regional Development in Southern California.* Berkeley, CA: University of California Press.

Smith, N. (1992) 'New city, new frontier', in M. Sorkin (ed.), *Variations on a Theme Park.* New York: Hill & Wang. pp. 61–93.

Soja, E. (1989) *Postmodern Geographies: The Reassertion of Space in Critical Social Theory.* London/New York: Verso.

Soja, E. (1992) 'Inside Exopolis: scenes from Orange County', in M. Sorkin (ed.), *Variations on a Theme Park.* New York: Hill & Wang. pp. 94–122.

Soja, E. (1996) 'Los Angeles 1965–1992: the six geographies of urban restructuring', in A.J. Scott and E. Soja (eds), *The City: Los Angeles and Urban Theory at the End of the Twentieth Century.* Los Angeles, CA: University of California Press. pp. 426–62.

Sonenshein, R. (1993) *Politics in Black and White: Race and Power in Los Angeles.* Princeton, NJ: Princeton University Press.

Sorkin, M. (ed.) (1992) *Variations on a Theme Park: The New American City and the End of Public Space.* New York: Hill & Wang.

Storper, M. and Walker, R. (1989) *The Capitalist Imperative.* Oxford: Blackwell.

Suisman, D.R. (1989) *Los Angeles Boulevard.* Los Angeles, CA: Los Angeles Forum for Architectural and Urban Design.

Tygiel, J. (1994) *The Great Los Angeles Swindle: Oil, Stocks, and Scandal during the Roaring Twenties.* New York: Oxford University Press.

Vigil, J. (1988) *Barrio Gangs: Streetlife and Identity in Southern California.* Austin, TX: University of Texas Press.

Wachs, M. (1996) 'The evolution of transportation policy in Los Angeles: images of past policies and future prospects', in A.J. Scott and E. Soja (eds), *The City: Los Angeles and Urban Theory at the End of the Twentieth Century.* Los Angeles, CA: University of California Press. pp. 106–59.

Waldie, D.J. (1996) *Holy Land: A Suburban Memoir.* New York: W.W. Norton.

Waldinger, R. and Bozorgmehr, M. (1996) *Ethnic Los Angeles.* New York: Russell Sage Foundation.

Weiss, M. (1987) *The Rise of the Community Builders: The American Real Estate Industry and Urban Land Planning.* New York: Columbia University Press.

Wolch, J. (1990) *The Shadow State: Government and Voluntary Sector in Transition.* New York: Foundation Center.

Wolch, J. (1996) 'From global to local: the rise of homelessness in Los Angeles during the 1980s', in A.J. Scott and E. Soja (eds), *The City: Los Angeles and Urban Theory at the End of the Twentieth Century.* Los Angeles, CA: University of California Press. pp. 390–425.

Wolch, J. and Dear, M. (1993) *Malign Neglect: Homelessness in an American City.* San Francisco, CA: Jossey-Bass.

Wolch, J. and Sommer, H. (1997) *Los Angeles in an Era of Welfare Reform: Implications for Poor People and Community Well-being.* Los Angeles, CA: Liberty Hill Foundation.

Yoon, I. (1997) *On My Own: Korean Businesses and Race Relations in America.* Chicago: University of Chicago Press.

5

ROAMING THE CITY: PROPER WOMEN IN IMPROPER PLACES

Hilary Radner

Consumerism produces a disputed terrain within cultural studies in general and within feminist scholarship in particular. This debate revolves around a question fundamental to the field of cultural studies as a whole: does consumption always work in the service of a hegemonic structure or are there ways in which consumption offers a space for resistance against the very structures that it would appear to represent?[1] The articulation of fashion within the broader context of feminine consumption is symptomatic of this larger debate. So called 'high fashion' offers a strikingly fraught example of the vagaries of culture and its relationship to hegemonic modes of social control. On the one hand, 'high fashion' is the prerogative of the wealthy and the privileged; on the other, in post-Second World War culture, high fashion clearly draws upon the subcultures of street life and of the avant-garde – subcultures generally thought to represent the extremes of social subversion by the dominant class in the USA.[2]

Initially within 'second wave' feminist scholarship, in so far as 'fashion' was tied to the social injunction that femininity be constructed in terms of a position in which the feminine was identified with 'to-be-looked-at-ness', fashion was discussed as an ideological institution designed to confirm the woman in her place within patriarchy and capital.[3] Thus Janice Winship comments critically in 1980 that consumer culture dictates that: '[a] woman is nothing more the commodities she wears: the lipstick, the tights, the clothes and so on are "woman"' (1980: 217). Elizabeth Wilson summarizes the general assumptions behind this position:

> In the nineteenth century fashion had come to be associated almost entirely with women's clothing, while men's clothes have since been perceived (inaccurately) as unchanging. Fashion as a mania for change could therefore the more easily be interpreted either as evidence of women's inherent frivolity and flightiness; or – the other side of the coin – as evidence of women's subjection and oppression. As argued most influentially by Thorstein Veblen, women's fashion was part of conspicuous consumption and reflected her status as property. (Wilson, 1990: 29)

In contrast, drawing on the work of scholars such as Angela McRobbie and Wilson herself (who is critical of Veblen), Jane Gaines queries in 1990:

'What better site for the disruption of the social order than the seeming scene of the origins of women's oppression?' (Gaines, 1990: 9). This query is indicative of a sea-change in feminist studies itself. Rather than positing the feminine consumer as a 'cultural dupe', scholars have attempted to understand how, within the larger structures of patriarchy and capital, female consumers have constructed 'tactics' of resistance.

Here, in using the term 'tactics', I borrow from the French poststructuralist Michel de Certeau, who introduces this last to suggest the dynamical nature of cultural production. In his model, the tension between strategies, which serve to reproduce economies grounded in commensurability, and tactics, which wander elsewhere, in an infinite complexity of counter-movements, can never be resolved. De Certeau describes these two positions:

> A strategy assumes a place that can be circumscribed as proper (*propre*) and thus serve as the basis for generating relations with an exterior distinct from it (competitors, adversaries, clientèles, targets, or objects of research) . . . a tactic insinuates itself into the other's place, fragmentarily, without taking it over in its entirety, without being able to keep it at a distance . . . tactics wander out of orbit, making consumers into immigrants in a system too vast to be their own, too tightly woven for them to escape from it. (de Certeau, 1984: xix)

Fashion itself, as all social practices, might be considered as an amalgam of tactics and strategies, one that foregrounds the paradox implicit in de Certeau's theory: tactics can only signify as such in opposition to strategies. My tactics could very easily become your strategies – the ones against which you will position your 'self' as a 'tactician' (to put it playfully). The strategies of the fashion house, which has as its goal to generate a set of relations with a demographically specific 'clientele' that define that clientele as such – a 'proper' woman of the upper classes – might also imply a set of tactics that define a designer as 'gay' and that thus move his designs, if only in passing, 'outside' a 'proper' heterosexist institution of femininity. Is feminine fashion inextricably linked (if only in passing) to the notion of the '*impropre*': the improper of the prostitute, or the *demi-monde* who thumbs her nose at the proprieties of bourgeois life, who refuses to take her proper place, that which is appropriate to her status as feminine within the social hierarchy?

Gaines's comment on what she terms 'genuine perversion' might be said to hold true for fashion in general, and high fashion in particular. She remarks that 'genuine perversion' represents: 'the muffled protests against oppression found in the very practices which seem to most graphically implement and spell out the patriarchial wish' (Gaines, 1990: 29). Gaines continues: 'the most constricting mode of dress might lead women to make erotic discoveries about their own bodies' (1990: 29). With this remark Gaines raises yet another significant issue – the manner in which heterosexuality itself is not a monolithic position. Within feminine culture, heterosexuality – its iconography – frequently might be best understood as providing an alibi for the feminine consumer who wishes to take her pleasure elsewhere. In the world of high fashion, heterosexuality operates more often than not as a 'cover story' that authorizes the production of other libidinal moments.[4] We might, then, talk about how heterosexuality 'poaches' upon other less legitimate pleasures in order to create an acceptable story for both men and women. This concept is implicit in Foucault's opposition between the couple as the socially legitimate sign of alliance and sexuality (and pleasure by extension) which explicitly structures itself against a regulating social architecture (Foucault, 1980: 106–7). Fashion clearly regulates the female body, its appearance, and its behaviour; and yet it is also tied to the pursuit of pleasure, of 'frivolity', within feminine culture.

'High fashion' occupies an especially difficult place within feminine culture, in that it clearly reproduces in an exaggerated form the fundamental tenets of a Veblen's analysis of feminine consumer culture. The fashionable woman is constructed through 'conspicuous consumption' as a spectacle that represents the wealth of the family – and of the patriarch that heads this family.[5] Yet 'fashion' as 'style' sets itself in opposition to a spectacle that is produced through expenditure alone. The fashionable spectacle is defined by an ineffable 'allure' that, at least seemingly, transcends vulgar excess. If 'fashionableness' is the goal of the 'nouveau riche', it is a goal that must always situate itself beyond her reach. Thus the discourse of 'fashion' – its 'tactics' as it were – resists translation into 'money' as a universal signifier.

We cannot explain the fashionable in terms of expenditure alone. As a result, the subject of high fashion occupies a paradoxical position vis-à-vis a social hierarchy regulated by capital. She is a member of the upper classes, economically, socially and culturally; however she does not automatically enjoy the privileges of this class, of her 'family', except by proxy. Furthermore, she must also represent that which cannot be 'bought'. As a sign, she functions within the discursive production of a myth that constructs a notion of 'class' that might exist outside economic hierarchy.[6]

One might say that as a subject the fashionable woman is articulated as such through an 'occulted dominant discursive class'. I use the term 'occulted dominant' to refer to the position that a woman might occupy, perhaps only temporarily, in which she is objectively neither poor nor marginalized. She is, nonetheless, economically dependent upon the labour or capital of another; in other words, she does not technically 'work'.[7] Her social and economic status are thus defined through her position within a patriarchal family; yet, this position does not prevent her definition as a subject within another discourse that situates itself against patriarchy. The occulted dominant discursive class, and here I borrow from intellectual historian Timothy Reiss, is defined by a set of practices 'composed of widespread activities . . . that escape analysis by the dominant model, that do not acquire "meaningfulness" in its terms, that are therefore in the strictest sense unthinkable' (Reiss, 1985: 11). Fashionableness – at least initially – was produced precisely by such a set of practices, deemed meaningless, a symptom of 'women's inherent frivolity and flightiness' in Wilson's terms, by the dominant class – that of men.

For 'men', then, clothing apparently (and only apparently) had no meaning. Thus the ostensible blindness of the male to the rhetoric of fashion (coupled with his vulnerability to its effects, the seduction of this invisible spectacle that is designed to capture his look) is one of fashion's defining features. The actress, whose attributes are vulgarly apparent, is not a fashionable woman. She may on occasion demonstrate 'style', as might the professional model; however, high fashion is the goal of the socialite rather than the actress, or the entrepreneur. The mavens of high fashion in the pre-Second World War years, such as Diana Vreeland, 'tactically'[8] made a career of 'it'; however, fashionableness in the hey day of *haute couture* was the proper aspiration of the *haute bourgeoisie* – a state to which ostensibly one was 'born' rather than one to which one aspired. Thus Diana Vreeland, in her capacity as the spokeswoman of fashion asserts: 'Of course, one is born with good taste' (1985: 161). The waning power of the *haute couture* in the post-Second World War years suggests a new feminine subject and a new erotics of fashion.

Thus an analysis of high fashion as public spectacle in the post-Second World War era offers a crucial insight into the narrative whereby a feminine consumer subject is defined and constructed. The stakes of this spectacle are perhaps most clearly delineated through the development of a genre in fashion photography termed 'Outside Fashion' by art historian Martin Harrison. This genre, Harrison argues, evolves in post-Second World War New York – thus simultaneously with the fall of the great European *couture* houses and the rise of the ready-to-wear market (Harrison, 1991, 1994). Harrison argues in the catalogue of a show hung by the Howard Greenberg Gallery:

> Women's fashion magazines were the first medium to present images of women for the consumption of women, rather than men, and the women depicted in these photographs – who after all represented their readers – began to be cast in active as opposed to the passive roles traditionally assigned to them in art. (Harrison, 1994)

Within Harrison's argument, the displacement of the fashion model from the studio to the outdoor *mise-en-scène* signified the construction of an 'active' as opposed to 'passive' feminine. This 'active' genre emphasizes the contradictions inherent in fashion photography that hinge upon the coincidence of seemingly inconsistent terms such as 'street' photography and high fashion; spectacle and activity; provocation and commercialism.

The fact that these images, discussed by Harrison, were transposed from their original setting in the fashion magazine to a New York gallery immediately raises a series of questions regarding the status of the fashion image and its relationship to art. The facility of this transposition indicates the difficulties inherent in an analysis of the genre: fashion photography is not 'popular' in the common sense of the term, but is clearly distinct from the category of 'art' photography. Unlike 'art', fashion photography obviously functions primarily within a marketplace that serves to sell clothes. It is only belatedly that one comes to think of fashion photography as a medium that sells itself as art, almost as an afterthought. Yet the boundaries between art photography and fashion photography have always been blurred, photographers themselves crossing easily between genres. Similarly, institutions such as Condé Nast, a major publishing house that specializes in magazines, and women's fashion magazines in particular, were among the first to promote art photography as such in the twentieth century, testifying to the difficulties that this non-genre presents for analysis. As 'art' the fashion photograph resists easy dismissal as mere commercial pap for the gullible consumer. However, as a promoter of fashion, and especially high fashion as the ultimate of consumer follies, the fashion photograph is rarely taken seriously.

Ultimately, as a commercial genre that itself follows 'fashion' and the dictates of art editors, it resists the requirement of contemporary high art, which arguably sees the work's fundamental goal as the expression of individual genius. Nonetheless, as the show 'Outside Fashion' suggests, the photographic image of fashion itself often circulates along other trajectories, in particular the trajectory of 'art', that are themselves 'outside' the fashion industry. In this sense, fashion photography might on occasion subvert the discourse of the very industry that spawned it as a genre. Martin Harrison comments:

> To describe any fashion photograph as 'anti-fashion' is a contradiction in terms.
> . . . But the history of fashion photography is punctuated with examples of
> photographers who have nobly (or irrationally) attempted to resist some of its
> obvious seductions. (Harrison, 1994)

The above statement underlines the specificity of the discourse surrounding the fashion photograph as a genre. On the one hand, it is a genre, its attributes who culturally defined; on the other, it is only the individual photographer who 'resists', following 'irrational' trajectories, but who also is seduced by the spectacle of fashion itself, as an 'improper' pleasure.

Indeed, Harrison's collection sets itself apart from other shows that might or might not include fashion photographs – in which it is the name of the photographer (Richard Avedon, Helmut Newton, William Klein, etc.) that lends legitimacy to the work. The work of individual photographers circulates easily within the discourse of art as the production of individual genius. Harrison, in his catalogue essay, continually returns to the notion of art as the manifestation of personal vision (thus his emphasis on the influence of Alexander Liberman as an art director and William Klein as a photographer); however, the show itself belies the concept by presenting a set of images defined through genre rather than authorship. Certainly, if the photographer William Klein pioneered the 'street' look in fashion photography, it was the lesser known Frances McLaughlin[9] or Karen Radkai who were equally responsible for furnishing *Vogue*[10] with these images of a new urban femininity. The show itself, as a collection of images, attests to one of the many contradictions that inform the fashion photograph as an aesthetic object: the images are legitimated as 'art' through the establishment of a tradition of 'authorship'; however, the social function of these images depends upon their cohesion as a genre independent of this same authorship.

Harrison himself establishes the significance of this show in three distinct ways that point to the ambiguous status of fashion and the fashion photograph. First, he underlines the relationship of the images with a potential consumer. Thus fashion photography becomes 'art' not through the act of creation but through a hypothetical act of reception.[11] Secondly, Harrison evokes the historical context of the genre in which the industry itself is crucial to its formal evolution. Thus the 1933 image that is said to have provided the seeds for the genre, which would flourish in the post-Second World War years, was commandeered by editor Carmel Snow. Harrison comments:

> [A] burgeoning new commodity she had to propagate was sports wear. Of all aspects of clothing, sports wear most clearly exemplified the modernist fascination with speed – streamlining, motor-racing, air travel, *movies* – all testified to the faster pace of urban life. (Harrison, 1994)

Martin Munkacsi, a sports photographer who 'creates' the historic image at Snow's request 'not only instructed his model to move, but to *run*' (Harrison, 1994). Thus the genre develops in response to a 'client' that required a new aesthetic to promote a new type of clothing. The effect of spontaneity is contrived, designed to articulate this new aesthetic of urban life, produced through a hierarchy of 'instructions', of stage directions, geared towards creating a certain market.

Thirdly, the genre is described as deriving from stylistic conventions, and techniques proper to mass culture (sports photography and journalism) rather than 'art'. Stylistically, the genre exploits the techniques of immediacy (and disposability) that characterize the mass media in general. Thus, the Munkacsi photograph of Lucile Brokaw is, according to Carmel Snow, 'the first action photograph made *for fashion*' (Harrison, 1994). The fact that this action is 'staged', 'made' rather than 'taken', affirms the duplicity of the moment. The model is there to be looked at – to sell the new 'sports-wear' look as well as a set of specific items. She is not an athlete or soldier performing a designated task with an external goal. She is there to represent something other than her 'self'.

Yet the contrast between this image and others of the period is undeniable. Brokaw seemingly moves outside the frame – her hand blurred, her leg extending beyond the formally inscribed field of the image. Her body is draped with a cloak – some sort of after-bathing apparel. Both the details of what one must assume is a bathing suit and the cloak[12] are obscured by the lines of movement. The body itself as an entity, defined by specific physical attributes, overwhelms the structural attributes and details of her outfit: the musculature of a thigh is sharply delineated, one white shoe visible at the bottom of the page, the neckline of the suit itself hidden, her crisp hair softened by air rushing past.

In clear counterpoint, a series of fashion photographs shot by Edward Steichen[13] that appeared in the 1 May 1927 issue of *Vogue* emphasizes the image as a process of containment: the model is triply framed by the page and then within the page itself. The photographs portray a woman carefully posed for the camera, immobile, her body fully and conspicuously displayed, captured in its entirety. It is a body that takes its identity from the clothes that cover it. Rather than asserting its independence, it is subsumed, rendered abstract, by the clothes that cover it. Every detail of her toilette is visible, including the details of jewellery and stockings. Here, the image functions as a means of enumerating a set of items, which assembled constitute the fashionable look. Stylistically the image draws explicitly on fashion illustrations that offered similar portraits of an anonymous model, or even actual details of hats, shoes, jewellery, accessories, etc.

The function of the traditional fashion image would seem to confirm the analysis of feminine consumerism pioneered by Veblen. Fashion served to encourage the purchase of a set of specified objects that if accumulated would signal the position of the woman. 'Style' could be easily emulated in so far as it manifested itself as a taxonomy of formal detail. Significantly, an advertisement for B. Altman and Company (a department store, with its own *Altman Magazine*) proclaims in the 1 May 1927 issue of *Vogue*: 'Correctly Dressed Women Have Authority.' The advertisement defines correctly dressed in the following terms:

> Well-dressed women of New York and Paris have given their cachet to certain lines, materials, colours, details of the mode for Spring. Thus, they have not only established what is immediately correct among all the tendril ideas advanced at the Paris Spring Openings; but they have also given the cues for future development of the mode.

The Altman advertisement concludes: 'Altman Fashions are for those who lead with an air of authority.' In emphasizing the formal attributes of a given 'look' (line, material, colour, detail), the advertisement underlines that 'style' is produced through the reproduction of a defined set of qualities. The last are not co-terminous with (but are not unconnected to) 'expenditure'. The advertisement, then, does not 'sell' style as such, but rather 'correctness', which produces 'authority'.

The notion that fashion and authority are related, that the one confers the other, both confirms and disputes the facile reduction of fashion to 'conspicuous consumption'. The articulation of a set of formal attributes that are visible and verifiable as such corresponds to the concept of 'conspicuous'. However, implicated in the term 'correctly dressed' is the issue of literacy. Literacy results from proximity to the geographical locations of authority – 'New York and Paris' as the City – but also (by proxy) from reading *Altman Magazine* and, by extension, *Vogue* itself. The 'authority' that this literacy confers, which the feminine consumer must externalize, make 'conspicuous', is in turn the result of this literacy – or rather its display.[14] In this sense high fashion exemplifies the means by which 'occulted discursive practices' construct alternative hierarchies of 'meaningfulness' while continuing to maintain a 'cover story' that seemingly corresponds to the dominant discursive practice. The fashionable woman may serve to confirm the status of her husband and/or family, but she also 'conspicuously' confirms her own status within a different hierarchy – a hierarchy that is not necessarily 'visible' to those outside. Thus the fashionable woman may use 'fashion' tactically in a bid for pleasure and power against patriarchy; however, she may also use it strategically to establish and maintain her position within the social hierarchy of the upper classes.

From Harrison's perspective, the flourishing of the genre inaugurated by Munkacsi marks out a position of greater freedom and power than that offered by the strategies of Steichen, which recall a long tradition of portraiture. In particular he notes (as pointed out above) that the new 'active' feminine is 'opposed to the passive roles traditionally assigned them [women] in art' (Harrison, 1994). Here, then, Harrison promotes fashion photography over 'art' because it offers 'active' roles for women. As I remark above, the contrast is undeniable. Certainly, in moving the model into the street, as does William Klein in his forays into fashion photography, the woman is positioned very differently than she is in the staged drawing-room of Steichen.

Similarly, the emphasis on so-called 'sports wear' or 'casual wear' implied a new physical freedom – a new relationship to the body, manifest in the notion of 'sports wear', 'causal wear', 'the little suit'. Sports wear, however, was also a symptom of the growth of Fordism in the fashion world. In 1926, American *Vogue* asked itself: would women agree to all wear the same dress? It was the designer who defined the *époque*, Chanel herself, credited with inventing the sports-wear look as well as the suit for women, *le costume*, who responded: 'Voici la Ford signée Chanel' – 'Here is a Ford signed Chanel' (Fottorino, 1995: 12).[15]

In post-Second World War culture, that question could no longer be asked: mass-produced 'ready-to-wear' dominated the market. These new fashions signalled the demise not only of the *haute-couture* house, but of dressmaking and tailoring as cottage industries and of the production of clothing as fashion within the home itself. It would be a mistake to assume that this transformation produced a more homogeneous fashion industry; the industry evolved along new lines that implied a national market in the USA.

Very briefly, the *haute-couture* house did not disappear but transformed its function, becoming a franchise broker and an advertising organ for ready-to-wear lines. Dressmakers and tailors disappeared but slowly. There are still women who make extra money by copying cheaply the more expensive ready-to-wear designs of the larger firms. There are also small firms that produce *couture*-inspired clothing that sell nationally but directly to small boutiques (e.g., Jacqueline West, Martha Egan, Kate Spade); lesser known franchise lines that copy the New York or Paris look of lines such as Ralph Lauren, or Agnès B (e.g., Ann Taylor, The Limited, Structures, etc); department store lines that offer less extreme, less expensive versions of the internationally visible ready-to-wear lines (such as DKNY, Anne Klein II, CK, etc).

The importance of the new 'ready-to-wear' lines in terms of the analysis offered by Harrison is that they represented a shift away from formal evening gowns and a European 'look' as fashion concerned itself with day-wear and in particular 'working' clothes. This shift implied another setting, a new *mise-en-scène* for the fashionable woman. By the 1960s, it was the so-called 'working girl' who set fashion standards. Suburban housewives adopted the suit and the little black dress as their 'party' wear. For practical and aesthetic reasons the formal attire of the socialite (though still important to the scene of fantasy that fashion magazines offer their readers) no longer was constructed as the locus of 'correctness' and 'authority'.[16] The woman liberated from the drawing-room apparently wanders freely on the city streets.

In a 1958 William Klein photo (included in show curated by Harrison), the model seems to be moving towards the camera. Her suit, simple and minimal, does not impede her movement; she is not set apart as an *objet d'art* to be regarded with reverence, pleasure and attention; she is one among many making her way with the other inhabitants of the street. Klein's image cannot be contained by its frame; a figure in the foreground, in soft focus, seems to lurch towards the viewer, recalling the claustrophobia of the metropolitan crowd, whether Paris (depicted here) or New York. The model's legs are cropped by the bottom frame; much of the suit is in shadow; she is partially obscured by another stroller walking away from the camera. Like the model in the Munkacsi photograph discussed above, she seems on the verge of moving beyond the image – purposively directed toward a goal. Through this movement the model makes visible a sense of agency that extends paradoxically beyond her function as image. She is captured only momentarily by the camera. She is an image in flight that defies stasis. The image is her 'trace' – it cannot represent 'her' as such.

The formal construction of space enhances the visual impression that the model's place is elsewhere, beyond the gaze of the camera. The vertical movement within the plane of the image constructs several layers of action, giving a depth of focus to the image that is absent in the photographs by both Munkacsi, in which the lines of the image move horizontally, and Steichen, in which the figure of the woman seems trapped and mounted within the frame of the image and the drawing-room decor. If the image of the model in the Munkacsi photograph moves the eye beyond the frame to the left, this movement empties the image, leaving only an expanse of water. The model alone animates the frame. In contrast, in Klein's image, the visual evidence of a space that extends beyond the purview of the camera is enhanced and underlined. The model's place is in the street, among the throngs of urban passers-by, extending infinitely beyond the location marked by the camera. Within seconds after the picture is taken, the model will find herself in the space behind the camera, a space which the camera can never define, which here becomes the street, and by extension the city itself. And the space now occupied by the model will be occupied by another. Let us not forget that this new space is nonetheless a spectacle staged for the camera. However, the spectacle that we see here moves us as viewer, like the nineteenth-century *flâneur*, from the drawing-room to the street.

The image of the *flâneur* has been widely discussed, thus I will not belabour his identity here except to say that if the department store destroyed the tradition of the *flâneur*,[17] it is perhaps re-invented, re-inscribed on the body of the women, in post-Second World War fashion photography. The models do not necessarily wander aimlessly (they are not *flâneuses*) but as often as not are directed, almost hurried. These images suggest not a world of endless leisure, as did the society photographs and Baudelaire's original *flâneur*, but one in which a woman's time is the time of labour – an exchangeable commodity. Certainly, Harrison is correct in asserting that within this new genre 'the women depicted in the photographs . . . began to be cast in active as opposed to the passive roles traditionally assigned to them in art' (1994). However, the story does not stop with this statement. No longer is fashion associated with the production of authority. On the contrary, fashion, increasingly, is represented by the adolescent body, defiantly youthful in appearance, its value calculated as the sum of its parts. Thus movement quickly becomes the strategy whereby the body is segmented and commodified as such.

In a section entitled 'Vogue's own boutiques' from the 1 April 1976 issue, we note that even the details of 'line and material' are shot and framed in a way that suggests a continuing movement that transports the image outside its frame. In a photograph that features a belt, the model moves her leg outside the frame. In another that features a leotard, the model is cropped at the bust and the knee, while striding horizontally, her hand on her hip. In the adjacent photograph, the skirt itself, worn by a model depicted from behind, framed at the bust and ankle, seems about to 'flip' out of the frame. The accompanying text reads: 'New York: Follow the flip of the hip.' The text enunciates the paradox of this new fashionable feminine identified with the city in general, here with New York. However, rather than representing a 'body of authority', she is segmented, articulated as fragments of that body. It is not soley a matter of reducing a women to a set of consumable parts as Marshall McLuhan pointed out in 1951; it is also a matter of constructing a narcissistic gaze that travels across the body from one point to another, in which the body, especially the youthful body, becomes the terrain of fashion.

The meaningfulness of this activity to the feminine subject is defined in relation to her own pleasure rather than in terms of producing a position within a given social hierarchy. The narcissistic involvement of the working girl produces another cover story that situates her firmly within a patriarchal norm, in which her narcissism reflects the projected fetishism of the masculine voyeur who takes up the terrain demarcated by fashion for his own pleasure. Not coincidentally, the proper and the improper – the career girl and the working girl – the woman in the streets and the streetwalker – become less and less distinguishable. This trend is most marked in the 1960s during which period fashion and seduction become seduction *tout court*. If the body that emerges is a minimized attenuated body, it is nonetheless a body that inhabits clothes as body. It refused effacement, asserting its identity much as does the model that can no longer be contained within the image. Significantly, during this period models developed an independent identity, a signature so to speak.[18] The model emerges, the supermodel, as an author in fashion discourse, as a recognizable and recognized agent in the production of the fashion spectacle. Harrison signals this transition by including the names of the models alongside those of the photographer in his attribution. Steichen's models remain anonymous, though the collection – the *couture* line – is noted.

I argue that this set of images discussed here poses more questions than it resolves. Thus, the discussion of fashion within cultural studies has been sparse and erratic, often 'ghettoized' as 'women's studies', or 'design': perhaps because fashion is a function neither of 'art' nor of 'mass consumerism', or neither social behaviour, nor representation – but is perhaps a function of all four. A brief comparison of Jennifer Craik's excellent study of fashion, *The Face of Fashion* (1994) and Cathy Griggers's influential article, 'A certain tension in the visual/cultural field: Helmut Newton, Deborah Turbeville, and the *Vogue* fashion layout' (1990), underlines this problem.

Craik, borrowing from theorists such as Foucault, Bourdieu and de Certeau, situates fashion as part of the practice of everyday life and the production of 'habitus'. Griggers turns away from fashion itself to focus on certain aspects of high fashion photography. The key terms that Craik uses to describe fashion as a cultural practice are negotiation and bricolage. She makes little distinction between representation and practice. Thus one of her major points is that there is a continuity between often termed 'traditional' forms of dress and 'fashion' as such within consumer culture. Griggers, on the other hand, focuses on representation. She draws the readers' attention to the production of 'auteur' photographers (such as those discussed above) and to an epistemological break that she sees represented in fashion photography, which she defines as symptomatic of a postmodern performance of gender. I hope that this analysis suggests the general validity of Griggers's point. Yet, Craik quite correctly points out that:

A fashion system embodies the denotation of acceptable codes and conventions, sets limits to clothing behavior, prescribes acceptable – and proscribes unacceptable – modes of clothing the body, and constantly revises the rules of the fashion game. Considered in this light, 'fashioning the body' is a feature of all cultures although the specific technologies of fashion vary between cultures. (Craik, 1994: 5)

Griggers, in contrast, explains that:

what is even more apparent in women's fashion photography is the symptomology of a body of discourse that bears her overtly as constative sign. This body is disjunctive, multiplicitous, both coextensive with other discursive fields and incommensurable, problematic, and paradigmatically postmodern. (Griggers, 1990: 78)

Griggers further elaborates that at least in certain fashion images: 'represented discourse . . . and the representing discourse are obviously at odds' (1990: 88). However, if we return to Harrison's statement, in which he notes that fashion illustration and photography developed to represent women for women, we must recognize that the specific forms of these two discourses (representing and represented – if we wish to retain Griggers's terms) do not suggest the clear division that is argued by Griggers.

Fashion, whether reproduced on the body or in a photograph, is always in the business of representing. In so far as the fashionable image functions as a sign, it must also refer to the represented. Similarly, the fashionable woman is always her 'self' for the gaze of another. To the degree that she also performs that representation, we must accord her a certain agency in the act of representation. In contemporary fashion, the scope of this agency is articulated through the rise of the fashion model as an independent contractor. As fashion photography develops among the lines inaugurated by Munkacsi and Snow, it is the model, the supermodel, that authors this moment of performance, which is then captured by the camera. Thus, in the last two decades we have witnessed the creation of the supermodel, a fashion professional, as the emblem of the fashionable woman.[19] If she does not replace, she certainly competes with the socialite as the incarnation of a certain feminine ideal. This ideal implies a position of authority within feminine culture that nonetheless moves the issue of feminine visibility outside the home into the improper spaces of the street, the city and the marketplace.

I return to my earlier point – this series of images collected by Harrison poses far more questions that it answers, testifying yet again to the ability of fashion photography to 'travel' outside the boundaries of the genre proper. Here I have attempted to demonstrate the complexity of fashion as a discourse, suggesting that it is precisely this complexity that enables fashion to function as the woman's accomplice in her expeditions within the public arena of authority and power, and as the guard at her drawing-room door within which she remains an ornament, an object rather than a subject. The constraints of time do not permit me to do much more than pose the problem of this complicity – a complicity that is necessarily complex, multiformed and perpetually re-negotiated – that is symptomatic of the position accorded the occulted dominant discourse within dominant discourse. However, if I have signalled the significance of fashion photography as a discourse capable of punctuating and transgressing a number of different cultural limits – that of gender, but also of art, of popular culture, of authorship and authority – I will have completed the task of this brief intervention.

Notes

1 See *Constructing the New Consumer Society* (Sulkunen et al., 1997) for a discussion of these issues within the larger context of race, class, nationalism, etc.

2 That both welfare and support for the arts have been jeopardized during the same period in the USA is not mere historical coincidence.

3 See Laura Mulvey's (1988) now classic articulation of the issue for an influential initial definition of these terms within the specific context of representation.

4 See, for example, the work of Danae Clark (1991), and Diana Fuss (1994) for a discussion of lesbian iconography in fashion magazines.

5 Thus traditional pre-Second World War society portraits included in fashion magazines typically represent wives, mothers and daughters. The representation of actresses, movie stars, etc. are relegated to another section of the magazine, as though these women were not part of 'society'. Post-Second World War magazines move towards a conflation of, or at least a confusion between, these two categories of the 'proper' and the 'improper'. In pre-Second World War magazines the categories are more or less systematically maintained.

6 I am referring here specifically to US culture in which there is arguably no clear tradition of class that is not directly linked to economic status.

7 Technically, she may be listed as a dependent on her husband's tax forms. I do not wish to belabour this point, since, historically, a woman may own a company on a tax form that is effectively controlled by her husband or her father.

8 Vreeland in her youth enjoyed a *'prix de jeune fille'* (loosely, the unmarried girl's discount, though Vreeland was neither a girl nor unmarried), because, implicitly, her innate style made her a good advertisement for the designer who clothed her. During and after the Second World War, at which point such prices were no longer offered, Vreeland was forced to turn 'professional' and formally work for the fashion industry (Vreeland, 1985: 154). Similarly, she presents her expertise on fashion as an accident of taste when Carmel Snow initially proposes that she work for *Harper's Bazaar*. Vreeland states that she 'dedicated hours and hours of very detailed time to (her) clothes'. However, she also tells Snow that she 'has never worked' (1985: 117).

9 In his book *Appearances: Fashion Photography since 1945*, Harrison himself comments on the significance of McLaughlin's work: 'Liberman saw in Frances McLaughlin, then only twenty-four years old, the ideal interpreter of junior fashions' (Harrison, 1991: 42). However, in the catalogue *Outside Fashion*, he dismisses her as 'adept at a gentler kind of urban naturalism' (1994).

10 For example, see *Vogue*, 15 April 1947 (141), and *Vogue*, 1 November 1954 (86).

11 Ironically, one image included in the show ('Mary-Jane Russell with Ice Cream', by Saul Leiter) was deemed too 'radical' for actual publication. The model is depicted consuming food with evident abandon and relish.

12 It can be no coincidence that Harrison himself fails to offer a precise enumeration of the clothing that in fact the photograph was designed to sell. He describes the image only in terms of a general category, alluding to a developing convention of fashion photography that represented 'lifestyle' as opposed to clothing as a set of specific items.

13 I owe my sense of the importance of this series to Martin Harrison who included an image from it in his book *Appearances, Fashion Photography since 1945* (1991).

14 I address some of these issues in greater detail in *Shopping Around: Feminine Culture and the Pursuit of Pleasure* (1995).

15 Valerie Steele cautions us to view the myth of Chanel with a certain scepticism. Steele explains that Chanel, as a popular icon, represents a number of trends in the development of twentieth-century fashion: 'Chanel was typical of the entire modernist movement. To the extent that she stands out, it is because she synthesized, publicized and epitomized a look that many other people also developed' (Steele, 1993: 122).

16 See the work of Valerie Steele (1996) and Ann Hollander (1994) for a discussion of the role of fantasy in fashion.

17 See the work of Anne Friedberg (1993) for a detailed discussion of the *flâneur*.

18 See Jean-Noël Liaut (1996) for a history of the development of the supermodel.

19 The importance of the supermodel is such that she commands enormous fees for fashion shows because as a supermodel she is likely to be photographed, or taped by the popular media while coincidentally wearing a designer's clothes. Unknown models do not elicit that same attention from the public, and thus cannot circulate a new look with the same efficacy and authority.

References

Clark, Danae (1991) 'Commodity lesbianism', *Camera Obscura*, 25–6: 80–201.

Craik, Jennifer (1994) *The Face of Fashion: Cultural Studies in Fashion*. London: Routledge.

de Certeau, Michel (1984) *The Practice of Everyday Life* (trans. S. Rendall). Berkeley, CA: University of California Press.

Fottorino, Eric (1995) *Le Monde*, Tuesday, 25 July: 12.

Foucault, Michel (1980) *The History of Sexuality, Volume 1: An Introduction* (trans. R. Hurely). New York: Vintage Books.

Friedberg, Anne (1993) *Window Shopping: Cinema and the Post-Modern*. Berkeley, CA: University of California Press.

Fuss, Diana (1994) 'The homospectatoral gaze', in S. Benstock and J. Ferriss (eds), *On Fashion*. New Brunswick, NJ: Rutgers University Press. pp. 211–32.

Gaines, Jane (1990) 'Introduction: fabricating the female body', in J. Gaines and C. Herzog (eds), *Fabrications: Costume and the Female Body*. New York: Routledge. pp. 1–27.

Griggers, Cathy (1990) 'A certain tension in the visual/cultural field: Helmut Newton, Deborah Turbeville, and the *Vogue* fashion layout', in *Differences: A Journal of Feminist Cultural Studies*, 2 (2): 77–103.

Harrison, Martin (1991) *Appearances: Fashion Photography since 1945*. New York: Rizzoli.

Harrison, Martin (1994) *Outside Fashion: Style and Subversion* (exhibition catalogue). New York: Howard Greenberg Gallery.

Hollander, Ann (1994) *Sex and Suits: The Evolution of Modern Dress*. New York: Kodansha International.

Liaut, Jean-Noël (1996) *Cover Girls and Supermodels: 1945–1965* (trans. R. Buss). London: Marion Boyars.

McLuhan, Marshall (1951) *The Mechanical Bride*. New York: Vanguarde Press.

Mulvey, Laura (1988 [1976]) 'Visual pleasure and narrative cinema', in C. Penley (ed.), *Feminism and Film Theory*. New York: Routledge. pp. 57–68.

Radner, Hilary (1995) *Shopping Around: Feminine Culture and the Pursuit of Pleasure*. New York: Routledge.

Reiss, Timothy (1985) *The Discourse of Modernism*. Ithaca, NY: Cornell University Press.

Steele, Valerie (1993) 'Chanel in context', in J. Ash and E. Wilson (eds), *Chic Thrills*. Berkeley, CA: University of California Press. pp. 118–26.

Steele, Valerie (1996) *Fetish: Fashion, Sex, and Power*. New York: Oxford University Press.

Sulkunen, Pekka, Holmwood, John, Radner, Hilary and Schulze, Gerhard (eds) (1997) *Constructing the New Consumer Society*. London: Macmillan.

Veblen, Thorstein (1912 [1899]) *The Theory of the Leisure Class: An Economic Study of Institutions*. New York: Macmillan.

Vreeland, Diana (1985) *D. V.* New York: Vintage Books.

Wilson, Elizabeth (1990) 'All the rage', in J. Gaines and C. Herzog (eds), *Fabrications: Costume and the Female Body*. New York: Routledge. pp. 28–38.

Winship, Janice (1980) 'Sexuality for sale', in S. Hall, D. Hobson, A. Lowe and P. Willis (eds), *Culture, Media, Language*. London: Hutchinson. pp. 217–26.

Part III
REFLEXIVE SPACE

6

NOT ALL THAT IS SOLID MELTS INTO AIR: MODERNITY AND CONTINGENCY

Heidrun Friese and Peter Wagner

In the view of the social sciences of some two or three decades ago, social life was seen to happen in *structures* or systems, and human beings were defined, if not even determined, by their roles and *interests* which could be derived from their position in the social order. True, there were differences between approaches that used these concepts for a critique of contemporary society and others that adopted a more affirmative position, often both a positive and positivistic one. However, what distinguished the former from the latter ones was that they identified contradictions of interests and roles rather than assuming harmonious interrelations – not much more. More recently though, such language has fallen out of fashion. Social life now appears to be ordered by meanings and beliefs; human beings live together in *cultures*, and they recognize the similarity or strangeness of the other not by their class locations but by their *identities* (for similar observations, see Lamont, 1992: 179–80; Griswold, 1994: xiii; Lash, 1994: 214–15; Smelser, 1997: ch. 3).

Conventionally, one may think of two reasons for the shift to have occurred, and for its likelihood to stay with us for a while. The first reason is *intellectual progress*. Could it be that scholars in the social sciences have ultimately realized how human beings really group together, and have overcome earlier misconceptions? The other reason is major *social change*. Maybe our societies were structurally ordered and were tied together by roles and interests until very recently, but have now changed towards a predominance of cultural relations and the grouping of individuals according to identities. Very bluntly, we may see here just a reflection of a change in the most visible social conflicts. Class struggle seems to have given way to national and ethnic strife; concern for equality appears to have been replaced or superseded by the assertion of the right to diversity.

It should not be entirely ruled out that the one or the other or a combination of the two explanations is indeed valid. Before any such conclusion can be reached, however, it seems to us that some rethinking of both the structural and the cultural language has to be undertaken. It is disturbing, to put it mildly, that this intellectual shift has occurred without an appropriately explicit debate about its merits. No elaborated arguments have been made to support either of the two above-mentioned reasons for the change. Should we see ourselves in the midst of a change of paradigm or of research programme, just like Thomas Kuhn or Imre Lakatos described it, when an established theorizing without being refuted is just gradually abandoned, because it no longer produces interesting findings and because a younger generation flocks away from it to other perspectives? While all this may well be the case, the least one could do is to reflect about the causes and consequences of intellectual shifts while they go on, and not leave this to historians of science. We will here just make one modest attempt.

Our main ambition is to discern some presuppositions of common modes of conceptualization and to show what effects those presuppositions may have on the analysis. Far from being able to offer better foundations for social theory, we will argue for the need for a theorizing that is reflexive of its presuppositions even while working with them (see Wagner, 1994; Friese, 1997). Reflexivity is the attempt to take a step back from current practices (Bauman, 1991: 272); as such, it gives a different perspective but no higher-order knowledge, and reflexive criticism should also be applied to the outcomes of the reflexive endeavour itself.

Modernity and Contingency

Any direct comparison of the structural and the cultural language is limited by the fact that it cannot recognize elements which both constructions have in common.[1] That is why we intend to direct attention to a third approach, to which both structural and cultural theorizing stand in a problematic relation. The recent intellectual shift did not occur as smoothly as we suggested above. At a closer look, an interim period can be identified, broadly the 1980s, in which structural analysis had already lost its power of persuasion but cultural analysis had not yet emerged as the successful contender for the succession.

There were some years of pervasive doubt whether the social world could at all be described in terms of a limited number of stable features. To some observers, often labelled postmodernists, it appeared to be of very limited intelligibility; to others, it just did not show the solidity and stability required to give a strong representation of it. For instance, Marshall Berman (1982) recalled the time-honoured view that modernity dissolves all stable linkages between human beings, that it introduces a social dynamics that will leave nothing untouched. 'All that is solid melts into air', as Marx and Engels had said in the *Communist Manifesto* (1848). Social life will thus become ever more contingent as modernity unfolds. And towards the end of the 1980s, Richard Rorty (1989) published what is probably the most comprehensive and consistent eulogy of such a view, his triple praise of the contingency of all human life, of language, community and selfhood. The assertion of principled contingency of the social world provides the third position, from which structural and cultural theorizing can be compared and commented upon. In its radical version, it is a position from which social analysis can probably not itself be pursued, but it is one which enables the reflexive considerations we deem necessary (for a related discussion, see Derrida, 1978: 292–3).

In a long-term perspective, the argument on increasing contingency may be considered one, if not the, guiding theme of much social theorizing – and even more so of the political philosophy of individualist liberalism. In the stock of the tradition of social theory,[2] we find the idea of a dissolution of 'community' and its transformation into 'society'. 'Society' gives much more room to individuation and individuality, though these individuals may be characterized by their roles and interests which are specific to their location in the social order. Somewhat later we find that modernization theory relaxes its idea of role-boundedness of human beings and ends on the theorem of individualization. Finally, poststructuralist theorizing, despite its self-image as a critic of the mainstream of social theory, can also be read as the latter's radical continuation assuming that the individual is ultimately dissolved, fragmented and dispersed. One way of reading modern social theory is to see it as being basically concerned with the increase of contingency in modernity.

However, this is only one side of the matter. If this observation were absolutely valid, social theory would seem to have chosen a very peculiar task. What is commonly considered as 'social' about human life tends to be weakened with increases of contingency, at least so it may appear. Social theory would then have selected a vanishing phenomenon as its object of consideration.[3] If truly all that is solid melts into air, social theory will be among the victims.

Indeed, after the bourgeois revolution that was supposed to melt everything into air, it was not least social theory, including Marxian theorizing, that was centrally concerned with identifying what was solid or could be made solid. Its rise was associated with concern about the incalculable effects of the bourgeois revolution. If there were no features in human life that imposed order somehow from the outside – via physical or biological determination, or via a religious or otherwise eternally conceived authority – and if human beings were to self-determine their individual and collective actions, to identify how they would do so became a question of key importance. The modes of human sociability, or, in other words, the form and nature of the ties between human beings, thus stood in the centre of interest in emergent social theorizing (see Wagner, 1995; Heilbron et al., 1998).

Conceptualizing Social Ties

There is no way of writing *about* social theory without already using socio-theoretical terms. Our own brief sketch of the history of social theory given above was based on at least two such terms, *human beings* and *relations between human beings*. A recognizable objective of this description was to be as unspecific as possible about the latter; this question will occupy us during the remainder of this chapter. To be so unspecific with regard to one key term, however, and to yet write in a comprehensible language, we had to be adamant with regard to the other key term. It is indeed here presupposed that the bodily existing human being, though not a foundation in an ontological or methodological sense, is a phenomenon of some key interest to social theory, a phenomenon around which theorizing may sensibly go on.

To assume that human beings in their bodily existence are a highly relevant unit in social analysis does not presuppose that they are proto-typical bourgeois-humanist subjects. The 'hypostatization of the individual in the conception of the subject as the main form of social reality marks one extreme' of social theorizing, as Marlis Buchmann writes, the 'dismissal of the subject as pure fiction [. . .], the other. Both ways of looking at the individual are one-sided interpretations of social reality, insofar as they reify one element in the development of advanced industrial society and neglect the other' (Buchmann, 1989: 75). Thus, neither the much-debated 'end of the individual' or 'end of the subject' nor the dominance of the rational and autonomous individual that is hailed in economic and rationalist approaches enter as an assumption into the argument. Both are possible, though extreme, findings at the end of the analysis. But it is even difficult to imagine that the absolute predominance of the one or the other extreme conception would result from any specific socio-cultural analysis. Rather, they mark the space over which the human condition may be traced.

This view on human beings in social theory generates, or implies, the second key term we needed in our introduction as well as the way we dealt with it. If it is not postulated that human beings are either autonomous or totally submerged, then they have relations to other human beings, linkages whose form and nature we do not know beforehand. This may be called the assumption of *sociality*. It emerged very early in what became known as social theory, and much of this theorizing has been occupied ever since with determining more specifically what the nature of this sociality is (see Heilbron, 1995: 72–7).

Most of such social theory made fairly strong assumptions about the relations between human beings, but these assumptions were also fairly diverse, even contradictory. Many of the recurrent controversies in the social sciences – such as between individualism and collectivism, between determinism and voluntarism or, indeed, between structural and cultural analysis – can be discussed in terms of different assumptions about these relations. In our attempt to review the shift from a predominantly structural social analysis to a predominantly cultural one in the light of the contingency theorem, three assumptions about social relations are particularly important, assumptions about their *form*, their *impact* and their *stability*.

The form of social relations tells us something about the way groupings of human beings form and what holds them together; the notion of impact of social relations is meant to indicate whether those forms determine human action; and the notion of stability refers to their persistence over time. If strong responses to all three issues are given, if human beings form stable collectivities with common modes of interaction which persistently determine their individual actions, then human social life shows very little contingency. We shall discuss the sustainability of these assumptions in turn.

The Form of Social Relations: Boundedness and Coherence

Two of the major modes of relating human beings to each other that were conceptualized in social theory were the structural or cultural linkages mentioned above. In the sociological tradition, the term *social structure* refers to relations of social characteristics – as diverse as age, wealth and income, election behaviour – to each other within and across categories.[4] Such relations are analysable but they may well be unknown to the persons themselves (e.g., the impact of somebody's position in a demographic structure on professional opportunities may be unknown to the person concerned). However, even if they may be partially unknown, positions in a social structure shape the *interests* of persons, or the roles they will assume, who are thus tied together by structural characteristics (group or class interests). The problematic relation between the structure which 'objectively' shapes interests and the views on their interests which the persons themselves hold has been a standard topic of such structural sociology (neo-Marxist or otherwise).

The term *culture*, in contrast, refers to commonly held beliefs, norms, values and ways of doing things. In some sense, at least, people thus always know cultural traits of their lives, though they possibly may not explicate them unless asked, or they may be unaware of the range of people with whom they share them.[5] In many cases, however, cultural analysts argue, people have some view and sense of the community they are a member of, this sense being called *collective identity*. This identity, then, this sharing of beliefs and practices, constitutes a social tie in a cultural perspective.[6]

If there was, then, a recent shift in hegemony from the structural to the cultural mode of reasoning, it does not necessarily entail much, since there are important similarities between them. Structure as well as culture *can* be seen as objective entities existing regardless of the consciousness and the volition of their member human beings. Both would then also be regarded as macro-phenomena with firm *boundaries* and, often, their specific modes of maintaining *coherence* or, as the more common term was, integration.

During the recent resurgence of cultural theorizing, however, a number of different perspectives were developed. We shall have to distinguish between two quite different guiding threads, which intermingle in the new fashion of cultural analysis. On the one hand, cultural analysis emerged as a *response to the deficiencies of structural reasoning*. Such analysis would try to take the contingencies and uncertainties of social life better into account than structural theorizing did. Doubts had risen as to the existence and objectivity of the supposed 'structures'. A broad movement of rethinking set in which argued not least for reflexivity in sociology, for instance in the works of Anthony Giddens and Pierre Bourdieu. Social constructivism in areas such as gender and science studies, a turn to 'micro-histories' in the historical sciences, and increased emphasis on the openness of language leading to a plurality of modes of representing the social world are other parts of this movement. Though the conclusions drawn from such reconsiderations vary between and even within any of those approaches, most of them attach considerable importance to the meanings human beings give to their practices (that is why they may be labelled 'cultural' in a broad sense), and they all have in common to see social linkages as much less clearly established and unequivocally identifiable than most earlier thinking did. In this sense, some might want to see these theoretical openings as paving the way for the theorem of contingency.

On the other hand, cultural analysis was also revived as a means to *counter the supposed weaknesses of the contingency perspective*. Even though it may not be social structures, something solid remained in the social world that did not melt into air, namely ties of cultural belonging. Though remaining in the continuity of traditional views on culture, this thinking has been considerably modified, too. In contrast to structural theory, which assumes that people within a given macro-phenomenon are *different*, since they have (groupwise) different locations therein, cultural analysis keeps maintaining, despite some sophisticated arguments on cultural complexity (Hannerz, 1992), that people are rather *alike* in a given culture (and differ from members of other cultures). Given obvious limits to sustain empirically such a view for, for instance, current nations, the possibility of several cultures on a given territory, of sub- and countercultures has been introduced. Or, inversely, it has been emphasized that cultures may extend over large spaces without covering them completely (as national cultures were supposed to do). Obvious examples are Jewish culture, or the 'culture of science', but those cultures that were the traditional objects of anthropology, like the Samoan culture, have also been analysed as 'multilocal cultures' in such a perspective, thus trying to emphasize the double feature of spatial extension through migration and maintenance of ties of belonging (Sahlins, 1995).

Despite this relaxation of earlier assumptions, however, many of these analyses remain confined to some of the limiting connotations of the term culture. As James Clifford puts it,

> culture, even without a capital c, strains toward aesthetic form and autonomy. . . .
> The inclusive twentieth-century culture category . . ., this culture with a small c
> orders phenomena in ways that privilege the coherent, balanced, and 'authentic'
> aspects of shared life. Since the mid-nineteenth century, ideas of culture have
> gathered up those elements that seem to give continuity and depth to collective
> existence, seeing it whole rather than disputed, torn, intertextual, or syncretic.
> (Clifford, 1988: 232; see also Archer, 1988: xv)

Some cultural analysts may want to argue that, while the criticism may still be valid for much of the work done in this field, there is no need to retain such a view of culture as a whole. The analysis of 'cultural practices' may replace the one of 'cultures'. If there are varieties of differently conceived linkages between human beings, there is no reason why they should lead to a bounded, coherent collectivity.[7] Such a conclusion, though, would hit a core element of cultural analysis and introduce a degree of indeterminacy which endangers the whole enterprise. The presupposition of boundedness and coherence is dear to many theorists not least because it provides an important link to political theory.

In general, political theorizing demands criteria for determining the extension of the polity as well as the depth of political regulation, that is the identification of entities of representation both for the constitution of a polity and within a polity. Liberal-individualist political theory does not provide such criteria, it depends on social and/or cultural analysis in this respect. Our suspicion is that the second intellectual shift we described above, from postmodernism to cultural theory, is not mainly supported by empirical insights, but rather by a desire to end what came to be seen as a political indecisiveness produced by postmodernism.[8]

Nothing is wrong, in principle, with trying to move beyond indecisiveness. However, one needs to look very carefully where one is going. The result of a *normative* assessment of the current move depends very much on what cultures and identities are in focus (ranging from feminist to nationalist and elsewhere), and how these cultures and identities are conceptualized. We will not deal with these issues here,[9] since we think some *analytical* questions need to be openly confronted beforehand.

To avoid misunderstandings, it may be useful to state explicitly at this point that it is not our intention to deny that many of the recent analyses have brought important insights.[10] Neither do we want to claim, in conceptual terms, that the notions of structural and cultural linkages between human beings should be entirely abandoned. What we try to argue instead is that there have been serious conceptual flaws in the ways such phenomena have been dealt with in conventional social analysis, and that these flaws have not completely been overcome in more recent debates. Though a significant movement of reconceptualization has started, in particular in the first kind of above-mentioned approaches, it is now important that it be carried further rather than partially withdrawn, as is the tendency in some works of the second kind. In the remainder of this chapter we shall try to sketch what such carrying further might entail.

The Impact of Social Relations: Determination and Interpretation

Social and cultural theory used to share rather strong assumptions about social linkages, at least before these more recent debates. They both tended to assume – in quite analogous ways – that there are *predominant* types of linkage and that these linkages basically *determine* the size and shape of the collectivity that is relevant to individual human beings as well as to the individuals' behaviour. The simple guiding assumption was that people who find themselves in similar positions to others, in structural analysis, or who think alike, in cultural analysis, will tend to act alike and/or see themselves as part of a group. This conclusion is arrived at by coupling a term denoting a *collectivity* of human beings somehow linked to each other (related to each other, or belonging together), described as a macro-phenomenon (structure or culture respectively), to a sister term denoting basic orientations of human beings which provide the *linkage* between members of this collectivity (interest or identity respectively).

A key question here is obviously the mode of coupling the orientations of human beings to the collectivity of which they are (supposed to be) a part. In traditional versions of structural and cultural reasoning this coupling was an assumption. One may even hold that it is an essential part of the sociological mode of explanation. By interrogating the impact of social relations, we try to loosen the conceptual link and open the issue to analysis.[11] In this sense, high-impact social relations shape decisively – the conventional term was 'determine' – the orientations and actions of human beings; low-impact relations do not. The task of sociological research, then, is to identify whether relations have a low or high impact.

There are two related but quite different issues at stake here. At first, it may seem that a presupposition has been transformed into an *empirical question*, which then generates its own research programme. Cultural analysis is opened to the identification of a possible multiplicity, and even inconsistency, of values and beliefs a person may hold and of overlapping boundaries of 'cultural communities' with regard to different beliefs, including – as mentioned above – the possibility that cultures may not be territorially based, or that cultural practices might not cohere. If such research concludes on diversity, plurality and inconsistency of values and beliefs that individuals and groups hold, as it often does nowadays, the idea of a direct relation between culture and action is strongly challenged. However, beyond challenging the earlier presupposition, very little can be added to an understanding of human action on this road alone.[12]

The relation between beliefs and action is not a mere matter of holding some action-relevant belief, but of actualizing it in a given situation. The *situated interpretation* decides which of a number of cultural resources a person has at her or his disposal are activated to deal with an exigency to act. Principally, no resource is unequivocally destined to serve in a given situation; and every situation is in need of interpretation. Structural-functionalist sociology has made a modest attempt to take the multiplicity of situations and interpretations into account by introducing the idea of 'multiple role-sets', but it has ended in the same dead end as class analysis, because it was unwilling to relinquish the strong relation between social status and role. Or in other words, it could not envisage a conceptual openness as to which interpretations apply to which situations but has maintained a pre-established conception of this linkage. In contrast, this issue has been more fruitfully addressed in the interactionist tradition of sociology. Rarely, however, have the conclusions for sociological reasoning at large been fully spelt out.

Taken seriously, the conclusions from these reflections demand to renounce 'any conception that regards the unity and cohesion of a group as the product of a substantive similarity between its members and of an objectively shared interest' (Boltanski, 1990: 70). This is not to deny or rule out that there may be 'limited spaces of action in which the permanence of a universe of objects and routines guarantees stability and similarity of conduct' (Thévenot, 1990: 57). But the presupposition that 'a unanimity or similarity of behavior' results from people being 'subject to common material constraints or well mastered by shared ideas (beliefs, representations)' (Thévenot, 1993: 276) entails a restrictive definition of action that is incapable of dealing with either doubt and uncertainty or creativity in human interaction.

Heuristically, one may want to distinguish two types of situations in social life. There are indeed such 'moments in which the activities of persons hold together, [people] adapt to each other and achieve agreement over an order of things, moments that tend to allow for notions of objective constraint, social norm, equilibrium, successful communication, fulfillment of the speech act and the like.' But there are also those 'moments in which unrest dominates the scene and reveals disputes over what is at stake, moments of uncertainty, of more or less critical doubt' (Thévenot, 1990: 57–8). The important insight is that the latter, not the former, make for the analytically more general case. The latter should not be treated as a deviant case of the former; rather, the former emerges from the latter through creative human action.

Rather than treating societies as naturally bound by a common history or as cohering by the force of functional exigencies, such a perspective will direct attention towards 'the immense historical labour that is necessary to unite disparate beings around the same system of representation, to constitute the reality of such a heterogeneous ensemble, to inscribe it into dispositions by an intensive effort of objectification and to endow it with a common interest' (Boltanski, 1990: 70; on the preceding, see also Wagner, 1994).

This is not to say that functional exigencies or common history could not play a role in shaping a society. Indeed, the 'historical labour', which went into, say, the creation of a national compulsory unemployment insurance in Germany, is an effort a group of people have embarked upon in common to deal effectively with a situation defined as problematic. That the struggle was long and the issue contested does not preclude that the new rules create an order of representation that is likely to be accepted by people societywide (in the specific case, this actually did not immediately happen). A situation of dispute and uncertainty can be transformed into one of greater consent and certainty that may reign over a significant historical period (Zimmermann, 1996). However, as the current questioning of both the viability and the justifiability of compulsory insurance shows, the rules of an institution only reign if they are constantly re-enacted. There are no unequivocally superior solutions to social problems; and common history itself does not explain anything.

The Stability of Social Relations: Reality and Possibility

Having already questioned the link between common history and common practice as a foregone conclusion of much of cultural analysis in the preceding section, we shall now point to an important implication of this presupposition, which will enable us to get a third requirement for reconceptualization in social theory into focus. For the purpose of the argument only, we will imagine an empirical 'case' in which our earlier two requirements are fulfilled. This would be a context in which, at the time of analysis, members of a given collectivity tend to converge in their statements about their beliefs as well as in their interpretations of a situation and in their ways to deal with a situation. In such a case, may one say that there is a shared representation of the social world, and may cultural analysis justifiably want to provide a mirror image of this world? Even for such a very special case, such terminology and such ambitions are problematic, because 'representation requires a suppression of time; mirroring necessitates a standing still' (Game, 1991: 21).

As long as one assumes that the social world is truly solid, *ontologically* solid, the suppression of time may appear unproblematic. And for a long time it was almost a founding assumption of (at least, important variants of) social science that a substantive social ontology is both needed and possible. More recently, however, the problematic character of this claim went no longer unnoticed, and attempts were made to introduce temporality into social theory. Pierre Bourdieu (1979) turned the temporal aspect of social life into a cornerstone of his critique of structuralism. Margaret Archer (1988) introduced agency together with temporality into cultural theorizing by exactly making a distinction between cultural practices, in her terms: Social-Cultural Interaction, and a coherent cultural order, the Cultural System. And Michèle Lamont (1992: 183), to give just a short series of examples, criticized the assumption of a 'stable set of actors' over time even in Bourdieu's analyses.

Despite the considerable merits of such works, there are further, yet hardly noticed implications that go with the need for an empirically more open understanding of the stability of social relations. Basically, the more recent analyses argue that cultural practices may differ between two points in time with regard to all their key characteristics: the size and composition of the cultural community, the substance of the beliefs and values, the importance of those beliefs and values for actions. Some analyses, like Archer's, specifically underline that it is, or at least may be, the agential capacities of the people that bring these changes over time about.

Saying this, however, appears to imply that the notion of culture, and analogously the one of structure, no longer performs the theoretical task for which it was created in the first place. Culture and structure were introduced, as we argued above, to allow a focus on coherence and stability of human social behaviour. Once these certainty-providing phenomena were identified, they permitted theorists to conclude on expectations as to the future behaviour of human beings. If cultural practices are now seen as potentially variable over time in all the above-mentioned respects, then such conclusions are no longer possible. We seem to be back to the theory of contingency, and to the insight into the impossibility of social theory.

To avoid such a conclusion – and there are good grounds to avoid it – it is necessary to rework further the idea of temporality of human action. To do this, we will for a moment revert to the conventional assumption of cultural theorizing that common history may explain the existence and the stability of collectively shared orders of beliefs. One of the problems with this statement is that, strictly speaking, there is no 'common history' but always a multitude of experiences which all differ the one from the other. The evocation of 'common history', as for instance in nationalism, is an operation that is always performed in the respective present. It is a specific representation of the past, reworking it with a view to creating commonalities. As such, it may indeed 'work', it may create the idea of belonging among human beings in the present. But it is not the past, as 'common history', that produces this effect, but the present interaction between those who propose to see the past as shared and those who are convinced by this reasoning and accept it for their own orientation in the social world.

Such a view might be taken to downplay the importance of history for social analysis. Indeed, we were admonished (at the Berlin TCS conference at which this volume originated) for producing a typically postmodernist 'ideology of the present'. However, this seems to be a strong misreading of both postmodernism (whatever that may exactly be) and of our proposal. From Nietzsche to Derrida (if that is a postmodernist lineage), the questioning of the status of the present and reflections about the interpretative appropriation of history have been key concerns. And our own intention is exactly to open social analysis to a more adequate understanding of temporality and historicity.

Currently, many works still fall into the trap of either resorting to a-temporal snapshots of the social world or using history to explain the present in a deterministic way. In the former case, so-called empirical evidence, say, the views respondents voice in interviews, is synchronically analysed as present facts without any consideration of their historical construction and their possibly limited durability. This is true theoretical presentism, and a rather modernist invention at that. In the latter, the analyst, working in the present, selectively appropriates the past to explain this present. Given that the identification of continuities between past and present is a methodological a priori in this approach, it becomes impossible to say whether the coherence of the analysis is an effect of the selection or indeed the result of causally effective linkages between past and present actions (de Certeau, 1988; Friese, 1994, 1996).

There are certainly no methodological highways that bypass the epistemological obstacles on the way to dealing with historicity more adequately. The only viable conceptualization, however, is to see the relevance of 'history' for present actions as a combination of 'traces' of past action in the present, such as a building whose physical structure will both enable and constrain present action, and of the appropriation of the 'past' in the minds of present beings, its endowment with action-relevant meaning. Cultural practices may leave imprints, such as inscriptions in the body of the pugilist from training and fight, as emphasized by Loïc Wacquant in his latest research. But any 'culture' is also a representation of the past in the present, whose relevance for present action is subject to appropriation and interpretation by present human beings.

It is not least in the situated interpretation of their own past experiences that human beings create a 'gap between past and future' (Arendt, 1961: 3) which enables them to make a distinction between reality and possibility which neither presentist empiricism nor structural or cultural determinism can grasp. The present world is neither just there nor predetermined in the past; it is the creation out of a plurality of possibilities which existed at the moment before.

Contingency and Solidity of the Social World

Nothing of what we said, thus, amounts to adopting a version of the theorem of contingency. However, reflecting on the possibility of utmost contingency of human action allows us to identify principled shortcomings of more conventional social theorizing, both in its structural and its cultural varieties. The widespread adoption of the cultural approach in current social analysis risks being not much more than a change of fashion. Despite the relaxation of some of the strong assumptions of cultural analysis, the danger is that the problematic analogies between structural and cultural theorizing will reassert themselves against the more reflexive tone in some recent contributions.

Thinking about contingency, then, should not lead social theorists to abandon the attempts, characteristic of their field, to understand linkages between human beings. Rather, it is a means to emphasize the issues of form, impact and stability of such linkages as permanently open questions of social theory and research, including the question of their very intelligibility or, at least, describability in terms of a social science.

One does not have to assume that there are no stable linkages at all, that everything is contingent and in flux, a position often associated with sociological postmodernism. But rather than rushing to replace one kind of terminological hegemony by another, one should seriously conceptualize the kind of social linkages that may be stable, extended and create collectivities as compared to others that tend to remain fluid, narrowly confined and changing between persons.

The intellectual shifts we described at the outset, from structural theorizing through the emphasis on contingency to cultural theorizing, entailed a double move. First, all that was solid seemed to melt into air. Then, that situation appeared unsustainable, both analytically and politically; too much of what was solid had melted into air. We continue to think that not all that is portrayed as solid in social theory and research has ever been so. And that we should devote more attention to ask what solidity might mean in the social world.

Notes

We would like to thank Michèle Lamont and Neil Smelser for helpful comments on an earlier draft of this chapter.

1 Beyond the recent shift which is in the centre of our interest here, both modes of construction obviously have a long history in the human sciences (see Wagner, 1998), and the direct comparison of structural and cultural analyses is part of the sociological stock in trade (for a useful recent example, see Wuthnow, 1992).

2 The key terms we will need are used in confusingly variable ways in the literature. 'Social theory' is meant here in comprehensive terms, referring to every theorizing interested in relations between human beings. It specifically includes both of what we call 'structural' and 'cultural' theory.

3 And if there is a reflexive impact of social theory on the world, then, even more perversely, it may be regarded as enhancing the dissolution of its own object, which tends to disappear, not least, under the analytical gaze of the sociologist, to rephrase a common conservative reasoning.

4 In the tradition of structural anthropology, the term more profoundly refers to basic, and mostly unconscious, ways of ordering the social life.

5 The difference between the two kinds of theorizing on this point has implications for the role of the theorist, an issue we will only mention but not elaborate on in this chapter.

6 Some readers may want to dispute whether these views on structure and culture are still held. We shall come back to this question. For a general confirmation, one may consult Light and Keller (1985), which is a fairly open-minded sociology textbook. For recent contributions which raise issues related to ours, see Sewell (1992) and Emirbayer and Goodwin (1994).

7 For an ambitious critique, see Turner (1994). Searle (1995) resorts to biological explanation for 'collective intentionality', which is at the root of bounded social institutions.

8 The relation between political and intellectual positions is never unequivocal. Thirty years ago, the term 'structure' had a rather critical flavour and 'culture' a conservative one. This relation has almost been reversed.

9 For comprehensive discussions see Assmann and Friese (1998). What is at stake here, politically speaking, is what could be termed the inevitability of (some kind of) liberalism.

10 We should also at least mention two important kinds of reasoning which do not neatly fit our categorization. Daniel Bell's *Cultural Contradictions of Capitalism* (1976) and Fredric Jameson's *Postmodernism, or the Cultural Logic of Late Capitalism* (1991) link cultural to structural factors by means of a theoretical reflection on contradictions and affinities. As stimulating as the reading of these works may be, they are but very thinly rooted in empirical observations. In contrast, works such as Pierre Bourdieu's *Distinction* (1984) and, more comprehensively, Michèle Lamont's *Money, Morals and Manners* (1992) connect cultural to structural phenomena via sophisticated empirical designs and thus open a way to discuss interrelations without imposing the one on the other.

11 For the use of the term 'strength' for a quite similar purpose, there referring to symbolic boundaries, see Lamont, 1992: 181-2.

12 One might envisage cultural analysis going the same path of increasing empirical sophistication which has led structural analysis to concepts such as 'contradictory class locations' (Eric Olin Wright), which keep asking the same question – how is structure related to action? – but have robbed themselves of any possibility to answer it.

References

Archer, Margaret S. (1988) *Culture and Agency: The Place of Culture in Social Theory*. Cambridge: Cambridge University Press.

Arendt, Hannah (1961) *Between Past and Future*. New York: Viking.

Assmann, Aleida and Friese, Heidrun (eds) (1998) *Identitäten*. Frankfurt: Suhrkamp.

Bauman, Zygmunt (1991) *Modernity and Ambivalence*. Cambridge: Polity Press.

Bell, Daniel (1976) *The Cultural Contradictions of Capitalism*. London: Heinemann.

Berman, Marshall (1982) *All that is Solid Melts into Air: The Experience of Modernity*. New York: Simon & Schuster.

Boltanski, Luc (1990) *L'amour et la justice comme compétences: trois essais de sociologie de l'action*. Paris: Métailié.

Bourdieu, Pierre (1979) *Le sens pratique*. Paris: Minuit.

Bourdieu, Pierre (1984) *Distinction: A Social Critique of the Judgment of Taste*. London: Routledge & Kegan Paul.

Buchmann, Marlis (1989) *The Script of Life in Modern Society: Entry into Adulthood in a Changing World*. Chicago: University of Chicago Press.

Clifford, James (1988) *The Predicament of Culture*. Cambridge, MA: Harvard University Press.

de Certeau, Michel (1988) *The Writing of History*. New York: Columbia University Press.

Derrida, Jacques (1978) 'Structure, sign and play in the discourse of the human sciences', in *Writing and Difference*. London: Routledge & Kegan Paul. pp. 278-93.

Emirbayer, Mustafa and Goodwin, Jeff (1994) 'Network analysis, culture, and the problem of agency', *American Journal of Sociology*, 99 (6) (May): 1411-54.

Friese, Heidrun (1994) 'Zitationen der Geschichte: zur (Re)Konstruktion von Vergangenheit in einem sizilianischen Ort', *Historische Anthropologie* 2 (1): 39-62.

Friese, Heidrun (1996) *Lampedusa: historische Anthropologie einer Insel*. Frankfurt: Campus.

Friese, Heidrun (1997) 'Geschichte im Alltag', in Jörn Rüsen and Klaus E. Müller (eds), *Historische Sinnbildung*. Reinbek: Rowohlt. pp. 328-52.

Game, Ann (1991) *Undoing the Social: Towards a Deconstructive Sociology*. Milton Keynes: Open University Press.

Griswold, Wendy (1994) *Cultures and Societies in a Changing World*. Thousand Oaks, CA: Pine Forge/Sage.

Hannerz, Ulf (1992) *Cultural Complexity: Studies in the Social Organization of Meaning*. New York: Columbia University Press.

Heilbron, Johan (1995) *The Rise of Social Theory*. Cambridge: Polity Press.

Heilbron, Johan, Magnusson, Lars and Wittrock, Björn (eds) (1998) *The Rise of the Social Sciences and the Formation of Modernity*. Dordrecht: Kluwer (Sociology of the Sciences Yearbook, vol. 20).

Jameson, Fredric (1991) *Postmodernism, or the Cultural Logic of Late Capitalism*. Durham, NC: Duke University Press.

Lamont, Michèle (1992) *Money, Morals and Manners: The Culture of the French and American Upper-Middle Class*. Chicago: University of Chicago Press.

Lash, Scott (1994) 'Expert systems or situated interpretation? Culture and institutions in disorganized capitalism', in Ulrich Beck, Anthony Giddens and Scott Lash (eds), *Reflexive Modernization*. Cambridge: Polity Press. pp. 198–215.

Light, Jr., Donald, and Keller, Suzanne (1985) *Sociology* (4th edn). New York: Knopf.

Rorty, Richard (1989) *Contingency, Irony, Solidarity*. Cambridge: Cambridge University Press.

Sahlins, Marshall (1995) '"Sentimental pessimism" and ethnographic experience, or, Why culture is not a disappearing "object"', contribution to the conference 'The Coming into Being and Passing Away of Scientific Objects', Max Planck Institute for the History of Science, Berlin, September.

Searle, John (1995) *The Construction of Social Reality*. New York: Free Press.

Sewell, Jr., William H. (1992) 'A theory of structure: duality, agency and transformation', *American Journal of Sociology*, 98 (1) (July): 1–29.

Smelser, Neil (1997) *The Problematic of Sociology: The Berlin Simmel Lectures*. Berkeley, CA: University of California Press.

Thévenot, Laurent (1990) 'L'action qui convient', in Patrick Pharo and Louis Quéré (eds), *Les formes de l'action: sémantique et sociologie (Raison pratiques no. 1)*. Paris: Editions de l'EHESS. pp. 39–69.

Thévenot, Laurent (1993) 'Agir avec d'autres: conventions et objets dans l'action coordonnée', in Paul Ladrière, Patrick Pharo and Louis Quéré (eds), *La théorie de l'action: le sujet pratique en débat*. Paris: CNRS. pp. 275–89.

Turner, Stephen (1994) *The Social Theory of Practices*. Chicago: University of Chicago Press.

Wagner, Peter (1994) 'Dispute, uncertainty and institution in recent French debates', *Journal of Political Philosophy*, 2 (3): 270–89.

Wagner, Peter (1995) 'Sociology and contingency: historicizing epistemology', *Social Science Information/Information sur les sciences sociales*, 34 (2): 179–204.

Wagner, Peter (1998) 'Certainty and order, liberty and contingency: the birth of social science as empirical political philosophy', in Johan Heilbron, Lars Magnusson and Björn Wittrock (eds), *The Rise of the Social Sciences and the Formation of Modernity*. Dordrecht: Kluwer (Sociology of the Sciences Yearbook, vol. 20). pp. 239–61.

Wuthnow, Robert (1992) 'Cultural change and sociological theory', in Hans Haferkamp and Neil J. Smelser (eds), *Social Change and Modernity*. Berkeley, CA: University of California Press. pp. 256–76.

Zimmermann, Bénédicte (1996) 'La constitution du chômage en Allemagne: mise en forme d'une catégorie nationale de politiques publiques (1871–1927)'. PhD thesis, Institut d'études politiques, Paris. (Paris: Editions de la Maison des Sciences de l'Homme, forthcoming.)

7

MOVING CULTURE

Ron Eyerman

A growing interest in culture, understood as symbolic frameworks of meaning, can be noted among scholars of social movements (see for example, McAdam, 1994; Johnston and Klandermans, 1995). It is no doubt possible to trace this interest to what Richard Rorty and others have called the 'linguistic turn' in philosophy and how it has affected the theory and practice of social science. Here one could include discussion of such recent developments as constructivism and the emergence of postmodern social theory in the wake of the language-based structuralism of the late 1970s. Also included could be the 'post'-structuralism that followed and, finally, the passing of what Habermas has called the 'philosophy of consciousness'. Such would make for an interesting exercise in the history of contemporary ideas or, perhaps, as in Habermas's hands, provide the stepping off point for a new 'theory of communicative action'.

It is also possible to see this new interest in culture by social movement theorists in light of a synthesis of European and American traditions, as a sort of positive by-product of the globalization of academic work. When, in a now classic article, Jean Cohen (1985) stylized two 'paradigms' of social movement research, and then attempted to synthesize them, she was giving voice to processes which had been in motion since the end of the Second World War (Eyerman and Jamison, 1991). The collective behaviourist tradition, which had dominated American research on social movements until the 1960s, had by the 1980s given way to the organizational analysis and rational choice approach of resource mobilization theorists as the hegemonic leader in the field. This was matched on the other side of the Atlantic by a concern with interest mobilization and a focus on questions of power and domination. Common to both was that social movements, actors and organizations were approached 'from the outside', that is, as objects to be explained in terms of individual or collective strategies. The prime concern was the success or failure of movements, as measured through their longevity, power and influence. The latest edition to this body of literature is Sidney Tarrow's *Power in Movement* (1994), which may well become its canonical text.

From this perspective, if they are considered at all, the meanings social movement actors bring to a situation and how these meanings affect both the process of collective identity formation within a movement and the wider culture of the society in which it emerges are treated as matters of secondary importance to the exercise of power in bringing about social change. That the alteration of 'meaning', the struggle to 'define the situation', might itself be a major aspect of power and social change has, until recently, only rarely been considered.

Frame Analysis

This lack of concern with meaning by social movement theorists, especially where this concerns the struggle to define a situation, has been recognized by McAdam (1994) and given new direction by Roger Friedland (1995). There is no need to go into here why or how this has occurred. Suffice it to say that what Cohen helped identify as the 'identity paradigm', which she associated with Habermas and Alain Touraine, and which has since been recast as the 'new social movement approach' by Alberto Melucci and others, effectively challenged the hegemony of the small, but powerful circle of resource mobilizationists, a camp which includes several variations as well as internal tensions. That this essentially European-based approach should be gaining ground represents a sort of coup for European sociology in what has been an American field. A direct result of this hegemonic struggle and the new configuration of 'power in movement (research)' is the notion of 'frames' (itself an American innovation) and the process of framing as central to both meaning and culture in social movements. *Social Movements and Culture* (Johnston and Klandermans, 1995) is the most recent expression of this new hegemonic configuration.

In a recent article, Doug McAdam (1994) traces the origins of the notion of frame to Erving Goffman (see also Johnston, 1995). Even its American roots go deeper, however, back to the symbolic interactionism formulated by Herbert Blumer in the 1930s, which itself drew inspiration from G.H. Mead.[1] In *Frame Analysis* (1974), Goffman begins a discussion of how actors in everyday situations arrive at a definition of their situation, that is, how actors 'make sense' out of experience. He writes: 'I assume that definitions of a situation are built up in accordance with principles of organization which govern events – at least social ones – and our subjective involvement in them; frame is the word I use to refer to such of these basic elements as I am able to identify' (Goffman, 1974: 10–11). American social movement theorists have since taken this as a starting point for the analysis of how social movements provide vehicles for the framing of reality, that is, how movements become sources of 'alternative' frames for interpreting reality. In his 1994 Presidential Address to the American Sociological Association, William A. Gamson (1995) noted that 'students of social movements emphasize the importance of collective action frames in inspiring and legitimating actions and campaigns' (Gamson, 1995: 13). Such 'collective action frames', or what McAdam refers to as 'movement cultures', are now seen as central to the identity formation of social movements and to its understanding, its 'framing', of its adversaries.

One problem can immediately be identified in this approach to meaning and 'culture': it is at once too general and too specific. It is too general in that its phenomenological starting point begins at the highest level of abstraction, where all human understanding can be said to be 'framed'. This is the level at which Kant spoke about the basic 'categories of all experience'. From the most abstract, the social movement adaptation tends to move directly to the most concrete, to the ways in which 'frames' are constituted within specific movements. To continue with a previous example, following the example of Snow and Benford (1988, 1992), Gamson (1995) turns immediately to the ways in which mass media are central to the process of the construction of adversary frames.[2]

At this 'I was framed' level, what tends to be ignored is all that falls between, specifically, the historical and what will be called the traditional. It is here that present framing interacts not with the basic structures of human experience, but with previously 'framed' experience.[3] Such framing is the result of both personal experience and the collective memory and objectifying practices we commonly associate with the concept of culture. Traditions, inherited ways of interpreting reality and giving meaning to experience, are constitutive of collective memory and thus of interpretative frameworks of meaning. In a following section I will outline a way of conceptualizing tradition, in conjunction with forms of art and music, as networks of meaning that are collectively formed and passed on between individuals and generations. Such traditions, often embodied in ritual practices, can serve as a basis for social movement activity, both as resource mobilization and as emotionally infused frameworks of meaning and interpretation. They can also serve as invisible links between individuals and between movements, bridging time and space as well as generations.

As constitutive of culture, aesthetic forms of symbolic representation are media of tradition and collective memory. As inherited frameworks of meaning and interpretation, art and music, for example, can serve as resources upon which social movements can draw in mobilizing and organizing protest and, at an even deeper level, they can provide the basis for (re)defining a situation. As structured frameworks of meaning, traditions form 'cultural' or symbolic networks which accompany or underpin 'material' networks, organization, friendship circles, neighbourhoods, and so on, which much of current social movement theorizing concerns itself with. As carrier or vehicle of tradition, music and art are bearers of images and symbols which arouse emotion, which provoke interpretation, and which can form a basis upon which action, even that narrowly defined as political, occurs.

The Cultural Praxis of Social Movements

Cultural praxis can be thought of as an aesthetic extension of what has been called the cognitive praxis of social movements (Eyerman and

Jamison, 1991; see also Lash in Beck et al., 1993). Where cognitive praxis called attention to the constitution of consciousness within social movements, and the role of movement intellectuals as its producers, cultural praxis focuses on the role of the aesthetic in meaning construction and the creation of collective identity within and between social movements.

Two levels can be identified to cultural praxis in social movements: a pre-political, (sub)cultural dimension and an overtly political dimension. With pre-political I mean the everyday processes of meaning construction, where art and music can be important sources of (sub)cultural identification as well as the 'framing' of reality; thus they can provide a latent and even invisible resource upon which political movements can draw. I agree with Murray Edelman when he writes 'contrary to the usual assumption – which sees art as ancillary to the social scene, divorced from it, or, at best, reflective of it – art should be recognized as a major and integral part of the transaction that engenders political behavior' (Edelman, 1995: 2). Art, especially in what Walter Benjamin termed the age of mechanical reproduction, and which today has become electronic and global, provides a resource of images which can promote 'political impulses' and be the sources of politically motivated actions. With this in mind, we take a wide understanding of art, a central part of culture, in that it operates at 'that level at which social groups develop distinct patterns of life, and give expressive form to their social and material life experience' (Hall and Jefferson, 1975: 10), and in a broader sense 'tradition', which forms part of a context, a relatively amorphous milieu out of which social movements take form.

The second level concerns the more overt use of cultural artefacts, songs, and artworks for example, as tools for the mobilization of protest and social solidarity. On this level, which I will illustrate through an analysis of the song 'We Shall Overcome', Serge Denisoff (1972) identified types of what he called 'protest songs' based on their function in giving voice to dissent, which in part can be directly connected to social movements. The first type of protest song is magnetic, attracting the non-participant or reinforcing the commitment level of adherents. Its structure is such that it encourages participation, building around known and catchy melodies, repeating verses, sing-along, simple chords, etc. And it carries a political message. Here the verbal, the singing and the text are central, the music is only secondary, a means to the message. The second type Denisoff identified is the 'rhetorical', which focuses attention on individual indignation and dissent, but offers no solution. Rhetorical songs place some emphasis on lyrics, but allow more space for musical sophistication and skill. Other types could also be mentioned, such as marching songs for instance, songs which tell the history of a movement or the story of an important event, and songs of strength, courage and solidarity, which are more than 'magnets' in Denisoff's categorization.[4]

It should be said in this connection that songs are more than texts which carry ideas, they are also performances, a form of ritualized practice in and through which meaning and significance is embedded. This gives more force to music as a carrier of collective memory, tradition, in that music is pregnant with meaning at more than the cognitive, literal level. Music embodies tradition through the ritual of performance. It can empower, help create collective identity, a sense of movement, in an emotional and almost physical sense. This is a force which is central to the idea and practice of social movements.

Tradition and Ritual

The twin concepts of tradition and ritual are keys to understanding the cultural praxis of social movements. Tradition has generally been seen as the opposite of social change, and therefore what 'progressive' social movements are against. They have been viewed as habitual forms of behaviour, legacies of the past that tend to impede innovation and hold back progress. In social theory as well as in 'progressive' political ideologies, traditions have been characterized as conservative, even reactionary, ways of life that the forces of modernity have set out to transcend. The so-called modern project and its corresponding forms of rationality have thus often been portrayed as a battle against the past, a future-oriented struggle to free society from the constraints of culture.

Tradition, as Edward Shils (1981) reveals in his history of the concept, refers to the coexistence of past and present. Tradition can be understood as a set of beliefs or practices that are passed from one generation to the next and which affect the practice and interpretation of life. 'Tradition', Shils writes, 'is whatever is persistent or recurrent through transmission' (1981: 16). This process of passing on traditions can be consciously done, even 'invented', or more unconsciously transmitted through ritualized practice.[5] Making tradition conscious, that is, the articulation of 'persistent or recurrent' practices as 'tradition', has been central to the role intellectuals have played in social movements. In part, it is the articulation, this naming and making conscious, which distinguishes tradition from custom or habit, which are similar in that they all deal with recurrence. Custom refers to beliefs and practices that are less articulated than tradition, less durable and more short lived, and thus more easily altered. Habits, on the other hand, usually refer to individuals and not groups or entire societies, which can be said of both tradition and custom. Traditions, even those of oral cultures, can be written about, talked about and consciously, that is reflexively, chosen, while habits and customs are routinized and taken for granted. As such, they can be practised but not easily adopted.[6]

As the carrier of (past) traditions, music bears (bares!) images and symbols which help frame (present) reality. Music carries many traditions, as it is the historical outcome of a range of social forces and processes, local cultures, personal, commercial and political interests, and so on.[7] In that sense, music is part of what Gene Bluestein (1994) has called 'poplore', the syncretic process through which modern cultures are formed. Because it is the bearer of many traditions, the images and symbols music gives rise to are open ended, not closed and determinant. This is something that distinguishes music from ideology. As it is being defined here, as bearer of tradition, carrier of images and symbols, music and ideology have things in common. Ideology, which can be defined as an ready-formed system of interpretation, which explains why things are as they are (Eyerman, 1981), also is composed of images and symbols which provoke emotional response and which provide a basis for framing or interpreting reality. The difference is that while both encourage interpretation and action through symbolic representation, ideology is more direct in what it does. Music suggests interpretation, ideology commands it. Ideology tells one what to think, how to interpret and what to do; music is much more ambiguous and open-ended, and like any art form contains a utopian element. Music, like art generally, opens experience to the potentials and potentialities of life, but does not necessarily proscribe or even describe them. Admittedly, this can be a fine line and there is certainly a point where music becomes ideology or propaganda and ceases to be art. The two however can, and should, be distinguished.

Art and music carry traditions in the form of images and symbols which evoke response and help frame interpretation and action. This is how the past comes to the present. Social movements create a context in which the traditions carried through art become actualized, reinvented and revitalized. There must, however, be some fit, some congruence between the traditions carried in a particular art form, or, to be more specific, form or piece of music, and the ideas and ideals of an emerging social movement. Just as not any political ideology will fit any social group or individual, not every type of music or cultural artefact, like a song, will fit any social movement. Musical traditions embody particular experiences and frameworks of meaning, even contain utopian images of possible futures, which limit their reinvention. It is hard to imagine American country music, which emerged out of the everyday experience of a rural white working class, being used to mobilize a black protest movement. The small town, rural 'family values' such music often contains would much more likely be heard at a conservative, white rally or public function. This works in the other direction as well. While the song 'Swing Low Sweet Chariot' can be sung by crowds at English football matches (as was pointed out to me when this chapter was presented at the *Theory, Culture & Society* conference at Berlin), it is hard to imagine the same for 'We Shall Overcome', an equally old gospel song. While both have similar roots (and perhaps also similar 'utopian images'), the latter has become part of the ritualized practice of a distinct political tradition; its singing at a football match would most likely evoke feelings of anger and disgust, of meaning out of place, if the intended affect was not meant to be ironic or agitating in a consciously political way.[8]

Ritual

Singing a song such as 'We Shall Overcome' at political demonstrations is a ritual event, just as singing 'Solidarity Forever' or the 'International' at union meetings or on the First of May is. Such pre-ordained ceremonies serve to reunite and to remind participants of their place in a 'movement' and also to locate them within a long-standing tradition of struggle and protest. The affect here is probably more ideological than utopian. Like tradition, ritual is central to the construction of meaning. Ritual can be defined as 'an action which dramatizes and re-enacts the shared mythology of a social group' (Small, 1987: 75). In his study of vernacular music, Christopher Small (1987) shows how African slaves in the USA created rituals which enabled the preservation of dignity, even 'the celebration of identity' under conditions of great deprivation. For cultural and historical reasons, music formed the central part of these rituals. What was accomplished and preserved through the ritual performance of music was the affirmation of unity in variety, a sense of community. 'It was musicking and dancing, those twin rituals of affirmation, of exploration and celebration of relationships, with their unique power to weld together into a higher unity the contradictory experiences of sorrow, pain, hope and despair' (Small, 1987: 87). On Small's account, it is this which gives music its power and explains why other groups, in very different circumstances, can be so powerfully affected by it.

Like tradition, ritual has often been relegated by social theorists to the long-forgotten past, and to the more 'primitive' societies of the present (for an exception among social movement researchers, see Taylor and Whittier, 1995). Such a danger even remains in an analysis such as Small's, cited above, if one sees in African American music remnants of a 'primitive' past. However, as recent research and theorizing in what has come to be called cultural studies has revealed, rituals are very much part of meaning construction even in the most modern or postmodern social reality. In the form of ceremony at public events like sporting matches or political campaigns, ritual practices, such as saluting a flag, or specified forms of address, help mark the significance of an occasion and, in the process, solidify a group through creating a sense of common experience. Rituals, Durkheim argued, are central to the constitution of social solidarity and to the creation and maintenance of social order. Rituals perform a similar function in social movements, in that central process of the formation of a collective identity.

The meaning of ritual performance is not given, however, as a Durkheimian functional analysis might lead one to believe. In her study of the interplay between art and politics in turn-of-the-century Barcelona, Temma Kaplan (1992) reveals how the same rituals, popular street festivals, could serve two entirely opposite political functions. 'They [the festivals] could express or encourage local solidarity or internal struggle, celebration or opposition' (Kaplan, 1992: 1). For the established political and religious authorities, these ritualized events were intended to reaffirm and legitimate their established power and authority. But such authorities cannot control how the same events were interpreted and used by those who participated. In this case rituals that were intended to reaffirm authority, actually contributed to the reverse, as participants, including the group of rebellious artists of which the young Picasso was a part, used the occasions to promote alternative visions and group solidarities.

Drawing on the work of Victor Turner, Richard Schechner (1993) discusses ritual as a form of resistance and rebellion to established ideas and practices, rather than as an aspect of their reproduction. In terms of the aesthetic praxis of social movements, his analysis of 'liminality', a term taken from Turner (1969) which refers to individual or collective states or periods of transition between ordered structure, in which actors 'lose themselves' in ritualized performance is very useful. Such periods can themselves be more or less ordered and structured, like the festivals and carnivals studied by Kaplan or the more spontaneous mass demonstrations choreographed by social movements. Schechner's examples of the latter include the anti-war marches in the USA in the 1960s and 1970s and the democracy movement in China as it surfaced in Tiananmen Square in 1989. As opposed to Kaplan's example, where popular forces redefined an established ritual practice to their own ends, Schechner's examples are of movements creating the possibility to express both their rebellion and their (utopian) desire for freedom through ritualized performances, song, dance, nakedness and sexuality, and so on. In the space opened by the movement, established constraints can be cast off and 'freedom' expressed. The ideals of the movement are thus objectified, embodied and expressed in practices which can be seen, learned and transmitted to others. In the age of global media this transmission can involve billions.[9]

Cultural Praxis in Practice

The New Negro Movement

> I do not doubt that the ultimate art coming from black folk is going to be just as beautiful, and beautiful in largely the same ways, as the art that comes from white folk . . . but the point today is that until the art of black folk compels recognition they will not be rated as human. (W.E.B. Du Bois, 1986)

In the 1920s, the USA experienced a great upsurge of creative activity among African-Americans. Centred in the industrial cities of the North, what could be called a black public sphere emerged as urban areas expanded to accommodate the waves of migrants arriving from the southern regions of the country. Within the neighbourhoods which were created or transformed, small clubs and meeting halls, restaurants, cinemas, theatres and dance halls sprung up in the teeming black sections of Chicago, Detroit, Cleveland and Philadelphia. Forms of popular entertainment were created as the newly arrived refitted their traditional cultures

to fit the urban environment and style of life.[10] At the same time, a
growing interest in black history, literature and art could be found within
the small groups of educated, African-American middle class. These two
processes were interconnected, in part through a range of magazines,
journals and newspapers which served to link together this wide-ranging
and socially diverse racial community. Through such media, 'race leaders'
and intellectuals sought to influence the formation of a new collective
identity, both within and outside the social movements, which included the
nationalistic movement associated with Marcus Garvey and the integra-
tionist National Association for the Advancement of Colored People
(NAACP) whose leading intellectual was W.E.B. Du Bois, a Harvard-
educated sociologist and editor. A central focus of this identity formation
concerned the meaning and form of 'culture' and its use as a medium and
symbol of political and moral practice.

To many participants and observers in the mid-1920s it seemed as if a
new age was dawning in the USA. A 'New Negro', sophisticated, urbane
and above all imbued with a sense of racial pride, was said to be replacing
the stereotyped ignorant country bumpkin, the 'nigger' and the subservient
'Uncle Tom', and other symbolic representations white America loved to
hate, and which many African-Americans themselves appeared to accept as
the inevitable outcome of the cultural politics of racial distinction in the
USA. Art was one of the major weapons in this cultural struggle. As one
'race leader' expressed it at the time, 'through his artistic efforts the Negro
is smashing [an] immemorial stereotype faster than he has ever done. . . .
He is impressing upon the national mind the conviction that he is an active
creator as well as a creature . . . that his gifts have been not only obvious
and material, but also spiritual and aesthetic' (James Weldon Johnson,
quoted in Cruse, 1967: 34).[11]

While this sense of change was experienced more or less across the urban
North, for reasons having as much to do with its being a centre of cultural
production than the number of blacks living there (in 1920 there were
152,467 blacks living in New York City, up from 91,709 in 1910; this
would explode to 327,706 by 1930. The numbers in Chicago, Detroit and
Cleveland were expanding at an even quicker rate. Figures from Wintz,
1988: 14), New York City became the locus of this cultural revitalization.
That section of upper Manhattan known as Harlem, a former rural
paradise which offered country-style living to New York's wealthiest
families as late as the 1910s, was quickly evolving into a 'black metropolis',
a cultural centre, and an urban ghetto at one and the same time.[12]

In the consciousness of its actors, whose core was made up by a loose
coalition of about 20 people – artists, writers, musicians and poets – and
for hundreds of others on its periphery, what came to be called the Harlem
Renaissance was a symbol of the promise of black America. Even if its
activist core was small, its potential impact was great, especially given the
thrust provided by linkage with the culture industry in New York City.
More than a movement, one historian writes, 'the Harlem Renaissance was

basically a psychology – a state of mind or an attitude . . . a consciousness (of participating) in a new awakening of black culture in the United States' (Wintz, 1988: 2).[13]

Taking both a longer perspective and a wider view on the components of social change, and on the meaning of culture and politics, the Harlem Renaissance can be viewed as a political movement, or, better, as a cultural movement with a political effect, in a quite different way from even the 'integration through art' strategy championed by some intellectuals. This would entail interpreting social change in terms of gradual shifts in values and attitudes, which occur over the long term and involve the cumulative effect of a complex array of social forces, including, of course, artistic and more directly political movements. This, in effect, brings the long and the short term, and the 'political' and 'cultural', together within the framework of historical sociology, while at the same time illustrating the aesthetic dimension of the cultural praxis of social movements.[14]

The cultural praxis of the Harlem Renaissance sought to effect the very nature and meaning of experience – how the (black) self was to be understood and to identify the role of art and the artist in that attempt to (re)define the situation of African-Americans. While the movement itself may have been small and short-lived, the artefacts it produced, as well as the traditions it recalled and invented, laid the groundwork upon which not only individual African-Americans could draw, but also later social movements.

The struggle over the meaning and place of culture had both internal and external aspects. Internally, the struggle took the form of 'Old' versus 'New' Negroes, between youth and the establishment. The Harlem Renaissance was a youth movement in addition to being a cultural political movement. From this point of view, many of the leading intellectuals of the period, even those who championed the movement, were considered 'Old' Negroes, measured in terms of age, social standing and ideology. They were considered part of an earlier generation of middle-class Negro 'professionals' and 'race leaders' whose concerns lay first of all with being recognized and accepted by the white community. For the new generation they were part of the problem, not the solution, even if some, such as the philosopher Alain Locke whose anthology *The New Negro* (1925) is usually seen as the first attempt to draw together the 'movement' under one roof, were sympathetic to the younger generation's explorations into areas of popular culture such as jazz and the blues, which others of the older generation found embarrassing and degrading.

Although primarily concerned with political integration, when the Old Negro leaders discussed 'culture' as a strategic medium for integration the concept was limited to the fine arts. Indeed, this notion of culture was also central to Locke's New Negro and his understanding of the Harlem Renaissance. Most of the older generation of Negro leaders shared the European cultural prejudices of the whites they sought acceptance from: real culture was high culture and serious music was classical music, composed and performed by those with formal training.[15] Those who stood outside this designation were entertainers and the untrained players who maintained the oral folk traditions of the rural and slave past. At best, the latter were tolerated as representatives of a bygone age; at worst, as an embarrassment and a constant reminder and reproduction of unfavourable racial stereotypes. Robert S. Abbott, the editor and founder of the *Chicago Defender*, the city's leading black newspaper, wrote on its pages in the 1930s:

> At sometime during our intellectual maturity we are expected to have in our repertoire something more than 'St James Infirmary', 'Minnie the Moocher', and All God's Chillun Have Shoes'. . . . We must train ourselves to enjoy formal music, symphony concerts and chamber music. Such music tends to purify the senses and edify the imagination. It helps to refine the feelings by appealing to our higher aesthetic selves. (Quoted in Spenser, 1993: 113)

Also writing in the *Defender*, Lucius C. Harper wrote:

> While we have failed in these fundamental instances [gleaning political recognition from whites], we have succeeded in winning favor and almost unanimous popularity in our 'blues' songs, spirituals, and 'jitterbug' accomplishments. Why? . . . Our blues melodies have been made popular because they are different, humorous and silly. The sillier the better. They excite the primitive emotion in man and arouse bestiality. He begins to hum and moan and jump usually when they are put into action. They stir up the emotions and fit in handily with bootleg liquor. They break the serious strain of life and inspire the 'on with the dance' philosophy. (Quoted in Spenser, 1993: 114)

The same applied to literature – the Negro writers preferred by the older generation were those who wrote of protest or, in more popular literature, with a message of moral and economic uplift, similar to those Horatio Alger tales that the white ethnic population enjoyed. The new generation associated with the Harlem Renaissance was the first to turn inward, to write expressively about emotions, including the psychological effects of racism, and to write realistically about African-American life. These were themes which tended to embarrass the older generation. Regarding James Weldon Johnson, an important figure in the transition between the Old and the New Negro, Cary Wintz writes:

> the major problem that confronted blacks [in the 1920s] was no longer how to deal with prejudice but how to achieve racial identity [think of Jean Cohen here, the two 'paradigms' can also be two strategies]; the major task of black writers was not to expose racial injustice but to uncover, describe, and possibly explain the life of American blacks. . . . [B]efore the 1920s most black writers avoided detailed and realistic descriptions of the colorful life of lower-class urban blacks because they believed that depicting the squalor and vice of ghetto neighborhoods would only reinforce negative racial stereotypes. They usually described blacks in middle-class settings and emphasized the similarities between white and black society. (Wintz, 1988: 67)

There was thus a gap between the elite and the masses that encompassed the meaning and aim of culture as well as income and social standing.[16]

The new generation was working out its own aesthetic, something that would form a central part of the cognitive praxis of its collective identity-formation. In literature and art, this would mean a search for 'authenticity' and truth, a turn to realism and away from the uplifting romanticism of the older generation. It meant the realistic portrayal of Harlem street life in Claude McKay's *Home to Harlem* (a best seller in 1928, which for Du Bois was an expression of the 'debauched' rather than the 'talented' tenth), the use of dialect and street slang in the blues-inspired poetry of Langston Hughes, the folk tales and stories collected and transformed by Zora Neale Hurston, and the primitivism and the naïve realism in the painting of Palmer Hayden and William H. Johnson. In addition, the new generation was more open to the 'mediated' repro-duction of culture than their elders. Like youth movements of the 1960s, participants and supporters were much more open to accepting various forms of cultural expression and reproduction (Eyerman and Jamison, 1995). Radio and recording had begun to play an important role in promoting the fusion of cultural forms and genres, as well as in their dispersion. Like its latter-day counterparts, this new generation in the 1920s was more accustomed to listening to music in a mediated form and probably more open to converging styles and transgressions than its elders. Langston Hughes, one of the central figures of the Harlem Renaissance had no difficulty fusing jazz and poetry, or of writing poems in rural dialect (something which marked the older generation and which the Old Negro elite looked down upon), thus mixing the 'high-brow' and the 'low-brow' genres, as well as musical and literary forms. Nor did he have difficulty taunting those who did:

> Let the blare of Negro Jazz bands and the bellowing voice of Bessie Smith singing Blues penetrate the closed ears of the colored near-intellectuals until they listen and perhaps understand. . . . We younger Negro artists who create now intend to express our dark-skinned selves without fear or shame. (Quoted in Floyd, 1993: 9)

This short discussion of the New Negro Movement and the Harlem Renaissance was meant to illustrate the cultural praxis of social movements. In this case, the 'social' movement was, in the eyes of many current social movement theorists, a 'cultural' and therefore not a 'real' movement, since political power was not its motivating force. Part of my point has been to challenge that very distinction and notion of social movement. The broader aim, however, was to show that the struggle of meaning, how the world is to be understood, is a central part of what social movements are all about. As Roger Friedland puts it: 'the meaning of society is very much at stake in all important social movements' (1995: 2). I would only question the adjective 'important'. It is my contention that what I have called cultural praxis, the struggle over meaning, which also includes an aesthetic dimension, is part of the definition of that which we identify as social movements.

Music and the Civil Rights Movement

> A pamphlet, no matter how good, is never read but once, but a song is learned
> by heart and repeated over and over; and I maintain that if a person can put a
> few cold common sense facts in a song, and dress them up in a cloak of humor to
> take the dryness off them, he will succeed in reaching a great number of workers
> who are too intelligent or too indifferent to read a pamphlet or an editorial on
> economic science. (Joe Hill, quoted in Reagon, 1974: 54)

'Learned by heart and repeated over and over', that is the basic process
of tradition and what ritual performance is all about. And singing and
songs, as bearers of traditions, are thus powerful weapons in the hands of
social movements. That aspect of cultural praxis and level of aesthetic
practice, where tradition provides a resource upon which social movements can draw, can be illustrated through the historical role of music in
African-American life. Beginning with the slave-songs, music has provided African-Americans with a way of expressing and communicating
under conditions of great oppression. While the distinction is a matter of
controversy, in both their sacred and secular forms, these songs carried a
message of hope and transcendence through decades of struggle even
after formal emancipation.[17]

It was these songs that formed the basis for the 'freedom songs' which
were so important during the civil rights movement in the 1950s and early
1960s. Bernice Johnson Reagon writes: 'the songs of the slaves represented
a body of data that remained present in the Black community to be used in
future crisis situations' (Reagon, 1974: 38) and

> On many occasions, the new moved from the old in the midst of Movement
> activity. This evolutionary process was possible because the structure of the
> traditional material enabled it to function in contemporary settings. There was
> continuity with some traditional lyrics being changed for statements of the
> moment. These transformed songs were used in conjunction with older songs to
> convey the message that the struggle of Blacks had a long history. (Reagon,
> 1974: 96)

The evolution of 'We Shall Overcome', which Bernice Johnson Reagon
provides in her work on the role of music in the civil rights movement,
provides an instructive example of the power of tradition in social
movements. That song, which began as a spiritual, was picked up by the
labour movement and eventually, through contact between labour
movement and civil rights activists at the Highlander Center in Tennessee
in the early 1960s, was transformed into the anthem of the civil rights
movement and, eventually, used by similar movements around the world.

Tracing the 'history' of that song is an instructive exercise in how
tradition and ritual links social movements, providing an invisible river of
embodied cultural practices, as well as ideas and images, between movements and generations of (potential) activists. 'We Shall Overcome'
emerged out of the collective tradition created by African slaves in the
USA. It first appeared in written form in a collection made in 1901 as 'I'll
Be All Right, I Will Overcome'. It would soon appear, along with other

spirituals, in sheet music form, as this genre achieved a degree of popularity, as church music created a new market. A major shift occurred in the 1940s when the song was taken up by the black Tobacco Workers' Union as part of its mobilizing campaign during labour conflicts in the south. The title was changed to 'We'll Be All Right, We Will Overcome' in the process, as the collective pronoun replaced the singular, reflecting a shift in the locus of redemption, if not from sacred to secular, at least from singular to plural. In 1947 a second major shift occurred as the song was transformed into a white union-organizing song at the Highlander Center in Tennessee. Symbolically, the title was altered to the more grammatically correct 'We *Shall* Overcome', probably by the Harvard University drop-out Pete Seeger, then active at the Center, which served as an institutional base in the struggle to keep alive the union movement traditions in the extremely hostile rural south.[18] It was at the Highlander Center, which not only was one of the very few institutions of its kind, but also one of the few to recognize the value of music to social movements, where the song was eventually passed back to blacks and the civil rights. In 1959 a workshop was organized to teach traditional union movement songs to young activists in the school desegregation movement in nearby Knoxville, among them, 'We Shall Overcome'. They carried it further into the streets and prisons of the south, and of course modified its form of presentation in the process. Eventually recorded by popular folk-singers like Joan Baez, the song has become part of a global culture of dissent and is usually sung in a ritualized way, as a sing-along, with the audience linking arms as they sing. In the USA the traditional call and response technique of African-American musical culture is also usually used. Here the leader, such as Pete Seeger in one of many live recorded versions, 'calls' a verse and the audience responds with the by now well-known chorus.

'We Shall Overcome' and other songs associated with the civil rights movement provide an illustration of the second level of the aesthetic dimension, where songs help mobilize protest and create group solidarity in specific situations. Bernice Johnson Reagon (upon whose research the above discussion draws) writes of its early stages: 'music supplied the cohesiveness to the masses of people of the Montgomery Bus Boycott; it conveyed the essence and unity of their movement' (Reagon, 1974: 93). In the process, many traditional songs were transformed. For example, 'Onward Christian Soldiers', a Christian hymn, became the most popular marching and fighting song within the movement context. Again, 'Out of the pressure and needs involved in maintaining group unity while working under intense hostility and physical opposition, the Sit-in Movement developed its culture. Music was the mainstay of that culture' (Reagon, 1974: 101). Mary King, active in the Student-Non-violent Coordinating Committee (SNCC), the student arm of the civil rights movement in its early phase, wrote in her memoir *Freedom Song*, 'the repertoire of "freedom songs" (sung at demonstrations) had an unparalleled ability to evoke the moral power of the movement's goals, to arouse the spirit, comfort the afflicted, instill courage and commitment, and to unite disparate strangers into a "band of brothers and sisters" and a "circle of trust"' (King, 1987: 23).

Conclusion

With the examples provided by the Harlem Renaissance and the civil rights movement, I hope to have illustrated the importance of what I have called a social movement's cultural praxis. This importance works on various levels: one deeply rooted, where reality is interpreted and experienced, and another, more on the surface, where situations are defined and acted upon. Here, what I have called tradition and ritual operate to provide bridges between movements and generations of activists. Traditions, illustrated through the example of music and art, form part of collective memory which carries ways of seeing and doing between past and present and between individuals in the past and present. Rituals – symbolically pregnant performances – embody the ideas and orientations contained in traditions, providing also a structured link between movements and generations. The New Negro Movement and the Harlem Renaissance, and the history of the song 'We Shall Overcome', were intended as illustrative examples of the aesthetic praxis of social movements. The literature and artworks of the former originated and helped to embody a tradition, a way of defining 'blackness', which would serve as the basis upon which other movements would later draw. Tracing the history of the song 'We Shall Overcome' was meant to illustrate how music can also link movements, across time and racial barriers, and contribute to the creation and continuation of a culture and 'habitus' of protest. In terms of social movement theory, the aim has been to elaborate the notion of culture as is currently being debated, to illustrate the role of tradition and ritual in linking movements and individuals. Protest may very well occur in visible waves and cycles, but there are invisible links between them. The concept of culture currently in use by social movement theorists, even those attempting to break out of traditional frames of analysis, is much too narrowly conceived to capture the depth of a movement's aesthetic dimension and cultural praxis.

Roger Friedland writes: 'It is not a question of whether ideas matter, but when, how and what do they materialize; and not whether matter idealizes, but when, how and what it does' (1995: 34). Ideas and traditions of protest matter when social movements revitalize them. They can be revitalized, I have suggested, because they have become objectified as matter, as cultural artefacts, in songs and other symbolic representations that we call art. The cultural praxis of social movements is the mobilization of the traditions contained in art and music. A question to explore is how and under what conditions do traditions and ritual practices serve as a basis for social change, rather than reproduction. This is the challenge and the task of a cultural sociology of social movements.

Notes

Earlier versions of this chapter were presented at the 2nd Annual *Theory, Culture & Society* Conference, Berlin, August 1995 and at the Social and Cultural Movements Seminar at Lund University. I would like to thank those present for their perceptive comments and criticisms. Johanna Esseveld deserves special mention in this regard. Funding by the Swedish Research Council for the Humanities and Social Sciences (HSFR) made both the chapter and its presentation possible. The ideas expounded here have now been expanded and elaborated upon in Ron Eyerman and Andrew Jamison (1998).

1 In previous work (Eyerman and Jamison, 1991), Blumer's importance for social movement research was discussed in relation to the collective behaviour approach. Here a bit more can be added about the symbolic interactionist perspective he helped formulate. According to Blumer, symbolic interactionism rests on three premises: (1) 'that human beings act towards things on the basis of the meanings that the things have for them'; (2) 'that the meaning of such things is derived from, or arises out of, the social interaction that one has with one's fellows'; (3) 'that these meanings are handled in, and modified through, an interpretative process used by the person in dealing with the things he encounters' (Blumer, 1969: 2). Human action in other words, is mediated through a symbolic framework which gives it meaning, whether that action be concerned with objects or with other human beings. Things and actions are understood, get their meaning, through shared symbolic networks made up of symbols (language) and expections of behaviour (roles). It is assumptions like these which led to Goffman's (Blumer's colleague at the University of California, Berkeley, for many years) analysis of frameworks of meaning and how they affect individual behaviour.

2 Todd Gitlin (1980) used a similar approach in his study of how media framing affected the general public's perception of American New Left, and also that movement's own self-understanding.

3 In addition to these social movement theorists, Murray Edelman (1995) provides an interesting account of the role of art in the 'framing' of reality. As opposed to Gitlin, whose concern is with those who make the news, that is the ways in which journalists 'frame' reality, Edleman's concern is with the receivers. He writes, 'the models, scenarios, narratives, and images into which audiences for political news translate that news are social capital, not individual inventions. They come from works of art in all genres: novels, paintings, stories, films, dramas, television sitcoms, striking rumors, even memorable jokes. For each type of news report there is likely to be a small set of striking images that are influential with large numbers of people, both spectators of the political scene and policy makers themselves' (Edelman, 1995: 1).

4 There is more to music and movements than can be captured within a functional perspective which focuses on the use made of music within an already existing movement. Music, it can be shown, maintains a 'movement' even when it no longer has a visible presence in the form of organizations, leaders, demonstrations, and can be a vital force in preparing the emergence of a movement. Here the role and place of music needs to be interpreted through the framework of meaning, where tradition and ritual are understood as forms of identity and identification, as encoded meaning, rather than through a mechanistic functionalism of the sort Denisoff applied. Of the few sociologists concerned with social movements to recognize the importance of the symbolic in the formation of collective identity Francesco Alberoni (1984) and Alberto Melucci (1989: esp. chs 3 and 4) stand out. Alberoni (1984: 8) discusses the processual 'succession and degradation' between social movement and institution with reference to the theories of Max Weber and Emile Durkheim. Alberoni calls attention to how actors within social movements, which in his terms begin with 'the nascent state and ends with the reestablishment of everyday-institutional order' (1984: 221), tend to reinterpret the past in terms of present needs for mobilization in a process he calls 'historicization'. The latter 'questions anew every act and every decision and considers open to appraisal the decisions of legendary and historical figures. . . . In historicizing the past, the nascent state also historicizes the present' (1984: 60–1). One example Alberoni offers is that of the Black Muslim movement

in the USA, of which he writes, 'the choice of the Islamic religion represented a search for a past which would clearly distinguish the new movement from the black Christian movements that had predominated until then. . . . Thus both sides are responsible for the formation of cultural traditions' (1984: 243). While not directly addressing the importance of tradition or the reinterpretation of the past in relation to a theory of social movements, Melucci (1989) does stress the importance of meaning and the symbolic in the process of collective identity formation within social movements. Neither Alberoni nor Melucci, however, discuss the role of music in relation to social movement identity formation.

5 Eric Hobsbawm's now classic statement on the invention of tradition can be found in his introduction to *The Invention of Tradition* (1983). Hobsbawm's notion of tradition as something that gives symbolic value to customary practices has much in common with the point of view being developed here. For me, however, Hobsbawm puts too much stress on 'invention', on manipulation from above, and too little on the power of resistance 'through ritual'.

6 Bourdieu's studies of education and taste, which take 'tradition' seriously as a major force in the reproduction of social hierarchy, though couched within the perspective of 'objective' social science, are coloured by this dichotomy. In his scheme, social practices and frameworks of evaluation, 'traditions' in Shils's terms, are transmitted from one generation to the next through socialization processes which lie somewhere between conscious strategies and more or less unconscious habits. To capture this process of social reproduction, Bourdieu prefers the term 'habitus' to tradition. Habitus is similar to tradition in that it entails embodied practices in addition to the transmission of cognitive frameworks determining criteria of 'taste'. Bourdieu's habitus links expressed individual preferences, in art, music, food, etc., not only to social categories, such as status groups and classes, but also to the past, in his case to childhood socialization, but with the underlying assumption that this is historically rooted as part of structurally generated class 'cultures'. On this reading, the concept of habitus, like the concept tradition, calls attention to the significance of the past for the present. Like tradition, habitus is more than habit; both lie somewhere between the unconscious and the conscious, between the body and the mind, between behaviour and action, and most importantly for our purposes, between the past and the future.

Since Bourdieu is more interested in explaining social reproduction than social change, he makes no mention of social movements in developing the concept of habitus. He thus has no interest in analysing under what conditions habitus or tradition might themselves change or even form the basis of rebellion and thus social change at a societal level (Sewell, 1992; Friedland, 1995). However, armed with the notion, it is easy to find examples of habitus within existing social movements, in ritualized demonstrations and meetings, in the performance of speeches, songs and slogans, which serve to reconstitute the collective and to initiate new generations. Within some national political cultures it would be quite easy to identify a 'habitus' of protest and rebellion, as embodied in the ritualized practice of individuals and groups. Such practices help to embody 'the movement' in activists, shape their practices and their tastes, in the same way that the conspicuous consumption of classical music or eating 'French' cuisine can be said to embody the reproductive strategies of certain segments of the middle class. Such a habitus could also link generations, such as the 'red-diaper babies', the children of old-left parents who were instrumental in the formation of new left in the USA in the early 1960s. In this and other cases which could be called upon, music and art played an important role, as they helped constitute the tastes and habits, the habitus of rebellion. Singing songs such as 'We Shall Overcome', whose history I shall shortly trace, was important in linking generations and movements between the 1930s and the 1960s, as was a certain taste for 'political' art.

7 The folklorist Robert Cantwell (1992) provides an insightful conception of musical tradition in discussing Bill Monroe, the founder of bluegrass music in America. He writes:

> Though bluegrass music, like other kinds of popular music, reflects the various social and commercial influences that worked upon it during its formative period, it stands securely upon a traditional foundation which, if we could somehow uncover it, would show itself to be as abstract as a grammar, and just as mysteriously linked on the one hand to the values

of a culture and on the other to the structure of human thought. . . . A traditional fiddler recalls the melodies he has heard around him, offering his own elaborations, combinations, and variations upon them; he finds that the circle of his memory intersects others', so that something independent reveals itself – the 'tradition' – which compels his loyalty because it is apparently so much larger and more enduring than he is. What he has discovered, in fact, is sure evidence of an otherwise imperceptible interconnectedness in the human community, a community without which there would be no 'tradition'. (Cantwell, 1992: 16)

8 Musical analysts interested in the links between culture and politics have pointed out that a song text and its performance is multi-layered. Different messages can be extracted and the same song performed in radically different social and political contexts through the separation and selecting of these various layers. In the case of 'Swing Low, Sweet Chariot' for example, its swaying rythmic cadence can be divorced from its spiritual meaning to fit a football crowd.

9 As Schechner (1993) shows, the old order also has embodied its 'aesthetic dimension'. His analysis of the Chinese example, where the 'ordering' of Tiananmen Square as a symbolic space, the rectangular layout and so on, are all revealingly discussed in a chapter entitled 'The Street is the Stage'. In expressing its own aesthetic, the movement restructured, if only for a moment, the official culture. Thus it was a 'democratic' movement in more than the usual, political, meaning.

10 A budding black-owned film industry was influential in creating this public sphere and was helped along by it. Cinemas were part of the arena of public life in the expanding black communities, and were themselves made commercially possible by the new audience which created a demand for its products. Writing about the Chicago-based and black-owned Micheaux Film and Book Company, founded in 1918 and perhaps the third black-owned film company in the USA, Mark A. Reid (1993) writes:

Micheaux's action films, like other cultural productions of the Harlem Renaissance, were imaginative reflections of a proud, aggressive New Negro whose new morality condoned retaliatory action against white racist aggressions. New cultural 'objects' such as black action films were created for this group of urbanized, race-conscious blacks who were learning to lessen their need for approval by White America. Blacks were becoming politically and culturally aware consumers, and the black market required products tailored to their new sensibilities. (Reid, 1993: 11–12)

Like the literary and pictorial works of the core Renaissance group, Micheaux's films covered topics not previously ventured upon in cinema. His 1920 film *Within Our Gates* included a racial lynching. Later films depicted anti-Semitism as well as racism, while *The Brute* (1920) depicted the urban, black underworld and a black boxer who fought against lynching. Yet, as Reid notes, 'Despite the moral worthiness of the film's two topics, self-conscious black critics denounced "scenes of crap games, black dives, wife-beating, and women congregating to gamble" for portraying the New Negro as less than human' (1993: 13).

In the early 1920s, black independent filmmaker William Foster had recognized that there was a black audience that was interested in black-oriented art. Activists in the 1960s Black Arts Movement, such as Larry Neal, 'argued that the first wave of black independent filmmakers, such as Foster and other creative artists of the Negro Renaissance, did not address . . . [themselves] to the mythology and the life styles of the Black Community' (Reid, 1993: 75). (Neal's remarks can be found in Addison Gayle Jr (ed.) (1972) *The Black Aesthetic*. New York: Doubleday.)

11 In the Preface to the first edition of his anthology *The Book of American Negro Poetry* (1922), Johnson wrote:

The Negro in the United States has achieved or been placed in a certain artistic niche. When he is thought of artistically, it is as a happy-go-lucky, singing, shuffling, banjo-picking being or as a more or less pathetic figure. The picture of him is in a log cabin amid fields of cotton or along the levees. Negro dialect is naturally and by long association the exact instrument for voicing this phase of Negro life; and by that very exactness it is an instrument with two full stops, humor and pathos. So even when he confines himself to purely racial themes, the Aframerican poet realizes that there are phases of Negro life in the United States which cannot be treated in the dialect either adequately or artistically. Take, for example, the phases rising out of life in Harlem, that most wonderful Negro city in the world. I do not deny that a Negro in a log cabin is more picturesque than a Negro in a Harlem flat, but the Negro in the Harlem flat is here, and he is but part of a group growing everywhere in the country, a group whose ideals are becoming increasingly more vital than those of the traditionally artistic group, even if its members are less picturesque. What the colored poet in the United States needs to do is something like what Synge did for the Irish; he needs to find a form that will express the racial spirit by symbols from within rather than by symbols from without, such as the mere mutilation of English spelling and pronunciation. He needs a form that is freer and larger than dialect, but which will still hold the racial flavor; a form expressing the imagery, the idioms, the peculiar turns of thought; and the distinctive humor and pathos too, of the Negro, but which will also be capable of voicing the deepest and highest emotions and aspirations, and allow of the widest range of subjects and the widest scope of treatment. (From Huggins, 1995: 300)

12 The two sides of this process are not often discussed together. The activists in the Renaissance tended to glorify the cultural possibilities and downplay or even ignore, except as it became a basis for their literature or art, the poverty and the overcrowding that also characterized Harlem in the late 1920s. *Black Metropolis* is also the title of the classic study of Chicago by St Clair Drake and Horace Clayton from 1945. Jon Michael Spenser (1993: 109ff.) discusses this book in relation to the blues.

13 From the point of view of current social movement theory, whether we interpret the Harlem Renaissance as a cultural movement or as a political movement depends to a great extent on our theory of social change and the meanings we attribute to culture and politics. If we conceive of change in terms of an abrupt rupture which results, at least to an important extent, from the conscious efforts of organized, 'politically' motivated groups, then the Harlem Renaissance will appear as a 'cultural' movement, with little or no transformative effect on politics (the state). From this perspective, which is probably the dominant one regarding the Harlem Renaissance, some of that movement's key actors, the poet Langston Hughes for example, became 'political' in the early 1930s when they associated with the Communist Party, and only after the 'cultural' movement had waned (Cruse, 1967; and Huggins, 1995, discuss these issues).

From this perspective also, the 'cultural' movement that was the Harlem Renaissance, delayed or even prevented a 'political' movement from emerging among African-Americans during the heyday of the late 1920s. Seen from a more traditional perspective, especially from the point of view of the Marxist theory dominant at the time, focusing creative energy on 'culture' tended to divert attention from 'politics', unless that is, this 'culture' had a clear political message. If any political consequences are granted the Harlem Renaissance at all (from this perspective), they would concern its role in a general strategy to be found among the contemporary Negro elite (or leadership, depending upon one's ideological perspective) which aimed at assimilation and acceptance through the arts: if Americans could be show, it was argued, that blacks were a creative and talented race, that would make assimilation all that easier. As Paul Robeson, one of the greatest African-American singers of that and any other era, said at the time, 'it is through our artistic capacity that we will best be recognized . . . it is through art we are going to come into our own' (quoted in Duberman, 1989: 72). Robeson was on the periphery of the Harlem Renaissance, but the views he expressed here were those of its core group as well. This artistic achievement to advance the race, as Martin Duberman, Robeson's biographer, notes, was individual, 'not organized, collective action'.

14 By 'aesthetics' I mean a social practice, not merely a theory about the meaning of art. This is how I understand Bourdieu's notion of 'distinction', which links taste (in art and music, for example, to an ordered hierarchy of meaning and to strategic processes of social exclusion and inclusion. In the 1920s, the upper stratas of the African-American community developed different strategies concerning the meaning and use of 'black' culture with reference to the dominant white community. At another level of analysis, it can be said that social movements have an aesthetic dimension in the 'cognitive praxis' of their identity-formation (Eyerman and Jamison, 1991). Culture and cultural products are necessary tools in the

formative struggle of constructing a collective identity, around which what we call 'social movements' evolve. In the new social movements of the 1950–1960s, for example, distinct forms of music, recorded and live, were an essential ingredient in the process of movement creation (Eyerman and Jamison, 1995).

15 It is true that Du Bois had written sympathetically and with great feeling about the 'sorrow songs' of the slaves. Still, in his role as race-leader, he remained encased in a European system of values when it came to culture. For this generation of high educated Negroes, an extremely small minority, it would be difficult to be otherwise. Even to offer a sympathetic hearing to the 'folk music' of the rural, uneducated black population was considered avant-gardist, in their circles. For the majority of their peers, such forms of 'culture' were an embarrassment.

16 Lawrence Levine (1977, 1988) has argued the point of view that there existed a long-standing culture of rebellion in African-American life, which can be traced back to the slave-songs and other forms of cultural expression. This would make the claim that the 'new Negro', armed with his positive valuation of the race, was indeed 'new'.

Regarding Du Bois, many have remarked upon his 'hate' or distaste for the blues and other forms of popular entertainment as enjoyed by blacks.

17 In discussing the difference between European and African folk music, Christopher Small writes: 'The European folk musician usually thinks of him or herself not as a creator of songs, but as a transmitter' (1987: 42). To the extent this can be said to be true, it is very much in line with Bourdieu's notion of habitus, discussed above. The individual singer is a traditional singer of traditional songs, and the same is as true for 'classical' music and folk music, that is for written and orally transmitted music. The stress is on the individual (or collective in the case of a symphony) performance, and how well or badly the received music is transmitted. And on the 'integrity of a music-object', which implies the assumption that the 'power of original creation is rare, [where] a clear-cut distinction between those who perform and those who listen . . . (Small, 1987: 43). This is contrasted to the African musician who 'thinks of music primarily as action, as process, in which all are able to participate' (1987: 45). If true, it provides insight into the tensions in the revival of American folk music. Where on the one side the performer, such as the 'political' Pete Seeger, works hard to include the audience in the singing, that is to break with the 'tradition' of performance and the barrier between performer and audience, and on the other side there is the 'purist' Mike Seeger who interprets 'traditional' music in the traditional way: playing old tunes on old instruments in a virtuoso way.

18 In April 1995 I attended a memorial celebration at the Highlander Center where Pete Seeger and Bernice Johnson Reagon, among a host of others, sang their songs of union organizing and civil rights struggle. It was there that the idea behind this chapter suddenly became clear. At the Berlin meetings I played recorded versions of 'We Will Overcome' and 'We Shall Overcome' to help illustrate the convictions and the differences.

References

Alberoni, Francesco (1984) *Movement and Institution*. New York: Columbia University Press.
Beck, Ulrich, Giddens, Anthony and Lash, Scott (1993) *Reflective Modernity*. Cambridge: Polity Press.
Bluestein, Gene (1994) *Poplore*. Amherst, MA: University of Massachusetts Press.
Blumer, Herbert (1969) *Symbolic Interactionism*. Englewood Cliffs, NJ: Prentice-Hall.
Cantwell, Robert (1992) *Bluegrass Breakdown: The Making of the Old Southern Sound*. New York: Da Capo Press.
Cohen, Jean L. (1985) 'Strategy or identity: new theoretical paradigms and contemporary social movements', *Social Research*, 52 (4): 663–715.
Cruse, Harold (1967) *The Crisis of the Negro Intellectual*. New York: Quill.
Denisoff, R. Serge (1972) 'Evolution of the protest song in America', in R. Serge Denisoff and Richard Peterson (eds), *The Sounds of Social Change*. Chicago: Rand McNally.

Drake, St Clare and Clayton, Horace (1945) *Black Metropolis*. New York: Harper & Row.
Duberman, Martin (1989) *Paul Robeson*. London: Bodley Head.
Du Bois, W.E.B. (1986 [1926]) *Writings*. New York: Library of America.
Edelman, Murray (1995) *From Art to Politics*. Chicago: University of Chicago Press.
Eyerman, Ron (1981) *False Consciousness and Ideology in Marxist Theory*. Highland Hills: Humanities Press.
Eyerman, Ron and Jamison, Andrew (1991) *Social Movements: A Cognitive Approach*. Cambridge: Polity Press.
Eyerman, Ron and Jamison, Andrew (1995) 'Social movements and cultural transformation: popular music in the 1960s', *Media, Culture and Society*, 17: 449–68.
Eyerman, Ron and Jamison, Andrew (1998) *Music and Social Movements: Mobilizing Traditions in the Twentieth Century*. Cambridge: Cambridge University Press.
Floyd, Jr., Samuel A. (ed.) (1993) *Music and the Harlem Renaissance*. Knoxville, TN: University of Tennessee Press.
Friedland, Roger (1995) 'Interested meanings/meaningful interests'. Unpublished paper.
Gamson, William (1995) 'Hiroshima, the Holocaust, and the politics of exclusion', *American Sociological Review*, 60 (1): 1–20.
Gayle, Addison (ed.) (1972) *The Black Aesthetic*. New York: Doubleday.
Gitlin, Todd (1980) *The Whole World is Watching*. Berkeley, CA: University of California Press.
Goffman, Erving (1974) *Frame Analysis*. Cambridge, MA: Harvard University Press.
Hall, Stuart and Jefferson, Tony (eds) (1975) *Resistance through Rituals*. London: Hutchinson.
Huggins, Nathan Irvin (1995) *Voices From the Harlem Renaissance*. New York: Oxford University Press.
Johnson, James Weldon (ed.) (1922) *The Book of American Negro Poetry*. New York: Harcourt Brace.
Johnston, Hank (1995) 'A methodology for frame analysis: from discourse to cognitive schema', in H. Johnston and B. Klandermans (eds), *Social Movements and Culture*. London: University College of London Press.
Johnston, Hank and Klandermans, Bert (eds) (1995) *Social Movements and Culture*. London: University College of London Press.
Kaplan, Temma (1992) *Red City, Blue Period*. Berkeley, CA: University of California Press.
King, Mary (1987) *Freedom Song*. New York: Quill.
Levine, Lawrence (1977) *Black Culture and Black Consciousness*. New York: Oxford University Press.
Levine, Lawrence (1988) *Highbrow Lowbrow: The Emergence of Cultural Hierarchy in America*. Cambridge, MA: Harvard University Press.
Locke, Alain (ed.) (1925) *The New Negro*. New York: Boni Press.
McAdam, Doug (1994) 'Culture and social movements', in Enrique Larana, Hank Johnston and Joseph Gusfield (eds), *New Social Movements*. Philadelphia: Temple University Press.
Melucci, Alberto (1989) *Nomads of the Present*. Philadelphia: Temple University Press.
Reagon, Bernice Johnson (1974) 'Songs of the Civil Rights Movement 1955–64: a study in culture history'. PhD Dissertation, Howard University (available through the University of Michigan Dissertation Service).
Reid, Mark A. (1993) *Redefining Black Film*. Berkeley, CA: University of California Press.
Schechner, Richard (1993) *The Future of Ritual*. London: Routledge.
Sewell, Jr., William (1992) 'A theory of structure: duality, agency, and transformation', *American Journal of Sociology*, 98 (1): 1–29.
Shils, Edward (1981) *Tradition*. London: Faber and Faber.
Small, Christopher (1987) *Music of the Common Tongue*. London: Calder Press.
Snow, David A. and Benford, Robert D. (1988) 'Ideology, frame resonance, and participant mobilization', in Bert Klandermans, Hans Kriesi and Sidney Tarrow (eds), *From Structure to Action*. Greenwich, CT: JAI Press.
Snow, David A. and Benford, Robert D. (1992) 'Master frames and cycles of protest', in

Aldon Morris and Carol Mueller (eds), *Frontiers of Social Movement Theory*. New Haven, CT: Yale University Press.

Spenser, Jon Michael (1993) *Blues and Evil*. Knoxville, TN: University of Tennessee Press.

Tarrow, Sidney (1994) *Power in Movement*. Cambridge: Cambridge University Press.

Taylor, Vera and Whittier, Nancy (1995) 'Analytic approaches to social movement culture: the culture of the women's movement', in H. Johnston and B. Klandermans (eds), *Social Movements and Culture*. London: University College of London Press.

Turner, Victor (1969) *The Ritual Process*. London: Routledge and Kegan Paul.

Wintz, Cary D. (1988) *Black Culture and the Harlem Renaissance*. Houston, TX: Rice University Press.

8

RADIATED IDENTITIES: IN PURSUIT OF THE TEMPORAL COMPLEXITY OF CONCEPTUAL CULTURAL PRACTICES

Barbara Adam

In the age of nuclear power, cultural theorists and social scientists share the fate of radiation with a global community of beings for whom radiation works silently and visibly from within. For them as for everybody else, radiation proceeds outside the reach of their senses: it is known only to their cells. Im/material[1] and beyond the capacity of perception and sensibility, it affects our collective present and long-term future, our own and other species' daughters and sons of a thousand years hence. It is dispersed in time and space and marked by complex temporalities and time–space configurations. Its life-cycles of decay span from nano seconds to millennia. This means its time horizon, too, exceeds human capability and concern. Furthermore, radiation permeates all life-forms to varying degrees and disregards conventional boundaries: skin, clothes and walls, cities and nations, the demarcation between the elements. Its materiality thus falls outside the traditional social sciences' and philosophies' definition of the real, outside a conception that has been absorbed as unquestioned norm into the everyday understanding of 'Western' culture: real is what is material and this in turn is defined by its accessibility to the senses. Invisibility, vast variable time-spans of decay, networked interdependence and the fact that effects are not tied to the time and place of emission, therefore, make radiation a cultural phenomenon that poses problems for traditional ways of knowing and relating to the material world. Radiation is, of course, only one example of contemporary phenomena and processes that work invisibly beyond the capacity of our senses. Chemicals, the ozone, air and water pollution are some of the other such industrially pro- and induced phenomena and processes that share these characteristics. All are recognizable only once they materialize through symptoms and once they have been identified through the mediating loop of science. Without the artificial sensory extension of laboratory science and medicine, therefore, cultural theorists and social scientists, in common with lay people, are dependent on second-hand, thus collectivized, experience and knowledge for the identification and definition of such processes and phenomena.

Thus, there arise questions about how to relate and respond to these in/
visible yet central aspects of contemporary culture on the one hand, and
how to conceptualize and take account of them in the routine practices of
everyday life and cultural theory on the other.

Like many who follow the theoretical developments in the natural
sciences, I am seduced by the transformative power of the key concepts
that emerge from the various versions of chaos theory, quantum theory
and the mathematics of fuzzy logic:[2] by their emphases on un/certainty,[3]
contingency, temporality, scale, reflexivity, non/proportionality, connectivity, wholeness and the many shades of grey instead of choices between
black or white, yes or no, one or zero. Their theoretical revision resonates
with my efforts to overcome the conceptual heritage of the Enlightenment
in analyses of contemporary global/izing culture (Adam, 1990, 1995a, 1996,
1998). Not the detail and not the mathematical precision of those theories,
however, but their conceptual insights and their general unsettling of the
theoretical *status quo* proved helpful for my endeavour to theorize contemporary, technologically induced phenomena and processes that lie
outside the grasp of the Enlightenment episteme.

In this chapter I focus on the nuclear accident at Chernobyl as an
exemplar of contemporary phenomena and processes that pose problems
for some of the basic assumptions of classical theory. This environmental
disaster bore all the hallmarks of a chaotic 'event', as defined by the
various forms of chaos theory: out of the explosion emerged order of a
kind that was un/predictable. Its processes were non/linear and non/
proportional. It demonstrated the importance of scale, intensity and
amplification.[4] And yet, to understand that event and its aftermath in
socio-cultural terms requires that we take note of features that do not play
a part in the scientific theories of chaos. Crucial among these are the
invisibility of radiation and the complex, contextual *temporality* that
emerge from the disaster, its implications, and cultural responses. In order
to bring to the fore the conceptual and practical difficulties that have to be
faced in encounters with in/visibility and complex temporality, I first give a
brief outline of the theoretical context and the principle assumptions
associated with the Enlightenment episteme that underpin everyday
conceptualizations of reality in 'Western culture'. In the next section of the
chapter I explore cultural responses to Chernobyl and the associated im/
materiality of radiation. In the third section I consider the temporal complexity of the disaster and its aftermaths. This is followed by a discussion
of implications for conceptual cultural practices and some concluding
reflections.

Knowledge in the Context of Global/izing Culture

The social sciences encounter deep structural problems when they engage
with global/izing cultural processes and phenomena, be they of an

environmental, financial, political or technological kind. These difficulties are historically rooted in the origins of the social sciences and their strong ties with industrial development and the rise of nation-states on the one hand, and with the demarcation of the social from the natural sciences on the other. While the material and living world in its macro and micro dimensions was considered the subject matter of the natural sciences, culture, with its 'modern' institutions, was deemed the bounded meso realm of social science research. This separation of the disciplines and the clear delimitation of knowledge, however, is proving unsustainable where globally networked processes transcend national boundaries and historical time scales, where the industrial way of life refashions nature, and where this industrialized nature impacts on culture, alters living conditions, and affects the health and survival of human beings and other life-forms. In other words, it becomes inappropriate to uphold the definitional and conceptual boundaries when macro and micro, long- and short-term, cultural and natural processes intermesh to such an extent that they mutually implicate each other; when, as Hayles (1990: 16) argues, 'the epistemic ground' on which contemporary culture rests has changed.

The successes as well as the hazards of industrialization, we need to appreciate, have their roots in a particular way of understanding and relating to the human and natural environment. In addition to the separation of culture from nature, the achievements and their associated dangers can be traced to the operationalization of specific conceptual practices, most particularly the reduction of complex, interdependent processes to their component parts and functions, the isolation of things and linear event chains from their contextual interdependencies, and the imposition of the mathematical grid of a linear-perspective vision on the phenomena under investigation. This particular world view is strengthened by the conception of time as empty and neutral as well as its use as a standardized, quantified medium for exchange. What we recognize as the unintended dangers of industrialization therefore constitutes the inescapable shadow of the successful operationalization of that understanding. It is the darker down-side to such technological feats as mineral exploitation, the heat-engine, electronic communication, chemistry in food production and medicine. As materializations of a particular conception of reality, these products of scientific knowledge in turn feed back into our understanding of phenomena and processes. Deeply embedded in our culture, they shape our habits of mind and thus determine and delimit our imagination and theories, the hopes and fears that guide our actions. Technology, argues Romanyshyn, is 'the enactment of the human imagination on the world'. Through it, we not only 'create ourselves' but actually live 'our fantasies of service and control, our images of exploration and destruction, our dreams of hope and nightmares of despair' (Romanyshyn, 1989: 10). As such, this technologically infused understanding is in need of being scrutinized for its historical relevance, whether it is still appropriate, that is, to the structurally new features of global/izing culture, to the phenomena and processes created on the basis of this understanding but transcending its reach. Conceived in isolation, that is, the 'products' transform the logic of their inception through interaction, interpenetrations and networked implication. As these assumptions of classical science have been absorbed into everyday knowledge to such an extent that they have become the hegemonic conceptual practice of industrial culture, it is important to examine them for their contemporary relevance. A brief outline of these assumptions will suffice here as they are already extensively elaborated in the literature of the sciences, the humanities and the arts.[5]

To begin with, the practice of reduction and the assumption of linearity affect our understanding in a way that makes it difficult, if not impossible, to grasp global/izing processes. To achieve the desired reduction, classical science relies on mathematical descriptions and technological metaphors. Their combined application banishes chaos, complexity, temporality, disorder, context, connectivity and creativity from the analysis. Thus, classical mathematical description smoothes out irregularities, works with temporal symmetries were past and future are irrelevancies, and is taken to provide statements of truth and probability. In the mode of classical science, phenomena are explained through a scheme of cause and effect and represented by linear differential equations, first introduced in Newton's laws of motion where, irrespective of the phenomena in question, the principle of proportionality applies: small changes produce small effects while big changes bring about big effects. Dramatic, large-scale events, moreover, are understood as the accumulation and sum of a vast number of small event chains. Equipped with such conceptual principles, scientists (of whatever discipline) are not only able to generalize from one event and equation to another but also to predict future events.

Technological metaphors such as the clock, heat-engine, telegraph, camera, and the computer, in turn, represent an abstract world of interacting parts, a universe that can be taken apart and reassembled, a world of cogs, levers and reversible motion. Through them, complexity is conceived in purely quantitative terms; that is to say, it is merely the sheer number of 'parts' in even the tiniest 'chunk' of reality that make chaos probable, predictability difficult and reversibility *in practice* virtually impossible.[6] Temporality, that is change, is eliminated from that vision through the theoretical development of reversible motion and measurements conducted on a before-and-after basis; through the former, classical science denies any directionality to time and through the latter it eliminates change from the analysis. In both cases, time is de-temporalized. With the development of thermodynamic theory towards the end of the last century, time is re-temporalized but nature remains de-naturalized, lifeless: the temporality of thermodynamic theory refers to entropy and the unidirectional behaviour of dead matter, to its change towards heat-death, but it does not account for growth, creativity, the increase of order and autopoiesis, the central characteristics of nature and life. The reductionist-linear vision thus represents nature in pieces and pieces of nature, a laboratory nature abstracted from context and the networked give-and-take of inter-actions.

These assumptions and their operationalization in technology are intimately tied to the linear perspective, a way of seeing and viewing the world that was first developed in the fifteenth century as an artistic technique to represent three-dimensional space on a two-dimensional plane. Today, that vision permeates an understanding that came to fruition in (Western) industrial culture. It is a way of knowing that places viewers and objects horizontally on the same plane while positioning those viewers as spectators outside the frame of reference, thus transforming them from temporal participants at the centre of things to externally constituted observers of a universally valid spatio-visual reality. It imposes order on complexity. On the other side of the window and with their gaze fixed on the distant vanishing point, those observers cast no shadow; their contexts, bodies and sensualities are lost in irrelevance. The subject matter, in turn, is not only treated as an object of information but as a legitimate subject for fragmentation. Thus, Romanyshyn, in his excellent, wide-ranging study, talks of the linear perspective as 'the eye of fragmentation' (1989: 216) and shows persuasively that the window functions as geometric grid for a world subject to inspection. It is, he argues, a world purified of all but quantity and it serves the purpose of decomposing the whole into parts (1989: 216). As such, the linear perspective vision is an excellent prepara-tion for scientific explanation and a central conceptual base for tech-nological development.

> It [the world] has become primarily a visual matter, well on the way toward becoming a bit of observable, measurable, analysable data, readable as a com-puter print-out, for example, or perhaps as a blip on a radar screen. Indeed, so many of our technological instruments emphasise this feature of visibility – microscope, telescope, camera, television – that we might venture to say that our sense of reality has nearly become identical with our ability to render something visible. . . . We live in a diagnostic age and to diagnose something is literally to know something through seeing it. (Romanyshyn, 1989: 184)

The eye of the camera can be seen as the ultimate realization of that vision: monocular, neutral, detached and disembodied, it views the world at a distance, fixes it with its stare, and separates observer from observed in an absolute way. With the invention of the cine-camera this immobilized universe is re-animated, static frame by static frame, creating simulated motion from vast numbers of isolated frozen images, but still negating the sensual world of the contextual, embodied viewer. This linear-perspective has been centrally absorbed as a cultural norm and with it reality and 'truth' have become rooted in an a-temporal realm of space and vision. It is therefore not surprising that a number of cultural commentators have theorized the implications of the visual emphasis for understanding indus-trial culture.[7]

Finally, in this overview of the conceptual context of global/izing industrial culture, it is important to note that the traditional (social) scientific mode of knowing tends to eclipse the body. This is because nature in general and the body in particular are intensely temporal, characterized by ageing and growth, creativity and self-renewal, by periods of intense activity interspersed with times of calm, by consciousness, feeling and emotionality – all those aspects of reality that have been negated by scientific reduction, denied reality status by linear causality and banished from the linear perspective vision. This mode of understanding is effectively limited to the cultural *products* of human activity – its technology and institutions, for example – and thus finds both the living, contextualized body and nature in its autopoietic, transient and creative form located outside its frame of reference and capability. As decontextualized spectacle and as specimen subject to fragmentation, mechanization and quantification, body and nature are *reinvented* to suit the classical science mould. Cinderella's glass slipper would be an appropriate image for this reconstruction of nature to fit the conceptual cage of classical science: reduction, simplification, causal relations, machine parts, and the window ethic. Alternative visions were offered by the Romantics and Vitalists of the previous century;[8] yet, the stresses between assumptions and subject matter were not yet of a level that would create sufficiently widespread public mistrust in that vision. Today, however, we find ourselves surrounded by events, processes and phenomena that place the classical system of thought under almost intolerable strain. The symptomatic products of the products – radiation, pollution and global warming, for example – have outgrown the limiting framework of their inception. To illustrate these stresses in conceptual cultural practice and to show the complexity of cultural responses, I use as an example the nuclear disaster at Chernobyl, an event that has affected people across the globe and deeply unsettled Europeans in particular.

Im/materiality and Mediation of an Invisible Threat

On the morning of 28 April 1986 workers at a nuclear reactor 100 kilometres north of Stockholm registered abnormally high levels of radiation, a reading which was soon to be confirmed by other stations across Scandinavia. These measurements were the first indication of an event that would send shock waves through the European nations and cast its long shadow over present and future communities across the globe. The Swedish measurements, though unmistakable and confirmed by others, could not provide (accurate) information about the source of the radiation; they merely indicated that 'something, somewhere, was releasing huge amounts of radioactivity in the atmosphere' (May, 1989: 280). It was not until the next day that Moscow television issued a brief, three-line statement from the USSR Council of Ministers that informed viewers of an accident at the Chernobyl nuclear power station and assured the public that 'measures are being taken to eliminate the consequences of the accident' (May, 1989: 280; McNair, 1988: 140). Thus, while the Scandinavian measurements and others that followed were based on 'first-hand' information, everything we know about the incident is a retrospective construction built up from a number of predominantly secondary sources: two Soviet (preliminary) reports to the International Atomic Energy Agency (IAEA) and the International Nuclear Safety Advisory Group (INSAG), a number of articles and television programmes by journalists, and analyses by social scientists and scientific specialists.[9] Similarly, our knowledge of the consequences of the disaster is principally gained through the mediating loop of scientific interpretations and media representation. Thus, we know that on 26 April 1986 reactor number 4 exploded in the Ukrainian nuclear power plant at Chernobyl.[10] The particular atmospheric conditions at the time sent a radioactive plume 1,500 metres into the atmosphere (Bunyard, 1988: 35) and diffused its radiation across the whole of Europe and beyond, falling as nuclear rain and contaminating all life at the level of cells in ways that elude sensory perception and scientific certainty. The outcome was, and still is more than 10 years later, environmental destruction of enormous spatial and temporal proportions and untold numbers of *dead in degrees*: there and then, a bit later, tomorrow, and some time in some elastic future somewhere.

Interpretations about causes and reasons for the disaster – the materialization of the impossible – varied enormously. Analyses differed with perspective and analytical framework, with the time frame imposed on the event, with political and scientific interests, and with the degrees of implication and affliction.[11] Reports on Chernobyl were replete with comments about miscalculations, non-anticipated consequences, wrong predictions, over- and underestimations, profound and irresolvable disagreements between experts. Not surprisingly, the advice given to people in affected areas varied tremendously, ranging from maximum restrictions to silence which meant effectively 'carry on as normal'. Some affected populations were told not to consume locally produced milk and vegetables, some to stay inside, others to avoid drinking rain water. Some authorities withdrew from circulation all known affected produce while others simply raised the acceptable level of radiation (Aubrey et al., 1991). These different and irreconcilable reactions demonstrate the difficulty of responding to complex, in/visible, im/material processes that are unbounded by future time and space. We can appreciate the nature of the problem when we consider with Beck:

> What would have happened if the weather services had failed, if the mass media had remained silent, if the experts had not quarrelled with one another? No one would have noticed a thing. We look, we listen further, but the normality of our sensual perception deceives. In the face of this danger, our senses fail us. All of us – an entire culture – were blinded even when we saw. We experienced a world,

unchanged for our senses, behind which a hidden contamination and danger occurred that was closed to our view – indeed, to our entire awareness. (Beck, 1994: 65)

In Kiev, Chernigov and Gomel – all cities within a 100 km radius of the Chernobyl plant – the May Day celebrations were going ahead as normal on the day that the radioiodine content in the air was at its peak (Aubrey et al., 1991: 147, 150) when in other years the parade had been cancelled due to rain. The people of Pripyat, the town where most of the workers of the nuclear plant lived, were not evacuated until 26–36 hours after the disaster, which means they were moved during the period of maximum height of radiation fallout. Another 90,000 people were evacuated after they had received between eight and eleven days of massive doses of radiation. Others as far away as 200+ km from the site of the accident were evacuated three and four years later because they too were approaching the new *raised* permissible maximum dose of life-time radiation per person. Further afield, and more than nine years after the accident, some 20 farms in North Wales were still under quarantine and new 'hot spots' are still being discovered.

This difficulty (and the convenience as far as the authorities are concerned) to accept something invisible as real applied to the unprotected workers involved in the clean-up operation, to the mothers who nourished their children with contaminated food and sent them outside (to go to school, to play outside, to watch or take part in parades), to Government and Local Authority officials near and far away from the damaged reactor who fail/ed to respond to the danger. It applied to the reindeer herders of Sweden, Finland and Norway and the sheep farmers of North Wales who had to be told by scientists and government officials that their animals and their land, their lives and livelihoods were contaminated by radiation. They all were and still are affected by something im/material they can't see, touch, feel, taste or hear, something in/visible that requires the extra-sensory perception of scientific instruments to accord it status of material reality. Without scientific measuring instruments radiation is 'known' only to our cells and we can recognize it only when it shows itself as symptom: when we can *see* the dying children, the congenital deformities in all affected species, the mutated plants, orange-coloured pine forests without needles; when we become aware of the lack of bird song; when we experience the eerie sounds and feel the ghostly quality of deserted villages and dead forests. Finally, no one knows with certainty what is left in the entombed reactor and whether, in Medvedev's (1990) words, 'the radioactive volcano is really dead' (quoted in Aubrey et al., 1991: 150).

The in/visibility and mediation of this technologically constituted reality affect the sovereignty of the self, family, nation, species, earth.

Without sovereignty over our senses, the dream of privacy is non-existent. Our notions of individuality, of self-determination of one's life, are founded upon personal access to reality. To the extent to which we are cut off from this access, we are driven – in the full flower of individualism – into a collective existence at the height of modernity. (Beck, 1995: 66–7)

Beyond the reach of our senses, radiation perforates the boundaries of person, species and earth and thus places humans and other life-forms in a new relation to each other, emphasizes their communality. It extends to the depth of our being and the furthest reaches of our connectedness, from quantum self to the universe, from cell to brother pine and sister meson, our evolutionary ancestors and relations. As the implicate order of interconnections becomes recognizable, so spatio-temporal location loses definition. With the dispersal of radiation across time and space, in other words, there is no longer an unambiguously clear answer to the question, 'where and when am I?' Moreover, there is no escape from involvement: observers, experts and analysts – the mediators of the Chernobyl disaster – were not merely describing objective facts from the disembodied neutral position of spectator outside the frame of reference. On the contrary, their presence and their reports *constituted* and *created* for a global audience an otherwise invisible and unknowable event. Through their presence and their interpretations spectators were implicated in the 'materialization' of that reality as it, in turn, settled invisibly in their cells.

At one level, therefore, only what was written and communicated through the media became real, giving the event the textual quality and status Derrida (1984) has written about with reference to nuclear war in 'No Apocalypse, Not Now'. At the local level, however, this 'textuality' was experienced and *lived* – in most cases with bitter and long-term consequences. In the immediate aftermaths of the explosion, two people died and many suffered severe burns and radiation sickness. Evacuated families lost homes and possessions and had to endure severe hardship before they were resettled 'in safety' just outside the 30 km danger zone. All are dying – bit by bit and in degrees – nothing textual about it for them. Those further afield, moreover, live with the *words* and their effects: agricultural produce destroyed, animals slaughtered for the fur trade or confined to specified, bounded parcels of land, livelihoods threatened. Depending on country and location within, the effects are interpreted differently and tied to widely varying policies and dictates. That is to say, the radiation, its source and its silent damage to the cells are the same but the particular contexts and temporalities play a crucial role in constituting the realities differently. While scientists disagree over facts and prognoses and politicians play with 'safe levels', the people at the receiving end of the worst of the Chernobyl fallout 'know' that the cancers, the congenital deformities, the ill health and the premature deaths are the outcome of the explosion: lack of scientific proof and the inability of experts to establish causal chains are irrelevant as far as they are concerned. Such incompatible perspectives and the mixing of traditional roles, however, are not unique to the Chernobyl disaster; rather, they characterize every nuclear and chemical incidence of this century be they of a military, civil or mixed nature.

Focus on the contextual temporality of the event allows us to shift analyses from the Procrustean bed of classical science assumptions and dualistic conceptions – danger or safety, order or chaos, measurement or experience, dead or alive – to an understanding of complexity and implication.

Temporal Complexity as Cultural Practice

In the classical mode of analysis, events take place *in* time and time is utilized to establish their chronology – their date, duration and order. Moreover, in that form, time is employed unproblematically in the singular. It is used to measure change on a before-and-after basis and implicated in statements about cause and effect. Finally, questions tend to be raised about reversibility and costs associated with the duration of effects. This means time is constituted quantitatively and external to the event. Like the historical time analysed in Ermarth's *Sequel to History* (1992), it is abstract and neutral, characterized by a 'flight from the concrete' (1992: 31) and operationalized by disembodied, 'no-body', experts and narrators. Time conceived in this way is ideally suited to complement the principle assumptions of classical science practice: of linear causality, abstraction, reduction and reversibility.

The nuclear disaster at Chernobyl and its effects, however, stretch that mode of analysis to its limits and show the inadequacy, paucity and poverty of that cohesive vision: how could we possibly identify causes when actions and reactions of operators and technology interacted according to different time scales, principles and goals, at different speeds and with incompatible timing; when symptoms were/are not tied to the time and place of the accident but permeate/d the globe to varying degrees; when futures are created then and now for thousands of generations hence; and when the periods of decay of radioactive materials stretch from a few seconds to millions of years? How could we establish effects when those subjected to radiation fallout from the Chernobyl accident tend to show no visible signs of injury, when the power to destroy life and health is achieved silently from within, is transferred to subsequent generations and is quite unlike the wounds sustained in conventional accidents? Traditionally, cause and effect are linked in time and space – not so with the effects of radiation.

> Radioactive chemicals can now be found in the organs, tissues and bones of every individual in the Northern Hemisphere, and the contamination from past nuclear explosions will continue to cause environmental and health problems for hundreds of thousands of years, even if all nuclear activities stopped today. (Bertell, 1985: 56)

How could we differentiate between radiation from the accident at Chernobyl, natural background radiation, radioactive pollution from nuclear testing, and leakages from nuclear power stations across the world? In a situation where the 'effect' is not confined to the region and time of its emission but pollutes water, land and air across the globe and where the entire earth community of living beings is implicated and affected to varying degrees for an open-ended period by the consequences of the industrial world's nuclear proliferation in general and the accident at Chernobyl in particular, the traditional (social)scientific quest for proof and causes becomes inappropriate, and our understanding of the relation between the past, present and future in need of revision. We will have to ask different questions, understand from a multitude of perspectives, and keep one eye on the future and the other on the past in a rather complicated way. We need simultaneously to peer into the future and the past while recognizing the interpenetration and inseparable, mutual implication of what we conventionally understood as the past, present and future.

To be able even to begin to make sense of the cultural complexity of the Chernobyl disaster and its ramifications, time has to be liberated from its classical mould and understood in new ways. It has to be disentangled from its standardized, neutral, quantitative use and re-embedded and contextualized in the particular experiences, actions and meanings in question. Like the invisible radiation, time is internal to processes, thus not accessible to the senses. It too materializes through symptoms, that is, it becomes visible through the unidirectionality of ageing and growth, of explosion, fallout, contamination, mutations, deformations, thyroid complications, leukaemias and other cancer deaths. This in/visibility, im/ materiality and internality, moreover, needs to be grasped in relation to the convention of using time as a standardized, external measure and exchange value. Not the replacement of classical time therefore, but its transformation is the task (see Adam, 1995a). It needs to be conceived as a multivariate with each variant implicating all the others. At the very least, therefore, we would be concerned with time, temporality, tempo, timing, duration, sequence, and rhythmicity as the mutually implicating structural aspects of time.

At the most general level, time refers to the frames and boundaries within which we act and conduct our daily lives, construct chronologies and histories, establish biographies and mark key events. Time in this sense means the cultural convention of time measured in minutes, hours, days, years, generations and periods of historical, archaeological and geological dimensions. It is also the external, standardized, historical and scientific framework under which we assemble and systematize some elements and eliminate others. As such, 'it is a means of connecting entities and filing them away' (Latour, 1993: 75). This convention of a standardized, external framework enables us to establish moment by moment the actions leading to the fatal accident, fix the time of explosion, chart the fallout as it moved across Europe, tie it to specific dates, and temporally map the pattern of its changing intensities.

A very different picture emerges, however, when we allow time to become coextensive with events and processes. Tied to position, time becomes temporal and the framework of observation relative. With contextualized time we can take account of differences in experience and handle variation in intensities and rhythmicity, in speed, pace and pressure. Despite discernible overall patterns of contamination and damage, every person, animal and plant is affected differently. The existence of radiation 'hot spots', for example, means that there are differences not just between farms but even between single fields and areas within. Moreover, not just the symptoms but their temporal progression is unique: unidirectional, irreversible, but contextually unique. Moreover, time as function of position brings the seemingly objective spectators into the frame and acknowledges their implication in the subject matter. It is both a more honest and a more disconcerting conceptual/theoretical position to take: as participants in the midst of things we forego the 'security' of contemplating events in tranquillity from some no-time, no-where, no-body position of historical and scientific objectivity. This shift in conception transforms the classical time from sole contender to one framework among many and it acknowledges the conventionality of its hegemonic position. The central importance of this shift, however, lies in the stress on agency and practice, in the realization that every one of us and each of our actions count.

Temporality, as distinct from time, is established in the classical mode of analysis on the basis of before-and-after measurement; that is, you determine and fix two points in time and the measured difference constitutes change: measure radiation on two consecutive days and the difference between the two measures marks the level or degree of change, thus temporality. A second feature of the classical approach to temporality is the express belief in reversibility. Talk of 'undoing mistakes', 'reversing trends and decisions', 'getting the land back to what it was before' illustrates that particular assumption. A third characteristic is the understanding of processes in terms of cause-and-effect chains where input and output stand in a 1:1 proportional relation to each other: when you knock over a full wine glass you spill the wine and stain the surface, you might even break the glass, but the event is bounded in time and space.

The Chernobyl disaster calls these assumptions into question, necessitates their qualification, and requires conceptual revision. First, the before-and-after measurement could not tell us anything about differences within the frame and it is silent with respect to anything that lies beyond those two points: it pronounces on the difference between two fixed points – nothing more. Even when lots of these measures are collected at very short intervals so that a semblance of process is achieved, the outcome is still as far removed from temporality as the reconstituted sequence of fixed frames in cinematography is from 'real' movement. Secondly, the experiences associated with Chernobyl make it both easier and more difficult to recognize reversibility as an illusion. On the one hand, the invisibility of radiation makes it hard to believe in the threat and its ongoing destructive action at the level of cells. As grass and plants begin to grow again, the wishful belief in reversibility, that is, a return to a previously 'safe' condition, is all too tempting. On the other hand, however, the dying children and young grown-ups in their prime, the deformities, the general deterioration of health and the realization that this accident has cast a shadow over the future of people yet to be born shows the belief in reversibility to be a misplaced theoretical construct that bears no resemblance to the lives of people who have been subjected to massive and intense doses of radiation. Further afield in the hills of Cumbria and North Wales the farmers, too, might have been guided by the hope that this invisible threat may be quickly washed into the soil to a depth where it no longer materializes on the surface as contamination, thus 'restoring' the land to its pre-radiation condition. But here to, the belief in reversibility has been shaken: radiation is proving to be 'stickier' than previously thought (Aubrey et al., 1991: 139–42). Farmers, consumers and parents had to come to terms with the half-lives of radioactive materials – periods of decay that extend from the imperceptible short to the unimaginably long – and with the material's variable passage through bodies. Not just the use but the quality of land has altered. Daily practices had to be adjusted. Personal relations have changed: between affected farmers and those whose land escaped the critical dose of fallout, their surrounding communities, their local and national organizations. For many, their livelihood was (and in some cases still is) threatened to a point of no return. They 'know' that their land, their animals, their own bodies, and their relationships are *ir*reversibly transformed: every aspect of their lives has been touched in a way that relegates the belief in reversibility to the never-never land of dreams and wishful thinking. Thirdly, radiation is not bounded in time and space; it disperses systemically, permeating the material and living world invisibly, and it materializes as symptom in un/predictable temporal and spatial positions. Moreover, the amount of emission is not proportional to radiation symptoms: in some species, individuals and areas of land, radiation works stronger and/or quicker than in others. Thus, the traditional way of understanding temporality loses its pertinence when confronted with nuclear processes and needs to be extended to embrace contextuality, irreversibility and non-proportionality.

An additional feature of the classical approach to time is its fundamental separation of time from temporality. That is to say, from the classical perspective you cannot focus on time and temporality simultaneously. Similar to Heisenberg's Uncertainty Principle, emphasis on the one means losing sight and definition of the other. To do both aspects justice, we have to oscillate between them, deal with them in sequence – not so when we conceptualize time as a function of position and coextensive with events. In the latter case the complexity of times is implicated in that which is explicated at any one moment. Detaching time from temporality, the classical mode of analysis associates time with culture and temporality with the processes of nature which means it simultaneously separates culture from nature and the body. Radiation, however, makes us aware of the shared bases of existence. Threatening life at the level of cells, it ignores the boundaries between levels of being and species, nature and culture. It thus brings to the fore the networked connectivity of earthly existence, the unity of being and becoming, time and temporality, the link of the one to the whole, the common origin and destiny. With respect to time and temporality, therefore, nuclear processes unsettle the classical assumptions of dualism and proportionality, the dependence on cause-and-effect chains and the associated reliance on proof. Time lags, in/visibility, im/materiality, networked interconnectivity, and contamination in other times and places associated with the Chernobyl nuclear explosion make the classical theories of time and temporality unworkable.

Finally, the complexity of time is incomplete without the further incorporation of tempo, timing, rhythmicity and the interpenetration of past, present and future in any one moment of analysis (see Adam, 1995a). That is to say, when we focus on one of these aspects of time we must not lose sight of the others as important constituents of the subject matter under investigation. Thus, for example, any cultural analysis of the Chernobyl disaster should not isolate the timing of operators' actions from other time factors: from decisions about the date and time of the test with respect to the May Day celebrations and in relation to the fuel cycle,[12] from concerns with the tempo, duration and sequencing of processes, actions and reactions, and from the timing of specific newspaper reports, particularly those in the Western press and responding actions by Soviet government and local authority officials.[13] The delay in providing as much information as possible in order to assist the authorities in their responses to the crisis, for example, is centrally implicated in the way the disaster was handled not only in the Ukraine and in Byelorussia but also in the countries of Northern Europe that lay in the path of the nuclear cloud on the move. In Britain, for example, the more stringent safety measures were only introduced *after* radiation levels had fallen significantly with the result that there was no longer any need to follow Germany and Holland in their ban of the sale of milk and other farm produce beyond, that is, restrictions on the slaughter and sale of lambs for human consumption. Thus it matters when events happen, where and in what context, at what speed, in what sequence, over what duration, at what intensity, and under what conditions and pressures. Moreover, past and future are always implicated in decisions: past transgressions of safety measures, the history of animosity and mistrust between East and West, widely differing predictions and scenarios, recommendations about not having children, as well as the tragic future of generations yet to be born play an irreducible part in the Chernobyl disaster and its aftermaths. Finally, and contrary to chaos theory, recognition of temporal complexity and the principle of implication call into question the assumption of 'initial conditions', that there is, or could ever be even in principle, an originary, point-like, simple, measurable condition. It suggests instead that implication and temporal complexity are irreducible and inescapable principles of cultural processes, that there can be no reduction, that the belief in 'initial conditions' belongs firmly in the classical realm of scientific abstraction.[14]

The point here is that the complexity of Chernobyl and its aftermaths is not accessible to the classical mode of temporal analysis. Both content and interrelation matter; in isolation the neutral dates and the accuracy of time tell us nothing. Rather, time and date receive their meaning from the contextualized complexity, infinite in its manifestations, and in need of interpretation and representation. This brief discussion shows that the focus on time provides an indication of how a shift in conception is tied to potentially more appropriate contemporary cultural practice. It offers a point of departure from the popular classical science approaches to global/izing phenomena such as the radiation fallout from Chernobyl.

Relativity of Measure, Greying of 'Facts'

Chernobyl, like many other contemporary phenomena of its kind, demonstrates the need for new conceptual practices; it discomfits the Enlightenment episteme. Its complexity, in/visibility and im/materiality, its globalizing tendency and perforation of spatial and temporal boundaries, and the inescapable need for mediation affect what is considered scientific fact. Collectively, these facets reduce the power of measurement, delimit the truth value of data, and severely curtail the utility of proof: black and white 'truths' shade into grey. Factual knowledge becomes partial, provisional and demarcated by its measurements, interpretations and representations. I mentioned earlier that only a small number of authorities acted fast enough to protect their citizens from the consumption of milk contaminated during the height of radioactive fallout. By not taking readings at the earliest possible point, milk was not considered unsafe. The effects of this neglect have been felt across the world: contaminated milk powder from Britain, the European Community and Poland found its way to Malaysia, Brazil, Nepal and Ghana (May, 1989: 290–1; Aubrey et al., 1991: 141). However, it neither follows that the reported and detected incidences exhaust the cases of contaminated milk being sold and consumed, nor that they give an indication of the actual amount of contaminated milk in circulation: the measure gives no insight into the size of the problem. The same conclusion applies to the contamination of land and water, animals and people. Since not every square metre of land and cubic metre of water has been (or ever could be) measured and since not every animal and person, present and future has been (or ever could be) examined for the full range of possible problems and since measurements have not been (and could not be) conducted on a daily or even hourly basis before and since the accident, we have no means of knowing the extent of the problem. We can't even be sure that the worst contaminated areas and beings have yet been spotted. With complete cover of measurement an impossibility, scientists rely on mathematics, models and theory to establish 'truth' and 'proof' while expediency plays a substantial role in defining the boundaries of 'safety'.

The sensitivity of the measure, we have to appreciate further, depends on both its temporal and spatial scale. Traditional 'factual' and representational knowledge, however, is indifferent to scale. It was only through Einstein's Theories of Relativity that the importance of the time-frame of observation made a difference at very high speeds; and through the establishment of the physical theories of chaos that the inextricable involvement of scale began to be accepted for the observation for complex systems.[15] These theoretical developments led to a subtle shift towards relativity and the realization that the scale of measure influences not only what is visible but also what is considered to constitute a problem and what is deemed to be an appropriate response. That is to say, if we change the measure and classificatory principle, we get different results for the same events. Thus, 'facts', 'proof' and 'truth' clearly belong to the absolutist, representational framework of meaning used by theorists, politicians, lawyers and policy-makers who continue to use the language of absolutes for phenomena that scientists have begun to recognize as fundamentally tied to the framework of observation and thus relative.

Acknowledgement of our dependence on the framework of observation, on scale and on measurement, however, makes the contamination no less real; it simply recognizes its contested nature: May (1989: 284–7) gives a chilling account of the uncertainty and the lack of expert knowledge on the effects of Chernobyl; Aubrey, Grunberg and Hildyard (1991) chart the conflicting expert opinions and document the widespread practice of doubling and trebling the levels of 'safety' while Beck (1992a) points out that because risks and hazards depend for their existence on the knowledge we have about them, they can be 'changed, magnified, dramatised or minimised' and are thus 'particularly *open to social definition and construction*. Hence the mass media and the scientific and legal professions in charge of defining risks become key social and political positions' (Beck, 1992a: 23). The scientific becomes inherently cultural and political. Again, we have to recognize connections and interdependencies where classical theories work with abstractions and isolated phenomena.

In the light of these observations, what meaning can be attached to identity and the definition of safety? The perception of identity as unique and bounded by time and space is in need of revision when the damage of radiation, at the level of cells and bases of existence, is shared un/equally by all, when radiation disregards the boundaries of bodies, locality, nation and species, and when it both affects and is transferred to an unknown number of future generations. The effect on the meaning of safety is even stronger. In Chernobyl, after the accident, 'safety' began outside the 30 km exclusion zone around the damaged reactor: danger inside, 'safety' outside – until, progressively, safety levels of contamination were raised and safe zones extended. Four years later, the authorities were still identifying whole communities who had exceeded the 'safe' level of contamination and were thus in need of evacuation. At the conceptual level, either-or assumptions still pervade official thinking while individual and society, nature and culture, safety and non-safety, contamination and non-contamination, knowledge and ignorance shade into each other, interpenetrate. Often experts and lay persons exchange their roles when local people give vital information to those in charge of defining and pronouncing on danger and safety. The black-and-white language of proof and certainty clearly has no place in the globalized world of nuclear power and radiation where death comes in degrees, a cell at a time, and where damage materializes in many guises – sometime, somewhere but in certain places more likely than others.

There is some predictability but this is based on principles other than those of classical science; it is not extrapolated from fixed before-and-after knowledge of the past but rooted in understanding of relationships and the inherent openness of processes, developments that suggest nevertheless that some outcomes are more probable than others. It recognizes, for example, that risk analysis can inform about dangers but that the converse is not true. That is to say, low probability is not the same as making a statement about safety: anything not entered as data for the initial condition can pull the outcome in unpredictable directions. The assumption that risks are knowable, measurable and predictable – the basis of safety claims for nuclear power plants – clearly has been proven wrong and inappropriate with the Chernobyl explosion which has shown that 'impossible' outcomes are not only possible but likely.[16] The emerging 'perceived wisdom' recognizes that nuclear reactors are *not* inherently safe but depend on a large number of active safety and support systems and it appreciates that our knowledge of hazards is in principle incomplete because it is impossible to quantify, measure and predict the human factor, model and anticipate all possible event chains and test all safety systems (Gruppe Ökologie (1986), Hanover, extracted in Aubrey et al., 1991: 173). Despite the relative *measured* safety of nuclear power to date, therefore, cultural practice in the nuclear age means coming to terms with an inherent threat, now and for an indefinite future.

Reflections

The explosion at Chernobyl has demonstrated the limit of classical assumptions associated with science and the industrial way of life to a large number of people in Europe and beyond. Because it was a social drama that involved real people making decisions, being heroic, suffering slow deaths, grieving for their children, and fearing for those yet to be born, the in/visibility and the im/materiality of the cultural-environmental global processes and their implications became real for all who were touched by the disaster and all those willing to see. When the control of atomic energy went so catastrophically wrong, the conceptual tools of classical science came tumbling down with the explosion: the insistence on proof based on unbroken causal chains, the expectation of proportionality, the dependence on sense data, thus on materiality and visibility, the reliance on objectivity and neutrality, the habit of abstraction and reduction, the search for simplicity, the status of laboratory knowledge, and the separation of culture from nature. Networked, global connectedness is demonstrated when action by workers in Ukraine can threaten the livelihood of farmers in North Wales and when, in turn, their milking of cows radiates babies in Malaysia. This unsettles traditional conceptions of identity. Moreover, Chernobyl pressed home the shared basis of existence: in the threat, the communality of vulnerability and needs was inescapable. It made visible the unbroken wholeness across space and time, the im/material connection below the surface. It showed us not as observers but implicated participants whose actions matter because they construct reality – here and now, everywhere and all time.

Notes

This research was conducted with the support of the ESRC through a fellowship (1994–96) under the Global Environmental Change Initiative. I would also like to thank Klaus Kümmerer and Tom Weissert for their comments on an earlier draft of this chapter and to acknowledge the influence on this work of my reading over the years of quantum theory, chaos theory and, more recently, the mathematics of fuzzy logic. With respect to those influences on this chapter I would want to cite most specifically Briggs, J. and Peat, F.D. (1989) *Turbulent Mirror*. New York: Harper & Row; Hiley, B.J. and Peat, F.D. (eds) (1987) *Quantum Implications: Essays in Honour of David Bohm*. London: Routledge; Kosko, B. (1994) *Fuzzy Thinking: The New Science of Fuzzy Logic*. London: Flamingo/HarperCollins; Zohar, D. and Marshall, I. (1993) *The Quantum Society: Mind, Physics and a New Social Vision*. London: Bloomsbury.

1 Im/material is to indicate that radiation is material in the physical sense, that is, as it acts at the level of cells, but immaterial from the perspective that ties materiality to sense data, to availability to the human sense, perception and consciousness.

2 See Gleick, 1987; Briggs and Peat, 1989; and Hayles, 1990 for excellent summaries and discussions on the various forms of scientific theories grouped under the umbrella term of chaos theory; Capra, 1976; Bohm, 1983; Zohar, 1983, 1991; Hiley and Peat, 1987; and Zohar and Marshall, 1993 for accessible accounts of quantum theory; and Kosko, 1994 for fuzzy logic.

3 I use this form of textual expression whenever I want to indicate that a phenomenon or process cannot be captured by just one side of its either-or characteristics, that is to say, when certainty and uncertainty, linearity and non-linearity, visibility and invisibility, for example, are not mutually exclusive alternatives but simultaneously present and thus in need of being conceptualized as one.

4 See note 2 for references to the various forms of chaos theory.

5 In addition to my own writing on the full range of this subject matter (Adam, 1988, 1990, 1995a, 1995b, 1998), I refer the reader to Capra (1982), Prigogine and Stengers (1984) and Briggs and Peat (1985) for their analyses of mechanism; to Beck (1992a, 1992b and 1994) for conceptions of the risk society; to Ermarth (1992, 1995) for analyses of historical time; and to Romanyshyn (1989) for elaborations of the linear perspective – he provides a summary of the implications of that vision on pages 54–6.

6 For discussions on complexity, reversibility and Bolzmann's work on probability, see Eigen, 1983: 37–41; Prigogine and Stengers, 1984; Briggs and Peat, 1985: 22–3 and 146–8; Adam, 1990: 168.

7 See Arendt, 1958: 265–7; Romanyshyn, 1989; Ermarth, 1992; Adam, 1995a: 131–2, as examples of cultural commentators who have theorized the implications of the visual emphasis for understanding the industrial way of life.

8 For an excellent study on the Romantic and Vitalist movements, see Wilshire, 1968.

9 Much of this material is collected in a special two-volume information pack, edited for *The Ecologist* by Aubrey et al., 1991.

10 For my brief account of the disaster I draw on Bunyard, 1988; Dörner, 1989: 47–57; May, 1989: 280–92; and the extracts in Aubrey et al., 1991 (which include Aubrey, 1991; *Energy Economist*, 1990; and Roche, in *SCRAM*, 1990). It is important to note, however, that not the technical detail but the conceptual principles involved are of interest to the analysis presented in this chapter.

11 For these different interpretations I refer the reader to such excellent publications and studies on the subject matter as Aubrey et al., 1991 and Medvedev, 1990.

12 Medvedev (1990; reported in Aubrey et al., 1991: 145) points out that the test was conducted at the end of the reactor's first fuel cycle which meant there were three billion curies of radionucleides in the reactor core which created additional hazards once things had begun to go wrong.

13 McNair (1988) devotes a whole chapter of his book *Images of the Enemy* to the timing of Soviet press reports on the Chernobyl disaster. As I already noted above, the first indication of unusually high levels of radiation came from Scandinavian sources, while the first Soviet statement did not appear until 72 hours after the explosion. The fact that the Western press was first to report on this matter placed the Soviet authorities in a defensive position, needing to respond to and counter an avalanche of ever more extreme Western media speculation. This situation of accusation, denial and counter-accusation lasted until 6 May, 10 days after the explosion, when Gorbachov's *glasnost* approach seems to have won through and the first informative and self-critical reports began to appear in the Soviet media.

14 This interpretation is supported by quantum theory which has shown that the deeper physicists probe the quantum realm, the more they encounter complexity and inexplicable forms of temporality. See Capra, 1976; Bohm, 1983; Zohar, 1983; Adam, 1990: 55–60.

15 For discussions of scale and relativity, see Adam, 1995a: 160–5; Hayles, 1990; and Ingold, 1993.

16 For extended discussions on social risk analysis, see Beck, 1992a and 1992b; Dixon, in Aubrey et al., 1991: 200–10; Gruppe Ökologie, in Aubrey et al., 1991: 170–92; and for the shifting positions of French and US officials on the safety of nuclear power plants, see May, 1989: 280–91.

References

Adam, B. (1988) 'Social versus natural time: a traditional distinction re-examined', in M. Young and T. Schuller (eds), *The Rhythms of Society*. London: Routledge & Kegan Paul. pp. 174–97.

Adam, B. (1990) *Time and Social Theory*. Cambridge: Polity Press; and Philadelphia: Temple University Press.

Adam, B. (1995a) *Timewatch: The Social Analysis of Time*. Cambridge: Polity Press; and Williston, VT: Blackwell.

Adam, B. (1995b) 'The temporal landscape of global/ising culture and the paradox of postmodern futures', in B. Adam and S. Allan (eds), *Theorizing Culture: An Interdisciplinary Critique after Postmodernism*. London: University College of London Press. pp. 249–60.

Adam, B. (1996) 'Technology–ecology connection and its conceptual representation', in J.T. Fraser and M. Soulsby (eds), *Dimensions of Time and Life: The Study of Time VIII*. Boston, MA: International University Press. pp. 207–14.

Adam, B. (1998) *Timescapes of Modernity: The Environment and Invisible Hazards*. New York and London: Routledge.

Arendt, H. (1958) *The Human Condition*. Chicago: Chicago University Press.

Aubrey, C. (1991) 'Journey into the danger zone', in *Meltdown: The Collapse of the Nuclear Dream*. London: Collins & Brown.

Aubrey, C., Grunberg, D. and Hildyard, N. (eds) (1991) *Nuclear Power: Shut It Down!* (Vols 1 and 2). London: Ecologist.

Beck, U. (1992a) *The Risk Society*. London: Sage.

Beck, U. (1992b) 'From industrial society to risk society: questions of survival, social structure and environmental enlightenment', *Theory, Culture & Society*, 9: 97–123.

Beck, U. (1995) *Ecological Enlightenment: Essays on the Politics of the Risk Society*, trans. Mark Ritter. Atlantic Highlands, NJ: Humanities Press.

Bertell, R. (1985) *No Immediate Danger: Prognosis for a Radioactive Earth*. London: The Women's Press.

Bohm, D. (1983) *Wholeness and the Implicate Order of Chaos*. London: ARK.

Briggs, J. and Peat, F.D. (1985) *The Looking Glass Universe*. London: Fontana.

Briggs, J. and Peat, F.D. (1989) *Turbulent Mirror*. New York: Harper & Row.

Bunyard, P. (1988) 'Nuclear energy after Chernobyl', in E. Goldsmith and N. Hildyard (eds), *The Earth Report: Monitoring the Battle for our Environment*. London: Beazley.

Capra, F. (1976) *The Tao of Physics*. London: Fontana.

Capra, F. (1982) *The Turning Point*. London: Wildwood House.

Derrida, J. (1984) 'No apocalypse, not now (full speed ahead, seven missiles, seven missives)', *Diacritics*, 14: 20–31.

Dixon, I. (1991) 'The risks of accidents', in C. Aubrey, D. Grunberg and N. Hildyard (eds), *Nuclear Power: Shut It Down!* Vols 1 and 2. London: Ecologist. pp. 200–10.

Dörner, D. (1989) *Die Logik des Misslingens*. Hamburg: Rowohlt.

Eigen, M. (1983) 'Evolution and Zietlichkeit', in A. Peisl and A. Mohler (eds), *Die Zeit*. Munich: Oldenburg. pp. 35–57.

Energy Economist (1990) 'World status: Chernobyl revisited', (May), in C. Aubrey, D. Grunberg and N. Hildyard (eds) (1991), *Nuclear Power: Shut It Down!* Vols 1 and 2. London: Ecologist. pp. 144–9.

Ermarth, E. (1992) *Sequel to History: Postmodernism and the Crisis of Representation*. Princeton, NJ: Princeton University Press.

Ermarth, E. (1995) 'Ph(r)ase time: chaos theory and postmodern reports on knowledge', *Time & Society*, 4: 91–110.

Gleick, J. (1987) *Chaos: Making a New Science*. London: Penguin.

Gruppe Ökologie (1986) 'International nuclear reactor hazard study', in C. Aubrey, D. Grunberg and N. Hildyard (eds) (1991), *Nuclear Power: Shut It Down!* Vols 1 and 2. London: Ecologist. pp. 170–92.

Hayles, K. (1990) *Chaos Bound: Orderly Disorder in Contemporary Literature and Science*. Ithaca, NY: Cornell University Press.

Hiley, B.J. and Peat, F.D. (eds) (1987) *Quantum Implications: Essays in Honour of David Bohm*. London: Routledge.

Ingold, T. (1993) 'The temporality of landscape', *World Archaeology*, 25: 152–74.

Kosko, B. (1994) *Fuzzy Thinking: The New Science of Fuzzy Logic*. London: Flamingo/HarperCollins.

Latour, B. (1993) *We have Never been Modern* (trans. C. Porter). London: Harvester.

May, J. (1989) *The Greenpeace Book of the Nuclear Age: The Hidden History; the Human Cost*. London: Gollancz.

McNair, B. (1988) *Images of the Enemy*. London: Routledge.

Medvedev, Z. (1990) *The Legacy of Chernobyl*. Oxford: Blackwell.

Prigogine, I. and Stengers, I. (1984) *Order out of Chaos*. London: Heinemann.

Romanyshyn, R.D. (1989) *Technology as Symptom and Dream*. London: Routledge.

SCRAM (1990) 'The legacy of Chernobyl', (June), in C. Aubrey, D. Grunberg and N. Hildyard (eds) (1991), *Nuclear Power: Shut It Down!* Vols 1 and 2. London: Ecologist. pp. 150–1.

Wilshire, B. (1968) *Romanticism and Evolution*. New York: G.P. Putnam's Sons.

Zohar, D. (1983) *Through the Time Barrier: A Study of Precognition and Modern Physics.* London: Paladin.

Zohar, D. (1991) *The Quantum Self.* London: Flamingo.

Zohar, D. and Marshall, I. (1993) *The Quantum Society: Mind, Physics and a New Social Vision.* London: Bloomsbury.

Part IV

CARTOGRAPHIES OF NATION

9

TRIUMPHALIST GEOGRAPHIES

Michael J. Shapiro

Cartographic Violence

Contemporary cartographic practices are ahistorical. The dominant representations provide names and jurisdictional boundaries, but the violence that attended the pacification which the maps express is unavailable to the gaze. Much of the 'spatial history' frozen in today's maps resulted from the direction choosing, naming and inhabiting of 'discoverers, explorers, and settlers' (Carter, 1987: xxi). And while continuing, postcolonial struggles give the geopolitical map much of its contemporary dynamic, the 'world' presented to us in maps appears wholly quiescent. Cartographers remain largely complicit with both the original conflictual acts of settlement and the more recent forms of state pacification. In short, the maps reproduce the state-centric structure of global recognition.[1]

What are most notably absent in the recent history of cartography are alternative spatial stories which, if heeded, would have produced alternative cartographies and affirmed the historical existence of peoples whose collective coherences and spatial practices are overcoded in modern maps. Since the Renaissance, cartographers have largely dehistoricized maps, displacing the cosmological and political dynamics of pre-Renaissance maps – stories of spatial creation and incorporation – with static geometries and impressions of timeless boundaries. In contrast, many Fourth World maps, especially those produced by Mesoamerican cultures, 'register space according to sequence of encounter' (Brotherston, 1992: 82).

Although the contemporary static cartography, the geopolitical map of nation-states, is dehistoricized, it is nevertheless lent support by a familiar historical narrative, one in which the state is represented as an unambiguously positive, evolutionary accomplishment. This narrative is belied by the conjunctural history of cartography; there have been alternative, pre-state system maps that have survived.[2] For example, in his struggle against the Mexican state, Emiliano Zapata drew upon local maps of areas that had been drawn by peoples resisting 'capitalist invasion' prior to this century (Brotherston, 1992: 83). By and large, however, the map of the state system dominates not only because of the power of states over their populations but also because of the way that state power is recognized in dominant political narratives. State power is celebrated not only in its self-representation as an evolutionary achievement but also in the idea that the state represents a triumph of culture over nature as the peoples from the continent of Europe imposed a model of space and a structure of political economy on the rest of the planet.

There are a variety of sources to which one could turn to treat the rationales of this latter part of the story, but for purposes of illustration, I focus here on the flourishing of liberal theory in the nineteenth century. Ironically, at the same time they were elaborating the dignity and autonomy of the individual in Europe, liberal theorists were legitimating the disparagement and destruction of peoples on its periphery. For example, Alexis de Tocqueville could not condone slavery – it was immoral for one [man] to own another – but, as Tzvetan Todorov (1990) has noted, Tocqueville felt that it was perfectly reasonable for one people to own another people. His report on the Algerian colony constitutes a firm justification for repressive colonial rule, based on his presumption that France was a superior 'civilization' (Tocqueville, 1840).

The remarks of Tocqueville's contemporary, John Stuart Mill, on civilization and non-intervention are also instructive and paradigmatic, for they issue from the pen of a canonical nineteenth-century liberal, who is even more identified with the value of liberty. Mill's devaluing of the collective coherence of indigenous peoples operated within a state-oriented cartography. Indigenes had been deprived of respect in different geographical imaginaries in earlier centuries. For example, the Jesuits of the seventeenth century in the New France (Eastern Canada) had universalized a model of sacred space to deny the significance of indigenous spirituality, and the Puritans in New England had imposed a spiritual geography that also virtually unmapped indigenous peoples. Cotton Mather's 'Exact Mapp of New England and New York' is exemplary in this respect. It contained sections labelled 'Indian Country', 'Nipnak' and 'Country of Narragansett', but was largely 'ethically cleansed',[3] using English names and church steeple icons to represent each town.[4]

Mill universalized a different global understanding, the European state model of space to deny tribal nations significant presence in general and nationhood in particular. First, in his essay on 'civilization', Mill employed the venerable discourse of savagery but gave it a new spatial spin; he located Native Americans as a thinly scattered, disordered people: 'a savage tribe consists of a handful of individuals, wandering or thinly scattered over a vast tract of country' (Mill, 1962a: 46). Denying that 'savages' even have a society he stated that 'in savage communities, each person shifts for himself; except in war . . . we seldom see any joint operations carried on by a union of many; nor do savages find pleasure in each other's society' (1962a: 46).

Then, addressing himself to the issue of non-intervention, Mill surmised that their asocial character is enough to disqualify them from significant claims to either being a coherent collectivity or being eligible for recognition on the basis of their land use. Summoning, finally, a European notion of property to cap his argument for non-recognition – savages fail to practise a notion of property in the British legalistic sense – he stated that savages have no basis for nationhood; they have no 'rights as a *nation*, except a right to such treatment as may, at the earliest possible period, fit them for becoming one' (Mill, 1962b: 378). Mill's argument here is precisely the practice of self–other identity construction that constituted, in Derrida's terms, the 'advance' of the European, which took no heed of 'other headings' (Derrida, 1992).

Apart from its immediate legitimation for colonization, Mill's interpretative complicity with the European 'advance' exemplifies more generally the interrelationship of spatial practices and political and ethical sensibilities. To be an object of moral solicitude and a subject with eligibility to act within the domain of the political, one must occupy space and have an identity that commands a recognition of that occupation. Mill's dismissal of the first American peoples is simply the modern, state-oriented cartography of violence. His geographic imaginary was both state- and Anglo-centric; he constructed his world on the basis of a radical home–colony separation.

In his autobiography, for example, he manifests a remarkable aphasia with respect to his career as an administrator of India for the East India Company.[5] For purposes of his self-representation, Mill's audience was wholly English; the centre of global space is England, and everything on the pale has diminished significance. Mill's 'profound unlooking' (Shetty, 1994: 138) was a form of representational violence that was a family tradition. His father, James Mill, had already consolidated a disparaging view of the Indian example of colonial alterity in his *History of British India*. In effect, James Mill elaborated his construction of India's caste system into a discourse that produced a 'symbolic invisibility of the peoples of India' (Suleri, 1992: 19).

The Mill family did not monopolize the nineteenth-century discourse on global inequalities. John Stuart's account of his life was more generally complicit 'in reproducing the Victorian Geography of cultural difference' (Shetty, 1994: 144). To disclose the structure of this kind of spatial complacency and ethico-political insensitivity, Gilles Deleuze and Felix Guattari have represented the confrontation between the emerging state system and various colonized and tribal peoples with a geometric metaphor. The coming of the state, they suggest, created a disturbance in a system of 'itinerant *territoriality*' (Deleuze and Guattari, 1987: 209). While the normative geometry of these itinerantly oriented societies takes the form of a set of non-concentric segments, a heterogeneous set of lineage-based power centres integrated through structures of communication, the state is concentric in structure, an immobilized pattern of relations controlled from a single centre.

The state-oriented geometry produces a univocal code, a sovereignty model of the human subject which overcodes all segmental affiliations. For this reason, those, like Mill, schooled in the geometry of the state, cannot discern a significant social and political normativity in segmentally organized groups. They see no collective coherence in peoples with a set of polyvocal codes based on lineage. In short, having changed the existing geometry, linear reason of state dominates, privileging what is sedentary and disparaging and arresting what moves or flows across boundaries. It sedentarizes labour and counteracts vagabondage, giving the nomad no space for legitimate existence (in various senses of the word space).[6]

This lack of legitimacy of non-state peoples continues to be reflected in the inattention to spatial practices and marginalized identities in contemporary political and ethical discourses. Specifically, among what are silenced within state-oriented societies are alternative stories, the narratives through which non-state and diasporic peoples struggle to maintain and achieve collective coherence and spatial identity. In the context of what Deleuze and Guattari call the state geometry, such peoples are unable to perform effectively recognized identities; they are not a significant part of modern political conversations. Such cartographic, and by implication, ethnographic violence forecloses conversation. This violence of state cartography is powerfully conceptualized in Paul Carter's (1987) account of the European encounter with Australian aboriginal peoples.

The European state system's model of space involved boundaries and frontiers, and its advance during its colonizing period pushed frontiers outward. During the process of the 'stating' of Australia (Dillon and Everard, 1992), when the European spatial imaginary was imposed, those on the other side of the frontier, the Aborginals, were given no place in a conversation about boundaries. Carter suggests a different frame for treating boundaries. The boundary could be seen as 'a corridor of legitimate communication, a place of dialogue, where differences could be negotiated' (Carter, 1987: 165). Indeed, by regarding a boundary 'as the place of communicated difference' (1987: 163) instead of proprietary appropriation (the European model), the Europeans would have summoned a familiar practice from the Aborigines. For Aborigines, boundaries are '*debatable* places' (Carter, 1987: 265), which they treat as zones for intertribal communication.

As is well known, however, Australia was ultimately 'settled', and the boundaries served not to acknowledge a cultural encounter but to establish the presence of the Europeans, practically and symbolically. This violence, which substituted for conversation, is already institutionalized in the form of what is represented as 'Australia' just as other names and boundaries on the dominant, geopolitical world map are rigidified and thus removed from the possibility of encounter. To the extent that community, society, and nation fail to reflect the otherness within, we have a cartographic unconscious in the form of an unreflective linear narrative. Carter offers an alternative to this unconscious, stating that 'nothing could be less appropriate to the evocation of historical space than the one way logic of positive chronology' (1987: 293), and adding more elaborately:

> A spatial history does not go confidently forward. It does not organize its subject matter into a nationalist enterprise. It advances exploratively, even metaphorically, recognizing that the future is invented. Going back, it questions the assumptions that the past has been settled once and for all. (Carter, 1987: 294)

The various discourses springing from the cartographic unconscious against which Carter writes are legion. In order to disclose it effectively, it is necessary to unread the geopolitical map and begin the process of writing another one. As Carter implies, this is a process without limit. As a first step, a brief historical intervention, aided by some of Joseph Conrad's insights, will initiate my attempt to disrupt the USA's geopolitically oriented national imaginary.

Militant Geographies

Joseph Conrad understood well the 'violence of representation' that is a part of some geographic imaginaries.[7] Under the general rubric of 'imperial geography', he proposed a chronology of geographic perspectives that accompanied and legitimated various stages in the process of the European colonization of various parts of the world. His various stages ran from 'geography fabulous', based on myths of the new world, through 'geography militant', coinciding with the invasions, to 'geography triumphant', expressed in the subsequent cartographic representations of the European settlements (Conrad, 1926).

While there are abundant examples of the articulations involved in Conrad's second stage, I am struck by the perspective of the Dutch traders as they explored the coasts of the 'New World'. The Dutch traders, who established the first colonial settlement on Manhattan Island, were connected to a trading company – the Dutch West India Company – that Emmanuel Wallerstein aptly described as an 'aggressive semipiratical body' (1980: 51). While the East India Company was controlled by Amsterdam merchants who were 'partisans of peace', the West India Company was run by a coalition of Netherlanders who were 'colonizing and warlike' (Wallerstein, 1980: 51).

This privateering spirit was reflected unambiguously in the language with which the West India Company's treasurer, Isaac de Rasieres, described the land around Sandy Hook (now Long Island) at the time of his July 1626 landing. From his ship, not irrelevantly named 'The Arms of Amsterdam', he saw a sandy reef, which he described as 'a musket shot broad' and narrows the width of which was, he added, 'about a cannon shot' (Jameson, 1990: 103). The trader's gaze, directed by the martial spirit evident in his figuration, clearly belonged to that period in the imperial mapping of new worlds that Conrad so perceptively called 'geography militant'.

While one could easily elaborate on this militant stage of imperial geography, my concern in this chapter is more with Conrad's ultimate stage, 'geography triumphant'. This stage coincides with the consolidation of a European nation-state system. It is important to recognize, however, that this consolidation has never been total. As a result, at the level of representation, various expressions of state legitimation consist of narratives aimed at masking the second stage of imperial conquest. In order both to deflect the grievances of indigenous peoples and to impose an orderly model of a consensual national culture on what are various aspects of disorder and centrifugal senses of affiliation, national stories are told that recast militancy and aggressivity as heroism and self-sacrifice. Sensing that the 'geography triumphant' has never been wholly uncontested, national stories endlessly repeat the process of consolidation; they perform national unity. My focus here is on one such performance, Theodore Roosevelt's (1989) telling of the triumphant movement westward of 'the English-speaking peoples', a story that continues to be a primary part of the dominant 'American' imaginary.

Narrative Contentions

The process of 'constituting Americans' (Wald, 1995), especially struggles over how the national story should be written to connect personhood with national identity, has been particularly contentious during periods in which the boundaries of the self have been altered. Theodore Roosevelt's gloss on 'the winning of the West' was written during a period in which the boundaries of the working body were being extended. Specifically, Roosevelt's role in attempting to author American nationhood and personhood is associated with a crisis of masculinity at the turn of this century. As the industrial age increasingly lent mechanical extensions to the working body, there were expressions of concern about the depletion of masculinity. Such significant cultural actors as Thompson Seton, a co-founder of the scouting movement, concerned themselves during this period with the craft of making men as an 'antidote to anxieties about the *depletion* of agency and virility in consumer and machine culture' (Selzer, 1992: 149). As it is put in the first *Boy Scouts of America* handbook, it is necessary 'to combat the system that has turned such a large proportion of our robust, manly, self-reliant boyhood into a lot of flat-chested cigarette smokers, with shaky nerves and doubtful vitality' (Selzer, 1992: 149).

The anxieties expressed at the time were organized around a confusion of agency, as 'men' enacted their work with the increasing aid of mechanical prostheses which, on the one hand, extended bodily capacities but, on the other, ambiguated issues of agency and value. Telling the American story as the story of the 'winning of the West' was among Roosevelt's solutions to what he saw as this crisis.

Not surprisingly, various recent anti-immigration alarmists have invoked Roosevelt's mythic treatment of the Euro-American movement westward. For example, Peter Brimelow does so explicitly; his assertions about the threat of recent immigrants to what he constructs as an American 'core culture' invokes Roosevelt's mythologizing as if it were an ethnohistorical investigation that traces a 'perfectly continuous history' of Anglo-Saxon settlement (Brimelow, 1995: 210). Brimelow's purpose is to argue that, as regards important nation-building epochs, 'America' has been effectively ethnically homogeneous; the westward settlement of English-speaking people, he avers, quoting Roosevelt without criticism, was 'the crowning and greatest achievement', having made America part of the 'heritage of the dominant world races' (Brimelow, 1995: 210). Thus, for Brimelow, the threat of non-whites and non-English speakers is to a cultural homogeneity seemingly established by the Rooseveltian fable.

E.A. Ross, an immigration alarmist writing much earlier in the century, also worried about the 'loss of political like-mindedness' engendered by the addition of immigrant aliens, but for him the primary threat was to the American bloodlines, which he imagined had been created by the rigours of the Western adventure ('The blood now being injected into the veins of our people is "sub-common"' (Ross, 1914: 285)). Thus, for example, he thought that Jews make poor Americans because they are not fit to haul canoes through the wilderness:

On the physical side the Hebrews are the polar opposite of our pioneer breed . . . it will be long before they produce the stoical type who blithely fares forth into the wilderness, portaging his canoe, poling it against the current, wading in the torrents, living on bacon and beans, and sleeping on the ground, all for 'fun' or 'to keep hard'. (Ross, 1914: 290)

Roosevelt's *The Winning of the West* (1989) certainly supports the inferences of these two differently situated but exemplary immigration alarmists, but there is another element of his legendary history that bears scrutiny. There is a remarkable disjuncture in Roosevelt's text, a telling economy of 'Indian' presence and absence in the West. Constructed in part as a spatial history, Roosevelt's fable depopulates the western landscape, referring to the Native American-occupied West as part of 'the world's waste spaces' (1989: 17). In so far as 'Indians' had a significant presence during the 'spread of the English-speaking peoples' (1989: 17), it was only as occasional visitors:

The white settler has merely moved into an uninhabited waste; he does not feel that he is committing a wrong, for he knows perfectly well that the land is really owned by no one. It is never even visited, except perhaps for a week or two every year. (Roosevelt, 1989: 119)

However, in the places where Roosevelt's analysis becomes an ethno-history (albeit a legendary one), the West becomes repopulated with 'savage and formidable foes' (1989: 30) against whom 'the English race' maintains its integrity by driving them off or exterminating them rather than, like the Spanish in other colonial venues, 'sitting down in their midst' and becoming a 'mixed race' (1989: 30). In its pseudo-ethnohistorical moments, *The Winning of the West* is a romantic *soldatesque* in which brave pioneers fight their way westward, impeded at every step by the Indians' 'fierce and dogged resistance' (1989: 40) until they gain what is rightfully theirs. But, when justice becomes the focus in the text – 'the settler and pioneer have at bottom had justice on their side' (1989: 119) – the 'fierce and dogged' foes again disappear, and what has been conquered turns out to have been merely 'nothing but a game preserve for squalid savages' (1989: 119).

The economy of presence and absence for Native Americans in Roosevelt's text, produced at the end of the nineteenth century, is evident in the historical production of American civics and history texts through-out the past two centuries. Reflecting Roosevelt's pseudo-ethnohistory and his concern with Americanization, civics texts from the early part of this century emphasized Anglo-Saxon accomplishments, devoting, for example, more space to Sir Francis Drake than to Spanish 'discoverers' and concentrating on English rather than French colonists (Fitzgerald, 1979: 77). And, not surprisingly, the 'rediscovery' of Anglo-Saxon roots in the texts coincided with a significant influx of non-English immigrants (1979: 78).

By contrast, in the early nineteenth century, when there was less cultural anxiety about the constitution of Americans, the civics texts in the 1830s and 1840s represented 'North American Indians' as important people despite their not being Christians (Fitzgerald, 1979: 90). Later in the nineteenth century, however, they become 'savage, barbarous and half-civilized' (1979: 91) and as the Anglo-Saxon revival in the texts proceeds in the early twentieth century, they become lazy and child-like, until they disappear in the 1930s, not to return until the 1960s as 'ethnics' and the 1970s as objects of official policy (1979: 91).

Ethnohistorical Challenges

Roosevelt's drama of the English-speaking people versus the 'squalid savages' deserves critical scrutiny not only because it has been appropriated in Brimelow's recent anti-immigration tract, but also because it is radically contradicted by both the history of 'English-speaking peoples' and the history of the Euro-Native American encounter in the West. It should be noted, first of all, that the 'English' spoken by these people who supposedly won the West was not a cultural property that divided the Anglo-Saxons from other peoples. Indeed, the history of English, like the history of any 'people', is a history of acculturation and co-invention. What Roosevelt called a perfectly continuous history of English-speaking people looks discontinuous, interculturally provoked, and often accidental and arbitrary from the point of view of the articulate noises they have made.

What has been historically produced as 'English' is not only the product of dialects brought to England by Jutes, Saxons and Angles, but also the languages of Romans, Scandinavians and Celts, in an earlier period (Baugh and Cable, 1951: 72) and French in a later period (1951: 93). The history of English in England is a history of the linguistic amalgamations following invasions and other cultural encounters. Without going into an elaborate philological analysis, a focus on the various episodes of the latinization of English is telling. Three historical epochs are primarily involved. First was the Roman conquest which brought classical Latin into the language mix in Britain, then the spread of Christianity, which infused medieval Latin into English, and then the development of Renaissance science, which added significantly more Latin to English (1951: 93).

The story of what H.L. Mencken called 'the American language' is similarly telling (1943). What Roosevelt called a perfectly continuous history of English speakers was more aptly described by Mencken as 'two streams' of English. American English diverged from the English variety as a result of new circumstances, for example, the need to describe unfamiliar landscapes and weather (Mencken, 1943: 3) and as a result of the contacts among people speaking different languages: French, Dutch, German, Spanish, African-Americans and Native Americans (1943: 108). Not only did the mixing of peoples produce new words, but also the circumstances of the encounters produced new contexts for old words, changing their meanings (1943: 121). American English had diverged significantly by 1812, and as a result, 'almost every English traveler of the years between the War of 1812 and the Civil War was puzzled by the strange signs on American shops' (1943: 12).

Most significantly for purposes of confronting Roosevelt's story of the 'winning of the West' by the 'English-speaking peoples', despite attempts to standardize American English in order to build a unique national culture (Noah Webster's primary motivation),[8] what resulted was a hybrid tongue, a product of cultural encounters, with Native American language speakers among others. As Mencken noted, 'the earliest Americanisms were probably borrowed bodily from Indian languages' (1943: 104), and it remains the case that many place names, animal and food names, as well as action and situation words come from Native American languages.

Rather than having been merely driven off, Native Americans left lasting cultural markers on 'America'. Apart from contributions to American English, Native American agricultural practices, alliance strategies, military technologies and methods, and other cultural practices helped create what are now both European and American institutions and practices.[9] Certainly, many of the Native American cultures became to some extent Europeanized, but it is also the case that English colonial culture became, in part, Indianized, with lasting historical effects (Axtell, 1981: 273).

In addition, and in direct contradiction to Roosevelt's fable, Native Americans have had a significant cooperative role in constituting the 'America' that was shaped as it was extended westward. A genealogical, as opposed to legendary, account of the constitution of the Native American Other by Euro-Americans reveals an initial period of in some ways respectful 'foreign relations' (despite European conceits about cultural superiority). For roughly 150 years before 'American independence', colonists negotiated agreements with Native Americans as if they were other nations worthy of recognition, and the various Native American nations (nations which were dispersed into autonomous rather than centralized tribal collectives) were important players in the struggles among different European colonials (Rossignol, 1995: 219).

Native Americans were resituated as domestic hindrances during the Jacksonian period, when Congress and the President, supporting Euro-American demands for territory, chose to ignore the earlier treaties and subsequent legal decisions that had granted tribes a degree of nationhood with respect to their territorial practices (Washburn, 1964: 119). And various forms of American 'knowing' accompanied the political impetus for the changing construction of the Native American. American anthropology, for example, was deeply implicated in the process through which Native American peoples had their identities reordered as they were changed from 'nations' into 'races', where, in the context of the former, Euro- and Native American relations were 'foreign policy' and in the context of the latter, 'domestic policy'. After a period of ambiguity in which 'American governments and ethnographers vacillated ambivalently in their conceptualization of Indian Otherness' (Borneman, 1995: 667), both were ultimately complicit in wholly domesticating 'Indians' within sociological and cultural frames that effaced the national frontiers of the North American Continent.

Roosevelt's spatial history to the contrary notwithstanding, the winning of the west involved, among other things, the changing of a legal frontier into a domesticated region with an accompanying alteration of the western ethnoscape. Moreover, while Roosevelt represented the movement west of the 'English-speaking peoples' as a series of violent conquests, in which 'The Indians have shrunk back before the advance only after fierce and dogged resistance' (Roosevelt, 1989: 39), ethnohistorical inquiry reveals instead a cultural encounter at a frontier that served as a 'school' (Axtell, 1981: 133), in which Native Americans assisted Euro-Americans in their adaptation to an unfamiliar landscape. The spatial encounter was cooperative as well as violent and in many ways co-productive: 'Indians and Old World invaders met, traded, and fought, sometimes with each other, sometimes with themselves. As they struggled to control a particular corner of the continent, they created new landscapes, new property systems, new social relationships, and new political institutions' (Cronon et al., 1992: 7).

The Euro-Native American cooperation was more extensive than what was ultimately produced as various ways of living *in* the West. Despite the

popular assumption that the West was 'won' by overcoming Indian resistance, in various ways, Native Americans assisted in the Euro-American
westward advance. The myth of the self-reliant, pioneer/Indian fighter
which has been a significant part of the legendary American nation-
building story, is belied by historical investigations into the effects of 'The
Covenant Chain', a treaty between Iroquois nations and the Euro-
American colonists. The confederation between the Iroquois and the
colonists not only helped the English colonists defeat the French (as well as
helping to keep the peace between colonists and Native Americans in the
eastern zones) but also helped to open the western regions for English
settlement.[10]

Francis Jenning's collaborative story of the movement westward dispels
a series of mythic construction of American nation-building: the one that
arrogates all significant achievements to the 'white race', the one that
constructs American institutions as culturally homogeneous, and most
essentially, the Rooseveltian myth of the 'Indians' as barriers to westward
expansion.[11]

Conclusion

The legitimacy of the contemporary nation-state cartography is supported
in part by a series of nation-building narrative performances. While it
remains unclear if the age of nationalism is near an end, one of its primary
legacies remains well entrenched. The story of a unified national culture,
designed to legitimate the ethnic and spatial boundary policing of the
modern state, retains its force. As a result, contemporary 'strangers in the
land', for example, are constructed as threats to legendary and anach-
ronistic national imaginaries. The account I have offered – of the highly
contingent and often arbitrary commingling of peoples and the resulting
co-inventions responsible for what have been historically rendered as
autonomous cultural achievements – is meant as an intervention. The aim,
at the level of writing, has been to disrupt such national imaginaries, and,
at the same time, to offer an alternative language and thus an alternative
moral geography.

State stories are generally consolidating discourses on national culture.
But while much of official culture has been constituted as narratives aimed
at performing the consolidation of the nation, various modalities of
popular culture have offered alternatives. For example, one recent film,
John Sayles's *Lone Star*, is pertinent here because it constitutes a dramatic
intervention into the historical construction of the American West. The
story takes place in a Texas town that contains a Mexican American
majority but is dominated by Anglo officials. The heroic legends surrounding the battle of the Alamo hang heavily over the town, estranging Euro-
and Mexican Americans. Contention over how to represent that and other
histories of the area is revealed in a scene at a school board meeting where

Anglo board members complain about the alternative, Mexican readings of western history being provided by teachers at the local high school. The problem of contested national and state legends that divide people is paralleled by the problem of a local legend. The Anglo-dominant city council plans to honour a deceased, legendary sheriff, Buddy Deeds, by naming a park after him, over the protests of the more politicized segment of the town's Mexican American community. The legend's son, Sam, is now the (ambivalent) sheriff. When a body is discovered – that of the former sheriff, with whom Sam's father had exchanged threats – Sam's investigation, which takes the form of uncovering a complicated set of local biographies, suggests that Buddy Deeds may have committed a murder.

Buddy turns out not to have committed the murder, however, his legend is compromised in a much more interesting way. Sam discovers that Buddy Deeds had a long-term affair with a Mexican American woman, Mercedes, and is the father of Mercedes's daughter, Pilar, with whom Sam had been romantically involved as a teenager. Buddy had forcibly ended the relationship. Sam has re-established a romantic relationship with Pilar after returning as sheriff 25 years later.

In various other ways, the ethnoscape turns out to be less divided than one first imagines; the boundary between Mexican and Anglo, which dissolves as we learn the personal biographies, is also challenged at the level of more aggregate politics. At the level of Sam's personal story, Pilar, as noted, is his half-sister, a product of Buddy Deed's affair with Pilar's mother, Mercedes. At another level, Sam learns about the complex Mexican–American cultural transactions that national boundaries cannot inhibit. During his murder investigation, he also discovers the fragility of the Mexican–US border, across which many of the relevant characters in his story have travelled, for example Pilar's mother, Mercedes, her first husband, and various other significant actors in the town's history. Sam is reminded at one point of the border's arbitrariness by a used tyre merchant in Mexico, a former 'illegal alien' who had lived for a while on the American side of the border. The man asks Sam to cross a line he draws in the sand on his lot and then tells him how much less power his interrogation has on one side versus another.

The story of the production of the town's ethnoscape produces further ambiguities. The Anglo political structure is shadowed by a black political structure in which Otis Payne (O), the black proprietor of a bar, serves also as an unofficial major of the black community. Both O and Hollis, the Anglo major of the town, turn out to have been involved in the personal history of Buddy Deeds. Both were present when Hollis, then a sheriff's deputy, not Buddy Deeds, shot the old sheriff to prevent him from killing O. Apart from his work, his unofficial political activities, and his implication in the personal histories of the town, O is also interested in the history of 'his people'. He is descended from mixed, black slave and Seminole ancestry, and has created a small museum, honouring black/Seminole fighters who resisted the tribe's expulsion from Florida and subsequently fought for and against Mexicans, Americans and various 'Indian' tribes.

O is also caught up in a complicated personal story because his estranged son, now an army colonel in charge of the local army base, is back in town. O finally meets his grandson to whom he tells the story about how the family contains 'mixed blood'. But, O notes, in a remark central to what the film conveys, 'blood only means what you let it'. Like O, Sam and Pilar don't let it mean too much; they remain romantically involved despite their 'blood' relationship.

Sayles does not want it to mean too much either. And he wants us to forget certain [hi]stories, for example that of the Alamo and other stories that allow the border between Mexico and America, and between Anglos, Mexicans and blacks to mean too much: 'sometimes you just have to forget history' (Sayles, 1996: 58). He enacts this sentiment by the way he constructs the historical development of the composition of the town. It turns out to have a surprising ethno-political history that doesn't mean too much in its daily life. As Sayles puts it:

> As *Lone Star* started to evolve, I wanted to have these three communities; we were basically in a part of Mexico that someone had drawn a line underneath and made into America, but the people hadn't changed. The Anglos got to run things, but it was still basically a Mexican town. (Sayles, 1996: 60)

Sayles is not alone in his artistic/political enactments, and progressive cinema is but one kind of intervention in the border policing mentality. In another venue of the Mexican–US border a group of artists who call themselves ADOBE LA ('Architects, Artists and Designers Opening the Border Edge of Los Angeles') have produced installations, performances and documentaries about immigrant life that intervene in the imaginative construction of American versus Mexican nationality (Davis, 1995: 33). They refer to themselves as 'coyotes with sketch books and video cameras' who advocate 'the "Tijuanization of LA"' (1995: 36).

Finally, the abjection of various others in the name of a unified and therefore threatened national culture can only be resisted if the so-called triumph of the nation-state system is retold. Rather than seeing that retelling as an epic task, however, perhaps we can view it as the need to conceptualize significant events, to point to episodes that have the effect of disrupting historicism in general and triumphalist narratives in particular.[12]

One such episode is described by the Mexican writer, Carlos Fuentes. His story provides an appropriate exemplar of the kind of disruption to which I have referred. Lost while driving with friends in the state of Mirelos, Mexico, Fuentes stopped in a village and asked an old peasant the name of the village. 'Well, that depends', answered the peasant. 'We call the Village Santa Maria in times of peace. We call it Zapata in times of war' (Fuentes, 1982: 61). Fuentes follows with a meditation that reveals the historical depth of forms of resistance to a homogeneous national story and culture. He identifies an aspect of centrifugal otherness that has existed relatively unrecognized within modernity's system of state sovereignties. Claiming that the peasant has existed within a narrative trace that tends to be uncoded in the contemporary institutionalized discourses on space, he notes:

> The old campesino knew what most people in the West have ignored since the seventeenth century: that there is more than one time in the world, that there is another time existing alongside, above, underneath the linear time calendars of the West. This man who could live in the time of Zapata or the time of Santa Maria, depending, was a living heir to a complex culture of many strata in creative tension. (Fuentes, 1982: 61)

By encountering an alterity that is at once inside and wholly outside the particular narrative within which his social and cultural self-construction has been elaborated, Fuentes is able to step back from the story of modernity that is continually recycled within the nation-state-oriented discourses on time and space: 'What we call "modernity" is more often than not this process whereby the rising industrial and mercantile classes of Europe gave unto themselves the role of universal protagonists of history' (Fuentes, 1982: 64).

Face-to-face with an otherness that these 'protagonists' – those who have managed to perform the dominant structures of meaning – have suppressed, Fuentes is able to recover the historical trace of that otherness, and on reflection to recognize that the encounter must yield more than mere affirmation for the models of subjectivity, time, and space that affirm the coherence of a national people. Most significantly, the encounter produces a disruption of the totalizing conceptions that have governed contemporary state societies – for example, the illusions that they are unproblematically consolidated and that they have quelled recalcitrant subjectivities.

Notes

1 The complicity of cartographic practices in the dominance structure of colonial discourse is discussed in Graham Huggan (1989).

2 'Conjectural history' is what Fernand Braudel (1977) opposes to the linear histories, which presume that contemporary practices have wholly displaced their predecessors.

3 The map is at the beginning of Mather's history of the New English Church, *Magnalia Christi Americana*. Much of this discussion is based on William Boelhower's commentary on the work, and the expression 'ethnically cleansed' is his (1993).

4 The map can be read as a clearing away to establish a colonial settlement, as Boelhower (1993: 392) has noted.

5 'Aphasia' is Sandhya Shetty's expression in her masterful reading of the silences with respect to India in Mill's autobiography (1994).

6 The conceptual language of this section derives from Deleuze and Guattari's discussion (1987).

7 The issue of the 'violence of representation' is treated in Jacques Derrida's reading of the thought of Emmanuel Levinas (1978).

8 Webster's role is noted in both Mencken (1943: 9) and in Baugh and Cable (1951: 360ff.).

9 See, for example, the catalogue of Native American contributions presented in Jack Weatherford (1988).

10 See Francis Jennings (1984: xvii). As Jennings notes, the five-nation Iroquois participation in the Covenant Chain involved a division of labour. For example, Mohawks were Keepers of the Eastern Door and Senecas Keepers of the Western Door. Ultimately, Iroquois diplomacy, rather than their mere military cooperation in the war with the French, set the stage for English westward migration. As Jennings puts it, 'English sovereignty claims westward depended primarily on Iroquois accomplishments' (1984: 173). Attention to the cooperative aspects of the story of settlement, in which Iroquois and other Native American peoples helped to facilitate movement westward and shape American practices, violates mainstream political and anthropological theory. From the point of view of political theory and consequently 'American' political history, the Covenant Chain is not recognized as part of the US nation-building story because 'there is no existing theory or ideology that has room for it' (1984: 38). What takes up all the room, he notes, is the traditional sovereignty discourse which requires an unambiguous cultural centre. The cooperative story violates anthropological theory because 'it does not fit an evolutionary scheme of any kind because it was unique' and it does not fit a functional approach either when applied to given cultures because it was 'bi-societal and bi-cultural' (1984: 39).

11 As Jennings summarizes it: 'Despite the fascination of European observers and writers with the otherness of Indians, it was human similarity that created great institutions of commerce and politics through which Indians guided Europeans to the interior and collaborated in their exploitation of its vast resources' (1984: 367–8).

12 When I speak of conceptualizing events, I am suggesting, against an essentialist historicism, that such 'events' are not lying in wait for us; as Deleuze and Guattari put it, 'the concept speaks the event' (1994: 21).

References

Axtell, James (1981) *The European and the Indian*. New York: Oxford University Press.

Baugh, Albert C. and Cable, Thomas (1951) *A History of the English Language* (4th edn). London: Routledge.

Boelhower, William (1993) 'Stories of foundation, scenes of origin', *American Literary History*, 5: 391–428.

Borneman, John (1995) 'American anthropology as foreign policy', *American Anthropologist*, 97: 663–72.

Braudel, Fernand (1977) *Afterthoughts on Material Civilization* (trans. Patricia M. Ranum). Baltimore, MD: Johns Hopkins University Press.

Brimelow, Peter (1995) *Alien Nation*. New York: Random House.

Brotherston, Gordon (1992) *Book of the Fourth World*. New York: Cambridge University Press.

Carter, Paul (1987) *The Road to Botany Bay*. Chicago: University of Chicago Press.

Conrad, Joseph (1926) 'Geography and some explorers', in *Last Essays*. New York: Doubleday, Page. pp. 1–21.

Cronon, William, Miles, George and Gitlin, Jay (1992) 'Becoming West', in William Cronon, George Miles and Jay Gitlin (eds), *Under and Open Sky: Rethinking America's Western Past*. New York: W.W. Norton. pp. 3–27.

Davis, Mike (1995) 'Learning from Tijuana', *Grand Street*, 56: 33–6.

Deleuze, Gilles and Guattari, Felix (1987) *A Thousand Plateaus* (trans. Brian Massumi). Minneapolis, MN: University of Minnesota Press.

Deleuze, Gilles and Guattari, Felix (1994) *What is Philosophy?* (trans. Hugh Tomlinson and Graham Burchell). New York: Columbia University Press.

Derrida, Jacques (1978) 'Violence and metaphysics', in *Writing and Difference* (trans. Alan Bass). Chicago: University of Chicago Press. pp. 79–153.

Derrida, Jacques (1992) *The Other Heading: Reflections on Today's Europe* (trans. Pascale-Anne Brault and Michael B. Naas). Bloomington, IN: Indiana University Press.

Dillon, C. Michael and Everard, Jerry (1992) 'Stat(e)ing Australia: squid jigging and the masque of state', *Alternatives*, 17: 218–312.

Fitzgerald, Frances (1979) *America Revised*. Boston, MA: Atlantic Monthly.

Fuentes, Carlos (1982) 'Writing in time', *Democracy*, 2: 61.

Huggan, Graham (1989) 'Decolonizing the map: post-colonialism, post-structuralism and the cartographic connection', *Ariel*, 20: 115–31.

Jameson, J. Franklin (ed.) (1990) *Narratives of the Netherland, 1609–1664*. Bowie, MD: Heritage Books.

Jennings, Francis (1984) *The Ambiguous Iroquois Empire*. New York: W.W. Norton.

Mencken, H.L. (1943) *The American Language*. New York: Alfred A. Knopf.

Mill, John Stuart (1962a) 'Civilization', in Gertrude Himmelfarb (ed.), *Essays on Politics and Culture*. Garden City, NY: Doubleday. pp. 45–76.

Mill, John Stuart (1962b) 'On non-intervention', in Gertrude Himmelfarb (ed.), *Essays on Politics and Culture*. Garden City, NY: Doubleday. pp. 368–83.

Roosevelt, Theodore (1989) *The Winning of the West*. New York: G.P. Putnam's Sons.

Ross, Edward Alsworth (1914) *The Old World in the New*. New York: Century.

Rossignol, Marie-Jeanne (1995) 'Early isolationism revisited: neutrality and beyond in the 1790s', *Journal of American Studies*, 29: 29–38.

Sayles, John (1996) '"I don't want to blow anything by people": interviewed by Gavin Smith', *Film Comment*, May–June: 58.

Selzer, Mark (1992) *Bodies and Machines*. New York: Routledge.

Shetty, Sandhya (1994) 'John Stuart Mill's "India": liberalism in an age of colonial domination', *Lit*, 5: 135–54.

Suleri, Sara (1992) *The Rhetoric of English India*. Chicago: University of Chicago Press.

Tocqueville, Alexis de (1840) *Report on Abolition of Slavery in French Colonies*. Boston, MA: James Monroe.

Todorov, Tzvetan (1990) 'Tocqueville's nationalism', *History and Anthropology*, 4: 357–71.

Wald, Priscilla (1995) *Constituting Americans: Cultural Anxiety and Narrative Form*. Durham, NC: Duke University Press.

Wallerstein, Immanuel (1980) *The Modern World System* Vol II: *Mercantilism and the Consolidation of the European World-Economy 1600–1750*. New York: Academic Press.

Washburn, Wilcombe E. (ed.) (1964) *The Indian and the White Man*. New York: New York University Press.

Weatherford, Jack (1988) *Indian Givers*. New York: Fawcett/Columbine.

10

THE ANTI-REFLEXIVIST REVOLUTION: ON THE AFFIRMATIONISM OF THE NEW RIGHT

Göran Dahl

According to many, indeed too many to mention, the world has gone wrong. Suffering, discontents, protest and critique go hand in hand with the everyday-life acceptance of taking care, getting enough money, etc. But during the last decade we have seen the return of a furious attack on the all too 'Western' character of the West. This attack comes from a 'new right' which deploys many ideas once formulated in Weimar Germany, often labelled as the 'conservative revolution'. Most explicitly, this attack, or counter-movement, is present in France and Germany. Here I want to make an attempt to grasp the 'meta-political' sources in this kind of political thinking, the personal affects and experiences that drive people to a new radical right. I have focused on what seems to be the central feature: the fear of, and turning against, reflexivity, which may end in a pathological hyperreflexivity. By doing this, I think I also clarify one more reason why the ideas of the new right might attract more and more people. I also want to demonstrate some connections between 'conservative revolution', 'technocratic conservatism', radical conservatism and the new right, and how the critique of reflexivity can be found in many separate discourses: political thinking, theology and psychiatry. The connection is the stress on anti-reflexivity, which makes visible that all of these traditions of thought together constitute a strong critique of modernity. First of all, I have to give a preliminary definition of 'reflexivity' and 'anti-reflexivity' since their meanings can differ.

Reflexivity and Anti-reflexivity

'Reflexivity', especially nowadays, can have different meanings, so let us go back to basics. George Herbert Mead (1947: 99) has a notion on 'delayed reaction', which I think covers the same area as I will do when talking about 'reflexivity'. It is worth quoting him in full:

> Our ideas of or about future conduct are our tendencies to act in several alternative ways in the presence of a given environmental situation. . . . Ideas, as

distinct from acts, or as failing to issue in overt behavior, are simply what we do not do; they are possibilities of overt responses which we test out implicitly in the central nervous system and then reject in favor of those which we do in fact act upon or carry into effect. . . . Intelligence is largely a matter of selectivity.

Delayed reaction is necessary to intelligent conduct. The organization, implicit testing, and final selection by the individual of his overt responses or reactions to the social situations which confront him and which present him with problems of adjustment, would be impossible if his overt responses or reactions could not in such situations be delayed until this process of organizing, implicitly testing, and finally selecting is carried out. (Mead, 1947: 99)

Thus, delayed reaction takes place in time, where the individual can make use of his or her social, cultural and normative competences. He or she can make judgements which can be rationally argued for, and also predict possible reactions to his or her actions and propositions.

To defend reflexivity is a classic intellectual strategy. However, this does not force us to deny and de-emphasize non-reflective activity. For example, the abilities of playing ball-games, having sex, etc. can be destroyed by reflection.[1] And if you suffer from insomnia problems, the worst you can do is to start thinking about them. Ecstasy belongs to the realm of life where thinking indeed plays a minor role. As long as we discuss individual matters, non-reflexive activity does not cause any problems. However, things look different when we move to the collective level.

On a collective social level there can also be reflexivity. According to many social theorists (Giddens, 1991; Beck, 1992; Lash, 1993) we now live in the second form of modernity where institutions (governments, corporations, etc.) have to take into account the effects of, and reactions to, their actions. So far so good. However, what really bothers me is *collective anti-reflexivity*. When, for example, the leading Russian rightist Aleksandr Dugin (1992) talks about the 'collective unconscious',[2] where the collective includes only its own *ethnos*, he wants to replace modern, individual reflexivity with an irrational pre-cognitive sense of belonging to a nation. Not reflexivity, but pure reflex is the goal, when Russians are supposed to form an 'organic democracy', that is a functioning body where the brain works without reflexion. The large mass is asked to give up subjective identities and rational capacities. When the nation or the state demands something, there is no room for delayed responses, since these entities should be sacred, that is beyond reflection. There is also the imperative of not missing the chances of the moment, a moment that will perhaps never appear again. This is probably one of the strongest causes for Heidegger's affiliation with the Nazis. Hitler was a revelation. A 'no' to him could mean that the moment could be lost (Safranski, 1994). More on this later. I now turn to Nietzsche, whose conception of reflexivity is so sophisticated that it has been used and interpreted in the totally contrary direction.

Nietzsche and Reflexivity

In any context discussing reflexivity and the critique of it, it is impossible to avoid Freidrich Nietzsche.[3] Nietzsche is often ambivalent, and can be interpreted in opposite ways. However, I think that it is most correct to place him among those who defend reflexivity, although he often discusses the necessity of non-reflective ecstasy. In *Twilight of the Idols* (1983b: 93f.), he criticizes liberal institutions as being decadent, precisely for the reason that they lack reflexivity; they are institutionalized and reified to the extent that they fly above any reflexivity. Modern men, for Nietzsche, live too lightly, instead of too heavily. Thus he laments: 'one lives for today, one lives very fast, one lives very irresponsibly: it is precisely this which one calls "freedom"' (1983b: 93f.). The same could also be said when Nietzsche criticizes 'faith' in moralists, priests and philosophers. Nietzsche apparently treated 'conscious hypocrites' as higher sort of men than 'believers', per-haps because the former still indulge in reflexivity (1983b: 96). Nietzsche's 'perspectivism' has been given a good description by Antonio: 'It chal-lenges reifications, clarifies the limits of rationality, opens multiple realities to view, and enchances particularity' (1995: 18). Nietzsche also dislikes 'fast' readings, and pleads for 'slow' readings, since these give us a chance to understand better and reflect more. To sum up, Nietzsche's vision was the wise *and* happy sovereign individual.

As for his rightist readers, and there were a lot of them, they became interested because they experienced nihilism very strongly, and thought that Nietzsche could offer a solution. Thus, they never saw his plea for true individuality, only the fascination for the non-reflective, turned this into a plea for ecstatism and combined it with Nietzsche's critique of the bourgeoisie and its love for the abstract.

Some authors have argued that there is an undertone of the cult of the Dionysian element in his whole authorship. For them, Nietzsche seems to appreciate the playfulness that only the mature Superman is capable of. This man has forgotten, in a literal sense, about seriousness and is able to create new values that are taken for given, not created though social-reflexive processes. Perhaps the most anti-reflexivist interpreter ever was Ludwig Klages (Klages, 1969; Fellman, 1993; Aschheim, 1994), who wanted to go back to a pre-modern natural stage where nothing was put in question, where man stood rooted in his soil with no reason for ques-tioning anything. For Klages, the origin of human consciousness was a result of disturbing original forms of life and sensations. As Aschheim puts it: 'Seele . . . represented the possibility of an authentically lived life – the overcoming of alienated intellectuality in favour of a new-found earthly rootedness' (1994: 80f.).[4]

To put it simply, for Nietzsche, 'intellectualism' was one of the most striking symptoms of the sickness of the modern world, a world where man is obsessed with exact observations, calculation, expectations, etc.[5] One point that Nietzsche seems to have is the inability of modern man to forget.

Let us start with his famous work on the *Zur Genealogie der Moral* (Nietzsche, 1924). Here, one of his main theses is that the basic distinction between good and evil is not given us by nature or god. Rather, man has to be taught it in a very cruel way. The distinction is forced upon man, for example, by whipping him so hard that he will not be able to forget it. This way it is incorporated, and in addition to his project to find a new culture 'beyond good and evil', Nietzsche also finds a terrorist aspect in memory. The noble person has been enslaved by the slaves, he is no longer able to answer with the spontaneous 'yes' to whatever he likes, while the 'no' comes from the slave morality, the 'evil' or bad (1924: §11). This inability results, for example, in a bad conscience. In short, it is bad to *life*, as Nietzsche writes in his *Untimely Meditations*:

> Thus: it is possible to live almost without memory, and to live happily moreover, as the animal demonstrates; but it is altogether impossible to *live* at all without forgetting. Or, to express my theme even more simply: *there is a degree of sleeplessness, of rumination, of the historical sense, which is harmful and ultimately fatal to the living thing, whether this living thing be a man or a people or a culture.* (Nietzsche, 1983a: 62)

To emphasize what Nietzsche seems to mean here results in a one-sided reading of him because he also defends the necessity to remember 'at the right time'. Although Nietzsche thus might be read as a balanced writer, emphasizing the need of both memory and forgetfulness, I think I am hardly exaggerating when I claim that his radical rightist readers tend to see more of the 'Dionysian' pole than the 'Apollonian'.[6] For example, in *Twilight of the Idols* he talks of being 'true to my nature, which is *affirmative* and has dealings with contradiction and criticism only indirectly' (Nietzsche, 1983b: 64). Here once again sophisticated, he is critical to the exaggerated seriousness and 'objectivity' of modern people. Thinking mechanically, reflecting too much forces man to repeat, creating nothing: '"We must take things more cheerfully than they deserve; especially since we have for a long time taken them more seriously than they deserve." – So speak brave soldiers of knowledge' (Nietzsche, 1983c: 227). Thus, it would be extremely hard to transform him into a defender of reflexive modernity. The path that Klages took seems to be a more reasonable option, from the intellectual anti-intellectualist point of view. Nietzsche is one of the founders of modern philosophy, and in what follows I locate some of his heirs in so far as they relate to the anti-reflexive affect. That is, the radical right that combines the anti-bourgeoisie effect and the critique of the homogenization of culture with anti-reflexivism, that is an attempt to create impulse-driven actions within a nationalist, mythic framework.

The *nouvelle droite* in France

In France, the 'new right' has been almost synonymous with the writer and editor Alain de Benoist. It is rather well known that he tries to apply Antonio Gramsci's sketch of the struggle of cultural hegemony to a rightist context. Obviously, the left was in certain aspects successful in doing this for their purposes. Of course, it did not conquer the political power, but nowadays it is quite dominating, at least if you believe what the new right says,[7] in the newspapers, television, the book market and what is still left of a 'public sphere'. The central concept in Benoist's discourse is 'culture'. He wants to restore the value of what he sees as lost, (Indo-)European, that is pre-Judaic-Christian culture. Culture is also the primal battlefield of hegemony. He wants to stop 'the reduction of all *cultures* (*Kulturen*) to a single "*world-civilization*" (*Weltzivilisation*)' (Benoist, 1985: 33). Thus, in his foregrounding of culture, its opposite, civilization, is also hinted at. Of course, these concepts are used in their classical German conservative sense. Culture stands for spiritual growth, civilization for materialism, atomism, individualism and economism, and, particularly important in this context, for hyperintellectualism. For the new right in France, universities and schools are seen as factories, where people learn a lot, but forget why they should. This leads to a paralysation of thinking: 'I know people that have learnt so much that it makes them unable to write anything. . . . Today, one has doubt. And more important, one has anxiety over doing the wrong thing' (Benoist, 1985: 31). Instead of bringing order to the world, intellectualization leads to an inner chaos where nothing is possible. The domination of economy, regarded as 'the base' in both liberalism and Marxism, strengthens this tendency since it is the best example of reflexivity: calculations, expectations, etc. Benoist's *nouvelle droite* differs from the 'old' right: 'Between the true right and the economist right, writes Julius Evola, there is no identity, rather a total contrast' (Benoist, 1985: 143). The saviour is culture, and the over-civilized culture has to be brought back home to its roots, to the popular culture of a homogenized territory. Reflexivity means reduction, one sees only the abstract, general side in a world of differences. It is hard, if not impossible, to reflect upon the unique and concrete, that which just 'is' and nothing more. Hence, Benoist pleas for 'ethnopluralism' against 'world-civilization', a world where each 'culture' (ethnic, religious, racial, etc. belonging) has the right to develop in its safe territory.[8] Since 'culture' is the centre of everything, it is in this place that he anchors his form of concrete, radical conservatism.

This strategy, 'cultural struggle', has been politically realized in Austria, where the leader of the ultra-nationalist Freiheitlische Partei Österreichs, Jörg Haider, has written a whole book on it (Haider, 1994). It is striking how central 'culture', as a point of reference and orientation, has become during the last decades. Maybe Fukuyama (1992) is right in one respect, namely the victory of capitalism. Even in 'socialist' countries like Vietnam and China the economy is basically capitalist. In the Western world, social democracy is busy cutting down welfare costs in order to make the capitalist economy run more smoothly. Even if the class society has not disappeared, at least it has been redefined.

Sociology has not only described, but also been part of this process. Pierre Bourdieu (1988), for example, has put down a tremendous work in order to show how style, taste and consumption are signs and creators of class differences. The most frequent example is Gerhard Schulze's (1993) concept of the 'Erlebnisgesellschaft', a society where everyone hunts new sensations, illusions, play, etc. He dates the birth of this society back to 1968 when cultural features like the length of the hair, musical taste, etc. came into the foreground due to the end of scarcity in the Western world and the rise of mass consumption. It now seemed like not power and economic wealth, but taste was what made people differ from each other. I say 'seemed' because the change was due to a new sensibility to aesthetic matters.

Even if sociology, like every discourse, has a constructive, practical aspect, this description of course also represents something real. During the Cold War and the happy days of the welfare state project, the role of economy as generating action and identity was over-emphasized, and the ideological dimensions of the political turbulence of the late 1960s also. Thus, aesthetic and cultural aspects were almost hidden. But as soon as 'culture' turns a central point of orientation they become visible, of course, and we run the opposite risk if social and political aspects are viewed as expressions of culture. I am not critizing Bourdieu's and Schulze's different approaches here; on the contrary, especially Schulze's work is illuminating in many respects.

Schulze, a German sociologist, takes Ulrich Beck's (1992) thesis on 'individualization' as given. That is, a post-industrial condition where individuals have to construct their own biographies without being able to use social norms which could give rise to a self-evident identity. Less and less is 'given' or transmitted from the social and historical context. However, Schulze shows that this does not mean the end of the social – new communities, groups and contexts are formed due to similarities in taste. New forms of competition might then occur where the goal is not primarily to secure political or economic interests, but the hegemony of a definition of what kind of taste, which sensations and what consumption can satisfy the aesthetic needs.

On the one hand, therefore, Schulze might be blinded by the culturalist light, and on the other hand, he might be describing new central processes in society. In this context, he is interesting because he obviously dislikes what he sees. Individualization does not only mean freedom, but also the burden of living without self-evidence. There is too much contingency and so individuals have to reflect too much, worry too much about themselves. He thinks that a revival of cyclical time might help here, that is, we can take what was given yesterday as still valid today, recognize repetition instead of hunting for the new.[9] Reflexivity is part of the problem, not the solution.

The New Culturalism

This process of culturalism has been strengthened by recent developments. The waves of immigration resulting in large ethnic minorities in most

European countries have given rise to the problem of difference and the 'need' for understanding and translation.[10] The media, the legal system, and what is left of the public sphere have defined the problem as 'multi-culturalism', the fact that there exists many different ethnic groups in the same places and at the same time. This condition is defined as the coexistence of different 'cultures', and culturalism includes the reduction of the individual to a member of a specific collective. In this way, the dialectical processes remain hidden.

When people immigrate from different countries, it is, of course, easiest to get in contact with those who speak the same language and have a similar habitus. Due to structural facts and prejudices resulting in high degrees of unemployment and poverty, they start identifying with each other. This identification is strengthened by legislation and education, and so they become defined as specific 'minorities' identified by an essential characteristic construct: their shared 'culture'. The fact that it is almost impossible to change anything on an individual level also makes people from the same 'culture' stick to each other. Of course, this development has been most visible in the USA – the step from wanting 'civil rights' to 'black power', from individual equality to the rights of a collective.

The claims from different minorities in the USA – gays, lesbians, blacks, women, Hispanics, etc. – are often summed up as 'identity politics'. After Marxism, which reduced the individual to a member of a class, a new reductionism appeared, in order to appoint him or her a member of a minority collective. Since Marxism had almost nothing to say about the effects of racism and sexism, deeply felt by their victims, people gathered in the new social movements to change an oppressive reality.

Identity politics paradoxically embraces both relativism and foundationalism at the same time. There are different truths for each minority, but as a member of a specific group or minority, one has privileged access to its criterias of truth. Thus, only as a member can one know the history of oppression and the refusal of what one regards as equal rights. What we see here is cultural relativism in new clothes. Not only the postmodernists, but also the European new right influence the development of identity politics.

From postmodernism come the ideas of the death of 'the grand meta-narratives' and the abandoning of the idea of a permanent and homogeneous subject. Postmodernism has also advocated a 'standpoint epistemology', that is criterias of 'truth' depend on what group you belong to. Even a sensible philosopher like Richard Rorty belongs to this group here: 'To be ethnocentric is to divide the human race into the people to whom one must justify one's belief and the others. The first group – one's *ethnos* – comprises those who share enough of one's belief to make fruitful conversation possible' (Rorty, 1991: 30). Such arguments are used both by minority groups and radical conservatives, a truly anti-liberal argument.

From radical conservatism comes the emphasis on the fundamental differences between 'cultures' and the impossibility of translation and the non-desirability of a mixed 'world-civilization'. The more difference is observed and constructed, the more fertile becomes the soil for radical conservative ideas, with their longing for separation of the different 'cultures'. From both postmodernism and radical conservatism comes what Walter Benjamin called the 'aesthetization of politics', of turning politics into a matter of beauty, disregarding rational discourses on freedom, solidarity and justice. Fascination thus becomes more important than rational judgements.

Technocratic Conservatism

The critique of reflexivity and the call for a more authentic culture can be found in many discourses, and I now turn to 'technocratic conservatism', which refers to the standpoints that three former radical conservatives – Arnold Gehlen, Helmut Schelsky and Hans Freyer – developed after the last World War. Their conservatism was 'deradicalized' (Muller, 1987), that is, they no longer saw any radical utopias and alternatives to a modern, differentiated and complex society. In this context, technocratic conservatism is interesting, since it thought that reflexivity was a burden, and that contemporary society had already 'solved' this problem. The solution was that modern institutions had institutionalized the necessary minimum of reflexivity so that ordinary people did not have to bother about complex matters.

In his postwar works, Arnold Gehlen stresses that the unsecure, unstable human being needs institutions to secure him or her from the dangers of reflexivity. Institutions at the same time alienate and release people, but alienation is not only negative, it is also positive objectification, which creates a distance to too much reflection. When one asks for 'meaning' something is already false (Terkessidis, 1995: 26f.), so this way people are freed from the eternal asking and having troubles.

In a famous broadcast discussion from 1965, Gehlen and Adorno discussed the subject 'Is sociology a science of human beings?' (Adorno and Gehlen, 1975). Adorno's arguments makes Gehlen's sociology more visible. One dominant, underlying theme is the rise of modern institutions and the problem of reification. Their different ideas are condensed in a short passage:

> *Gehlen*: Mr. Adorno, you see the problem of emancipation (*Mündigkeit*) here once again, of course. Do you really believe that the burden of fundamental problems, of extensive reflection, of errors in life that have profound and continuing effects, all of which we have gone through because we were trying to swim free of them – do you really believe one ought to expect everyone to go through this? I should be very interested to know your views on this.
>
> *Adorno*: I can give you a simple answer: Yes! I have a particular conception of objective happiness and objective despair, and I would say that, for as long as people have problems taken away from them, for as long as they are not

expected to take full responsibility and full self-determination, their welfare and happiness in this world will merely be an illusion. And it will be an illusion that will one day burst. And when it bursts, it will have dreadful consequences. (Safranski, 1998: 407–8)

While Adorno stresses his utopia of the possibility for mankind to take back the authority it has built into the institutions, Gehlen sees no problem here. The institutions protect man from worrying too much about the basic conditions and reproduction of his existence. 'I also think that the institutions protect man from himself. Surely this means a reduction of freedom' (Gehlen, in Adorno and Gehlen, 1975: 245). One conclusion Gehlen draws from this is that we should let the institutions ('secondary systems') think and worry, so that man only has to worry about that which is less problematic. Therefore, he has no utopia, like Adorno, of modern man as an enlightened and reflective person. On the contrary, when Gehlen observes modern reflexivity, he calls it 'the new subjectivism' (Gehlen, 1980). This means an obsession with inner life, which is talked about and discussed in a disciplined manner, where there is a 'relative lack of direct, naive, general emotionality' (Gehlen, 1980: 78). This is bad since it leads to a pathological 'overreflectiveness'.

In Freyer's and Schelsky's 'de-radicalized' postwar writings we find very similar themes and diagnoses. Of course, there are also differences, but in this context I choose to ignore them. For example, in Hans Freyer's work *Theorie des gegenwärtigen Zeitalters* from 1955, he writes that 'Der Mensch wird den Institutionen willig gemacht und ihnen angepaßt' ('man adapts to the institutions and accepts them'; Freyer, 1955: 89). Human beings are determined and created according to their functions and relations within the systems. Of course, this means alienation, but Freyer sees no problem with the system, the problem is if people do not adapt to the system.

So, for technocratic conservatism, we have self-reproducing systems that people have to learn to adapt to. History is no more. Instead, we now live in 'posthistory' (de Man, 1951; Gehlen, 1980; Jung, 1989). Nothing new that will surprise us will appear. Everything genuinely new has already been or happened. 'New developments, surprises, and genuine creativity are all still possible, but only within the area already staked out and only on the basis of the already given fundamental premises, which are no longer called into question' (Gehlen, 1987: 226). This also has implications for sociology: the mission to perform a 'diagnosis of the times' is no longer possible (Lichtblau, 1995). Finally, utopian thought is dead, and everyday man may resign and relax as everyday life goes on and on.

Technocratic conservatism was shocked by the student revolt in 1968. Schelsky (1975) accused the intellectuals of poisoning society, creating a new dividing line between intellectuals and work. Today, his diagnosis is echoed when 'the age of the elites' (Lasch, 1995) or 'the political class' is discussed.

The technocratic conservatives were, as I said, 'deradicalized' and cannot be blamed for having supported anti-democracy. Rather, they had no illusions on the possibility of a participatory democracy.[11] Only the elite-

governed society could defend freedom. Thus, one can count them among
'The Macchiavellians' (Burnham, 1943), to whom we can perhaps even add
Francis Fukuyama today.

Protofascism and the Conservative Revolution

The anti-reflexiveness of technocratic conservatism was something that,
even if it marked a deradicalization, was kept from the 'conservative
revolution', to which we can at least count the interwar Freyer. According
to Terkessidis (1995: 169), Ernst Jünger in the 1920s lamented that 'we' are
too 'ramosed', therefore 'the sap does not rise any longer into the tops'.

As always, Jünger's metaphors are interesting. Here, humankind, or
rather, the people, is like a tree. A tree has its roots (the favourite conservative metaphor) in the ground. However, the tree can be too ramosed.
In that case, the gardener (Jünger himself, social engineers, leaders) has to
prune it (a modernist view). The people should not bother too much,
instead the observer/leader takes care of that.

Just like the technocrat conservatives, Jünger says 'Yes' to reification
(Heidegren, 1995). What else would there be to choose from? What can be
done is to accept the historical development, not change it, but accelerate
it. Jünger loves actions and deed, these need no legitimation or reflection,
they are ends in themselves.

This aspect of Jünger's writings is most obvious in his proto-fascist works
from the 1920s. In the Weimar Republic Jünger did not feel at home. He did
not feel alive. Only feeling 'pain' (Jünger, 1995) made one feel alive.
Dostoevsky (1985) had the same point: only when one suffers from pain can
one feel human and know the 'being-there' (Bohatec, 1951: 269ff.). Suffering
is holy and magnificent since it brings us very close to life itself.

Nothing new or exciting was happening. A total mobilization was
already going on. The only problem was to get the proper 'banner', and
here the pilot or the photographer are the ideals. Getting the right 'banner'
requires that people are similar and can base a solidarity on this similarity,
that is, the similarity has to be obvious and clear to avoid reflection and
useless discussions.

Schmittian Radical Conservatism

There are striking similarities between Jünger's proto-fascist ideas and
those of his friend, Carl Schmitt. However, Schmitt tries to find a solution
by reading philosophy. Of most interest here is his work on, and
interpretation of Thomas Hobbes's main work, *Leviathan*.

Schmitt, the admirer of order, is extremely afraid of chaos, the state of
nature which, according to Hobbes, is the primal human condition. Therefore, there must be order, but, several hundred years after Hobbes: how?
The state must be the ordering principle. That is, of course, Schmitt's
answer. As Terkessidis (1995) has pointed out, the demand for order is

caused by the fear of chaos. Chaos is, of course, that state of nature where, according to Hobbes, everyone fights each other. Just like in Hobbes, Schmitt calls for the state to prevent this. The state is there to fill a void, something that is, like God, beyond questioning. But 1789, after Hobbes, marked the rise of reflexivity, institutionalized in the parliament. Therefore, Schmitt is against parliamentary democracy which settles discussions and compromises as norms. The task, according to Schmitt, is to construct and build a new state which is the organic expression of a people, and thus cannot be called into question. The state becomes the mythological and quasi-religious equivalent of the people. But it depends on a people as an organic community. This community can exist only if two premises are at hand: (1) a homogenized people, since then there are no reasons for different opinions, parties, interests; and (2) a negative, an enemy, must exist since we only can understand ourselves in relation to this Otherness. The first premise rests upon the will to define the essence of one's own people and to declare minorities as strange, or enemies. Here, Schmitt is a romanticist, postulating *volkisch* essences.

Schmitt's central distinction between friend and enemy as the central dimension in politics is famous. We can only know ourselves through the enemy, he says. The enemy has two dimensions. First, the general political dimension, which leads to cultural relativism, people standing against other people, and no universal principles at hand in order to judge which are right. The second, geopolitical dimension is Schmitt's concrete enemy, above all England, the Jews[12] and the USA. These enemies advocate 'universalism', which, according to Schmitt, means an ideological transformation of a particular interest into an absolute claim. Instead, every nation is, in its own eyes, superior to the other nation. Thus, each state should protect its own interests (its particular culture), and thus by definition has the right to exert influence in the surrounding territories, that is, to protect its *Großraum* (Schmitt, 1981).

Schmitt advocates 'concrete' analyses and finds that modern power and authority, society as a whole, is abstract. Even the state and the nation become abstract if they do not know where to go. Who are 'we' then? According to Schmitt, only 'the enemy' can provide such an answer. Then the state is determinated in a relationship. If we know whom we might fear, we can know what they fear of us, and during this exchange we can get to see ourselves. To recognize the enemy also means to recognize the possibility of war. In such a light, different kinds of 'peace projects', such as the UN and the EU, become suspect. When in the name of peace they attack Iraq, this was 'the first pacifist war' (Maschke, 1991). War can be in the service of peace only by taking refuse in the principle of 'humanity'. Then, according to Maschke, the enemy becomes a criminal, able to punish in a court, and not a brother with equal rights.

Schmitt and Schmittians have a point here, at the same time as they are totally crazy. Their point is that ideals like 'humanity' might conceal something more fundamental. But they do not escape from the dangers of fundamentalism this way. Logically, the state as they see it can only be based on similarity, and the 'different' is the enemy. The step to xenophobia and exclusion is obviously anything but gigantic.

A Schmittian slogan could be 'liberate the state!' The state should not be subordinated to ideals, the parliament, etc. No, it should incarnate the feelings – the language, culture and habits – of the people who live in the territory controlled by it. Reflexive intellectuality can, of course, exterminate these affects and feelings of organic communities.

Radical conservatives are, as many have pointed out, modernists.[13] Unlike the old conservatives, they say 'yes' to modern technology and efficiency. But they also differ from other modernist camps when they do not want to say 'yes' to reflexivity. Instead, they dream of a modernized illusion, the possibility that something – the nation and/or the state – just can 'be', exercising its power without being questioned. The new rightists do not seem to think that when God is dead, everything is permitted. Rather, nothing is possible (Benoist, 1985: 32). There must be an 'it is', a foundation. This foundation is not based on normativity, or transcendental criterias. 'It' is pure power and strength. It has not to be reflected upon, for if that happens it becomes clear that 'it' is nothing. It is real, as long as it stays (to use Jaques Lacan's concepts) real and imaginary.[14]

The rightists are close to the communitarian standpoint here: 'freedom' is nothing that can exist 'outside' communities (Kaltenbrunner, 1985: 71); freedom is the freedom to belong to something. The new and young conservatives are of the same opinion. Like the old ones, they practise political existentialism. For example, Roland Bubik (1995) mentions a fugue composed by Bach as a model for real freedom. The fugue has a strict structure and strict rules. However, within this frame the composer is free, and can therefore create real beauty.

Of course, I must make a small reservation here. There are communitarians and communitarians, and some of them regard themselves as leftists. These believe that communication is possible between cultures and communities – as opposed to what Rorty said above. Not only pure communication but also, for example, empathy might relate people to each other. Leftist communitarians also see the small community as the right place for the fundamental rights of citizens to develop (Ehnmark, 1994: 61f.). However, I would argue, in the European context right-wing communitarianism dominates.

The belonging to a community marks in what direction freedom can move. For example, 'The Nation' is a latent strong force, able to (bind) individuals together, making them members of an imaginary community. As Erich Fromm (1941) has written, there are two kinds of freedom: negative and positive. The negative one is the 'freedom from', that is freedom from slavery or injustice, while positive freedom is the freedom to create and develop. In this terminology, the radical conservatives do not plead for negative freedom, but for freedom from negative freedom, if positive freedom is to be realized.

Sacrifice

Another feature that can be related to the critique of reflexivity is the willingness to sacrifice something. The reason for this connection is of course the celebration of individual freedom in liberalism. In its most extreme form, liberalism wants the individual to have full sovereignty to do whatever he or she prefers. Even a social liberal like John Rawls (1971) stresses that nobody should be forced to sacrifice anything, even if the majority would benefit from the sacrifice. The strongest reaction against having to sacrifice anything, comes, according to Lasch (1995: 41), from the new class of cosmopolitans. These people do not belong to any community or nation, only to themselves. This is one important point in the communitarian critique of liberalism. A community rests on the willingness of the individuals to acknowledge its positive value, in other words, that freedom and the good demand the superiority of the community – while individual autonomy and self-preservation are subordinated values.

Although apologetical, Wolfgang Palaver (1995) has demonstrated that communitarianism and Carl Schmitt take similar standpoints here. The most obvious point in the critique of liberalism is the case of marriage and love – how can a marriage be possible without sacrifice? Undeniably, communitarianism has made clear some blind spots in liberal self-understanding, which is not to say that its own alternative would be without its own blind spots.

Anyway, there are clear parallels to Schmitt's thinking, and I think that Palaver is quite right to argue that 'Schmitt's critique of liberalism focuses on its anti-sacrificial attitude' (1995: 53). The state is everything for Schmitt, it is for the state that the individuals must sacrifice. This is necessary since a strong state with control of its territory needs an enemy. Without this prerequisite the end of politics is near, a pacified one-world civilization. And the end of politics also means the end of a meaningful life since a privileged relation between existence and politics is postulated (Schmitt, 1963).

Just like many communitarians, Schmitt's standpoint includes theological matters. As a Catholic, he despises Protestantism since it is the theological equivalent of economic and political liberalism. We could also add that Protestantism includes a more reflexive relation between the individual and God.

However, the most advanced discussion of sacrifice in a theological context is found in the works by René Girard. In his theory of mimetic sociability (Girard, 1977), he argues that the root of social cohesion in primitive societies stems from the scapegoat mechanism. When a tribe kills an outsider everything that happens after is comprehended as a result of the killing of a scapegoat and he is then worshipped as a god. This is the way the sacred is constituted, according to Girard. It is interesting to note that Emile Durkheim (1965) defines 'the sacred' as that which just 'is' and beyond reflection, while 'the profane' is that which can be reflected upon. The sacrifice in pre-Christian-Judaic religions was the killing of a human being and a sacred act. However, Judaism became the first religion not to sacrifice human beings, which could be another reason for Schmitt's anti-Semitism.[15] This move does not mean the end of sacrifice and the basic social bond, according to Girard. He claims that in the Bible there is a more human form for sacrifice than the killing of the scapegoat – the willingness to sacrifice one's own life in order to save the life of another person.

But today we find writers who recognize the primitive form of sacrifice as the only act that creates stable social cohesion. The first writer I am thinking of is Botho Strauss. In a famous essay (Strauss, 1993), he argues that the killing of foreigners is a degenerated form of the basic sacrifice. He criticizes modernity for having destroyed the memory of the past and mythical time. As Herzinger and Stein (1994: 200) show, in the end this means that if we do not want civil war, we have to accept blood sacrifice – an alarming sign of the times we live in, indeed. This form of critique of modernity and the Judaic–Christian civilization is also the reason for Benoist's (1982) paganism.

To sum up, I am not discussing whether there is real need for some kind of sacrifice in modern society. I have just wanted to demonstrate how the critique of reflexivity is connected to this issue. Sacrifice is beyond reflection, and means obeying God, law or community, it is not to be hindered by 'delayed reaction'. Reflection might lead to critical questions about the necessity of sacrifice. Therefore, some tendencies in society today might very well lead to a stronger anti-reflexive affect.

Pathological Hypermodernism and Hyperreflexivity

It is tempting to say 'yes' to radical conservatism – the quest for naïveté, innocence, creativity. There seems to be too much of intellect and reflexivity around. We might want to go back to an imaginary point where there is no reason to ask questions, but the price we would have to pay for this might be too high.

However, there are not only political and theological critiques of reflexivity. Even from psychiatry there comes a critique. In Louis A. Sass's work *Madness and Modernism* (1992), the author sees a clear parallel between social modernity, aesthetic modernism and schizophrenia. The strong dualism characterizing these phenomena, for example, between omnipotence and total passivity, can be traced back to Immanuel Kant who introduced a sort of doubling of consciousness (Sass, 1992: ch. 11). Here, consciousness is, on the one hand, everything, it constitutes the world, but it is also an object determined by, for example, the mechanism of cause and effect. This is an indicator of the widening rift between intellect and emotion. I do not want to make a long story too short, but Sass obviously sees modernity as a condition bred of too much reflection, or 'hyperreflection'. As I understand Sass, modernity is a cul-de-sac, where reflexivity only creates more and more reflexivity, thus deepening the rift between the two poles. Sass is no social critic, and has little to say about the cure, but of course modernity is a dead end, and authors like Heidegger and Wittgenstein can give clues to a possible answer since they look for a world before the existence of the dualistic consciousness, which might lead to the end of a homeless mind.

If Sass has no answer, another explorer of the human psyche, Rollo May (1991), has one simple and strong answer: back to the myths! In a demythologized world which in itself, according to May, leads to an increase in drug abuse and suicides, the only thing that can save man is the myth – myths of the meaning of life, its goal and origin. If reflected upon, they are destroyed. In certain ways, this is a wish to return to something lost, if not paradise, so at least to pre-modern patterns of thought, an attempt to escape 'the terror of history' (Eliade, 1974), in which man will find nothing but his historical existence, nothing mythological or eternal. This is also roughly in line with Schulze's 'cure' (see above): the revival of cyclical time.

Life-World or System?

Is there a life-world, that is a place for mutual understanding, questions and reflection? Of course, but does society need it in order to function? This is the central question in the controversy between the two giants of contemporary German sociology: Niklas Luhmann and Jürgen Habermas. As I see it, the similarities with the Adorno–Gehlen debate are striking. Gehlen and Luhmann share a truly anti-utopian attitude, while the opposite is true for Adorno and Habermas.

Adorno's 'negative dialectics' is, even if his main philosophical postwar work bears this title, not purely negative. He wants to keep the faith alive that everyday man can take responsibility for his own life. Habermas wants to see possibilities in the life-world to create new political arenas, making a democratization of what is now controlled by the system possible.

While Gehlen holds this for something negative, Luhmann does not understand how it can be relevant for sociology. The study of society, according to him, deals with the functioning of social systems and sub-systems. Among other mechanisms there is the 'reduction of complexity' (Luhmann, 1975), which transforms complex matters and problems into manageable problems. It works on a purely societal system-level, and has nothing to do with 'understanding' on a general level. The individual as a social being has no possibilities to reflect upon the whole. But this is Habermas's (and Adorno's) hope. Therefore, Habermas must place the life-world within sociological discourse, calling for a 'second modernity' that will secure the life-world from colonization and irrationalism. Whether Luhmann or Habermas is 'right' is an empirical question, I just wanted to note that the defence and rejection of subjective and intersubjective reflexivity constitutes a battle that has a long history and is still alive.

There truly seems to be a 'fascination of amorality' among many sociologists today, as Neckel and Wolff (1994) labelled the growing interest in Luhmann's works today. What works, not what is right, should be the object of contemporary sociology. This calls for observation and analysis, not so much for subjective or intersubjective reflection.

Conclusion

Thus, scepticism against widespread, individual reflexivity can be found in many camps. Most of us sometimes hate lack of spontaneity, inability to be more authentic and true to ourselves and complain of lacking a safe foundation. There seems only to be reflection upon reflection. My main point here has been to demonstrate that it is the new right who have described the problem and suggested a solution to it, and due to what I just said, there is a great potential for the new right to attract more people than it currently does.

The critique of reflexivity is as old as the recognition of its existence in modern Western thought. Saying this, and doing what I have done, that is, locating formations of thought where this criticism has been conceptualized, is rather easily done. More complicated questions are: (1) to ask what kind of social processes, developments and situations will favour this critique; (2) to discuss what results this will have.

1 The ethnification and culturalization of society might awake the longing for more 'organic' communities where the burden of reflection is annihilated. More is taken as given, having a 'sacred' nature.
2 Spontaneity might be institutionalized in post-industrial economic corporations where the need for new ideas is acute.

There *is* certainly a longing for the sacred, the 'it is'. But is it possible today to create a sacred 'state'? I think the chances are relatively small; rather, the market can provide sacred products – the identity industry, identity movements, new pseudo-sacred sects and churches, etc. Indeed, the modern world has turned into an inner world, where people go hunting solutions to their own life traumas. The public sphere has become fragmented and mediated by strange modes of communication where face-to-face inter-action and communication become obsolete (Sennett, 1978). But we have learned from history that such prophecies, whose function it is to give us security, might be radically false.[16]

Notes

The author wants to thank especially Robert Antonio, who once again gave me invaluable help. My gratitude also goes to Carl-Göran Heidegren, Adam Holm, Kang Chao, Ulf Lindberg and Frederik Stjernfelt for their very important comments.

1 Perhaps the best example of this is the Monty Python sketch where Germany meets Greece in a soccer game. Since the players are Hegel, Kant, Marx, Socrates, Plato, etc. there is a lot of thinking during the game, but very little ball-shooting.

2 This term stems from Carl Gustav Jung, who claimed that every *Volk* had its specific 'collective unconscious'. Thus he distinguished between the Aryan and Jewish dito. See *Res Publica*, 21 (1992) issue on 'Jung and Nazism'.

3 Talks and correspondence with Robert Antonio and Kang Chao helped me understand Nietzsche much better.

4 As Aschheim (1994) points out, C.G. Jung has a very similar interpretation of Nietzsche here.

5 See 'Our knowledge will take its revenge on us, just as ignorance exacted its revenge during the Middle Ages' (Nietzsche, quoted in Sass, 1992: 324).

6 The so called 'Asconians', that is the anarchists, libertarians, feminists, etc., united in the dance, at Monte Veritas in Ascona, Switzerland, during the first two decades of this century, can be regarded as true Dionysian Nietzscheans (see Green, 1986). On the rightist readings of Nietzsche, and how they had to transform him, see Aschheim, 1995.

7 I do not discuss the correctness of this proposition here, it is probably an exaggeration from the new right. However, I think that there is at least some truth in it: many of the former '68-leftists nowadays have important positions, especially in the mass media and at the universities. I can draw on my own experience. As a 'post-68', a younger person, I have experienced censorship and authoritarian 'knowing-better' exercised by this older generation.

8 In the end, de Benoist is a metaphysical fundamentalist: 'The Fatherland is the territory of a people and the land of its fathers. The people (*Volk*) is no abstract concept, the Fatherland no philosophical school. They are concrete realities' (1985: 75).

9 See the Marxist form of cultural criticism in the 1970s. For example Krovoza (1976) argues that there are limits to the capital logic of production (cumulative types of processes) and the reproduction of human beings, that is socialization, which represents non-cumulative types of process; Negt and Kluge (1974) argue for the necessity of pre-economic, social human beings capable to produce 'the emancipatory minimum'.

10 The need for 'understanding' and 'translation' is not 'out there'. The most recent example of this is the creation and separation of one language (Serbocroatian) into three (Serbian, Croatian and Bosnian) in the former Yugoslavia.

11 See the discussions on democracy, participation and elites between John Dewey and Walter Lippman (Westbrook, 1991).

12 In the original 1941 edition of *Land und Meer*, Schmitt's anti-Semitism is obvious. However, in the 1981 edition these passages are gone, without any mentioning of the omissions.

13 The first more well-known works to make this point were probably Herf (1980) and Bohrer (1978).

14 In a sense it is a matter of preventing a symbolic mediation. If so, it becomes possible to connect being and institution, to link the question of individual freedom to what the state can do. On these three concepts, see Lacan (1966).

15 This shows that anti-Semitism cannot only have emotional, but also intellectual reasons.

16 According to Max Weber (1964: 155) prophecies belong to the religious sphere, and the modern, scientific man should 'bear the fate of the times like a man'.

References

Adorno, Theodor W. and Gehlen, Arnold (1975) 'Ist die Soziologie eine Wissenschaft vom Menschen?', in Friedemann Grenz (ed.), *Adornos Philosophie in Grundbegriffen*. Frankfurt: Suhrkamp. pp. 225–51.

Antonio, Robert (1995) 'Nietzsche's antisociology: subjectified culture and the end of history', *American Journal of Sociology*, 101: 1–43.

Aschheim, Steven (1994) *The Nietzsche Legacy in Germany 1890–1990*. Berkeley, CA: University of California Press.

Aschheim, Steven (1995) 'Nietzsche and the German Radical Right 1914–1933'. Unpublished paper.

Beck, Ulrich (1992) *Risk Society*. London: Sage.

Benoist, Alain de (1982) *Heide-Sein*. Tübingen: Grabert.

Benoist, Alain de (1985) *Kulturrevolution von Rechts*. Krefeld: Sinus.

Bohatec, Josef (1951) *Der Imperialismusgedanke und die Lebensphilophie Dostojewskijs*. Graz/ Cologne: Herman Böhlam.

Bohrer, Karl Heinz (1978) *Die Ästhetik des Schreckens*. München: Carl Hanser Verlag.

Bourdieu, Pierre (1988) *Homo Academicus*. Cambridge: Polity Press.

Bubik, Roland (ed.) (1995) *Wir 89'er*. Frankfurt/Berlin: Ullstein.

Burnham, James (1943) *The Macchiavallians: Defenders of Freedom*. Chicago: Henry Regnery.

Dostoevsky, Fjodor (1985) *Anteckningar från källarhålet*. Stockholm: Atlantis.

Dugin, Aleksandr (1992) '"Organic" democracy prescribed for Russia', *Nash sovremennik*, 10: 139–47 (translated in *Current Digest of the Post-Soviet Press* 24 February 1993).

Durkheim, Emile (1965) *The Elementary Forms of Religious Life*. New York: Free Press.

Ehnmark, Anders (1994) *Den döda vinkeln*. Stockholm: Utbildningsförlaget Brevskolan.

Eliade, Mircea (1974) *The Myth of the Eternal Return*. Princeton, NJ: Princeton University Press.

Fellman, Ferdinand (1993) *Lebensphilosophie*. Reinbek bei Hamburg: Rowohlt.

Freyer, Hans (1955) *Theorie des gegenwärtigen Zeitalters*. Stuttgart: Deutsche Verlagsanstalt.

Fromm, Erich (1941) *Escape from Freedom*. New York: Holt, Rinehart & Winston.

Fukuyama, Francis (1992) *The End of History and the Last Man*. New York: Free Press.

Gehlen, Arnold (1980) *Man in the Age of Technology*. New York: Columbia University Press.

Gehlen, Arnold (1987) 'The crystallization of social forms', in V. Meja, D. Misgeld and N. Stehr (eds), *Modern German Sociology*. New York: Columbia University Press. pp. 218–31.

Giddens, Anthony (1991) *Modernity and Self-identity*. Cambridge: Polity Press.

Girard, René (1977) *Violence and the Sacred*. Baltimore, MD: Johns Hopkins University Press.

Green, Martin (1986) *Mountain of Truth*. Hanover, MA: University Press of New England.

Haider, Jörg (1994) *Die Freiheit, die ich meine*. Frankfurt/Berlin: Ullstein.

Heidegren, Carl-Göran (1995) 'Ernst Jünger's "yes" to reification'. Unpublished paper.

Herf, Jeffrey (1980) *Reactionary Modernism*. Waltham, MA: Brandeis University.

Herzinger, Richard and Stein, Hannes (1994) *Endzeit-Propheten oder Die Offensive der Antiwestler*. Reinbek bei Hamburg: Rowohlt.

Jung, Thomas (1989) *Vom Ende der Geschichte*. Münster: Waxman.

Jünger, Ernst (1995) 'Om smerten', *Kritik*, 114: 10–23.

Kaltenbrunner, Gerd-Klaus (1985) *Wege der Weltbewahrung*. Asendorf: Mut-Verlag.

Klages, Ludwig (1969) *Der Geist als Widersacher der Seele*. Bonn: H. Bouvier.

Krovoza, Alfred (1976) *Produktion und Sozailisation*. Hamburg: EVA.

Lacan, Jacques (1966) *Écrits*. Paris: Editions de Seuil.

Lasch, Christopher (1995) *Eliternas uppror*. Stockholm: SNS.

Lash, Scott (1993) 'Reflexive modernization: the aesthetic dimension', *Theory, Culture & Society*, 10: 1–23.

Lichtblau, Klaus (1995) 'Sociology and the diagnosis of the times or: the Reflexivity of modernity', *Theory, Culture & Society*, 12: 25–52.

Luhmann, Niklas (1975) *Soziologische Aufklärung 2*. Opladen: Westdeutsche Verlag.

Man, Hendrik de (1951) *Vermassung und Kulturverfall*. Bern: A. Francke.

Maschke, Günther (1991) 'Frank B. Kellogg siegt am Golf', *Siebte Etappe*.

May, Rollo (1991) *Ropet efter myten*. Stockholm: Rabén & Sjögren.

Mead, George Herbert (1947) *Mind, Self and Society*. Chicago: University of Chicago Press.

Muller, Jerry Z. (1987) *The Other God that Failed*. Princeton, NJ: Princeton University Press.

Neckel, Sighard and Wolff, Jürgen (1994) 'The fascination of amorality: Luhmann's system theory and its resonances among German intellectuals', *Theory, Culture & Society*, 11: 69–99.

Negt, Oskar and Kluge, Alexander (1974) *Offentlighed og erfaring*. Ålborg: NSU.
Nietzsche, Friedrich (1924) *Till moralens genealogi*. (*Zur Genealogie der Moral*.) Stockholm: Björck & Börjesson.
Nietzsche, Friedrich (1983a) *Untimely Meditations*. Cambridge: Cambridge University Press.
Nietzsche, Friedrich (1983b) *Twilight of the Idols*. Harmondsworth: Penguin.
Nietzsche, Friedrich (1983c) *Daybreak*. Cambridge: Cambridge University Press.
Palaver, Wolfgang (1995) 'Schmitt's critique of liberalism', *Telos*, 101: 43–71.
Rawls, John (1971) *A Theory of Justice*. Oxford: Oxford University Press.
Rorty, Richard (1991) *Objectivity, Relativism, and Truth: Philosophical Papers Vol. 1*. Cambridge: Cambridge University Press.
Safranski, Rüdiger (1994) *Ein Meister aus Deutschland*. Munich: Hanser.
Safranski, Rüdiger (1998) *Martin Heidegger*. Cambridge, MA: Harvard University Press.
Sass, Louis A. (1992) *Madness and Modernism: Insanity in the Light of Modern Art, Literature, and Thought*. New York: Basic Books.
Schelsky, Helmut (1975) *Die Arbeit tun die anderen*. Opladen: Westdeutscher Verlag.
Schmitt, Carl (1963) *Der Begriff des Politischen*. Berlin: Duncker & Humblott.
Schmitt, Carl (1981) *Land und Meer*. Köln-Lövenich: Hohenheim.
Schulze, Gerhard (1993) *Die Erlebnisgesellschaft*. Frankfurt/New York: Campus.
Sennett, Richard (1978) *The Fall of Public Man*. New York: Vintage Books.
Strauss, Botho (1993) 'Anschwellender Bocksgesang', *Der Spiegel*, 6: 202–7.
Terkessidis, Mark (1995) *Kulturkampf*. Cologne: Kiepenheuer & Witsch.
Weber, Max (1964) 'Science as vocation', in Hans G. Gerth and C. Wright Mills (eds), *From Max Weber*. New York: Oxford University Press. pp. 129–56.
Westbrook, Robert B. (1991) *John Dewey and American Democracy*. Ithaca, NY: Cornell University Press.

Part V
TRANSCULTURAL PLACE

11
TRANSCULTURALITY: THE PUZZLING FORM OF CULTURES TODAY

Wolfgang Welsch

> When we think of the world's future,
> we always mean the destination it will reach
> if it keeps going in the direction we can see it going in now;
> it does not occur to us
> that its path is not a straight line but a curve,
> constantly changing direction.
>
> (Ludwig Wittgenstein, *Culture and Value*, 1929: 3)

In the following I want to present a concept of culture which, I think, is appropriate to most cultures today: the concept of transculturality.[1] I will contrast it with three other concepts: first, with the classical concept of single cultures, and then with the more recent concepts of interculturality and multiculturality. I believe the concept of transculturality to be the most adequate concept of culture today – for both descriptive and normative reasons.

The Traditional Concept of Single Cultures

As is well known, the traditional concept of single cultures was paradigmatically and most influentially developed in the late eighteenth century by Johann Gottfried Herder, especially in his *Ideas on the Philosophy of the History of Mankind*.[2,3] Many among us still believe this concept to be valid.

The concept is characterized by three elements: by social homogenization, ethnic consolidation and intercultural delimitation.[4] First, every culture is supposed to mould the whole life of the people concerned and of its individuals, making every act and every object an unmistakable instance of precisely *this* culture. The concept is unificatory. Secondly, culture is always to be the *culture of a folk*, representing, as Herder said, 'the flower' of a folk's existence (Herder, 1966: 394 [13, VII]). The concept is folk-bound. Thirdly, a decided *delimitation* towards the outside ensues: every culture is, as the culture of one folk, to be distinguished and to remain separated from other folks' cultures. The concept is separatory.

All three elements of this traditional concept have become untenable today. First, modern societies are differentiated within themselves to such a high degree that uniformity is no longer constitutive to, or achievable for, them (and there are reasonable doubts as to whether it ever has been historically). T.S. Eliot's neo-Herderian statement from 1948, that culture is 'the *whole way of life* of a people, from birth to the grave, from morning to night and even in sleep' (Eliot, 1948: 31), has today become an obviously ideological decree.[5] Modern societies are multicultural in themselves, encompassing a multitude of varying ways of life and lifestyles.[6] There are vertical differences in society: the culture of a working quarter, a well-to-do residential district, and that of the alternative scene, for example, hardly exhibit any common denominator. And there are horizontal divisions: gender divisions, differences between male and female, or between straight and lesbian and gay can constitute quite different cultural patterns and life-forms. So already, with respect to this first point, the traditional concept of culture proves to be factually inadequate: it cannot cope with the inner complexity of modern cultures.

Secondly, the ethnic consolidation is dubious: Herder sought to envisage cultures as closed spheres or autonomous islands, each corresponding to a folk's territorial area and linguistic extent.[7] Cultures were to reside strictly within themselves and be closed to their environment. But as we know, such folk-bound definitions are highly imaginary and fictional; they must laboriously be brought to prevail against historical evidence of inter-mingling;[8] and they are, moreover, politically dangerous, as we are today experiencing almost worldwide.

Finally, the concept demands outer delimitation. Herder says: 'Everything which is still the *same* as my nature, which can be *assimilated* therein, I envy, strive towards, make my own; *beyond this*, kind nature has armed me with *insensibility, coldness* and *blindness*; it can even become *contempt* and *disgust*' (Herder, 1967a: 45). So Herder defends the double of emphasis on the own and exclusion of the foreign. The traditional concept of culture is a concept of inner homogenization and outer separation at the same time. Put harshly, it tends – as a consequence of its very conception – to be a sort of cultural racism.[9] The sphere premise and the purity precept not only render impossible a mutual understanding between cultures, but the appeal to cultural identity of this kind finally also threatens to produce separatism and to pave the way for political conflicts and wars.

To sum this up, the classical model of culture is not only descriptively unserviceable, but also normatively dangerous and untenable. What is called for today is a departure from this concept and to think of cultures beyond the contraposition of ownness and foreignness – 'beyond both the heterogeneous and the own', as Adorno once put it (Adorno, 1984: 192).

Interculturality and Multiculturality

Are then, perhaps, the concepts of interculturality and multiculturality more able to provide an appropriate concept of today's cultures? They apparently try to overcome some flaws of the traditional concept by advocating a mutual understanding of different cultures. Yet they are, as I will argue, almost as inappropriate as the traditional concept itself, because they still conceptually presuppose it.

Interculturality

The concept of interculturality reacts to the fact that a conception of cultures as spheres necessarily leads to intercultural conflicts.[10] Cultures constituted as spheres or islands can, according to the logic of this conception, do nothing other than collide with one another. Their 'circles of happiness' must, as Herder said, 'clash' (Herder, 1967a: 46); cultures of this kind must ignore, defame or combat one another.

The conception of interculturality seeks ways in which such cultures could nevertheless get on with, understand and recognize one another. But the deficiency in this conception originates in that it drags along with it unchanged the premise of the traditional conception of culture. It still proceeds from a conception of cultures as islands or spheres.[11] For just this reason, it is unable to arrive at any solution, since the intercultural problems *stem* from the island premise. The classical conception of culture *creates* by its primary trait – the separatist character of cultures – the secondary problem of a structural inability to communicate between these cultures. Therefore this problem cannot, of course, be solved on the basis of this very conception. The recommendations of interculturality, albeit well meant, are fruitless. The concept does not get to the root of the problem. It remains cosmetic.

Multiculturality

The concept of multiculturality is surprisingly similar to the concept of interculturality. It takes up the problems which different cultures have living together *within one society*. But therewith the concept basically remains in the duct of the traditional understanding of culture; it proceeds from the existence of clearly distinguished, in themselves homogeneous cultures, the only difference now being that these differences exist within one and the same state community.

The concept seeks opportunities for tolerance and understanding, and for avoidance or handling of conflict. This is just as laudable as endeavours towards interculturality, but equally inefficient, too, since from the basis of the traditional comprehension of cultures a mutual understanding or a transgression of separating barriers cannot be achieved. As daily experience shows, the concept of multiculturality accepts and even furthers such barriers. Compared to traditional calls for cultural homogeneity the concept is progressive, but its all too traditional understanding of cultures threatens to engender regressive tendencies which by appealing to a particularistic cultural identity lead to ghettoization or cultural fundamentalism.[12]

I cannot expand further on this point here. This would, for example, require distinguishing between the US-American and the European comprehension of multiculturalism and discussing their different histories, contexts and related problems. The basic point, however, is, in each case, that the concept implies and affirms the traditional conception of cultures as autonomous spheres, and that it's exactly this which emerges in present-day phenomena of separation and ghettoization.[13] It comes to light here just how fatal the outcome of recourses to the old concept of culture can be. The old cultural notion of inner homogeneity and outer delimitation engenders chauvinism and cultural fundamentalism.

Criticism of the traditional conception of single cultures, as well as of the more recent concepts of interculturality and multiculturality can be summarized as follows. If cultures were in fact still – as these concepts suggest – constituted in the form of islands or spheres, then one could neither rid oneself of nor solve the problem of their coexistence and cooperation. However, the description of today's cultures as islands or spheres is factually incorrect and normatively deceptive. Cultures *de facto* no longer have the insinuated form of homogeneity and separateness. They have instead assumed a new form, which is to be called *transcultural* in so far as it *passes through* classical cultural boundaries. Cultural conditions today are largely characterized by mixes and permeations. The concept of transculturality – which I will now try to explain – seeks to articulate this altered cultural constitution.[14,15]

Transculturality

Macro-level: The Altered Cut of Today's Cultures

First, transculturality is a consequence of the *inner differentiation and complexity of modern cultures*. These encompass – as I explained before – a number of ways of life and cultures, which also interpenetrate or emerge from one another.

Secondly, the old homogenizing and separatist idea of cultures has furthermore been surpassed through *cultures' external networking*. Cultures today are extremely interconnected and entangled with each other.[16] Lifestyles no longer end at the borders of national cultures, but go beyond these, are found in the same way in other cultures. The way of life for an economist, an academic or a journalist is no longer German or French, but rather European or global in tone. The new forms of entanglement are a consequence of migratory processes, as well as of worldwide material and immaterial communications systems and economic interdependencies and dependencies. It is here, of course, that questions of power come in. Consequently, the same basic problems and states of consciousness today appear in cultures once considered to be fundamentally different. Think, for example, of human rights debates, feminist movements or of ecological awareness which are powerful active factors across the board culturally.

Thirdly, cultures today are in general characterized by *hybridization*. For *every* culture, all *other* cultures have tendentially come to be inner-content or satellites. This applies on the levels of population, merchandise and information. Worldwide, in most countries, live members of all other countries of this planet; and more and more, the same articles – as exotic as they may once have been – are becoming available the world over; finally the global networking of communications technology makes all kinds of information identically available from every point in space.[17]

Henceforward there is no longer anything absolutely foreign. Everything is within reach. Accordingly, there is no longer anything exclusively 'own' either. Authenticity has become folklore, it is ownness simulated for others – to whom the indigene himself or herself belongs. To be sure, there is still a regional-culture rhetoric, but it is largely simulatory and aesthetic; in substance everything is transculturally determined.[18] Today, in a culture's internal relations – among its different ways of life – there exists as much foreignness as in its external relations with other cultures.[19]

Micro-level: Transcultural Formation of Individuals

Transculturality is gaining ground moreover, not only on the macro-cultural level, but also on the individual's micro-level. For most of us, multiple cultural connexions are decisive in terms of our cultural formation. We are cultural hybrids. Today's writers, for example, emphasize that they're shaped not by a single homeland, but by differing reference countries, by Russian, German, South and North American or Japanese literature. Their cultural formation is transcultural (think, for example, of Naipaul[20] or Rushdie) – that of subsequent generations will be even more so.[21]

Sociologists have been telling us since the 1970s that modern lives are to be understood 'as a migration through different social worlds and as the successive realization of a number of possible identities' (Berger et al., 1973: 77), and that we all possess 'multiple attachments and identities' – 'cross-cutting identities', as Bell put it (Bell, 1980: 243). What once may have applied only to outstanding persons like Montaigne, Novalis, Whitman, Rimbaud or Nietzsche,[22] seems to be becoming the structure of almost everybody today.

Of course, a cultural identity of this type is not to be equated with national identity. The distinction between cultural and national identity is of elementary importance. It belongs among the mustiest assumptions that an individual's cultural formation must be determined by his or her nationality or national status. The insinuation that someone who possesses an Indian or a German passport must also culturally unequivocally be an Indian or a German and that, if this is not the case, the person is without a fatherland, or a traitor to his or her fatherland, is as foolish as it is dangerous.[23] The detachment of civic from personal or cultural identity is to be insisted upon – all the more so in states, such as ours, in which freedom in cultural formation belongs among one's basic rights.

Wherever an individual is cast by differing cultural interests, the linking of such transcultural components with one another becomes a specific task in identity-forming. Work on one's identity is becoming more and more work on the integration of components of differing cultural origin. And only the ability to cross over transculturally will guarantee us identity and competence in the long run (see Welsch, 1992c).

To sum this up, cultural determinants today – from society's macro-level through to individuals' micro-level – have become transcultural. The old concept of culture misrepresents cultures' actual form, the type of their relations and even the structure of individuals' identities and lifestyles.[24] Every concept of culture intended to pertain to today's reality must face up to the transcultural constitution.[25,26] The gesture made by some cultural theorists, who prefer to cling to their customary concepts and, wherever reality doesn't yield to these, retreat to a 'well so much the worse for reality', is ridiculous.

Supplements and Outlooks

Having so far developed the general features of transculturality, I would now like to append some supplemental viewpoints and prospects.

Transculturality – Already in History

First, transculturality is in no way completely new historically. It has, to be sure, been the case to a larger extent than the adherents of the traditional concept of culture want to admit. They blindly deny the factual historic transculturality of long periods in order to establish the nineteenth-century's imaginary notion of homogeneous national cultures. Carl Zuckmayer once wonderfully described historical transculturality in *The Devil's General*:

> . . . just imagine your line of ancestry, from the birth of Christ on. There was a Roman commander, a dark type, brown like a ripe olive, he had taught a blond girl Latin. And then a Jewish spice dealer came into the family, he was a serious

person, who became a Christian before his marriage and founded the house's Catholic tradition. And then came a Greek doctor, or a Celtic legionary, a Grisonian landsknecht, a Swedish horseman, a Napoleonic soldier, a deserted Cossack, a Black Forest miner, a wandering miller's boy from the Alsace, a fat mariner from Holland, a Magyar, a pandour, a Viennese officer, a French actor, a Bohemian musician – all lived on the Rhine, brawled, boozed, and sang and begot children there – and – Goethe, he was from the same pot, and Beethoven, and Gutenberg, and Mathias Grünewald, and – oh, whatever – just look in the encyclopaedia. They were the best, my dear! The world's best! And why? Because that's where the peoples intermixed. Intermixed – like the waters from sources, streams and rivers, so, that they run together to a great, living torrent. (Zuckmayer, 1963: 930)

This is a realistic description of a 'folk's' historical genesis and constitution. It breaks through the fiction of homogeneity and the separatist idea of culture as decreed by the traditional concept.

For someone who knows their European history – and art history in particular – this historical transculturality is evident. Styles developed across the countries and nations, and many artists created their best works far from home. The cultural trends were largely European and shaped a network linking the states.

Cultural Conceptions as Active Factors in Respect of their Object

Conceptions of culture are not just descriptive concepts, but operative concepts.[27] Our understanding of culture is an *active factor* in our cultural life.

If one tells us (as the old concept of culture did) that culture is to be a homogeneity event, then we practise the required coercions and exclusions. We seek to satisfy the task we are set – and will be successful in so doing. Whereas, if one tells us or subsequent generations that culture ought to incorporate the foreign and do justice to transcultural components, then we will set about this task, and then corresponding feats of integration will belong to the real structure of our culture. The 'reality' of culture is, in this sense, always a consequence too of our conceptions of culture.

One must therefore be aware of the responsibility which one takes on in propagandizing concepts of this type. We should be suggesting concepts which are descriptively adequate and normatively accountable, and which – above all – pragmatically lead further.[28] Propagandizing the old concept of culture and its subsequent forms has today become irresponsible; better chances are found on the side of the concept of transculturality.

Cultural Annexability and Transmutability

The concept of transculturality aims for a multi-meshed and inclusive, not separatist and exclusive, understanding of culture. It intends a culture and society whose pragmatic feats exist not in delimitation, but in the ability to link and undergo transition. In meeting with other life-forms there are always not only divergences but opportunities to link up, and these can be developed and extended so that a common life-form is fashioned which includes even reserves which hadn't earlier seemed capable of being linked in. Extensions of this type represent a pressing task today.

It is a matter of readjusting our inner compass: away from the concentration on the polarity of the own and the foreign to an attentiveness for what might be common and connective wherever we encounter things foreign.

Transculturality sometimes demands things that may seem unreasonable for our esteemed habits – as does today's reality everywhere. But transculturality also contains the potential to transcend our received and supposedly determining monocultural standpoints, and we should make increasing use of these potentials. I am confident that future generations will more and more develop transcultural forms of communication and comprehension. Diane Ravitch reports an interesting example: in an interview, a black runner said 'that her model is Mikhail Baryshnikov. She admires him because he is a magnificent athlete.' Diane Ravitch comments: 'He is not black; he is not female; he is not American-born; he is not even a runner. But he inspires her because of the way he trained and used his body. When I read this, I thought how narrow-minded it is to believe that people can be inspired *only* by those who are exactly like them in race and ethnicity' (Ravitch, 1990: 354). Once again, we can transcend the narrowness of traditional, monocultural ideas and constraints, we can develop an increasingly transcultural understanding of ourselves.

Internal and External Transculturality

Furthermore, the individuals' discovery and acceptance of their transcultural constitution is a condition for coming to terms with societal transculturality. Hatred directed towards foreigners is (as has been shown particularly from the psychoanalytic side) basically projected hatred of oneself. One takes exception vicariously to something in a stranger, which one carries within oneself, but does not like to admit, preferring rather to repress it internally and to battle with it externally. Conversely, the recognition of a degree of internal foreignness forms a prerequisite for the acceptance of the external foreign. It is precisely when we no longer deny, but rather perceive, our inner transculturality that we will become capable of dealing with outer transculturality.[29]

Incidentally, Nietzsche was already a precursor of the subject-internal, as well as the societal transculturality which are topical today. Of himself he said that he was 'glad to harbour . . . not "one immortal soul", but *many mortal souls* within' (Nietzsche, 1980a: 386 [II 17]), and he coined the formula of the 'subject as a multitude' in general (Nietzsche, 1980b: 650). For Europe he prognosticated a process of increasing cultural intermixing:

> Commerce and industry, traffic in books and letters, the commonality of all higher culture, quick changes of locality and landscape, the present-day nomadic life of all nonlandowners – these conditions necessarily bring about a weakening

and ultimately a destruction of nations, or at least of European nations: so that a mixed-race, that of the European man, has to originate out of all of them, as the result of continual crossbreeding. (Nietzsche, 1984: 228 [475])

In Europe

a tremendous *physiological* process is taking place and gaining momentum. The Europeans are becoming more similar to each other; they become more and more detached from the conditions under which races originate that are tied to some climate or class; they become increasingly independent of any *determinate* milieu that would like to inscribe itself for centuries in body and soul with the same demands. Thus an essentially supra-national and nomadic type of man is gradually coming up, a type that possesses, physiologically speaking, a maximum of the art and power of adaptation as its typical distinction. (Nietzsche, 1989: 176 [242])[30,31]

Nietzsche, however, also considered such intermixing processes as ambivalent. He distinguished two possibilities: in general hybrid characters, since they 'have in their bodies the heritage of multiple origins', will 'be weaker human beings: their most profound desire is that the war they *are* should come to an end'; the happiness they yearn for will be 'the happiness of resting, of not being disturbed, of satiety'. Yet, in others, 'the opposition and war' in their nature 'have the effect of one more charm and incentive of life'; it is then that 'those magical, incomprehensible, and unfathomable ones arise', whose 'most beautiful expression' is found in men like Alcibiades, Frederick II or Leonardo da Vinci. Both types 'appear in precisely the same ages', they 'belong together and owe their origin to the same causes' (1989: 111f. [200]).

On the whole Nietzsche ultimately pleaded for future cultural mixing. Features of the erstwhile 'enigmas' would belong to tomorrow's normal type. Future culture would be one of intermixing, and the future person a polycultural nomad. Nietzsche had, in *Human, All Too Human*, already said, that one should 'work actively on the merging of nations' (Nietzsche, 1984: 228 [475]). And in his late years he spoke out acerbically against the relapse to 'nationalism', 'fatherlandishness' or 'soil addiction': 'What value could it have, now that everything points to larger and common interests, to goad these ragged self-ish feelings? . . . And that in a situation where *spiritual dependence* and denationalization leap to the eye, and the actual value and meaning of today's culture lies in mutual fusion and fertilization of one another!' (Nietzsche, 1980c: 92f. [235]).[32] Nietzsche can be considered as being a precursor of modern transculturality.

Link with Wittgenstein

Philosophically, the one person who provides the greatest help for a transcultural concept of culture, however, is Wittgenstein. He outlined an on-principle pragmatically based concept of culture, which is free of ethnic consolidation and unreasonable demands for homogeneity. According to Wittgenstein, culture is at hand wherever practices in life are shared. The basic task is not to be conceived as an understanding of foreign cultures, but as an interaction with foreignness. Understanding may be helpful, but it never is sufficient alone, it has to enhance progresses in interaction. We must change the pattern from hermeneutic conceptualizations with their beloved presumption of foreignness on the one hand and the unfortunate appropriating dialectics of understanding on the other hand to decidedly pragmatic efforts to interact. And there is always a good chance for such interactions, because there exist at least some entanglements, inter-sections and transitions between the different ways of life. It is precisely this which Wittgenstein's concept of culture takes into account.[33] Culture in Wittgenstein's sense is, by its very structure, open to new connections and to further feats of integration. To this extent, a cultural concept reformulated along Wittgenstein's lines seems to me to be particularly apt to today's conditions.

Transculturality in relation to Globalization and Particularization

Uniformization or New Diversity?

Let me turn to a final and crucial point. I want to respond to a potential misunderstanding. You might think that the concept of transculturality is tantamount to the acceptance of an increasing homogenization of cultures and the coming of a uniform world-civilization, and that it assents without objection to this development, while conspicuously conflicting with our intuitions of cultural diversity. But does transculturality really mean uniformization? Not at all. It is, rather, intrinsically linked with the pro-duction of diversity. Let me clarify this important point.[34]

As transculturality pushes forward, the mode of diversity is altered. If one doesn't recognize this, then one may – as some critics falsely do – equate transculturality with uniformization. For diversity, as traditionally provided in the form of single cultures, does indeed increasingly disappear. Instead, however, a new type of diversity takes shape: the diversity of different cultures and life-forms, each arising from transcultural per-meations.

Consider how these transcultural formations come about. Different groups or individuals which give shape to new transcultural patterns draw upon different sources for this purpose. Hence the transcultural networks will vary already in their inventory, and even more so in their structure (because even the same elements, when put together differently, result in different structures). The transcultural webs are, in short, woven with different threads, and in a different manner. Therefore, on the level of transculturality, a high degree of cultural manifoldness results again – it is certainly no smaller than that which was found between traditional single cultures. It's just that now the differences no longer come about through a juxtaposition of clearly delineated cultures (like in a mosaic), but result between transcultural networks, which have some things in common while differing in others, showing overlaps and distinctions at the same time.[35]

The mechanics of differentiation has become more complex, but it has also become genuinely cultural for the very first time, no longer complying with geographical or national stipulations, but following pure cultural interchange processes.

Moreover, these transcultural networks are more capable of affiliation with one another than were the old cultural identities. They include segments which also occur in other networks and thus represent points of affiliation between the different transcultural forms. So the new type of differentiation by its very structure favours coexistence rather than combat.

Flaws in the Globalization and the Particularization Diagnoses

It is, I think, the advantage of the transculturality concept over competing concepts that it explains uniformization and intermixing processes on the one side and the emergence of new diversity on the other side at the same time and by means of the same formula. Let me briefly demonstrate this compared to the two main competing diagnoses in the cultural field today: to globalization on the one hand and particularization on the other.

The concept of globalization assumes that cultures are becoming the same the world over (see Featherstone, 1990). Globalization is a concept of uniformization (preferably following the Western model), and of uniformization alone. But this view can, at best, represent half the picture, and the champions of globalization would have a hard time ignoring the complementary resurgence of particularisms worldwide.[36] Their concept, however, is by its very structure incapable of developing an adequate understanding of these counter-tendencies. From the viewpoint of globalization, particularisms are just phenomena which are retrograde and whose destiny it is to vanish.

But particularisms cannot in fact be ignored. The 'return to tribes' is shaping the state of the world just as much as the trend towards a world society.[37] The rise of particularisms is a reaction to globalization processes (see Robertson, 1987). It certainly creates an explosive situation, because the particularisms often refine themselves through the appeal to cultural identity to nationalisms, producing hatred, purification actions and war.[38] Enlightenment people don't like these particularisms. This is quite understandable. But not sufficient. As concerning as one may find these phenomena, we won't be able to get by without taking seriously the demand for a specific identity. People obviously feel compelled to defend themselves against being merged into globalized uniformity. They don't want just to be universal or global, but also specific and of their own. They want to distinguish themselves from one another and know themselves to be well accommodated in a specific identity. This desire is legitimate, and forms in which it can be satisfied without danger are to be determined and promoted.[39] Future cultural forms will have to be such that they also cater for the demand for specifity.

The Advantage of the Transculturality Concept

This brings me once more to the advantage of the transculturality concept over the competing concepts of globalization and particularization. The concept of transculturality goes beyond these seemingly hard alternatives. It is able to cover both global and local, universalistic and particularistic aspects, and it does so quite naturally, from the logic of transcultural processes themselves. The globalizing tendencies as well as the desire for specificity and particularity can be fulfilled *within* transculturality. Transcultural identities comprehend a cosmopolitan side, but also a side of local affiliation (see Hannerz, 1990). Transcultural people combine both.

Of course, the local side can today still be determined by ethnic belonging or the community in which one grew up. But it doesn't have to be. People can make their own choice with respect to their affiliations.[40] Their actual homeland can be far away from their original homeland. Remember Adorno's and Horkheimer's phrase 'Homeland is the state of having escaped' (Horkheimer and Adorno, 1994: 78).

Conclusion

With regard to the old concept of culture I have set out how badly it misrepresents today's conditions and which dangers accompany its continuation or revival for cultures' living together. The concept of transculturality sketches a different picture of the relation between cultures. Not one of isolation and of conflict, but one of entanglement, intermixing and commonness. It promotes not separation, but exchange and interaction. If the diagnosis given applies to some extent, then tasks of the future – in political and social, scientific and educational, artistic and design-related respects – ought only to be solvable through a decisive turn towards this transculturality.

Notes

1 For the first version of this conception, see Welsch (1992a). More detailed renderings are found in Italian (Welsch, 1992b), German (Welsch, 1994) and English (Welsch, 1996).

2 The work first appeared in four separate parts, each of five books, in the years 1784, 1785, 1787 and 1791, published by the Hartknoch Press in Riga and Leipzig. A first English edition (*Outlines of a Philosophy of the History of Man*) was published as early as 1800 in London.

3 Traditionally, the term 'culture' had a more restricted meaning. It was used only in combination with other notions such as 'animus', 'soul', or 'religion', designating the cultivation of specific capacities or habits related to these issues. Not until the late seventeenth century, with the natural rights scholar Samuel von Pufendorf, did 'culture' become a general concept claiming to encompass the whole of a people's, society's or nation's activities. It is only since then that the term has an absolute and autonomous usage (*the* culture) instead of its former relative usage. Herder follows Pufendorf's new general concept of culture which, due

to Herder's explication, has become so familiar that we usually are unaware of the fact that
for many centuries the notion of 'culture' had a rather narrow use.

4 I shall not take account of Herder's particularities here, but rather concentrate on the
typology of his concept of culture. For views on Herder's possible contemporary relevance, see
Mueller-Vollmer (1990).

5 The ethnology of the twentieth century also worked for a long time with the notion that
culture is a structured and integrated organic whole in itself. Ruth Benedict's book, *The
Patterns of Culture* (1934) is representative of this. From the 1960s and 1970s onwards doubts
about this premise were increasingly expressed (see Geertz, 1973). Margaret Archer called the
'myth of cultural integration' the dubious 'legacy of ethnology' (Archer, 1988: 2ff.).

6 I will expand on this point in more detail when discussing multiculturality.

7 'Every nation', Herder declared, 'has its *centre* of happiness *within itself* just as each
sphere its centre of gravity!' (Herder, 1967a: 44f.)

8 This was effectively noted by Ernest Gellner and Eric Hobsbawm: 'Nationalism is not
the awakening of nations to self-consciousness; it *invents* nations where they do not exist'
(Gellner, 1964: 168). '[T]he national phenomenon cannot be adequately investigated without
careful attention to the "invention of tradition"' (Eric Hobsbawm, 'Introduction: Inventing
Traditions', in Hobsbawm and Ranger, 1983: 14).

9 Lévi-Strauss – in a highly regarded speech to the UNESCO in 1971 – pointed out the
relevance of specifically cultural racism. 'Race' is, according to him, to be understood not so
much as the basis, but as a *function* of culture. Every culture, to the extent that it
autonomously develops itself and delimits itself from other cultures, tends to cultural racism
(Lévi-Strauss, 1983). For the strategic function of racism in the modern state, see Michel
Foucault (1991).

10 For this concept, see Wimmer, 1989; Mall and Lohmar, 1993.

11 J.N. Mohanty has demonstrated how mistaken this premise is. The 'talk of a culture
which evokes the idea of a homogeneous form is completely misleading. Indian culture, or
Hindu culture consists of completely different cultures. . . . A completely homogeneous
subculture is not to be found' (Mohanty, 1993: 118). 'The idea of cultural purity is a myth'
(1993: 117).

12 One complies with the maxim that cultures are to be their own – and they are exactly
this, above all, when contrasted with other cultures and contrasted with a common culture.
'Back to the roots' reads the magic formula, or 'only tribes will survive'. Salmon Rushdie once
articulated a similar danger when talking to his fellow Indian writers: '[O]f all the many
elephant traps lying ahead of us, the largest and most dangerous pitfall would be the adoption
of a ghetto mentality. To forget that there is a world beyond the community to which we
belong, to confine ourselves within narrowly defined cultural frontiers, would be, I believe, to
go voluntarily into that form of internal exile which in South Africa is called the "homeland"'
(Rushdie, 1991: 19).

13 See Kramer, 1990; Leggewie, 1990; Ravitch, 1990; Searle, 1990; Schlesinger, 1991;
Cohn-Bendit and Schmidt, 1992; Gallissot, 1993; Gutmann, 1994; Ostendorf, 1994; Takaki,
1994; Bernstein, 1995; Hollinger, 1995; Kaschuba, 1995; Kymlicka, 1995.

14 The prefix 'trans' in 'transculturality' has a double meaning. First, it denotes the fact
that the determinants of culture are becoming more and more cross-cultural. So, in the first
place, 'trans' has the sense 'across'. In the long run, however, the cross-cultural development
will increasingly engender a cultural constitution which is beyond the traditional, supposedly
monocultural design of cultures. So, while having the meaning 'across' with respect to the
mixed design of cultural determinants, 'trans' has the sense of 'beyond' with respect to the
future and compared to the earlier form of cultures.

15 I must admit that I took the term 'transculturality' to be a new one when I began
working on this topic in 1991. I have since learned that 'transculturality' – or at least the
adjective 'transcultural' – isn't quite so rare after all. But my usage of the term does not, as is
usual in an older tradition, target transcultural invariances. With this term I intend far more
to point out the specific structure of *today's* culture. As such, my perspective also distinguishes

itself from that of the research directed towards 'reciprocal anthropology', as pursued by the international alliance 'Transcultura'. They intend to bring about a dialogue between cultures' reciprocal interpretations. The conventional (or, in the meantime, well reflected upon) eurocentricism of anthropology and ethnology is to be outbid by the principle of reciprocating interpretations. Research in this direction is documented in the reader *Sguardi venuti da lontano: un'indagine di transcultura* (Le Pichon and Caronia, 1991).

16 Wherever we continue to speak of German, French, Japanese, Indian, etc. culture, what we really have in mind are *linguistic* or *state* borders – not genuinely cultural formations.

17 Places like Mammoth, a Californian ski station where you find numerous names such as St Moritz Road, Chamonix Place, Cortina Circuit, or Megeve Way (in the surroundings you also have a Matterhorn Peak), are curious examples of the trend to hybridization. One has the whole world (in so far as it counts for a specific purpose) in one place.

18 What's regionally specific has become decor, superficies, aesthetic enactment. This is, of course, one of the reasons for the eminent spread of the aesthetic noticeable today (see Welsch, 1993). One might, just once, seek out a Tirolean ski resort: Tirolean merely exists still as atmospheric enactment, as ornamentation. On the other hand, the basic structures – from the ski lifts through to the toilets – are exactly similar to those in French ski regions or at international airports. Significantly, the cuisine too has changed. What is put before one looks like and calls itself Tirolean Gröstl, Kasnocken or Schupfnudeln, but it is, corresponding with international standards, drastically calorie-reduced. In short, the appearance is still Tirolean, but in substance everything has changed. Originality exists only as an aesthetic production.

19 Sociologically viewed, this is a familiar fact today: '. . . people belong to many different cultures and the cultural differences are as likely to be *within* states (i.e. between regions, classes, ethnic groups, the urban and rural) as *between* states' (King, 1990: 409). '. . . [C]ultural diversity tends now to be as great within nations as it is between them' (Hannerz, 1992: 231). 'It is natural that in the contemporary world many local settings are increasingly characterized by cultural diversity. . . . and one may in the end ask whether it is now even possible to become a cosmopolitan without going away at all' (Hannerz, 1990: 249). From the philosophical side, Richard Rorty describes the disappearance of the difference between the intracultural and the intercultural as follows: 'Part of the force of Quine's and Davidson's attack on the distinction between the conceptual and the empirical is that the distinction between different cultures does not differ in kind from the distinction between different theories held by members of a single culture. The Tasmanian aborigines and the British colonists had trouble communicating, but this trouble was different only in extent from the difficulties in communication experienced by Gladstone and Disraeli. . . . The same Quinean arguments which dispose of the positivists' distinction between analytic and synthetic truth dispose of the anthropologists' distinction between the intercultural and the intracultural' (Rorty, 1991: 26).

20 'We cannot understand all the traits we have inherited. Sometimes we can be strangers to ourselves' (Naipaul, 1994: 9).

21 Amy Gutmann states that today 'most people's identities, not just Western intellectuals or elites, are shaped by more than a single culture. Not only societies, but people are multicultural' (Gutmann, 1993: 183).

22 Montaigne already stated: 'I have nothing to say about myself absolutely, simply, and solidly, without confusion and without mixture, or in one word'; '. . . we are all patchwork, and so shapeless and diverse in composition that each bit, each moment, plays its own game' (Montaigne, 1992: 242 and 244 resp. [II 1]. Novalis wrote that one person is 'several people at once' since '*pluralism*' is 'our innermost essence' (Novalis, 1983: 571 [107] and 250 [63] resp.). Or remember Walt Whitman's 'I am large . . . I contain multitudes' (Whitman, 1985: 84 [1314–1316]) or Rimbaud's 'JE est un autre' (Arthur Rimbaud, letter to Paul Demeny [15 May 1871] in Rimbaud [1972], pp. 249–54, here p. 250). For Nietzsche, see later.

23 This insinuation stems from the classical concept of culture is so far as this is folk-based and commands homogeneity.

24 Wherever this concept continues to be represented, it acts as a normative corset, as a coercive homogenization precept.

25 Ulf Hannerz's concept (or 'root metaphor') of 'creole cultures' and 'creolization' is quite close to my perspective of transculturality. 'Creole cultures come out of multidimensional cultural encounters and can put things together in new ways' (Hannerz, 1992: 265). 'Something like creole cultures', Hannerz suggests, 'may have a larger part in our future than cultures designed, each by itself, to be pieces of a mosaic' (1992: 267). In 1991 Michel Serres held an impressive plea in the spirit of transculturality (Serres, 1991). His thesis is that what matters for present-day culture and education is to transcend the traditional alternatives of own and foreign and to think in terms of intersection, mixing and penetration.

26 A further conceptual clarification may be helpful. The diagnosis of transculturality refers to a transition, or to a phase in a process of transition. It's a temporary diagnosis. It takes the old conception of single cultures as its point of departure, and it argues that this conception – although still seeming self-evident to many people – is no longer descriptively adequate for most cultures today. Instead, the diagnosis of transculturality views a present and future state of cultures which is no longer monocultural but cross-cultural. The concept seeks to grasp this transition conceptually. One point, however, might seem confusing in this talk of transculturality. It may even appear contradictory that the concept of transculturality which points to a disappearance of the traditional single cultures nonetheless inherently continues to refer to 'cultures', and to a certain extent even seems to presuppose the ongoing existence of such cultures – for if there were no longer such cultures, where should the transcultural mixers take their components from? The point can easily be clarified. The process of transition obviously implies *two* moments: the ongoing existence of single cultures (or of an old understanding of culture's form) *and* the shift to a new, transcultural form of cultures. With respect to this double character of the transition, it is conceptually sound and even necessary to refer to single cultures of the old type *as well as* to point the way to transculturality. But what will be the case after the transition has been made? Won't it, at least then, be contradictory to continue speaking of 'cultures' on the one hand and of 'transculturality' on the other? Not at all. Because the activity of weaving new webs will, of course, continue to take existing cultures as its starting point or reservoir for the development of further webs – but now these reference cultures themselves will already have a transcultural cut. The duo of reference cultures on the one hand and new cultural webs on the other remains, the difference however is that the reference cultures will now already be 'cultural' in the sense of 'transcultural'.

27 Generally, conceptions are schemata, with which we make our world understandable for ourselves and organize our actions. They preset grids and ways of viewing things which entail behavioural patterns and disturb facts. In this light, Deleuze determined the task of philosophy as being the creation of concepts: 'La philosophie . . . est la discipline qui consiste à *créer* des concepts' (Deleuze and Guattari, 1991: 10).

28 Hence critical reflections on cultural concepts, such as I undertake here, are – from time to time at least – necessary. No one would claim that an alteration of the concept *eo ipso* already alters reality. That would be overly simplistic idealism. But, conversely, the way in which the conscious and subconscious effectuality of cultural terms codetermines cultural reality should not be overlooked. The subcutaneous and officious effectuality of the old concept of culture – one thinks automatically, or even states explicitly that culture is to be homogeneous, national, etc. – contributes to separatisms and particularisms of the obsolete sort. Work on conceptual enlightenment is called for to counter this.

29 Freud had already pointed to an analogy between the inner topology of repression and the outer topology of the relation to strangers: '. . . the repressed is foreign territory to the ego – internal foreign territory – just as reality (if you will forgive the unusual expression) is external foreign territory' (Freud, 1973: 57). Julia Kristeva picks up on his insights: 'In a strange way, the stranger exists within ourselves: he is the hidden face of our identity. . . . If we recognize him within ourselves, we prevent ourselves from abhoring him as such' (Kristeva, 1988: 9). Against the appeal to 'roots', she says: 'Those who've never lost any of their roots, seem incapable of apprehending any word which could relativize their position. . . . The ear opens itself to objections only when the body loses the ground beneath its feet. To hear a

dissonnance, one must have experienced a sort of imbalance, a tottering upon an abyss' (1988: 29f.) – Adorno too had described as 'the better state' that 'in which people could be different without fear' (Adorno, 1993: 103).

30 I have portrayed Nietzsche's position in more detail in Welsch (1995b).

31 Herder, on the other hand, had vehemently opposed cultural mixing. He saw in this only decay: 'The *more countries drew together*, the culture of sciences, the *community* of orders, provinces, kingdoms and parts of the world grew; the more then, like all literature, poetry too gained influence in *space and surface*, the more it lost *thrust, depth and certainty*' (Herder, 1967b: 413).

32 Nietzsche indeed knew too of the constantly threatening danger of relapses: 'We "good Europeans" – we, too, know hours when we permit ourselves some hearty fatherlandishness, a plop and relapse into old loves and narrowness . . . hours of national agitations, patriotic palpitations, and various other sorts of archaizing sentimental inundations. . . . Indeed I could imagine dull and sluggish races who would require half a century even in our rapidly moving Europe to overcome such atavistic attacks of fatherlandishness and soil addiction and to return to reason, meaning "good Europeanism"'(Nietzsche, 1989: 174 [241]).

33 Following on from Wittgenstein, Peter Winch writes: 'Different aspects of social life do not merely "overlap": they are frequently internally related in such a way that one cannot even be intelligibly conceived as existing in isolation from others' (Winch, 1990: XVf.).

34 Similar views are forwarded by Mike Featherstone, who argues 'against those who would wish to present the tendency on the global level to be one of cultural integration and homogenization' (Featherstone, 1991: 146), and by Ulf Hannerz who says 'that the flow of culture between countries and continents may result in another diversity of culture, based more on interconnections than on autonomy' (Hannerz, 1992: 266).

35 Max Scheler had already pointed out the simultaneity of the adjustment between cultures and the increase in individual differentiation. He did this in a 1927 lecture entitled 'Man in the Era of Adjustment' (Scheler, 1958: 94–126). Scheler denoted the 'adjustment' as the 'inclusive trend of this era' (1958: 102).

36 Incidentally, it is by no means evident that globalization processes are correctly defined when they are only described as unilinear expansion of Western culture. One would, at the same time, have to be attentive to considerable alterations which the elements of the initial culture experience in their acquisition. Stephen Greenblatt has pointed out such ambiguities in the 'assimilation of the other'. He describes this, for instance, in the way the inhabitants of Bali deal with video technology in a ritual context: 'if the television and the VCR . . . suggested the astonishing pervasiveness of capitalist markets and technology, . . . the Balinese adaptation of the latest Western and Japanese modes of representation seemed so culturally idiosyncratic and resilient that it was unclear who was assimilating whom' (Greenblatt, 1991: 4). Hence not even with respect to economy – its paradigm sphere – does the globalization diagnosis seem to be fully appropriate. Ulf Hannerz discusses similar phenomena under the heading 'creolization': the uniform trends of a 'world culture', he demonstrates, are quickly bound into national or regional cultural profiles and thereby experience considerable diversification and transformation (see Hannerz, 1992: esp. 264ff.).

37 Recent years – especially where hegemonic superstructures have broken down – have often seen the emergence of small-state constructs. Moreover, on a higher level, beyond the particular cultures, large cultural alliances are forming which appeal to a cultural commonality – often one religiously based – and want to assert it politically. Samuel P. Huntington calls these large alliances 'civilizations' and outlines the future scenario of a 'clash of civilizations' (Huntington, 1993).

38 As understandable as it may be to recur to the resources of cultural identity (to the 'roots') in a situation of oppression from outside, since they represent a potential for resistance to foreign domination, the consequences are just awkward when the basis of resistance is retained unaltered at the moment of its victory and made the new state's *raison d'être*. It is then, under the appeal to cultural identity, that reactionary, anti-pluralist and tendencially totalitarian states come about. They exercise inner oppression just as they had previously been

oppressed from the outside. This danger was pointed out by Jean François Lyotard: 'Proud struggles for independence end in young, reactionary States' (Lyotard, 1988: 181 [262]). Over the past few decades this has been observable repeatedly in Africa and most recently in the disintegration of the Eastern sphere of power. Nation-states arose with exorbitant fictions of inner homogeneity and defences against outer heterogeneity (see Dahrendorf, 1991: 704). Already Popper, as early as 1945, had warned that the recourse to roots and tribes would lead to inner dictatorship: 'The more we try to return to the heroic age of tribalism, the more surely do we arrive at the Inquisition, at the Secret Police, and at a romanticized gangsterism' (Popper, 1950: 195).

39 In so doing, every more detailed look at particularisms – at their motives and their problems – shows that they will be capable of remaining stable to some extent only when they face up to the demands of plurality and the constitution of transculturality. They are internally affected by both in several ways. First, this is evident on the motivational level: the new particularisms obviously react to the overcoming of traditional identities by processes of cultural cross over. Secondly, any particularistic formation of identity finds itself confronted by the transcultural constitution of its own history. Within historical identities a certain identity must be selected, which is then declared to be *the* identity – alternatives exist however, and differing preferences of identity are sometimes at odds with one another within particularistic movements. Thirdly, it seems inconceivable that particularistic cultures might, in the long run, actually become homogeneous and remain protected against the rise of plurality within themselves. Not even totally closing the territorial and communicational borders could guarantee this, for even now there are already too many nuclei of plurality within each given culture. Fourthly, everyday life is characterized by transcultural elements everywhere, even where the most forceful identity rituals are found. Take potlatch as an example. Just as everything in the life of the First Nation People, this ritual too has changed drastically: today supermarket articles, telecommunications and T-shirts of famous universities belong to it. Even the representatives of this culture consider it highly questionable whether their ancestors would recognize today's practices as a continuation of the old ritual at all. In general, features of plurality and transculturality reach through to the core of particularistic identities. Therefore every particularism which simply tries to deny this plurality and transculturality and instead to establish forcefully monocultural purity – take fundament-alisms as an example – is to be criticized argumentatively, and pragmatically has poor chances of stability in the long run. Only those particularisms which acknowledge and permit plurality and transculturality can be granted long-term success.

40 As Amy Gutmann put it: 'Grant that we cannot stand outside of *any* culture. We need not therefore be standing inside of one and only one particular culture' (Gutmann, 1993: 192).

References

Adorno, Theodor W. (1984) 'Negative Dialektik', *Gesammelte Schriften* (vol. 6). Frankfurt-on-Main: Suhrkamp.
Adorno, Theodor W. (1993) *Minima Moralia: Reflections from Damaged Life.* London: Verso.
Archer, Margaret (1988) *Culture and Agency.* Cambridge: Cambridge University Press.
Bell, Daniel (1980) *The Winding Passage. Essays and Sociological Journeys 1960–1980.* Cambridge, MA: Abt Books.
Benedict, Ruth (1934) *The Patterns of Culture.* Boston and New York: Houghton Mifflin.
Berger, Peter L., Berger, Brigitte and Kellner, Hansfried (1973) *The Homeless Mind: Modernization and Consciousness.* New York: Random House.
Bernstein, Richard (1995) *Dictatorship of Virtue: How the Battle over Multiculturalism is Reshaping our Schools, our Country, and our Lives.* New York: Knopf.
Cohn-Bendit, Daniel and Schmidt, Thomas (1992) *Heimat Babylon: Das Wagnis der multikulturellen Demokratie.* Hamburg: Hoffmann & Campe.
Dahrendorf, Ralf (1991) 'Europa der Regionen?', in *Merkur*, 509 (August): 703–6.

Deleuze, Gilles and Guattari, Félix (1991) *Qu'est-ce que la philosophie?* Paris: Editions de Minuit.

Eliot, T.S. (1948) *Notes towards the Definition of Culture.* London: Faber and Faber.

Featherstone, Mike (ed.) (1990) *Global Culture: Nationalism, Globalization and Modernity.* London: Sage.

Featherstone, Mike (1991) *Consumer Culture and Postmodernism.* London: Sage.

Foucault, Michel (1991) 'Faire vivre et laisser mourir: la naissance du racisme', *Les Temps Modernes,* 46 (535): 37–61.

Freud, Sigmund (1973) 'New introductory lectures on psychoanalysis', in S. Freud, *The Standard Edition* (vol. XXII; ed. James Strachey). London: Hogarth. pp. 5–184.

Gallissot, René (1993) *Pluralisme culturel en Europe: culture(s) européenne(s) et culture(s) des diasporas.* Paris: L'Harmattan.

Geertz, Clifford (1973) *The Interpretation of Cultures.* New York: Basic Books.

Gellner, Ernest (1964) *Thought and Change.* London: Weidenfeld & Nicholson.

Greenblatt, Stephen (1991) *Marvelous Possessions: The Wonder of the New World.* Chicago: Chicago University Press.

Gutmann, Amy (1993) 'The challenge of multiculturalism in political ethics', *Philosophy & Public Affairs,* 22: 171–206.

Gutmann, Amy (ed.) (1994) *Multiculturalism: Examining the Politics of Recognition.* Princeton, NJ: Princeton University Press.

Hannerz, Ulf (1990) 'Cosmopolitans and locals in world culture', in M. Featherstone (ed.), *Global Culture: Nationalism, Globalization and Modernity.* London: Sage. pp. 237–51.

Hannerz, Ulf (1992) *Cultural Complexity: Studies in the Social Organization of Meaning.* New York: Columbia University Press.

Herder, Johann Gottfried (1966) *Outlines of a Philosophy of the History of Man.* New York: Bergman.

Herder, Johann Gottfried (1967a) *Auch eine Philosophie der Geschichte zur Bildung der Menschheit.* Frankfurt-on-Main: Suhrkamp.

Herder, Johann Gottfried (1967b) 'Ueber die Würkung der Dichtkunst auf die Sitten der Völker in alten und neuen Zeiten' [1778, first printed Munich: Strobl, 1781], in *Herders Sämmtliche Werke* (vol. 8; ed. Bernhard Suphan). Berlin: Weidmann, 1892; reprinted Hildesheim: Olms, 1967. pp. 334–436.

Hobsbawm, Eric and Ranger, Terence (eds) (1983) *The Invention of Tradition.* Cambridge: Cambridge University Press.

Hollinger, David A. (1995) *Postethnic America: Beyond Multiculturalism.* New York: Basic Books.

Horkheimer, Max and Adorno, Theodor W. (1994) *Dialectic of Enlightenment* (trans. John Cumming). New York: Continuum.

Huntington, Samuel P. (1993) 'The clash of civilizations?', *Foreign Affairs,* 72 (3): 22–49.

Kaschuba, Wolfgang (1995) 'Kulturalismus: Kultur statt Gesellschaft?', *Geschichte und Gesellschaft,* 21: 80–95.

King, Anthony (1990) 'Architecture, capital and the globalization of culture', in M. Featherstone (ed.), *Global Culture: Nationalism, Globalization and Modernity.* London: Sage. pp. 397–411.

Kramer, Hilton (1990) 'The prospect before us', *The New Criterion,* 9 (1): 6–9.

Kristeva, Julia (1988) *Étrangers à nous-mêmes.* Paris: Fayard.

Kymlicka, Will (1995) *Multicultural Citizenship.* Oxford: Oxford University Press.

Leggewie, Claus (ed.) (1990) *Multi Kulti: Spielregeln für die Vielvölkerrepublik.* Berlin: Rotbuch.

Le Pichon, Alain and Caronia, Letizia (eds) (1991) *Sguardi venuti da lontano: un'indagine di transcultura.* Milan: Bompiani.

Lévi-Strauss, Claude (1983) *Le regard éloigné.* Paris: Plon.

Lyotard, Jean-François (1988) *The Differend: Phrases in Dispute.* Minneapolis, MN: University of Minnesota Press.

Mall, Ram Adhar and Lohmar, Dieter (eds) (1993) *Philosophische Grundlagen der Interkulturalität*. Amsterdam: Rodopi.

Mohanty, Jitendra N. (1993) 'Den anderen verstehen', in R.A. Mall and D. Lohmar (eds), *Philosophische Grundlagen der Interkulturalität*. Amsterdam: Rodopi. pp. 115–22.

Montaigne, Michel de (1992) *The Complete Essays* (trans. Donald M. Frame). Stanford, CA: Stanford University Press.

Mueller-Vollmer, Kurt (ed.) (1990) *Herder Today*. Berlin: de Gruyter.

Naipaul, V.S. (1994) *A Way in the World: A Sequence*. London: Minerva.

Nietzsche, Friedrich (1980a) *Menschliches, Allzumenschliches II, Sämtliche Werke* (vol. 2; ed. Giorgio Colli and Mazzino Montinari). Munich: Deutscher Taschenbuchverlag.

Nietzsche, Friedrich (1980b) *Nachgelassene Fragmente: Juli 1882 bis Herbst 1885, Sämtliche Werke* (vol. 11; ed. Giorgio Colli and Mazzino Montinari). Munich: Deutscher Taschenbuchverlag.

Nietzsche, Friedrich (1980c) *Nachgelassene Fragmente: Herbst 1885 bis Anfang Januar 1889, 2. Teil: November 1887 bis Anfang Januar 1889, Sämtliche Werke* (vol. 13; ed. Giorgio Colli and Mazzino Montinari). Munich: Deutscher Taschenbuchverlag.

Nietzsche, Friedrich (1984) *Human, All Too Human: A Book for Free Spirits* (trans. Marion Faber). Lincoln and London: University of Nebraska Press.

Nietzsche, Friedrich (1989) *Beyond Good and Evil: Prelude to a Philosophy of the Future* (trans. Walter Kaufmann). New York: Vintage.

Novalis (1983) *Schriften*, vol. 3: *Das philosophische Werk II* (eds Paul Kluckhohn and Richard Samuel). Stuttgart: Kohlhammer.

Ostendorf, Berndt (ed.) (1994) *Multikulturelle Gesellschaft: Modell Amerika*. Munich: Fink.

Popper, Karl R. (1950) *The Open Society and its Enemies*. Princeton, NJ: Princeton University Press.

Ravitch, Diane (1990) 'Multiculturalism: E. Pluribus Plures', *American Scholar*, 337–54.

Rimbaud, Arthur (1972) *Œuvres complètes*. Paris: Gillimard.

Robertson, Roland (1987) 'Globalization theory and civilizational analysis', *Comparative Civilizations Review*, 17: 20–30.

Rorty, Richard (1991) 'Solidarity or objectivity', in *Objectivity, Relativism, and Truth*. Cambridge: Cambridge University Press. pp. 21–34.

Rushdie, Salmon (1991) 'Imaginary homelands' [1982], in *Imaginary Homelands: Essays and Criticism 1981–1991*. London: Granta Books. pp. 9–21.

Scheler, Max (1958) *Philosophical Perspectives*. Boston, MA: Beacon.

Schlesinger, Arthur M. (1991) *The Disuniting of America: Reflections on a Multicultural Society*. New York and London: W.W. Norton.

Searle, John (1990) 'The storm over the university', *The New York Review of Books*, 6 December: 34–42.

Serres, Michel (1991) *Le Tiers-Instruit*. Paris: Éditions François Bourin.

Takaki, Ronald (ed.) (1994) *From Different Shores: Perspectives on Race and Ethnicity in America*. New York and Oxford: Oxford University Press.

Welsch, Wolfgang (1987) *Unsere postmoderne Moderne*. Weinheim: VCH Acta humaniora.

Welsch, Wolfgang (1992a) 'Transkulturalität – Lebensformen nach der Auflösung der Kulturen', *Information Philosophie*, 2: 5–20.

Welsch, Wolfgang (1992b) 'Transculturalità: forme di vita dopo la dissoluzione delle culture', *Paradigmi. Revista di critica filosofica* (Special edition: Dialogo interculturale ed eurocentrismo X/30). pp. 665–89.

Welsch, Wolfgang (1992c) 'Subjektsein heute: Zum Zusammenhang von Subjektivität, Pluralität und Transversalität', *Studia Philosophica*, 51: 153–82.

Welsch, Wolfgang (ed.) (1993) *Die Aktualität des Ästhetischen*. Munich: Fink.

Welsch, Wolfgang (1994) 'Transkulturalität – die veränderte Verfassung heutiger Kulturen' in *Sichtweisen: Die Vielheit in der Einheit*. Weimar: Weimarer Klassik. pp. 83–122.

Welsch, Wolfgang (1995a) *Vernunft: Die zeitgenössische Vernunftkritik und das Konzept der transversalen Vernunft*. Frankfurt: Suhrkamp.

Welsch, Wolfgang (1995b) 'Nietzsche über die Zukunft Europas – Tyrannen oder Nomaden?', in *Sichtweisen: Völker und Vaterländer*. Weimar: Edition Weimarer Klassik. pp. 87–108.

Welsch, Wolfgang (1996) 'Transculturality – the form of cultures today', in *Le Shuttle: Tunnelrealitäten Paris–London–Berlin*. Berlin: Künstlerhaus Bethanien. pp. 15–30.

Whitman, Walt (1985) *Leaves of Grass* ('Song of Myself'). New York: Penguin.

Wimmer, Franz (1989) *Interkulturelle Philosophie*. Vienna: Passagen Verlag.

Winch, Peter (1990) *The Idea of a Social Science and its Relation to Philosophy*. London: Routledge.

Zuckmayer, Carl (1963) 'The devil's general', in *Masters of Modern Drama*. New York: Random House. pp. 911–58.

12

TOWARDS A MULTICULTURAL CONCEPTION OF HUMAN RIGHTS

Boaventura de Sousa Santos

For the past few years I have been puzzled by the extent to which human rights have become the language of progressive politics. Indeed, for many years after the Second World War human rights were very much part and parcel of Cold War politics, and were so regarded by the Left. Double standards, complacency towards friendly dictators, the defence of tradeoffs between human rights and development – all this made human rights suspect as an emancipatory script. Whether in core countries or throughout the developing world, the progressive forces preferred the language of revolution and socialism to formulate an emancipatory politics. However, with the seemly irreversible crisis of these blueprints of emancipation, those same progressive forces find themselves today resorting to human rights to reconstitute the language of emancipation. It is as if human rights were called upon to fill the void left by socialist politics. Can in fact the concept of human rights fill such a void? My answer is a qualified yes. Accordingly, my analytical objective here is to specify the conditions under which human rights can be put at the service of a progressive, emancipatory politics.

The specification of such conditions leads us to unravel some of the dialectical tensions which lie at the core of Western modernity.[1] The crisis now affecting these tensions signals better than anything else the problems facing Western modernity today. In my view, human rights politics at the end of the century is a key factor to understanding such a crisis.

I identify three such tensions. The first one occurs between social regulation and social emancipation. I have been claiming that the paradigm of modernity is based on the idea of a creative dialectical tension between social regulation and social emancipation, which can still be heard, even if but dimly, in the positivist motto of 'order and progress'. At the end of this century this tension has ceased to be a creative tension. Emancipation has ceased to be the other of regulation to become the double of regulation. While until the late 1960s the crisis of social regulation was met by the strengthening of emancipatory politics, today we witness a double social crisis. The crisis of social regulation, symbolized by the crisis of the regulatory state, and the crisis of social emancipation, symbolized by the crisis of the social revolution and socialism as a paradigm of radical social transformation. Human rights politics, which has been both a regulatory and an emancipatory politics, is trapped in this double crisis, while attempting, at the same time, to overcome it.

The second dialectical tension occurs between the state and civil society. The modern state, though a minimalist state, is potentially a maximalist state, to the extent that civil society, as the other of the state, reproduces itself through laws and regulations which emanate from the state and for which there seems to be no limit, as long as the democratic rules of law-making are respected. Human rights are at the core of this tension: while the first generation of human rights was designed as a struggle of civil society against the state, considered to be the sole violator of human rights, the second and third generations of human rights resort to the state as the guarantor of human rights.

Finally, the third tension occurs between the nation-state and what we call globalization. The political model of Western modernity is one of sovereign nation-states coexisting in an international system of equally sovereign states, the interstate system. The privileged unit and scale both of social regulation and social emancipation is the nation-state. The interstate system has always been conceived as a more or less anarchic society, run by a very soft legality, and even working-class internationalism has always been more an aspiration than a reality. Today, the selective erosion of the nation-state due to the intensification of globalization raises the question whether both social regulation and social emancipation are to be displaced to the global level. We have started to speak of global civil society, global governance, global equity. Worldwide recognition of human rights politics is at the forefront of this process. The tension, however, lies in the fact that in very crucial aspects human rights politics is a cultural politics. So much so that we can even think of human rights as symbolizing the return of the cultural and even of the religious at the end of the century. But to speak of culture and religion is to speak of difference, boundaries, particularity. How can human rights be both a cultural and a global politics?

My purpose here, therefore, is to develop an analytical framework to highlight and support the emancipatory potential of human rights politics in the double context of globalization, on the one hand, and cultural fragmentation and identity politics, on the other. My aim is to establish both global competence and local legitimacy for a progressive politics of human rights.

On Globalizations

I shall start by specifying what I mean by globalization. Globalization is very hard to define. Most definitions focus on the economy, that is to say, on the new world economy that has emerged in the last two decades as a consequence of the globalization of the production of goods and services, and financial markets. This is a process through which the transnational corporations have risen to a new and unprecedented pre-eminence as international actors.

For my analytical purposes I prefer a definition of globalization that is more sensitive to the social, political and cultural dimensions. I start from the assumption that what we usually call globalization consists of sets of social relations; as these sets of social relations change, so does globalization. There is strictly no single entity called globalization; there are, rather, globalizations, and we should use the term only in the plural. Any comprehensive concept should always be procedural, rather than substantive. On the other hand, if globalizations are bundles of social relations, the latter are bound to involve conflicts, hence, both winners and losers. More often than not, the discourse on globalization is the story of the winners as told by the winners. Actually, the victory is apparently so absolute that the defeated end up vanishing from the picture altogether.

Here is my definition of globalization: it is the process by which a given local condition or entity succeeds in extending its reach over the globe and, by doing so, develops the capacity to designate a rival social condition or entity as local.

The most important implications of this definition are the following. First, in the conditions of the Western capitalist world system there is no genuine globalization. What we call globalization is always the successful globalization of a given localism. In other words, there is no global condition for which we cannot find a local root, a specific cultural embeddedness. Indeed, I can think of no entity without such a local grounding. The only possible but improbable candidate would be airport architecture. The second implication is that globalization entails localization. In fact, we live in a world of localization, as much as we live in a world of globalization. Therefore, it would be equally correct in analytical terms if we were to define the current situation and our research topics in terms of localization, rather than globalization. The reason why we prefer the latter term is basically because hegemonic scientific discourse tends to prefer the story of the world as told by the winners. Many examples of how globalization entails localization can be given. The English language, as *lingua franca*, is one such example. Its expansion as global language has entailed the localization of other potentially global languages, namely, the French language.

Therefore, once a given process of globalization is identified, its full meaning and explanation may not be obtained without considering adjacent processes of relocalization occurring in tandem and intertwined with it. The globalization of the Hollywood star system may involve the ethnicization of the Hindu star system produced by the once strong Hindu film industry. Similarly, the French or Italian actors of the 1960s – from Brigitte Bardot to Alain Delon, from Marcello Mastroiani to Sofia Loren –

which then symbolized the universal way of acting, seem today, when we see their movies again, as rather ethnic or parochially European. Between then and now, the Hollywoodesque way of acting has managed to globalize itself.

One of the transformations most commonly associated with globalization is time–space compression, that is to say, the social process by which phenomena speed up and spread out across the globe. Though apparently monolithic, this process does combine highly differentiated situations and conditions, and for that reason it cannot be analysed independently of the power relations that account for the different forms of time and space mobility. On the one hand, there is the transnational capitalist class, really in charge of the time–space compression and capable of turning it to its advantage. On the other hand, the subordinate classes and groups, such as migrant workers and refugees, that are also doing a lot of physical moving but not at all in control of the time–space compression. Between corporate executives and immigrants and refugees, tourists represent a third mode of production of time–space compression.

There are also those who heavily contribute to globalization but who, nonetheless, remain prisoners of their local time–space. The peasants of Bolivia, Peru and Colombia, by growing coca, contribute decisively to a world drug culture, but they themselves remain as 'localized' as ever. Just like the residents of Rio's *favelas*, who remain prisoners of the squatter settlement life, while their songs and dances are today part of a globalized musical culture.

Finally, and still from another perspective, global competence requires sometimes the accentuation of local specificity. Most of the tourist sites today must be highly exotic, vernacular and traditional in order to become competent enough to enter the market of global tourism.

In order to account for these asymmetries, globalization, as I have suggested, should always be referred to in the plural. In a rather loose sense, we could speak of different modes of production of globalization to account for this diversity. I distinguish four modes of production of globalization, which, I argue, give rise to four forms of globalization.

The first one I would call *globalized localism*. It consists in the process by which a given local phenomenon is successfully globalized, be it the worldwide operation of transnational corporations (TNCs), the transformation of the English language into the *lingua franca*, the globalization of American fast food or popular music, or the worldwide adoption of American copyright laws on computer software.

The second form of globalization I would call *localized globalism*. It consists of the specific impact of transnational practices and imperatives on local conditions that are thereby destructed and restructured in order to respond to transnational imperatives. Such localized globalisms include: free-trade enclaves; deforestation and massive depletion of natural resources to pay for the foreign debt; touristic use of historical treasures, religious sites or ceremonies, arts and crafts, and wildlife; ecological dumping; conversion of sustainability-oriented agriculture into export-oriented agriculture as part of the 'structural adjustment'; the ethnicization of the workplace.

The international division of globalism assumes the following pattern: the core countries specialize in globalized localisms, while the choice of localized globalisms is imposed upon the peripheral countries. The world system is a web of localized globalisms and globalized localisms.

However, the intensification of global interactions entails two other processes which are not adequately characterized either as globalized localisms or localized globalisms. The first one I would call *cosmopolitanism*. The prevalent forms of domination do not exclude the opportunity for subordinate nation-states, regions, classes or social groups and their allies to organize transnationally in defence of perceived common interests and use to their benefit the capabilities for transnational interaction created by the world system. Cosmopolitan activities involve, among others, South–South dialogues and organizations, worldwide labour organizations (the World Federation of Trade Unions and the International Confederation of Free Trade Unions), North–South transnational philanthropy, international networks of alternative legal services, human rights organizations, worldwide women's groups networks, transformative advocacy non-governmental organizations (NGOs), networks of alternative development and sustainable environment groups, literary, artistic and scientific movements in the periphery of the world system in search of alternative, non-imperialist cultural values, engaging in postcolonial research, subaltern studies, and so on.

The other process that cannot be adequately described either as globalized localism or as localized globalism is the emergence of issues which, by their nature, are as global as the globe itself and which I would call, drawing loosely from international law, the *common heritage of humankind*. These are issues that only make sense when referred to the globe in its entirety: the sustainability of human life on earth, for instance, or such environmental issues as the protection of the ozone layer, the Amazon, Antarctica, biodiversity or the deep seabed. I would also include in this category the exploration of outer space, the moon and other planets, since the interactions of the latter with the earth are also a common heritage of humankind. All these issues refer to resources that, by their very nature, must be administered by trustees of the international community on behalf of present and future generations.

The concern with cosmopolitanism and the common heritage of humankind has known great development in the last decades, but it has also elicited powerful resistances. The common heritage of humankind in particular has been under steady attack by hegemonic countries, especially the USA. The conflicts, resistances, struggles and coalitions clustering around cosmopolitanism and the common heritage of humankind show that what we call globalization is in fact a set of arenas of cross-border struggles.

For my purpose in this chapter, it is useful to distinguish between globalization from above and globalization from below, or between hegemonic and counter-hegemonic globalization. What I called *globalized localism* and *localized globalism* are globalizations from above; *cosmopolitanism* and the *common heritage of humankind* are globalizations from below.

Human Rights as an Emancipatory Script

The complexity of human rights is that they may be conceived either as a form of globalized localism or as a form of cosmopolitanism or, in other words, as a globalization from above or as a globalization from below. My purpose is to specify the conditions under which human rights may be conceived as globalization of the latter kind. In this chapter I will not cover all the necessary conditions, but rather only the cultural ones. My argument is that as long as human rights are conceived as universal human rights, they will tend to operate as a globalized localism, a form of globalization from above. To be able to operate as a cosmopolitan, counter-hegemonic form of globalization human rights must be reconceptualized as multicultural. Conceived, as they have been, as universal, human rights will always be an instrument of Samuel Huntington's 'clash of civilizations', that is to say, of the struggle of the West against the rest. Their global competence will be obtained at the cost of their local legitimacy. On the contrary, multiculturalism, as I understand it, is a precondition for a balanced and mutually reinforcing relationship between global competence and local legitimacy, the two attributes of a counter-hegemonic human rights politics in our time.

We know, of course, that human rights are not universal in their application. Four international regimes of human rights are consensually distinguished in the world in our time: the European, the Inter-American, the African and the Asian regime.[2] But are they universal as a cultural artifact, a kind of cultural invariant, a global culture? All cultures tend to define ultimate values as the most widespread. But only the Western culture tends to focus on universality. The question of the universality of human rights betrays the universality of what it questions by the way it questions it. In other words, the question of universality is a particular question, a Western cultural question.

The concept of human rights lies on a well-known set of presuppositions, all of which are distinctly Western, namely: there is a universal human nature that can be known by rational means; human nature is essentially different from, and higher than, the rest of reality; the individual has an absolute and irreducible dignity that must be defended against society or the state; the autonomy of the individual requires that society be organized in a non-hierarchical way, as a sum of free individuals (Panikkar, 1984: 30). Since all these presuppositions are clearly Western and liberal, and easily distinguishable from other conceptions of human dignity in other cultures, one might ask why the question of the universality of human rights has become so hotly debated; why, in other words, the sociological universality of this question has outgrown its philosophical universality.

If we look at the history of human rights in the postwar period, it is not difficult to conclude that human rights policies by and large have been at the service of the economic and geopolitical interests of the hegemonic capitalist states. The generous and seductive discourse on human rights has allowed for unspeakable atrocities and such atrocities have been evaluated and dealt with according to revolting double standards. Writing in 1981 about the manipulation of the human rights agenda in the USA in conjunction with the mass media, Richard Falk spoke of a 'politics of invisibility' and of a 'politics of supervisibility' (Falk, 1981). As examples of the politics of invisibility he spoke of the total blackout by the media on news about the tragic decimation of the Maubere People in East Timor (taking more than 500,000 lives) and the plight of the hundred million or so 'untouchables' in India. As examples of the politics of supervisibility Falk mentioned the relish with which post-revolutionary abuses of human rights in Iran and Vietnam were reported in the USA. Actually, the same could largely be said of the European Union countries, the most poignant example being the silence that kept the genocide of the Maubere people hidden from the Europeans for a decade, thereby facilitating the ongoing smooth and thriving international trade with Indonesia.

But the Western and indeed the Western liberal mark in the dominant human rights discourse could be traced in many other instances: in the Universal Declaration of 1948, which was drafted without the participation of the majority of the peoples of the world; in the exclusive recognition of individual rights, with the only exception of the collective right to self-determination which, however, was restricted to the peoples subjected to European colonialism; in the priority given to civil and political rights over economic, social and cultural rights, and in the recognition of the right to property as the first and, for many years, the sole economic right.

But this is not the whole story. Throughout the world, millions of people and thousands of non-governmental organizations have been struggling for human rights, often at great risk, in defence of oppressed social classes and groups that in many instances have been victimized by authoritarian capitalistic states. The political agendas of such struggles are usually either explicitly or implicitly anti-capitalist. A counter-hegemonic human rights discourse and practice has been developing, non-Western conceptions of human rights have been proposed, cross-cultural dialogues on human rights have been organized. The central task of emancipatory politics of our time, in this domain, consists in transforming the conceptualization and practice of human rights from a globalized localism into a cosmopolitan project.

What are the premises for such a transformation? The first premise is that it is imperative to transcend the debate on universalism and cultural relativism. The debate is an inherently false debate, whose polar concepts are both and equally detrimental to an emancipatory conception of human rights. All cultures are relative, but cultural relativism, as a philosophical posture, is wrong. All cultures aspire to ultimate concerns and values, but cultural universalism, as a philosophical posture, is wrong. Against universalism, we must propose cross-cultural dialogues on isomorphic concerns. Against relativism, we must develop cross-cultural procedural criteria to distinguish progressive politics from regressive politics, empowerment from disempowerment, emancipation from regulation. To the extent that the debate sparked by human rights might evolve into a competitive dialogue among different cultures on principles of human dignity, it is imperative that such competition induce the transnational coalitions to race to the top rather than to the bottom (what are the absolute minimum standards? the most basic human rights? the lowest common denominators?). The often-voiced cautionary comment against overloading human rights politics with new, more advanced rights or with different and broader conceptions of human rights (Donnelly, 1989: 109–24), is a latter-day manifestation of the reduction of the emancipatory claims of Western modernity to the low degree of emancipation made possible or tolerated by world capitalism – low-intensity human rights as the other side of low-intensity democracy.

The second premise is that all cultures have conceptions of human dignity but not all of them conceive it as human rights. It is therefore important to look for isomorphic concerns among different cultures. Different names, concepts and *Weltanschaungen* may convey similar or mutually intelligible concerns or aspirations.

The third premise is that all cultures are incomplete and problematic in their conceptions of human dignity. The incompleteness derives from the very fact that there is a plurality of cultures. If each culture were as complete as it claims to be, there would be just one single culture. The idea of completeness is at the source of an excess of meaning that seems to plague all cultures. Incompleteness is thus best visible from the outside, from the perspective of another culture. To raise the consciousness of cultural incompleteness to its possible maximum is one of the most crucial tasks in the construction of a multicultural conception of human rights.

The forth premise is that all cultures have different versions of human dignity, some broader than others, some with a wider circle of reciprocity than others, some more open to other cultures than others. For instance, Western modernity has unfolded into two highly divergent conceptions and practices of human rights – the liberal and the Marxist – one prioritizing civil and political rights, the other prioritizing social and economic rights.[3]

Finally, the fifth premise is that all cultures tend to distribute people and social groups among two competing principles of hierarchical belongingness. One operates through hierarchies among homogeneous units. The other operates through separation among unique identities and differences. The two principles do not necessarily overlap and for that reason not all equalities are identical and not all differences are unequal.

These are the premises of a cross-cultural dialogue on human dignity which may eventually lead to a *mestiza* conception of human rights, a conception that instead of resorting to false universalisms, organizes itself as a constellation of local and mutually intelligible local meanings, networks of empowering normative references.

But this is only a starting point. In the case of a cross-cultural dialogue the exchange is not only between different knowledges but also between different cultures, that is to say, between different and, in a strong sense, incommensurable universes of meaning. These universes of meaning consist of constellations of strong *topoi*. These are the overarching rhetorical commonplaces of a given culture. They function as premises of argumentation, thus making possible the production and exchange of arguments. Strong *topoi* become highly vulnerable and problematic whenever 'used' in a different culture. The best that can happen to them is to be moved 'down' from premises of argumentation into arguments. To understand a given culture from another culture's *topoi* may thus prove to be very difficult, if not at all impossible. I shall therefore propose a *diatopical hermeneutics*. In the area of human rights and dignity, the mobilization of social support for the emancipatory claims they potentially contain is only achievable if such claims have been appropriated in the local cultural context. Appropriation, in this sense, cannot be obtained through cultural cannibalization. It requires cross-cultural dialogue and diatopical hermeneutics.

Diatopical hermeneutics is based on the idea that the *topoi* of an individual culture, no matter how strong they may be, are as incomplete as the culture itself. Such incompleteness is not visible from inside the culture itself, since aspiration to the totality induces taking *pars pro toto*. The objective of diatopical hermeneutics is, therefore, not to achieve completeness – that being an unachievable goal – but, on the contrary, to raise the consciousness of reciprocal incompleteness to its possible maximum by engaging in the dialogue, as it were, with one foot in one culture and the other in another. Herein lies its *dia-topical* character.[4]

A diatopical hermeneutics can be conducted between the *topos* of human rights in Western culture and the *topos* of *dharma* in Hindu culture, and the *topos* of *umma* in Islamic culture. According to Panikkar, *dharma*

> . . . is that which maintains, gives cohesion and thus strength to any given thing, to reality, and ultimately to the three worlds (triloka). Justice keeps human relations together; morality keeps oneself in harmony; law is the binding principle for human relations; religion is what maintains the universe in existence; destiny is that which links us with future; truth is the internal cohesion of a thing. . . . Now a world in which the notion of Dharma is central and nearly all-pervasive is not concerned with finding the 'right' of one individual against another or of the individual *vis-à-vis* society, but rather with assaying the dharmic (right, true, consistent) or adharmic character of a thing or an action within the entire theantropocosmic complex of reality. (Panikkar, 1984: 39)[5]

Seen from the *topos* of *dharma*, human rights are incomplete in that they fail to establish the link between the part (the individual) and the whole (reality), or even more strongly in that they focus on what is merely derivative, on rights, rather than on the primordial imperative, the duty of individuals to find their place in the order of the entire society, and of the entire cosmos. Seen from *dharma* and, indeed from *umma* also, the Western conception of human rights is plagued by a very simplistic and mechanicistic symmetry between rights and duties. It grants rights only to those from whom it can demand duties. This explains why, according to Western human rights, nature has no rights: for the simple reason that no duties can be demanded of nature. For the same reason, it is impossible to grant rights to future generations: they have no rights because they have no duties.

On the other hand, seen from the *topos* of human rights, *dharma* is also incomplete due to its strong undialectical bias in favour of harmony, thereby occulting injustices and totally neglecting the value of conflict as a way towards a richer harmony. Moreover, *dharma* is unconcerned with the principles of democratic order, with freedom and autonomy, and it neglects the fact that, without primordial rights, the individual is too fragile an entity to avoid being run over by whatever transcends him or her. Moreover, *dharma* tends to forget that human suffering has an irreducible individual dimension: societies don't suffer, individuals do.

At another conceptual level, the same diatopical hermeneutics can be attempted between the *topos* of human rights and the *topos* of *umma* in Islamic culture. The passages in the Qur'an in which the word *umma* occurs are so varied that its meaning cannot be rigidly defined. This much, however, seems to be certain: it always refers to ethnical, linguistic or religious bodies of people who are the objects of the divine plan of salvation. As the prophetic activity of Muhammad progressed, the religious foundations of *umma* became increasingly apparent and consequently the *umma* of the Arabs was transformed into the *umma* of the Muslims. Seen from the *topos* of *umma*, the incompleteness of the individual human rights lies in the fact that on its basis alone it is impossible to ground the collective linkages and solidarities without which no society can survive, and much less flourish. Herein lies the difficulty in the Western conception of human rights to accept collective rights of social groups or peoples, be they ethnic minorities, women or indigenous peoples. This is in fact a specific instance of a much broader difficulty: the difficulty of defining the community as an arena of concrete solidarity, and as an horizontal political obligation. Central to Rousseau, this idea of community was flushed away in the liberal dichotomy that set asunder the state and civil society.

Conversely, from the *topos* of the individual human rights, *umma* overemphasizes duties to the detriment of rights and, for that reason, is bound to condone otherwise abhorrent inequalities, such as the inequality between men and women and between Muslims and non-Muslims. As unveiled by the diatopical hermeneutics, the fundamental weakness of Western culture consists in dichotomizing too strictly between the individual and society, thus becoming vulnerable to possessive individualism, narcissism, alienation and anomie. On the other hand, the fundamental weakness of Hindu and Islamic culture consists in that they both fail to recognize that human suffering has an irreducible individual dimension, which can only be adequately addressed in a society not hierarchically organized.

The recognition of reciprocal incompletenesses and weaknesses is a condition *sine qua non* of a cross-cultural dialogue. Diatopical hermeneutics builds both on local identification of incompleteness and weakness and on its translocal intelligibility. In the area of human rights and dignity, the mobilization of social support for the emancipatory claims they potentially contain is only achievable if such claims have been appropriated in the local cultural context. Appropriation, in this sense, cannot be obtained through cultural cannibalization. It requires cross-cultural dialogue and diatopical hermeneutics. A good example of a diatopical hermeneutics between Islamic and Western culture in the field of human rights is given by Abdullahi Ahmed An-na'im (1990, 1992).

There is a long-standing debate on the relationships between Islamism and human rights and the possibility of an Islamic conception of human rights.[6] This debate covers a wide range of positions, and its impact reaches far beyond the Islamic world. Running the risk of excessive simplification, two extreme positions can be identified in this debate. One, absolutist or fundamentalist, is held by those for whom the religious legal system of Islam, the Shari'a, must be fully applied as the law of the Islamic state. According to this position, there are irreconcilable inconsistencies between the Shari'a and the Western conception of human rights, and the Shari'a must prevail. For instance, regarding the status of non-Muslims, the Shari'a dictates the creation of a state for Muslims as the sole citizens, non-Muslims having no political rights; peace between Muslims and non-Muslims is always problematic and confrontations may be unavoidable. Concerning women, there is no question of equality; the Shari'a commands the segregation of women and, according to some more strict interpretations, even excludes them from public life altogether.

At the other extreme, there are the secularists or the modernists, who believe that Muslims should organize themselves in secular states. Islam is a religious and spiritual movement, not a political one and, as such, modern Muslim societies are free to organize their government in whatever manner they deem fit and appropriate to the circumstances. The acceptance of international human rights is a matter of political decision unencumbered by religious considerations. Just one example, among many: a Tunisian law of 1956 prohibited polygamy altogether on the grounds that it was no longer acceptable and that the Qur'anic requirement of justice among co-wives was impossible for any man, except the Prophet, to achieve in practice.

An-na'im criticizes both extreme positions. The *via per mezzo* he proposes aims at establishing a cross-cultural foundation for human rights, identifying the areas of conflict between Shari'a and 'the standards of human rights' and seeking a reconciliation and positive relationship between the two systems. For example, the problem with historical Shari'a is that it excludes women and non-Muslims from the application of this principle. Thus, a reform or reconstruction of Shari'a is needed. The method proposed for such 'Islamic Reformation' is based on an evolutionary approach to Islamic sources that looks into the specific historical context within which Shari'a was created out of the original sources of Islam by the founding jurists of the eighth and ninth centuries. In the light of such a context, a restricted construction of the other was probably justified. But this is no longer so. On the contrary, in the present different context there is within Islam full justification for a more enlightened view.

Following the teachings of *Ustadh* Mahmoud, An-na'im shows that a close examination of the content of the Qur'an and Sunna reveals two levels or stages of the message of Islam, one of the earlier Mecca period and the other of the subsequent Medina stage. The earlier message of Mecca is the eternal and fundamental message of Islam and it emphasizes the inherent dignity of all human beings, regardless of gender, religious belief or race. Under the historical conditions of the seventh century (the Medina stage) this message was considered too advanced, was suspended, and its implementation postponed until appropriate circumstances would emerge in the future. The time and context, says An-na'im, are now ripe for it.

It is not for me to evaluate the specific validity of this proposal within Islamic culture. This is precisely what distinguishes diatopical hermeneutics from orientalism. What I want to emphasize in An-na'im's approach is the attempt to transform the Western conception of human rights into a cross-cultural one that vindicates Islamic legitimacy rather than relinquishing it. In the abstract and from the outside, it is difficult to judge whether a religious or a secularist approach is more likely to succeed in an Islamic-based cross-cultural dialogue on human rights. However, bearing in mind that Western human rights are the expression of a profound, albeit incomplete process of secularization, which is not comparable to anything in Islamic culture, one would be inclined to suggest that, in the Muslim context, the mobilizing energy needed for a cosmopolitan project of human rights will be more easily generated within an enlightened religious framework. If so, An-na'im's approach is very promising.

Diatopical hermeneutics is not a task for a single person writing within a single culture. It is, therefore, not surprising that An-na'im's approach, though a true *examplar* of diatopical hermeneutics, is conducted with uneven consistency. In my view, An-na'im accepts the idea of universal human rights too readily and acritically. Even though he subscribes to an evolutionary approach and is quite attentive to the historical context of Islamic tradition, he becomes surprisingly ahistorical and naïvely universalist as far the Universal Declaration goes. Diatopical hermeneutics requires not only a different kind of knowledge, but also a different process of knowledge creation. It requires a production of knowledge that must be collective, interactive, intersubjective and networked.

The diatopical hermeneutics conducted by An-na'im, from the perspective of Islamic culture, and the human rights struggles organized by Islamic feminist grassroots movements following the ideas of 'Islamic Reformation' proposed by him, must be matched by a diatopical hermeneutics conducted from the perspective of other cultures and namely from the perspective of Western culture. This is probably the only way to embed in the Western culture the idea of collective rights, rights of nature and future generations, and of duties and responsibilities *vis-à-vis* collective entities, be they the community, the world, or even the cosmos.

More generally, the diatopical hermeneutics offers a wide field of possibilities for debates going on, in the different cultural regions of the world system, on the general issues of universalism, relativism, cultural frames of social transformation, traditionalism and cultural revival.[7] However, an idealistic conception of cross-cultural dialogue will easily forget that such a dialogue is only made possible by the temporary simultaneity of two or more different contemporaneities. The partners in the dialogue are only superficially contemporaneous; indeed each of them feels himself or herself only contemporaneous with the historical tradition of his or her respective culture. This is most likely the case when the different cultures involved in the dialogue share a past of interlocked unequal exchanges. What are the possibilities for a cross-cultural dialogue when one of the cultures *in presence* has been itself moulded by massive and long-lasting violations of human rights perpetrated in the name of the other culture? When cultures share such a past, the present they share at the moment of starting the dialogue is at best a *quid pro quo* and at worst a fraud. The cultural dilemma is the following: since in the past the dominant culture rendered unpronounceable some of the aspirations of the subordinate culture to human dignity, is it now possible to pronounce them in the cross-cultural dialogue without thereby further justifying and even reinforcing their unpronounceability?

Cultural imperialism and epistemicide are part of the historical trajectory of Western modernity. After centuries of unequal cultural exchanges, is equal treatment of cultures fair? Is it necessary to render some aspiration of Western culture unpronounceable in order to make room for the pronounceability of other aspirations of other cultures? Paradoxically – and contrary to hegemonic discourses – it is precisely in the field of human rights that Western culture must learn from the South, if the false universality that is attributed to human rights in the imperial context is to be converted into the new universality of cosmopolitanism in a cross-cultural dialogue.

The emancipatory character of the diatopical hermeneutics is not guaranteed a priori, and indeed multiculturalism may be the new mark of a reactionary politics. Suffice it to mention the multiculturalism of the Prime Minister of Malaysia or the Chinese gerontocracy, when they speak of the

'Asian conception of human rights'. To pre-empt this move, two trans-cultural imperatives must be accepted by all social groups engaging in diatopical hermeneutics. The first one goes like this: of the different versions of a given culture, that one must be chosen which represents the widest circle of reciprocity within that culture, the version that goes farthest in the recognition of the other. As we have seen, of two different interpretations of the Qur'an, An-na'im chooses the one with the wider circle of reciprocity, the one that involves Muslims and non-Muslims, men and women alike. I think this must be done within Western culture as well. Of the two versions of human rights existing in our culture – the liberal and the Marxist – the Marxist one must be adopted for it extends to the economic and social realms, the equality that the liberal version only considers legitimate in the political realm.

The second transcultural imperative goes like this: since all cultures tend to distribute people and groups according to two competing principles of hierarchical belongingness, and thus to competing conceptions of equality and difference, people have the right to be equal whenever difference makes them inferior, but they also have the right to be different whenever equality jeopardizes their identity. This is a very difficult imperative to attain and to sustain. Multinational constitutional states such as Belgium approximate it in some ways. There is much hope that South Africa will do the same.

As they are now predominantly understood, human rights are a kind of esperanto which can hardly become the everyday language of human dignity across the globe. It is up to the diatopical hermeneutics sketched above to transform them into a cosmopolitan politics networking mutually intelligible and translatable native languages of emancipation.

This project may sound rather utopian, but, as Sartre once said, before it is realized an idea has a strange resemblance with utopia. Be it as it may, the important fact is not to reduce realism to what exists, in which case we may be constrained to justify what exists, no matter how unjust or oppressive.

Notes

1 Elsewhere, I deal at length with the dialectical tensions in Western modernity (Santos, 1995).

2 For an extended analysis of the four regimes, see Santos, 1995: 330–7, and the bibliography cited there.

3 See, for instance, Pollis and Schwab, 1979a, 1979b; Pollis, 1982; An-na'im, 1992.

4 See also Panikkar, 1984: 28.

5 See also Thapar, 1966; Mitra, 1982; Inada, 1990.

6 Besides An-na'im, 1990, 1992 see Dwyer, 1991; Leites, 1991; Mayer, 1991; Afkhami, 1995. See also Hassan, 1982; Al Faruqi, 1983. On the broader issues of the relationship between modernity and Islamic revival, see, for instance, Sharabi, 1992; and Shariati, 1986.

7 For the African debate, see Oladipo, 1989; Oruka, 1990; Wiredu, 1990; Wamba dia Wamba, 1991, 1992; Procee, 1992; Ramose, 1992. A sample of the rich debate in India is in

Nandy, 1987a, 1987b, 1988; Chatterjee, 1984; Pantham, 1988. A bird's-eye view of cultural differences can be found in Galtung, 1981.

References

Afkhami, Mahnaz (ed.) (1995) *Faith and Freedom: Women's Human Rights in the Muslim World.* Syracuse, NY: Syracuse University Press.

Al Faruqi, Isma'il R. (1983) 'Islam and human rights', *The Islamic Quarterly,* 27 (1): 12–30.

An-na'im, Abdullahi A. (1990) *Toward an Islamic Reformation.* Syracuse, NY: Syracuse University Press.

An-na'im, Abdullahi A. (ed.) (1992) *Human Rights in Cross-Cultural Perspectives: A Quest for Consensus.* Philadelphia: University of Pennsylvania Press.

Chatterjee, Partha (1984) 'Gandhi and the critique of civil society', in R. Guha (ed.), *Subaltern Studies III: Writings on South Asian History and Society.* Delhi: Oxford University Press. pp. 153–95.

Donnelly, Jack (1989) *Universal Human Rights in Theory and Practice.* Ithaca, NY: Cornell University Press.

Dwyer, Kevin (1991) *Arab Voices: The Human Rights Debate in the Middle East.* Berkeley, CA: University of California Press.

Falk, Richard (1981) *Human Rights and State Sovereignty.* New York: Holmes & Meier.

Galtung, Johan (1981) 'Western civilization: anatomy and pathology', *Alternatives,* 7: 145–69.

Hassan, Riffat (1982) 'On human rights and the Qur'anic perspective', *Journal of Ecumenical Studies,* 19 (3): 51–65.

Inada, Kenneth K. (1990) 'A Buddhist response to the nature of human rights', in C. Welch, Jr. and V. Leary (eds), *Asian Perspectives on Human Rights.* Boulder, CO: Westview Press. pp. 91—101.

Leites, Justin (1991) 'Modernist jurisprudence as a vehicle for gender role reform in the Islamic world', *Columbia Human Rights Law Review,* 22: 251–330.

Mayer, Ann Elizabeth (1991) *Islam and Human Rights: Tradition and Politics.* Boulder, CO: Westview Press.

Mitra, Kana (1982) 'Human rights in Hinduism', *Journal of Ecumenical Studies,* 19 (3): 77–84.

Nandy, Ashis (1987a) 'Cultural frames for social transformation: a credo', *Alternatives,* XII: 113–23.

Nandy, Ashis (1987b) *Traditions, Tyranny and Utopias: Essays in the Politics of Awareness.* Oxford: Oxford University Press.

Nandy, Ashis (1988) 'The politics of secularism and the recovery of religious tolerance', *Alternatives,* XIII: 177–94.

Oladipo, Olusegun (1989) 'Towards a philosophical study of African culture: a critique of traditionalism', *Quest,* 3 (2): 31–50.

Oruka, H. Odera (1990) 'Cultural fundamentals in philosophy', *Quest,* 4 (2): 21–37.

Pannikar, Raimundo (1984) 'Is the notion of human rights a Western concept?', *Cahier,* 81: 28–47.

Pantham, Thomas (1988) 'On modernity, rationality and morality: Habermas and Gandhi', *The Indian Journal of Social Science,* 1 (2): 187–208.

Pollis, Adamantia (1982) 'Liberal, socialist and Third World perspectives of human rights', in P. Schwab and A. Pollis (eds), *Toward a Human Rights Framework.* New York: Praeger. pp. 1–26.

Pollis, Adamantia and Schwab, P. (eds) (1979a) *Human Rights: Cultural and Ideological Perspectives.* New York: Praeger.

Pollis, Adamantia and Schwab, P. (1979b) 'Human rights: a Western construct with limited applicability', in A. Pollis and P. Schwab (eds), *Human Rights: Cultural and Ideological Perspectives.* New York: Praeger. pp. 1–18.

Procee, Henk (1992) 'Beyond universalism and relativism', *Quest,* 6 (1): 45–55.

Ramose, Mogobe B. (1992) 'African democratic traditions: oneness, consensus and openness', *Quest*, 6 (1): 63–83.

Santos, Boaventura de Sousa (1995) *Toward a New Common Sense: Law, Science and Politics in the Paradigmatic Transition*. New York: Routledge.

Sharabi, Hisham (1992) 'Modernity and Islamic revival: the critical tasks of Arab intellectuals', *Contention*, 2 (1): 127–47.

Shariati, Ali (1986) *What is to be Done: the Enlightened Thinkers and an Islamic Renaissance* (ed. Farhang Rajaee). Houston, TX: The Institute for Research and Islamic Studies.

Thapar, Romila (1966) 'The Hindu and Buddhist traditions', *International Social Science Journal*, 18 (1): 31–40.

Wamba dia Wamba, Ernest (1991) 'Some remarks on culture development and revolution in Africa', *Journal of Historical Sociology*, 4: 219–35.

Wamba dia Wamba, Ernest (1992) 'Beyond elite politics of democracy in Africa', *Quest*, 6 (1): 28–42.

Wiredu, Kwasi (1990) 'Are there cultural universals?', *Quest*, 4 (2): 5–19.

13

THE HYBRIDIZATION OF ROOTS AND THE ABHORRENCE OF THE BUSH

Jonathan Friedman

There are major changes sweeping the class organization of the world system. They became evident to me when I discovered that a certain way of representing reality, as hybridity was not a mere intellectual interpretation of the state of contemporary reality, but a politicized position. In the following I shall suggest that this identity and interpretation is an aspect of the emergence of a new global cultural elite or class faction that takes its form as particular state–class structures that pit a cosmopolitan elite against a nationalist 'red-neck' and, by definition, backward-looking working class, or remnants thereof. The representational logic of this development is one that is vertical and encompassing. Its vision of global reality is one in which the global itself is a place, located above and including the different local places of the world and which has emerged out of a more fragmented or localized world. This evolutionary logic applies to many statements concerning economic globalization as well as cultural globalization. The world is one place, structured by multinational capital whose project is to surpass the nation-state and create a world society, or at least a world working class. For this reason the following discussion contains two arguments, one concerning economic globalization and the other focused on the culture–class linkage.

Globalization in Economic Terms

Much has been made of the notion of globalization, understood as the increasing integration of the world under the aegis of increasingly central-ized forms of capital accumulation, of power over finance and production, and following this of markets, media and forms of dominance. I seek here simply to relate this appearance to what is another, perhaps more dynamic, reality of the global system.

The obvious aspect of the globalization process is the multinationaliza-tion of production via the development and dominance of transnational corporations (TNCs). There is a steady increase in the importance of TNCs in international trade. Such firms account for 80 per cent of international trade in the USA, and one-third of this trade is intra-firm. This indicates an increasing verticalization of, or integration of, various sectors under the aegis of single firms. Foreign direct investment (FDI) by the developed countries has increased cyclically but decidedly in the 1970s and 1980s. In the mid-1980s FDI increased three times faster than export trade. To understand this as a structural phenomenon, we might say that we are moving from a structure of national production coupled to international trade, to an internationalization of production itself. There are two phenomena that must be recognized here. First, there is an important technological change, an increase in the ability to move production processes via increasing modularization and greatly increasing productivity of transportation. This enables a general speed-up in the movement of production processes as well as new ways of dividing them up in space, a space which becomes increasingly cheaper and therefore less significant as a constraint and therefore more heterogeneous. It is clear that the spectacular development of information technologies is crucial in this 'time–space compression' and increasing sensitivity of capital movements. The capacity to globalize has thus increased significantly. But, the actual strategy of global capital movements has not changed in its basic structure. In other words, globalization does not occur because it is possible. Its engine lies in the differential gradient of profitability in the global arena, a gradient that can change rapidly and which channels movements of capital. The latter are movements of investment in sources of wealth in general and not merely production.

Now a main reason for FDI is to offset declining advantages of national production and export. Such a shift implies a relative decentralization of production from the home country to new hosts. It is not a modern invention although it has taken other forms in the past. Portfolio investment has been more important in the export of productive capital in the past, and this can be understood in terms of differences in the technology of transport, that is the capacity to export production. In such terms, there is nothing new in principle about the current globalized world. Forty per cent of the investment in the English Industrial Revolution came from Holland and Italy. The spread of railroads around the world, a major capital export, was the result of British and French investments in overseas production. The massive export of capital from Britain which had much to do with the industrialization of the USA at the turn of the nineteenth century had everything to do with a logic that has been a constant in the global system. Much of this shifting flow of capital has been related to changing cycles of hegemony in the centre of the Western world system: from the Mediterranean to Northern Europe, from Holland and Northern France to England, from England to Germany and the USA, from the USA to Western Europe and Japan after the Second World War, from the entire West to Eastern Asia, India and parts of Latin America. This last shift has been of a monumental character, a regional shift from West to East, Southeast and selected portions of the South. In our understanding, multinationalization of investment of wealth is related to, and productive of, declining hegemony. The form that it has taken is the globalization of production, and the multinationals seem to have gained considerably in power, as if a new level of global reality had emerged. But the fact is that as nation-states exist, and the level of welfare is still a national phenomenon, that is the degree to which capital investment tends to concentrate in one place or another. It is this clustering that makes it possible for Porter to argue for a comparative advantage of nations in an era of globalization. Thus the appearance of an increasing degree of multinationalization should not detract from our understanding of the differential regional flows of capital in the world system. In 1956 the USA had 42 of the top 50 corporations, a clear sign of hegemony over world production. In 1989 that number had dropped to 17. Europe as a whole has a larger number (21) of the 50 top firms today than the USA.

This would imply that the globalization of capital is a temporally delimited phenomenon or phase within a larger system rather than a general evolutionary phenomenon. It would in this case be related to the break-up of hegemonies, a process of fragmentation and decentralization of the accumulation of wealth in the larger system. Now in the contemporary situation there are clear markers of this process. While production and export have increased unabated since the 1960s, the developed market economies decreased their share of total world production from 72 to 64 per cent while developing countries more than doubled their share. Between 1963 and 1987 the USA has decreased its share of world manufacturing from 40.3 per cent to 24 per cent. Japan increased its portion from 5.5 per cent to 19 per cent in the same period. West Germany is stable around 9–10 per cent, but the UK declined from 6–5 per cent to 3.3 per cent. France, Italy and Canada have also declined somewhat in this period.

> It is especially notable that in the East and South East Asian NICs [new industrializing countries] manufacturing growth rates remained at a high level throughout the 1970s and 1980s whereas those of the leading developed market economies fell to half or less of their 1960s levels. (Dicken, 1992: 27)

Significant increases in Spain, Brazil, India and the NICs have been part of a larger process of decentralization of capital accumulation.

> Whereas in the first quarter of this century 95% of world manufacturing production was concentrated into only ten countries, by 1986 twenty-five countries were responsible for the same proportion of world output. (Dicken, 1992: 27)

In other words there is a trend toward decentralization of production in geographical terms.

> [M]anufacturing counted for only 19.8% of total exports in 1960 but for as much as 47% in 1988. In fact, by the end of the 1970s, for the very first time, the value of manufactured products exported from the developing market economies exceeded that of food and raw materials. After 1973 exports of manufactured

goods from the Third World grew at twice the rate of exports of raw materials. Without doubt the old international division of labour had been displaced. (Dicken, 1992: 27)

At the same time the world leaders lost shares in the total world export of manufacturing.

Table 13.1   *Percentage of world export of manufacturing*

	1963 %	1989 %
Japan	6	9
West Germany	15	11
UK	11	5
USA	17	12

And it is the centre that is the target market for this new production. Between 1978 and 1998 manufacturing exports to the USA increased from 17.4 per cent to 31.8 per cent. The process here is one where exported capital produces products that are re-imported to the centre. The trend here is to increasing competition, decentralization and a clear shift of capital accumulation to the East.

The model for my argument is that multinationalization of capital is a general process in periods of hegemonic decline. This is true of all commercial civilizations as well. For classical Athens and Rome the decentralization of production took the form of migration of artisans and merchants from the centre to specifically designated peripheral zones. In nineteenth-century capitalism it consisted in an increasing export of portfolio capital and today it takes the form of transnational production. Thus, I would argue, this is not a question of evolution so much as a question of cyclical decline and ascendancy, in the present case a general movement of productive capacity from the USA and Europe to the Far East, and a shift that has given rise to the concept of the 'Pacific Century'. This changing configuration is summed up by Bergesen and Fernandez:

> The network analysis of the national and industrial distribution of the world's 50 largest firms supports the idea that American dominance in world production is declining, and that competition between regions is increasing. The tripolar world economy is becoming a reality. Europe appears to increase the number of firms which compete with the United States, but the number of industries in which they compete stays constant. Japan and the NICs increase both the number of firms and industries which are in competition with the United States. (Bergesen and Fernandez, 1995: 24)

Thus the view that we are heading towards an increasingly integrated world, a globalized economy, is certainly a tendency in economic terms, but it does not necessarily mean that we are entering a new kind of world. The space of transnational capital and accompanying transnational institutions, clubs, classes and elites is certainly a part of the globalization process, but this does not account for the changes in regional distribution of accumulation and power in the world. Globalization, in other words, does not mean unification or even integration in any other way than increased coordination of world markets. Transnational corporations are, in important respects, the agents of the decentralization of wealth rather than its geographical concentration. And wealth, measured in consumption power, standard of living or whatever, is always geographically localized not global, not unless we all live in a third place called the global village. And where, one might ask, is that located? This argument is relatively simple. The world is still a geographically delimited place, and however virtual capital and communication has become, it still occurs between places, at least until virtual reality replaces the other one. What has happened in terms of trends is that the entire system operates at a faster rate, so that all the economic cycles have accelerated, including cycles of hegemony. This speed-up, primarily a result of the increasing productivity of information technology, is the major operator in the space–time compression that Harvey (1989) so clearly outlines. This in itself might have serious structural consequences, in so far as hegemonic stability with all of its political and cultural concomitants may prove to be an impossibility in the long run, but the underlying properties of the system remain the same, and this is at bottom a system of accumulation of abstract wealth that has been around for several thousand years. Thus two contradictory tendencies emerge. One is the historical shift in hegemony that we have outlined above. The other is a potential product of speed-up which would lead to the kind of implosive world city structure implied in the work of Sassen (1994, 1996).

Hybridity and the Ideological Matrix of Racism

Cultural globalization is correlative to the argument for economic globalization. The latter has taken on numerous forms during the past decade. A pervasive feeling and fear of many intellectuals has been the expected homogenization of the cultural organization of the world, by means of Western state intervention. This has been countered by arguments for local resistance, assimilation and finally hybridization. As a form of self-identification, hybridity harbours two inconsistencies: one growing out of the way the category is constructed; the other related to the social group that so identifies the world.

First, it should be recognized that hybridity is an old concept and one very central to writers on race in the nineteenth century and even earlier. Young's excellent discussion in *Colonial Desire: Hybridity in Theory, Culture and Race*, demonstrates the degree to which anti-'orientalist' discourse has vastly oversimplified the writings of this period and how modern self-declared hybrids are ensconced within the older framework of race:

'The question is whether the old essentializing categories of cultural identity, or of race, were really so essentialized, or have been retrospectively constructed as more fixed than they were' (Young, 1995: 27). Young argues that much of cultural studies is imprisoned in the same racial language that it seeks to criticize: 'If so, then in deconstructing such essentialist notions of race today we may rather be repeating the past than distancing ourselves from it or providing a critique of it' (1995: 27).

Now while there is clearly an historical gap in this argument, there is a certain logic to the concept of hybridity that merits our attention. This is aptly expressed in the 'diasporic' onslaught upon the nation which I have taken up above.

> But blood, which is to say, discourse about blood, ties us down and holds us in or out – and not only the kind of blood you are said to be born with, but also the kind of blood you shed. (Kelly, 1995: 477)

In this respect it should not be forgotten that race through most of the nineteenth century was a collection of cultural, behavioural and physical traits. No distinction was made between them and not all of them were necessary to classify the 'other'. So the new found term 'cultural racism' is none other than classical racism itself. The biological discourse of race is a twentieth-century phenomenon, itself related to the dissolution of the formerly more encompassing category. The attack on racism consisted in demonstrating that culture could not be genetically transmitted although it might be argued that it could be culturally transmitted. In this sense it is merely a question of the degree of ascription involved. Now there are two components to the racial argument. First is the notion that all X are bearers of a set of traits, physical or cultural. The second, stronger notion is that cultural traits are reducible to physical or biological traits. The second notion is racism proper. But any notion of the type 'all X are bearers of a distinctive set of traits which are inherited over time and thus ascriptive' belongs to a general family of essentialist discourse. Essentialism, however, need not be biological. But neither need it be wrong. Otherwise there are no such things as group-specific life-forms that have temporal continuity, no such thing as habitus. The problem, then, is not the attribution of a fixed set of properties to a given population, but the assumption that this set of properties is somehow not the result of practice but an inherent property of the individual members of that population. It is the substantivization of culture and the channelling of this substance into individuals as if it were a packet of recipes, codes or even knowledges that can be passed on like genetic material or blood to coming generations of individuals. If culture is carried in this way by individual subjects, it implies that a population's culture is only the individual bearer writ large.

It is this notion of culture that gives rise to the notion of hybridity and creolization. Cultures flow into one another and mix. And the more movement of culture in the world, by means of migration, media transmission, etc., the more mixture until finally we have a hybridized world equivalent in cultural terms to the economic globalization process. This can occur because cultures are substances that flow into one another from disparate origins producing mixtures that maintain the properties of those origins. This is, as Young suggests, a metaphorical extension of the discourse of race whose focus on hybridity foreshadows the current use of the term. In the struggle against the racism of purity, hybridity invokes the dependent, not converse, notion of the mongrel. Instead of combating essentialism, it merely hybridizes it.

Globalization as Hybridity

The 'birds-eye' view of the goings-on of the world may indeed convey an image of mixture and even of confusion, even if this is not the case for those who are observed (Ekholm and Friedman, 1995).

> How do we come to terms with phenomena such as Thai boxing by Moroccan girls in Amsterdam, Asian rap in London, Irish bagels, Chinese tacos and Mardi Gras Indians in the United States, or 'Mexican schoolgirls dressed in Greek togas dancing in the style of Isadora Duncan'. (Pietersee, 1995: 53)

What is it that we must come to terms with here? The problem would seem to be reducible to 'how do we identify' such phenomena, and as the phenomena are described as specific products, that is as cultural products, the question becomes 'How do we classify such phenomena?' This is a question asked by 'theoreticians' on race in the nineteenth century and by cultural diffusionists (also linked to the question of race, via migrations), that is how to map the world, put labels on things. But is it not striking that this intense preoccupation should appear today? What about blues, jazz, pasta and other potential hybrids of the past (Pietersee makes it clear that he understands hybridity to be a very general historical condition)? Is there more of this kind of thing nowadays or has something else happened? Could it be that the consciousness of mixture is simply a product of a genealogical turn in individual identity in a situation where the global has become a commonplace image in the media, a widely noted experience among Western middle classes? Could it be the product of the speed-up factor itself, Harvey's time–space compression coupled to a discourse of rootedness, that is the entanglement of the world's roots? Might one then want to draw this into a coherent account of the formation of a new 'elite' gaze produced in the experience of consumption of globally identified objects and images? And should we not then ask who it is who maintains such a gaze and produces the global images?

I would suggest that hybridity is very closely related to a major transformation of dominant ideology and that it is itself linked to the emergence of a new cosmopolitan elite. The intellectuals who so identify often have a powerful attraction to the media, both as subject of discussion and as willing participants. But this is not necessarily unauthentic. The relation of the intellectual to the world is one of contemplation, of objectification, of the external gaze. The experience of mixture, hybridity and even cultural confusion is the immediate experience of the postmodern tourist. This experience is based on the background of authenticity, the notion that in some past, locality/territory and culture hung together in separate units that are sometimes expressed in what is called the world mosaic. This leads to the quasi-evolutionistic model of world history as one of successive stages of global integration. The current stage is one in which culture has begun to overflow its boundaries and mingle with other cultures, producing numerous new breeds or hybrids.

The hybrid image is, I would suggest, a positioned representation of reality, and aside from its internal structure, it is a strangely spontaneous and unelaborated concept. It is, rather, a labelling device, an attempt to define the cultural state of the world. It is typical for hegemonic models that they generalize from one position to speak for the rest, and hybridism as a representation clearly harbours hegemonic intentions in so far as it translates a particular perception into a general interpretation.

The Cosmopolitan Connection

Cosmopolitans are a product of modernity, individuals whose shared experience is based on a certain loss of rootedness. It is for some a celebration of rootlessness and for others a powerfully ambivalent state of liberation versus alienation. Cosmopolitans identify with the urban, with the 'modern', with high culture which belongs to the world rather than the nation. They are the sworn enemies of national and ethnic identities since the latter are an absolute threat to their existence, even as they are part of the definition of the cosmopolitan, since the word has no meaning unless opposed to the local. Cosmopolitans have been around for a long time, of course, as long as commercial civilizations (Friedman, 1997). Cosmopolitanism is part of the very logic of modern individual subjective experience, based on alterity and distance to any particular world of meanings. It constructs a 'higher', more abstract knowledge of the world that acknowledges the local, by definition, while transcending it, also by definition. But while alterity is constitutive of modern experience, cosmopolitans actively engage alterity by translating it into geographical displacement. There is a difference, however, between modernist and the current, postmodernist, cosmopolitan. Modernist identity as an ideal type is anti-ethnic, anti-cultural, anti-religious. It works to maintain a self-experience in which alterity itself is transformed into sceptical rationalism, where nothing is taken for granted. The cosmopolitans of the turn of the century, and up to quite recently, were modernists. It was based on a striving for universal values and context freedom. The modernist nation-state was one which valued citizenship as formal membership and participation in the modern project, defined in terms of increasing standards of living, better knowledge in general, science in particular and high culture. As this system depended upon a hegemonic world order, which has now begun to dissolve, its modernist identity has also begun to dissolve.

Ernest Gellner (1994), in a very interesting discussion of the lives of Wittgenstein and Malinowski, both immigrants to England from the Hapsburg empire and its allies, described the modernist cosmopolitan in no uncertain terms. Wittgenstein, especially, represents the urban intellectual, totally dependent upon the imperial centre of Vienna, surrounded by rising nationalisms in the empire, movements of the locals, the red-necks, the unsophisticated. His own ambivalence and seeking after *Gemeinschaft* drove him to become a provincial school teacher, a total disaster for this master of the abstract, especially in the *Tractatus*. Wittgenstein was unable to resolve his problem in concrete terms, but this drove him to find a solution in philosophy, i.e. the philosophy of ordinary language, which became the substitute and symbol for the concrete lived experience that he could not attain via his modernist identity.

The decline of modernism has led to a situation where cosmopolitan ideology can no longer represent itself as higher, rational and abstract. What has been referred to as postmodernism is but one aspect of a more general shift of identity towards roots, identity that is somehow culturally fixed and a value in itself. In the first phase of intellectual reaction there was an onslaught on scientific knowledge, rationality, and high culture. It was part of an upsurge of the indigenous, the local, the cultural in general, as a form of tradition and traditional wisdom, all of which has taken the form of the re-emergence of that which had been repressed by modernism. The political form of this transformation is best expressed in multiculturalist politics and in its stronger form as indigeneity, a return to origins. It was part of a massive fragmentation of larger national and regional identities having both liberating and violently oppressive outcomes. But there is an absolute contradiction between cosmopolitan identity and this upsurge of strong local/territorial identities. The solution for the cosmopolitan, surely unconscious, was to invoke a more general yet not abstract identity. The intellectuals who struggled against modernism were not about to give up their cosmopolitan positions and become local generals. Cosmopolitanism minus modernism was the local solution and it took the form of hybridism: the position we are all mixed, and we intellectuals are the representatives of the hybrid world, the oppositional, liminal, betwixt and between, category busters that shall lead the new 'revolution'. This 'we are the world' hybridity is part of the evolutionary identity of the cosmopolitan, one that moves from lower to higher levels of 'cultural' integration.

The strength of the evolutionary bias is suggested by Hannerz (1996) when making the general claim that cosmopolitan formerly referred to national, elites located in national capitals as opposed to those sequestered in the hinterland. Is this the case with Paris and Vienna of the end of the last century? Gellner's discussion, at least, would seem to contradict such a proposal. There were, of course, national centres of high culture, descendants of the royal courts and their cultural activities, but these courts were themselves extraordinarily worldly and well travelled, great collectors of the things of the world and, of course, intermarried over all of Europe. On the contrary, the opposition between nationalists who often developed their own elites, and cosmopolitans was clearly marked. The new cosmopolitanism envisaged, perhaps normatively, by Hannerz, is defined as a kind of cultural connoisseur. As Lash and Urry put it:

> There is a search for and delight in contrasts between societies rather than a longing for uniformity. Hannerz also talks of the need for the cosmopolitan to be in a 'state of readiness, a personal ability to make one's way into other cultures, through listening, looking, intuiting and reflecting' (1990: 239). (Lash and Urry, 1994: 308)

They also criticize what appears to be a self-identification converted into objectivity:

> He draws a strong distinction between cosmopolitans and tourists, citing the main character in the film *The Accidental Tourist* who wrote travel books for anti-cosmopolitan tourists, people for whom visiting another country was largely a spectator sport. However, this contrast is overdrawn and rests upon the middle-class belief that their orientation to travel is far more sophisticated than to that of mere 'tourists'. (Lash and Urry, 1994: 308)

This cosmopolitanism has no content other than its encompassment of cultural difference. It is about 'being there' and knowing them in a way that can define a certain sophistication. It is a formal kind of cosmopolitanism without any project other than cultural hoarding or englobing itself. The older project was that of high civilization, high culture, high science. In the decline of modernism, which is also a decline of the intellectual public sphere, what is left is simply difference itself and its accumulation, a definition of a higher englobing level of identification. It is more global than previously, but this may be due to the fact that there is no collective project to occupy its members. They are not, as I said, going anywhere, nor do they want to. Thus the focal notion of creativity which characterized modernist science and art is replaced by hybridization. The former creativity was about the discovery process, the production of insights; the result was the unearthing of new connections in the real world, the founding of new gestalts. This was as true of the driving principles of art as of science (Lévi-Strauss, 1962). Nowadays, creativity consists merely in new blends, new creoles, new hybrids. This is the creativity advertising, of MTV and world music, not that associated with artistic or scientific originality.

Elements of Hybrid Resurgence

The subaltern school of Ranajit Guha has made innumerable and brilliant reinterpretations of the history of the marginalized and oppressed in Indian history. The general, Gramscian inspired, frame of their analysis is that the subaltern is usually repressed by the power of the colonial and postcolonial state and that which is repressed is an alternative *Gemeinschaft*, a culturally defined community. Its resurgence is the 'return of the suppressed' as 'a persistent human urge to form communities, which in effect emerges as a constant immanent critique of modernity and capitalism' (Hansen, 1995: 8). In Chatterjee's work this community is distinguished from its Western counterpart which, according to the latter, is an impoverished version due to the demolishing of community by capitalism.

> If the day comes when the vast storehouse of Indian social history will become comprehensible to the scientific consciousness, we will have achieved along the way a fundamental restructuring of the edifice of European social philosophy as it exists today. (Chatterjee, 1993: 169)

This is because colonialism was 'always dominant but never hegemonic' (Hansen, 1995: 9). The imperialist enemy stands as opposed to the indigenous and authentic communities of the East.

1	Western categories	$\longrightarrow$	1	Subaltern categories, hybridity
2	Rationalism	$\longrightarrow$	2	Holism
3	Colonialism	$\longrightarrow$	3	The 'third space'
4	Universalism (exclusive)	$\longrightarrow$	4	Encompassment (inclusive)

This authentic hybridity is the pre-colonial, pre-national cultural state of the world where there are no rigid boundaries of identification.

The discourse of hybridity is, as I have suggested here and elsewhere, positioned. It is cosmopolitan in its self-identification while being anti- or postmodern in so far as it rejects the abstract rationality of modernism. But the culturalist hybridity of postcolonial identity refers to a resurgence of something past, a pre-colonial hybridity, while the hybridity of most Western intellectuals is future-oriented and entirely postcolonial and postmodern (in the sense of locating itself at the end of the modernist world of the nation-state and its clear categories of identity). The homologies, however, are striking:

1 The pre-colonial becomes the postcolonial.
2 The pre-modern becomes the postmodern.
3 The hybrid is thus both pre- and postmodern.

The language is unabashedly Western and highly sophisticated, if not unentirely sophistic. Its Third World practitioners are most often residents of the West. One Third World intellectual resident in the USA has characterized this as follows:

> The current global condition appears in the discourse only as a projection of the subjectivities and epistemologies of First World intellectuals of Third World

origin: the discourse constitutes the world in the self-image of these intellectuals, which makes it an expression not of powerlessness but of newfound power. (Dirlik, 1992: 344)

And further,

> To insist on hybridity against one's own language, it seems to me, is to disguise not only ideological location but also the differences of power that go with different locations. Postcolonial intellectuals in their First World institutional location are ensconced in positions of power not only *vis-à-vis* the 'native' intellectuals back at home, but also *vis-à-vis* their First World neighbors here. My neighbors in Farmville, Virginia, are no match in power for the highly paid, highly prestigious postcolonial intellectuals at Columbia, Princeton, or Duke; some of them might even be willing to swap positions and take the anguish that comes with hybridity so long as it brings with it the power and the prestige it seems to command. (Dirlik, 1992: 343; note that Dirlik is himself employed at Duke University)

Hybridity is, in this view, an abstraction from the intellectual's cosmopolitan experience in an era devoid of modernist aspirations. '*Mélange*, hotchpotch, a bit of this and bit of that is *how newness enters the world*' (Rushdie, 1991: 394).

Now this is quite true of the world of Rushdie, with its bemused and musing distance from the migratory realities that make up his own life and that of his characters. But, unfortunately, *Khomeini denies this*[1] and the newness that entered the world after the Shah was of an entirely different order from the lighthearted cosmopolitanism described and advertised by Rushdie. In a world of multiplying diasporas, one of the things that is not happening is that boundaries are disappearing. Rather, they seem to be erected on every new street corner of every declining neighbourhood of our world. It is true that a little bit of this and that are flowing across all sorts of boundaries, but they are not being used to celebrate hybridity. Quite the contrary, they are incorporated and naturalized by group formation that strives to homogenize and maintain social order within its own boundaries. Now hybridization may indeed characterize this phenomenon when seen from afar, or above, the roaring crowd below in the street, its fruit stands, halal butcher shops, falafel stories, small groceries, world music and gangsta rap . . . and its all here outside the door. Why is this postmodern bazaar so bizarre, so strikingly intriguing? Does it evoke the laughter of 'matter out of place'? What would we have done in a medieval market in any of the larger cities of the world? These phenomena are only surprising and confusing if we expect to find a neatly classified world. There need not be less order and fewer boundaries 'down there'. It is only up here that it appears that way, and I can celebrate the view with my friends who share the same altitude. Pietersee, who by and large celebrates the equation of globalization and hybridity, is also forthright in denying the intellectual power of the concept. Criticizing Hannerz he states: 'Can we identify any culture that is *not* creole in the sense of drawing on one or more different historical sources' (Pietersee, 1995: 63). He too suggests that, if 'we accept that cultures have been hybrid *all along*, hybridization is in effect a tautology' (1995: 64), and concludes that 'the hybridization perspective remains meaningful only as a critique of essentialism' (1995: 64).[2] In other words, hybridization is a political and normative discourse, emphatically stated here by one of its best practitioners.

Postcoloniality and Cultural Elitism

The clearest indicator of the decline of hegemony in cultural terms is the rise of the postcolonial intellectual framework: a complex of key words of phrases that reorder the cultural reality of world systemic relations. The politicization of intellectual argument is central to this project, as is evident in Stuart Hall's reply to the critique made by Dirlik and cited above. His reply is part of an attempt to situate the concept of the 'postcolonial' which he does by claiming that it is both temporal and critical. It refers to an historical moment, a process of decolonization, but also to the internal decolonization that goes on incessantly both in colonial situations and long after them since the latter leave their 'traces' in the decolonized world. Thus the postcolonial refers to a kind of final yet continuous critique of the colonial in all of its forms, from the economic to the cultural. It involves a rethinking of the colonial as well:

> It follows that the term 'post-colonial' is not merely descriptive of 'this' society rather than 'that' of 'then' and 'now'. It re-reads 'colonisation' as part of an essentially transnational and transcultural 'global' process – and it produces a decentred, diasporic or 'global' rewriting of earlier, nation-centred imperial grand narratives. (Hall, 1996: 247)

This leads to an argument against what I understand to be the units of the colonial vision, based on nation-states and discrete territorial domains of empire. The postcolonial is about the diasporic consciousness.[3]

> Understood in its global and transcultural context, colonisation has made ethnic absolutism an increasingly untenable cultural strategy. It made the 'colonies' themselves and even more, large tracts of the 'post-colonial' world, always-already 'diasporic' in relation to what might be thought of as their cultures of origin. (Hall, 1996: 250)

What we arrive at, if I follow the argument literally, is an acceptance of the displacements of colonial expansion, a world of dispersal, of the transnational which harbours its own intellectual critique of the past.

> Hybridity, syncretism, multidimensional temporalities, the double inscriptions of colonial and metropolitan times, the two-way cultural traffic characteristic of the contact zones of the cities of the 'colonised' long before they have become the characteristic tropes of the cities of the 'colonising', the forms of translation and

transculturation which have characterised the 'colonial relation' from its earliest stages, the disavowals and in-betweeness, the here-and-theres, mark the aporias and re-doublings whose interstices colonial discourses have always negotiated and about which Homi Bhabha has written with such profound insight (Bhabha, 1994). (Hall, 1996: 251)

Two things: first the language, while possible to grasp, is increasingly vague and evocative and therefore open to numerous interpretations. But there is also an implicit agenda in the text. It runs like this: the voice from the periphery-now-in-the-centre, that is, the diaspora intellectual, says: 'First you colonized Me and I was dispersed and became transnational, and now I take on the identity that was bestowed upon me and use it as a weapon against essentializing discourses that were the core of the colonial era.' This is interesting to read but hardly convincing in its logic. After all, for decades the argument has been: 'First you colonized Me and I was dispersed and became transnational, and now I want to re-establish my former connection to my source, i.e. to turn my former pre-national space into a nation.' Now this argument makes just as much sense and in any case it has been a real agenda in much of the decolonization process. That ethnic absolutism has been made 'untenable' by all of this flies in the horrible face of the ethnic wars that are raging in substantial parts of the decolonized world.

One might ask whether or not the colonial ought to be understood in the same terms as the post colonial. Is the latter a state of being? Is it the colonized of Fanon's writing? Aren't there a lot of assumptions here and an inordinate amount of just that essentializing that postcolonials ought to avoid? Was there anything before the colonial world other than border-crossing, holistic and egalitarian society? The terms, colonial and post-colonial, are more like terms of self-identification. They have more sign value than empirical referential content. Could it be that postcolonial discourse, replete with its special vocabulary, is more a form of sociality or code for its adherents than an attempt to understand some aspect of the world. Hall's description belies such a possibility.

What, in their different ways these theoretical descriptions are attempting to construct is a notion of a shift or a transition conceptualized as the recon-figuration of a field, rather than as a movement of linear transcendence between two mutually exclusive states. (1996: 254)

What is described is a change in terms of reference; not the introduction of a new paradigm as such, but of a new language, a new field of discourse, reconfigured from the old. In order to account for this, the language itself becomes increasingly contorted.

To put this another way, all the key concepts in the 'post-colonial', as in the general discourse of the 'posts', are operating, as Derrida would put it, 'under erasure'. They have been subjected to a deep and thorough-going critique,

exposing their assumptions as a set of foundational effects. But his decon-
struction does not abolish them, in the classic movement of supersession, an
Aufghebung. It leaves them as the only conceptual instruments and tools with
which to think about the present – but only if they are deployed in their
deconstructed form. They are, to use another, more Heideggerean, formulation,
which Iain Chambers, for example, prefers, 'a presence that exists in abeyance'
(Chambers, 1994). (Hall, 1996: 255)

Alas!

Dirlik, who attacks what he sees as a hegemonic project of adaptation to
world capitalism, is complimented by Hall as a 'distinguished scholar of
modern China' and then criticized for his polemical ferocity. But this is
again turned into a compliment by Hall via an almost total agreement with
Dirlik's description of the world today in political economic terms,
including the national 'de-centring' of capital, the rebirth of native cultures,
the weakening of boundaries, the Confucian revival in East Asia, the
combination of homogenizing and heterogenizing. All of this, according to
Hall, is what the postcolonial is about. Even Dirlik's assertion that the
postcolonial critics seem totally blind to their own economic conditions
is accepted in stride, but it is simultaneously and quite nonchalantly
explained away as a mere reaction to the old-fashioned vulgar materialism
of a former reductionist Marxism. Where, precisely, is the problem with this
angry scholar? After all, 'Dirlik has therefore put his finger squarely, and
convincingly, on a serious lacuna in the post-colonial episteme' (Hall, 1996:
258). Hall seems disappointed. Damn it, we could have used this guy in
developing our 'episteme'. But then Dirlik goes and blows it by making the
class connection. Postcolonial discourse serves the 'cultural requirements' of
global capitalism. The postcolonial critics are 'unwitting spokespersons for
the new global capitalist order' (1996: 259). And suddenly the author is
accused of 'stunning (and one is obliged to say, banal) reductionism, a
functionalism of a kind which one thought had disappeared from scholarly
debate as a serious explanation of *anything*, that it reads like a echo from a
distant, primeval era' (1996: 259). Dirlik is arguing by association only, by
the fit of a certain discourse to a certain state of affairs. Young (1995),
whom I have referred to above, is similarly criticized for linking racism and
postcolonialist discourse via the concept of hybridity.

This is strange discourse, strange argument. Hall agrees with the analysis
but not with its implications concerning the relation between postcolonial
discourse and the larger system. No argument, however, is summoned;
only opinion and what might be interpreted as moral judgement. Hall's
way of discussing the issue is extraordinarily paternalistic in this respect. If
only Dirlik was on our side, on the side of the good, the postcolonial
episteme, then all could be forgiven, *but*, '. . . [w]e always knew that the
dismantling of the colonial paradigm would release strange demons from
the deep, and that these monsters might come trailing all sorts of sub-
terranean material' (Hall, 1996: 259). Who is the 'we' in this and to what
does the 'always knew' refer?

It is true that Dirlik falls back on functionalism, or rather a correlation, but his argument is aimed at identifying a real political issue, one that is dismissed, *in principle*, by Hall. I have argued that the global order is not New, but that its social composition is changing. I have argued that the postcolonial discourse of hybridity is not a function of global capitalism, since the latter has been around all the time. Rather, I have argued that this discourse is one that has identified with the cosmopolitan space of the global system and has vied for a hegemonic position within that space. This is not functionalism but, on the contrary, a hypothesis about competition within the highest echelons of the system. It is about factions of the elite and about the formation of intellectual hegemony. Hall's style of presentation does much to verify such an hypothesis.

The ease with which Dirlik is dismissed is indicative of another aspect of the current global transformation. It is based on a morally hierarchical classification in which certain words, arguments and propositions can be eliminated because they are quite simply morally or rather politically incorrect. Identifying acceptable codes of jargon, key words and attitudes replaces rational argument. This is part of the postmodernization referred to earlier. This is the kind of transformation that can make the epitome of political correctness, Stanley Fish, appear as a radical (against even his own remonstrations) and to sacralize the equation of power and knowledge, by subsuming the latter within the former. In this new elitism Fish is a true paragon of the relations described above: 'I am against blind submission because the fact that my name is attached to an article greatly increases its chance of being accepted' (Fish, 1988, cited in Jacoby, 1994: 183).

Transethnic Identity and the Myth of Cultural Creativity

The followers of hybridity theory have searched for a liberating creativity in 'complex, dynamic patterns of syncretism' (Gilroy, 1987: 13), and celebrate as best they can the 'inventive, border-transcending cultural creativity among immigrants' and the way it 'embodies, resistance to seg-regating definitions' (Ålund, 1992: 73). The argument harbours a series of rather simpleminded presuppositions:

1   Ethnic cultures are mixed/syncretic.
2   Such cultures challenge the mainstream and are better and gaining in force (the proof is in pop music which is becoming 'blacker').
3   The implicit goal of these cultures now understood as a kind of challenge and dynamism in the transformation of society . . . 'culture as a composite and challenging force' (Ålund, 1992: 79).

Much of this ideology, class conflict displaced to ethnicity, becomes the subaltern culture of today's cultural studies. Hebdige is aware of the general structural inversion involved here:

Ironically, those values conventionally associated with white working-class culture . . . which had been eroded by time by relative affluence and by the disruption of the physical environment in which they had been rooted were rediscovered, embedded in black West Indian culture. Here was a culture armoured against contaminating influences, protected against the more frontal assaults of the dominant ideology, denied access to the 'good life' by the colour of its skin. Its rituals, language and style provided models for those white youths alienated from the parent culture by the imagined compromises of the post-war years. (1983: 57)

But is this the same culture? The superficiality of the statement sacrifices cultural content to the researcher's definition of working-class resistance. Hebdige understands youth culture as a synthesis of 'those forms of adaptation, negotiation and resistance elaborated by the parent culture and others, more immediate, conjunctural, specific to youth and its situation and activities' (Hebdige, 1983: 56). In applying the notion of bricolage to her material on Yugoslav women in Sweden, Ålund argues for a combination or intersection of elements, some from the past and others from the present. There is a cultivation of the past by mothers, 'traditional female subculture of the Yugoslav village', stories of 'rebellions and communities from the past' (Ålund, 1992: 82), all of which is said to 'live on in immigrant communities through forms of resistance' (Ålund, 1992: 82). Girls travel to their 'real' homelands and have a desire to discover their origins, but they realize that they are not really at home there. Her circle of friends have similar problems.

To retain their identities in the multiethnic suburban tenements they actively had to create a cultural consciousness that was more comprehensive than that of their parents. Through its ethnic mix, this circle of friends not only represented most of what could be found in the local community, but also constituted a new kind of community, one which questioned and reworked both the traditional values of the new (Swedish) world and the established attitudes about masculinity/femininity, friendship/enmity, etc. of the 'old' world. (Ålund, 1992: 83)

Here we have retained identities and a kind of discussion of values from different ethnic groups. In her discussion she describes how the ethnically rooted frame of references becomes central for her subject's identity, even if it is 'reworked in the Swedish context' (1992: 83). The question is how? Where is the transethnic in all of this? She talks around the issue constantly, but do we ever get hold of any substantial transcultural social form? She stresses that such composites are not merely constructed from the cultural supermarket, but 'express a creative and constructive connection with the past' (1992: 84). Her interesting example of the appearance of vampires among Wallachian immigrants is described as a form of social control, and a desire to return to traditional authority as a means of maintaining solidarity in the group. The strengthening of roots becomes a central asset in negotiating immigrant existence.

There is no cultural mixture in these descriptions. On the contrary, we see competing social strategies and their resultant interpretations of social reality. But there is no description of new forms of community. Could it be that mixture expresses the outsider's view of a multicultural field. The metaphor of mixture is flat. It juxtaposes rather than exploring the articulation among different elements. This author, just as all other hybrid ideologues, takes refuge in literature to find her best examples, but even these are open to alternative interpretations. Kingston's *The Woman Warrior* explores a Chinese-American's voyage back to her roots, driven by magical forces of the ancestors and even leads to linkages to the 'barbarians' via a story of a kidnapping and subsequent discovery that impenetrable barriers can be broken and used as a resource. These tales of transcendence relate to *the way in which the intellectual embodies the cultures of 'others' in a superior combination*. But what do they say about the *social* world of multiculturalism?

The analysis becomes increasingly chaotic after this failure to establish a transcultural object. Modernity is alienation and the reaction is to search for something fixed, rooted, communal: youth are part of this reaction according to Ålund. On the one hand, the latter is characterized as healthy, but it also leads to authoritarian results: 'The ever present competition for social and cultural control of space frequently leads to a focus on youth violence, ethnic conflicts and their connection with each other' (Ålund, 1992: 89). But there is more, for

> [t]his longing can also be expressed in journeys across the boundaries of time, space and culture, in the search for new forms of grounded presence, both personally and collectively. It is on these journeys that the modern world shows its potential for transcendence and renewal. This is especially true of the young generation of immigrants, whose rediscovered ethnic consciousness constitutes an ever more comprehensive form of modern existence. (Ålund, 1992: 89)

The return to tradition among immigrants is redefined as a kind of cultural expansion. This is difficult to understand and it is not unpacked to make it comprehensible. The preoccupation with identity and difference is said to be creative in itself: 'In a climate of cultural tumult and social fragmentation, the interaction between ethnicity and modernity offers new pathways towards this kind of transcendence' (Ålund, 1992: 89). In this way a contradiction in terms is turned by a wave of the wand into its opposite. The formation of boundaries is identified with their transcendence. The vocabulary of this discourse belongs to the same family as that described above.

The key words on the side of good are: transcending, alternative, amalgamation, merging, composite, historical, anti-colonial, collective presence; and on the side of evil: authority, dominant cultural norms, racism.[4] But what is the content of this amalgamation and boundary transcending and what is the dominant cultural norm on the other side that is so readily associated with racism? There is quite simply no ethnographic evidence to support these broad classificatory statements. One senior researcher involved for many years in a similar framework comes to the opposite conclusion:

> I think that it will be difficult to find empirical evidence of this kind of 'creolized culture' (Hannerz, 1988) in the activities, experiences, and values of young people. This is particularly true if one searches for a pattern containing discernible and integrated 'cultural elements'. What would a mixture of Arabic Muslim, Latin American Catholic, and Swedish secular traditions look like in a group of teenage boys and girls? (Ehn, 1992: 142)

Kotsinas, in her work on immigrant dialects in Stockholm, asserts that while various pidgin dialects form, they become rapidly homogenized within specific youth groups, as they would have to do in order to serve as vehicles of communication. She refers to the language of mixed zones as an indicator of 'local united identity' (Kotsinas, 1992: 57). Another interesting aspect of these new dialects is that the foreign words for boys and girls introduced are often transformed obscene words, which might indicate the status relations involved in the formation of marginalized cultures. Work on Turks in Berlin also demonstrates the degree to which the internal dynamics of identification and world-definition aim at coherence. Schwartz in the same volume writes that '[t]he revitalization of traditions from their land of origin is readily recognizable in the recreational conduct of Turkish youths in Berlin' (Schwartz, 1992: 199). On the other hand, there is an identification with or at least use of 'symbols from lower-class Black America' which are 'dominant in the informal groups' (1992: 199). At the same time 'they show a clear desire to adapt to the life-style of their German peer groups' (1992: 199). Now this combination of cultural elements might be called hybridization, but it would tell us nothing about the processes involved. The use of symbols of Black America is part of a political identification mediated in pop culture. The reason for the popularity of such symbols must be analysed in its context and not simply interpreted as cultural creativity. Todd, in a comparative work on immigrants in Europe, discusses the way in which the Turkish family has become increasingly patrilineal in Germany due to the exclusion of Turks in German society (Todd, 1994: 179). The turn to fundamentalism from an essentially secularized background is also a specific cultural development among German Turks. Now such changes, which are accountable in terms of the immigrant context, cannot be understood in terms of cultural flows coming together in a given place. They are generated by the dynamics of identification in a context of social conflict. Caglar (1997) argues against the usefulness of concepts such as hybridization and hyphenation for understanding the real social processes involved in immigrant situations in which boundaries are paramount.

The phenomena described here are primarily about bounding. While the cultural products may seem mixed to the outsider, as social realities, the question of cultural hybridization is not part of the discourse. The latter is always and everywhere an observation of the researcher, an attribution of meaning to a world that bears no witness to that meaning. This is a normative discourse, an ideological discourse in the most elementary sense. Now one might retort that the mixture need not be recognized by those involved in the process, that it is an 'objective' process. But an objective hybrid culture is a self-contradiction, since no objective criteria for how to reckon the nature of hybridity are ever stated. In one sense, all culture is hybrid, and was probably always hybrid. If this is so, then the term has no operational significance, since it cannot differentiate between any two 'cultures'. If the term refers to a recent hybridization, well then it is a question of genealogies. How many generations do we reckon when determining whether or not to apply the term? And if Serbians claim purity in opposition to Bosnians, what does the objective reality of hybridity contribute to the situation? I would offer the following argument in discussing such problems.

1   All populations, no matter how bounded, are culturally mixed in terms of the genealogies of the meanings that they use. This fact has no significance in itself, except for those engaged in the exercise of cultural genealogy. This fundamental fact is what I refer to as the spaghetti principle.
2   It follows from this that hybridity only exists as a social phenomenon when it is identified as such by those involved in social interaction. This implies that where people do not so identify, the fact of cultural mixture is without social significance.
3   It follows from (2) that the problem of hybridity, as of purity, is a question of practices of identification. Who so identifies, when, and how? These are the fundamental issues.
4   The rise of a discourse of hybridity, creolization, etc. is a social phenomenon and not the reflection of a neutral fact that has finally been discovered. The discourse appears to be located among certain groups, usually cultural elites and harbours hegemonic pretensions, as suggested above.

Real Existing Hybridity

What are the social conditions for the existence of hybridity as a social reality, and not merely as a discursive construct? It should be apparent from the above discussion that such conditions exist where hybridity, diverse and mixed origins, are practised as a form of social identification. My general argument here is that hybridity is indeed a form of identity that is increasing today, but that this is a highly differential process, strongest in particular sectors of the global system. N.G. Canclini, is a spokesman for the emergence of hybrid cultures, especially in Latin America. In a study from Tijuana, which has become a vast city of more than one million inhabitants, with migrants from all over Mexico and with a constant border-crossing to California for day-wages, or longer-term employment, his research team worked on local self-identifications among journalists, artists and other cultural 'workers'. Here hybridity as an identity was self-evident. In an (apparently recorded) radio interview with the editor of a bilingual journal published in Tijuana and San Diego, we have the following excerpt.

> *Reporter*: If you love our country so much as you say you do, why do you live in California?
> *Gómez-Peña*: I am de-Mexicanizing myself in order to Mexicomprehend myself . . .
> *Reporter*: What do you consider yourself then?
> *Gómez-Peña*: Post-Mexica, pre-Chicano, pan-Latino, land-crossed, Art American . . . it depends on the day of the week or the project in question. (Canclini, 1995: 238)

Now Canclini also found reactions to this among Tijuana intellectuals who stress their local identity in opposition to those '"who have arrived recently and want to discover us and tell us who we are"' (Canclini, 1995: 239). Canclini's own perspective, based on his observation of the city, is decidedly hybrid, one of those 'laboratories of postmodernity' like New York or presumably Los Angeles. Several nods are made to the class relations involved and even, ever so slightly, to the larger global organization that might, as we should like to argue, generate this laboratory of multiculturalism. Canclini is primarily after the cultural product. It might have been interesting to have looked at some other perspectives, that is those of the migrants themselves, to see the degree to which such hybrid identification actually occurs in this highly differentiated population. What is important here, however, is the obvious fact of hybridity as a real social phenomenon, and not merely as Canclini's own perspective. The argument is simple, if it were only Canclini doing the identification, as is the case with which most of the literature in this area, then we would be dealing with his identification of others, a political act, of course, made from a particular position. But in this case we may be dealing with a conversation between analogous social positions, that of the cultural elites, both the researcher and his subjects. Now this is surely the reality of those who experience it, but it is not clear that it is the reality of others, and since the researcher comes from the same kind of social position as his subjects one might suspect that the assumption that cultural elites and migrant seasonal or day workers have the same kinds of identities is a gross conflation. But this is precisely the assumption made by Canclini, as by others, and it is this that may make it so popular among a certain American cultural anthropology. French culture, Brazilian culture, all are mixed cultures. Of course this is the case if it is the author of the text is doing the genealogical identification. Rosaldo, in his introduction to Canclini's book, makes the case as follows:

On the other hand, hybridity can be understood as the ongoing condition of all human cultures, which contain no zones of purity because they undergo continuous processes of transculturation (two-way borrowing and lending between cultures). (Rosaldo, 1995: xv)

In one sense this is trivial. Not only have cultural forms and elements been circulating around the world in recent times, they have been doing it for thousands of years! The fact that the process has speeded up may not be as significant as another issue – that of cultural identity. The universal fact of the diffusion of cultural 'elements' is not the central issue. But what people do with those elements. The usual fact that they make something of their own with the elements raises a new question, that of the social construction and identification of the final products. Now, whether or not we identify the global genealogies of the elements, the reality of the products and their construction belongs to those who do the cultural work. This means that hybridity is in the eyes of the beholder, or more precisely in the practice of the beholder. Experienced hybridity is one thing. To impose it on others as an 'objective' phenomenon is another. My argument is not new. The same kinds of discussions went on in linguistics some years ago when it was discovered that all languages were creole in so far as they continuously adapted new exogenous elements. Tell it to the English! Of course, in technical terms, creole can be seen as a transitional phase in which a new generation assimilates a second, reduced language (pidgin), as a first language. The process of transition is one of structuring, of elaborating a linguistic order. Carried over into culture this is a far more precise process than that currently promoted by anthropologists and cultural studies practitioners in which creolization and hybridization refer simply to the fact of mixture, to the blending of elements of mixed origins. The 'hamburger' is surely a hybrid, but what does this imply for American society and its cultures?

Hybridity as an objectified concept eliminates the tension and the real contradictions that might be said to exist at the borders, in the diasporas, in situations of social transformation. While metaphors such as liminality do stress the in-betweenness of the immigrant situation, they tend, paradoxically, to homogenize this in their celebration of just this state of affairs. In my own research material, as in that of others, the in-betweenness that is celebrated for its creativity by those who can afford to make use of it, is, for the larger majority of those involved, a field of contradictory forces, of misconstruals, and anxieties. People's lives may indeed span different worlds, and individuals may learn to cope with several worlds, but they still move from world to world and are not simply located at some ideal meeting point. This situation is compounded by the fact that the boundaries between worlds are not products of differential geographical origins. They are socially constructed and practised and can show up where we least expect them. Yugoslavia is surely a case in point. It has been said that social scientists refused to discuss ethnic differentiation there before it was already too late, on the grounds that it was assumed to be *mere* mythology. Hybridity is only significant where it is practised as a self-identification.

Hybridity as Absent and Hoped for Reality

There are older sources for the notion of hybridity that come, in fact, from American sociology. The first generation of Chicago School sociologists came to Hawaii and were very much taken by the multi-ethnic nature of the islands. They were studied extensively and intensively for several decades, everything from intermarriage rates, to dating behaviour, crime and spatial behaviour, in an informed attempt to understand the directions which the plantation-based society would take with increasing democratization as a result of incorporation into the American fold. One very respected sociologist, Andrew Lind, stated, following the Second World War, that

> [t]he mounting number of persons of mixed racial ancestry in the population makes the continued use of the ordinary racial designation untenable, and those charged with the keeping of Hawaii's vital statistics are disposed to set up a single, new category – the Cosmopolitans – for the innumerable varieties of mixed bloods which are emerging at the expense of the racial groups ordinarily listed. The 1950 census reveals that in addition to 73,885 persons of mixed Hawaiian ancestry – formerly classified as part-Hawaiians – there were 20,337 other racial hybrids in the population. The combined population of mixed racial ancestry constituted slightly less than one-fifth of the entire population of the Territory. (Lind, 1953: 6)

A hybrid category never took 'root' and the sociologists might be accused of conflating cultural heritage at best, and race or blood at worst, with ethnic identity. The sociologists gave up sometime in the 1960s, but the official state ideology of the multi-ethnic paradise continued and continues today in spite of increasing consciousness of the clear ethnic oppositions that characterize Hawaiian society. The interpretation of this wishful thinking-cum-ideological policy is, I would argue, rooted in the same question of social position. The sociologists were outsiders, striking roots in a place that had, since the turn of the century, denied that Hawaiians had any particular right to the land. There developed a saying that anyone who lived in Hawaii and had *aloha* was a true Hawaiian. There are several variants of this discourse but its core is constant. They stretch from the remarks of Judd (*Saturday Post*, 2 October 1880) to the attitude expressed by Kelly (1995) to the effect that the Japanese immigrants were at least the equals of the Hawaiians with respect to land claims, an easy proclamation for colonialists.

In a recent television talk show in which the popular issue of children of mixed marriages was taken up, a number of people discussed their mixed heritages, which were, in all cases, clearly demarcated. One youth claimed to the dismay of some of the others to be black: 'Oh yes my mother is white and I do love her, but I am black.' But why, he was asked. Because, he said: 'If I am mixed, then I have no history and no identity, no roots. I am nobody!'

Barth (1995) stresses the necessity of distinguishing between culture and ethnicity, a distinction that he has made famous. Culture can move anywhere and be handed down to anyone, but ethnicity is about social boundaries, not about the content of what is on either side of them, not about what can be transferred from one person, or region to another, but to the way it is identified in relation to a group. Hybridity is in large part a result of this simple confusion of categories.

Conclusion

There is a common evolutionism in the discourses of globalization. It has been assumed that we are now in the global stage of political-economic development. The world has become one place and there is a world society. We have evolved from tribal to national to regional and now to a global economic system. Globalization is not something that happens in particular conjunctures, but is a stage of world integration. There is some truth to the notion that the world is more globally connected than ever, but the fact of globality is not new. More importantly, the world is not now in the hands of multinational capital any more than it was a hundred years ago. What appears as a new stage, is, in my argument, the product of declining hegemony, the increasing export of capital and the decentralization of capital accumulation on a world scale. This decentralization is not an even process but has, I argue, demonstrated a clear gradient of movement of accumulation towards East and Southeast Asia. This has meant stronger polities in the East and a weakening of polities in the West, where fragmentation of nation-states and multiculturalism are expressions of this process. Globalization occurs and is an expression of declining hegemony. It implies the globalization of capital movements, commodities, and populations, the latter largely as a result of increasing availability of migration and increasing local instability and dislocation. In this process, cultural identity proliferates at all levels of the system. Indigenous movements have increased logarithmically, regionalism has grown rapidly, national identities have become increasingly ethnified, and immigrants have become diaspora societies. Above it all, in the global circuits of high culture, intellectual culture, media elites and diplomatic cores, there is a global identity, a cosmopolitan identity constructed on the basis of a multicultural world. It is a self-identified hybrid identity encompassing the cultural plurality of the world on which it is totally dependent for its self-definition. But as this is an all-encompassing identity it must define other people's realities for them. Hybridity becomes truth and national, local, ethnic and other restricted identities become backward, red-neck and nationalist. Global becomes equivalent to cosmopolitan and then to urban and hybrid.

World cities become world cultures and latter are not merely multicultural as a result of globalization, but truly hybridized as a result of fusion-integration. This is a new world, a new world of class, a new world of cosmopolitan consumption.[5] As a normative stance, hybridity requires interesting moral imperatives, not least a systematic solidarity with that which is unknown, on the grounds of a universal cultural tolerance or even engagement (see, for example, Levinas, 1971). Much of this discourse expresses a combined repudiation of that which is most at home in exchange for that which is most distant. It is a language of distinction and of distantiation from the local which is why it often celebrates the city or even the airport. And while intellectuals may celebrate border-crossing, the lumpenproletariat real border-crossers live in constant fear of the border and express a very different view of the matter. Without real borders, no border-crossing, without differentiation, no hybridization, and the fact of difference is not an autonomous cultural fact but the product of the practice of building walls, fences and boundaries.

Notes

1 'Two Crows Denies This' is a famous phrase from an article by Edward Sapir dealing with the issue of outsider versus insider representations of reality (Sapir, 1938).

2 I have argued that hybridity harbours no critique of essentialism because it is a derivative of essentialism. Arguing that cultures are creole merely pushes the essences back in some mytho-historical time frame when things were pure. This is inherent in the concept itself.

3 It should be noted that diasporas are not usually associated with hybridity, but, on the contrary, with extreme forms of precisely that essentialism, transnational ethnic identity that ought to be at odds with hybridity.

4 The actual terms are used as follows: '*boundary transcending* potential which emerges out of spiritual visits into historical, *past cultures* or contemporary, *alternative cultures*'; 'reservoir of *alternative knowledge*'; '*alternative cultural frames* of reference'; 'new *composite languages*'; '*complex forms* of transcultural communication'; '*struggle for control* over one's own existence *against authority, dominant cultural norms, racism* and discriminating control'; 'shared cultural experiences in *local communities* . . . unite *black and white* youth'; '*amalgamation* of cultural expressions (language, music and other forms of interaction)' which 'symbolizes mutuality in a common struggle to reconstitute a "*collective historical presence*" beyond the divisive, fragmented forms of existence in the inner cities'; '*ethno-cultural amalgamation*, which includes a dynamic *merging* of the legacy of *anti-colonial resistance* with new forms of struggle rooted in *modern urban contexts*'.

5 A well-known intellectual colleague explained to me that while he is negative about Germany, he bought a Volkswagen instead of a Saab, because the latter was constructed out of a high percentage of German parts while the former was entirely Mexican. The identity of objects is tricky business.

References

Ålund, A. (1992) 'Immigrant youth – transcultural identities', in C. Palmgren, K. Lövgren and G. Bolin (eds), *Ethnicity in Youth Culture*. Stockholm: Unit of Media and Cultural Theory, Stockholm University. pp. 73–94.

Barth, F. (1995) 'Ethnicity and the concept of culture', in D. Imig and P. Slavsky (eds),

Nonviolent Sanctions and Cultural Survival. Boston: Center for International Affairs, Harvard University.

Bergesen, A. and Fernandez, R. (1995) 'Who has the most Fortune 500 firms?: a network analysis of global economic competition, 1956–1989', *Journal of World-Systems Research*, 1 (12). http://csf.colorado.edu/wsystems/jwsr.html

Caglar, A. (1997) 'Hyphenated identities and the limits of "culture"', in T. Madood and P. Werbner (eds), *The Politics of Multiculturalism in the New Europe*. London: Zed. pp. 169–85.

Canclini, N. (1995) *Hybrid Cultures*. Minneapolis, MN: University of Minnesota Press.

Chatterjee, P. (1993) *The Nation and its Fragments*. Princeton, NJ: Princeton University Press.

Dicken, P. (1992) *Global Shift: The Internationalization of Economic Activity*. London: Chapman.

Dirlik, A. (1992) 'The postcolonial aura: Third World criticism in the age of global capitalism', *Critical Inquiry*, Winter: 328–56.

Ehn, B. (1992) 'Youth and multiculturalism', in C. Palmgren, K. Lövgren and G. Bolin (eds), *Ethnicity in Youth Culture*. Stockholm: Stockholm University.

Ekholm, K. and Friedman, J. (1995) 'Global complexity and simplicity of everyday life', in D. Miller (ed.), *Worlds Apart*. London: Routledge.

Fish, S. (1988) 'No bias, no merit: the case against blind submission', *PMLA*, 103: 739–48.

Friedman, J. (1997) 'Global crises, the struggle for cultural identity and intellectual pork-barreling: cosmopolitans, nationals and locals in an era of de-hegemonization', in P. Werbner (ed.), *Debating Cultural Hybridity*. London: Zed.

Gellner, E. (1994) 'Malinowski and Wittgenstein: impact of the Habsburg world on England'. Lecture given at Research School for Historical Anthropology/Sociology, University of Lund, Sweden, 3 October.

Gilroy, P. (1987) *There Ain't No Black in the Union Jack*. London: Hutchinson.

Hall, S. (1996) 'When was the post-colonial: thinking at the limit', in I. Chambers and L. Curti (eds), *The Post-Colonial Question*. London: Routledge. pp. 242–60.

Hannerz, U. (1988) 'American culture: creolized, creolizing', in *American Culture: Creolized, Creolizing and Other Lectures*. NAAS Biennial Conference, Swedish Institute for North American Studies.

Hannerz, U. (1996) 'Cosmopolitans and locals in world culture', in *Transnational Connections*. London: Routledge.

Hansen, T. (1995) 'Inside the Romanticist episteme'. Unpublished manuscript.

Harvey, D. (1989) *The Postmodern Condition*. Oxford: Blackwell.

Hebdige, D. (1983) *Subculture. The Meaning of Style*. London: Methuen.

hooks, b. (1995) *Killing Rage: Ending Racism*. New York: Holt, Rinehart & Winston.

Jacoby, R. (1994) *Dogmatic Wisdom: How the Culture Wars Divert Education and Distract America*. New York: Doubleday.

Kelly, John (1995) 'Blood and nation in Fiji and Hawaii', *Public Culture*, 7 (3): 475–97.

Kotsinas, Ulla-Britt (1992) 'Immigrant adolescents' Swedish in multicultural areas', in C. Palmgren, K. Lövgren and G. Bolin (eds), *Ethnicity in Youth Culture*. Stockholm: Unit of Media and Cultural Theory, Stockholm University.

Lash, S. and Urry, J. (1994) *Economies of Signs and Space*. London: Sage.

Lévi-Strauss, C. (1962) *La pensée sauvage*. Paris: Plon.

Levinas, E. (1971) *Totalité et infinité*. Dordrecht: Kluwer.

Lind, Andrew (1953) 'Changing race relations in Hawaii', *Social Process in Hawaii*, 17: 1–19.

Pietersee, J.N. (1995) 'Globalization as hybridization', in M. Featherstone, S. Lash and R. Robertson (eds), *Global Modernities*. London: Sage. pp. 45–68.

Rosaldo, R. (1995) 'Introduction', in N. Canclini, *Hybrid Cultures*. Minneapolis, MN: University of Minnesota Press.

Rushdie, S. (1991) *Imaginary Homelands*. London: Granta.

Sapir, E. (1938) 'Why cultural anthropology needs the psychiatrist', in *Psychiatry*, 1: 7–12.

Sassen, S. (1994) *Cities in a World Economy*. Thousand Oaks, CA: Pine Forge.

Sassen, S. (1996) *Losing Control: Sovereignty in an Age of Globalization*. New York: Columbia University Press.

Schwartz, J. (1992) 'The Turkish community in Berlin: youth cultures in the system of the German welfare state', in C. Palmgren, K. Lövgren and G. Bolin (eds), *Ethnicity in Youth Culture*. Stockholm: Unit of Media and Cultural Theory, Stockholm University.

Todd, E. (1994) *Le destin des immigrés: assimilation et ségrégation dans les démocraties occidentales*. Paris: Seuil.

Wallace, M. (1995) 'For whom the bell tolls: why America can't deal with Black feminist intellectuals', *Village Voice Literary Supplement*, November.

Young, R.C. (1995) *Colonial Desire: Hybridity in Theory, Culture, and Race*. London: Routledge.

14

NARRATING THE POSTCOLONIAL

Couze Venn

The questions which motivate my problematization of the postcolonial are the following: is it possible to retell the postcolonial in such a way as to open up a conceptual space for a settling of accounts with modernity that prepares the ground for imagining a radically different postmodernity? How far is the problematic of subjectivity and of identity central to this refiguration? In binding the theorization of the postcolonial with that of (post)modernity and of subjectivity, I am drawing lessons from a good deal of the important work already accomplished in rethinking late modern times that provides the already-said, allowing us to break with the terrain upon which a particular modernist vision of the world had been founded. I do not mean by this that we have somehow left behind the 'truths' that the occidental discourse of modernity had normalized, or that we have abandoned the life-world in which they have become instantiated. Far from it. For the danger today is the forgetting of the continuities of a certain modernity and the repetition of its violences. The danger is the more acute now that the restraining hold of liberal humanism no longer deters political action in so many places and that the ethical values inscribed in the 'grand narratives' that underwrote the project of modernity have become so fragile. Therein lies another interest guiding my approach in rethinking the postcolonial, namely, the search for some ethical component to validate the critique of the present, and the conviction that such an ethics is intrinsic both to rewriting the history of modernity and to the refiguration of being for a postmodern and properly postcolonial age.

The work to which I refer has already indicated the fruitfulness of pluralizing and disaggregating the discourse and the history of modernity. It has also become clearer that the history of colonialism and imperialism is affiliated with that of modernity and of capitalism, enabling us to reconstruct genealogies of the complex, mobile and contingent tripartite system of relations between them. A central proposition that informs my analysis of these relations is the view that a particular discourse of the subject functions as the suturing mechanism in the process of articulation of these relations. Much of my discussion will focus on the question of subjectivity and identity without, however, engaging directly with the issue of the 'politics of identity', since my questioning suspends the grounds of 'identity' through a number of deterritorializing moves. One such move is to locate critique from both the standpoint of an imprecise postcoloniality and the side of the aporias of modern Western thought.

Rewriting the Postmodern

If the debates about the postmodern have revealed anything, it is that the spectre of modernity continues to haunt all attempts to break away from its vision and its legacy. Whether it be a matter of salvaging the ethical and liberatory ideals of the project of modernity, as Jürgen Habermas (1987) has been advocating, or whether we are dealing with the critiques of the present from postcolonial or postmodern perspectives, the main analytical tools are borrowed from the theoretical terrain that they wish to abolish, so that the terms of the debate are ambivalently still framed by the discourses of modernity and of the Enlightenment. This is one more reason for not 'forgetting' modernity in the eschatological imaginary of endings, but instead to count its costs and to settle accounts with its history and its legacy. For Lyotard (1988), the temptation to forget is intrinsic to the narrative of modernity, for, in its very form, this narrative must period- ically 'start the clock back at zero' (Lyotard, 1988: 195) and, in this gesture, erase the preceding epoch, consigning it to the darkness of the 'prehistory' of the present. The implication is that the postmodern turn is one such point of periodization within the temporal stratagem of modern- ity, the repetition of a gesture of denial. Instead of the kind of discourse of the postmodern which writes off modernity, Lyotard argues for a rewriting of modernity that should take the form not of 'forgetting' but of a work of rememoration similar to 'working through' in the psychoanalytic experi- ence, that is, the refiguration of memory and of history that occurs in analysis and enables the analysand to deal with past traumatic events and with repressed knowledge. This work enables us to come to terms with the domain of the forgotten and the displaced without which we become locked into cycles of repetition and compulsion.

There is a second sense of the post of the postmodern which I would like to develop; I would locate it at the opposite pole of the tendency within the logocentric discourse of modernity to seek to accomplish the being of modernity by means of a *techne* – that is to say, an organic combination of knowledge and intention, an art of making and transforming that brings into being a desired world – that inscribes the modern subject's will to power in the instrumentality of a terroristic reason. This particular ratio is complicit with another temptation latent in the discourse of modernity: that for a totalizing narrative of being that would return the subject to the excess of desire invested in the metaphysics of presence. The metaphysics of presence seeks meaning by reference to a subject that would be present to itself, requiring no other to validate its existence as thinking being, or to authorize the knowledge it comes to of the world and of itself. It posits the fiction of a subject by itself, without borders, self-contained or rather containing within it everything that constantly threatens its loss and dissolution: openness to the other, the contingencies bound up with the temporality and the embodiment of being. The excess of its desire measures the excessive anxiety which being, thus abandoned to itself, must live. A totalizing narrative constructs a (w)holding space to contain the terrors of this being-for-itself. Or rather, it holds out the promise of overcoming contingency and finitude through a projection into the future whose already known trajectory traces a project that accomplishes the being of the metaphysics of presence through the agency of the logocentric subject.

The postmodern critique of logocentrism directs us towards a concept of modernity which recognizes its alliance with a process of emancipation that involves transformations at both the social and the subjective levels. The interesting aspect of this process, from the standpoint of examining modernity by reference to the being enframed by it, is that the trans-figuration of that being suggests a process in which the imagination works in a manner similar to its functioning in the Kantian analytique of the sublime. Lyotard (1988) hints at this process and develops it more fully in his reading of Kant's *Critique of Judgement* (Lyotard, 1994). I shall return to it below. A quite different problematic emerges here in which the rewriting of modernity is inscribed in the opening of the subject towards its ever-renewed process of becoming and towards the other. I take this to entail that the process of rememoration-refiguration is endless because 'the dispossession of the subject, its subjection to an heteronomy, is constitutive of it' (Lyotard, 1988: 201), which means to say that we are always-already in the process of being de-centred in relation to the domain of inter-subjectivity, in relation, therefore, to culture.

I cannot explain further in this chapter this decisive shift in our analysis of the postmodern, repeated, besides, in other texts (for example, Butler, 1993; Derrida, 1993; Elliott, 1996). I shall propose two considerations that will allow me to locate this shift in relation to postcoloniality. First, I think it is fruitful to examine how far the forgetfulness of the modern conscience is bound up with the violences that have accompanied the history of modernity, more specifically, the history of epistemic, psychic, ontological and physical violences that were projected on to the global terrain of colonialism and the space of modernity's 'others'.

Secondly, I want to begin to explore the idea that the discourse of modernity harbours at its heart a particular narrative of being, no doubt deeply aporetic, split between, on the one hand, a logocentrism allied to the metaphysics of presence and, on the other, a radical ontology that opens being to contingency and that apprehends the unpresentable, liminal and sublime character of what brings us to presence. Let me offer this passage of Jean-Luc Nancy as an indication of the line of thought that I am pursuing. Speaking about the economy of desire and pleasure, about the place of the gift in the work of art, and about what the work wishes to present, he says:

For presence is no longer the object of this desire, not the grasping of presence –
not even the desire's own presence unto itself – but just the coming preceding all
presence, beyond all presence. The burst of a presentation or its offering. In the
end, there is no more object of desire, and consequently, no more subject; it is no
longer a desire: it is something that burns, and it is a joy. (Nancy, 1993: 383–4)

What I think Nancy is trying to get at in this Heideggerian language is
the idea of being's projection of desire towards its object understood as an
anticipation of ecstasy and epiphany, that is, both the fulfilment and the
vanishing of the subject in jouisance; what is anticipated is something that
remains forever in the domain of deferred presence, something towards
which the subject grasps as what would confirm the subject's desire for
presence. The grasping-towards is itself the only gesture available to being
as its way of living this excessive desire. If we follow Derrida's (1982)
discussion of the aporia of time in 'Ousia and gramme', we could extend
the implications of the discussion to reveal the thematic of temporality
that underlies this way of speaking about subjectivity, for, the secret
object of desire is the impossible completeness of a transfixed 'now', the
'now' without borders, without trace, that would fix being within
presence, a desire that wishes to abolish the vanishing of the subject
because of the endless rush of time that condemns being to finitude. The
gesture is the trace of that desire: it harbours a promise of joy, and it is
endless.

I would like to tie up this line of thought with the project of the
becoming-subject instituted in the discourse of the Enlightenment, specifically, the Kantian project of the development of the subject from its
immaturity towards its maturity. This process is world historical, recruiting
the peoples of the world in the guise of a generalized humanity, in the
service of the underlying ontology. In a curious way, the aporias in
the West's discourse of being are refigured in the period of colonialism to
combine both a totalizing, even terroristic enterprise of subjection and
subjugation and a liberatory, ethical project driven by a self-reflexive
activity that has taken the terrain of aesthetics to be the site of a new
hermeneutics of the self. This connection itself conceals some very
fundamental features of modernity; their examination would reveal those
aspects of the discourse of modernity that one could retain in the
reconstruction of the grounds of a postmodern and postcolonial life-world.

The functioning of aesthetics in modern Western thought as the site of
the reconciliation of reason and ethics is to some extent overdetermined. In
every culture what is called 'art' is the space and the means for a community to express its deepest anxieties, its wildest hopes, its greatest joys,
its finest pleasures. It is the liminal place where the soul 'touches itself on
its inside part', to borrow a phrase from Toni Morrison's Beloved (1987). It
is not surprising that the search for the 'soul of black folk' has immersed
itself in the artistic products and forms like the novel, music, film, sculpture
and so on, in which both the West and 'its others' have voiced the
differently lived experience of modernity. Indeed, a work like Black Skin

White Masks (Fanon, 1970) invents a language which utilizes both fictional and analytical strategies in order to subvert both while putting them to work in constructing the ambivalent and hybrid space where something new or unsaid can be said. Fanon's work is also one of the few places, in what has come to be packaged as postcolonial theory, where the economic, political and cultural realities of colonialism are given equal prominence. My interest in examining the discourse of modernity from the standpoint of the postcolonial and by focusing on the aporetic character of the discourse arises from the possibility of rephrasing these connections as part of the task of thinking subjectivity differently.

A Problematic Postcoloniality

As a way of foregrounding these arguments I shall begin by briefly reviewing the discourse of postcoloniality in order to problematize a number of issues relating to (post)modernity. I think it is possible to group the massive production of narratives about the postcolonial in three broad categories. First, a story of the postcolonial as a period of modernization and of building or rebuilding the nation-state after decolonization. This is the common sense story and much neglected in the 'cultural studies' approach to the political and economic reality on the 'Third World', a neglect which leaves unexamined what this kind of narrative takes for granted, like the liberal-democratic form of the state or the desirability and normativity of the unproblematized notion of modernity that underlies the presuppositions of what 'development' means. Yet, this common sense view, enshrined in the education and training system, institutionalized in everyday practices of administration and management, directs policy and the economy. Its intelligibility is framed within a paradigm of modernization that has no space for the decolonization of mind for which Fanon and others have argued.

Secondly, there are the narratives scripted around the theme of the recovery and reconstruction of an imagined authentic community that colonialism and imperialism had ravaged, distorted, misrepresented and silenced. There is indeed much that needs to be recovered or revalued, the ordinary stuff of traditions, lost, surviving or imagined, invested in songs, stories, place-names, ceremonies and rituals and so on, the countless everyday monuments in which the past of a community is memorialized and made present. It is an important part of resistance that the living history of indigenous cultures remain visible and meaningful. It is understandable that those most threatened or marginalized by 'modernization' wish to invent a timeless zone of culture where an imagined original purity and wholeness of the community is preserved intact. The ancient desire for the phantasized plenitude of being gets locked into the dreams of real emancipations: a heady brew. The problem is that the appeal of essentialism and, in appropriate conditions, of fundamentalism, are difficult to avoid for those who imagine that the purity of race or culture transcends the incursions of history or for those whose strategies for reconstructing new identities continue to be in thrall to the specular gaze of their oppressors, entrapping them within the epistemological boundaries they wish to escape.

The third series explores the conditions of hybridity, convinced that all cultures are, in any case, heterogeneous, unmonolithic, mobile formations, as Edward Said (1993), among others, has argued. These narratives recognize the transformative effects of modernity and imperialism for both indigenous and metropolitan cultures. They recognize too the effects of domination and unequal power in the strategies that communities and individuals employ in coping with, surviving or resisting the encounter between cultures. An important theme concerns what is called 'double consciousness', that is to say, the sense of being at one and the same time Western and indigenous, belonging to both modernity and a vernacular culture. Frantz Fanon's and Bu Bois's analyses of splitting and of fractured identity provide the exemplary studies of the effects of Westernization and European racism on the (ex)colonized, teasing out the ambivalences lived by Europe's 'others' subjected to the epistemic, psychic and ontological violences that have been intrinsic to the Western imperial enterprise. More recently, a variety of insightful explorations such as in the work of Stuart Hall or those of Gilroy (1993a), West (1993), Appiah (1992) or Mercer (1993) have established the extent to which the polarities inscribed in the notion of the 'West and its others' misunderstand and distort the complexity of the identities forged in the long time of living with racism and making one's own a critical modernity. Women writers like Spivak (1988), hooks (1992), Minh-ha (1989), among a long list, have added the complications of gender to the question of subjectivity and of overcoming economic, racist and colonialist oppressions.

Nevertheless, the theme of splitting has continued to be a major focus in postcolonial times, transmuting the rift between cosmopolitan identity and the corporeal 'fact of blackness' that Fanon explored into questions of the 'in-betweenness' and hybridity of colonial and postcolonial cultural belonging (Bhabha, 1994). It highlights the vigilance that the 'state of emergency' of a normalized racism demands of those on the wrong side of the tracks, as hooks (1992) explored regarding everyday culture. For Bhabha, the hybridity bound up with empire is not a simple mix, but a way of living and narrating unequal and antagonistic cultural encounters that disrupt and disturb the authoritative gaze of the oppressor and the discourse of colonial hegemony. Here it is a recognition of the disjunctive temporalities and cultural spaces which form the life-world where tradition, modernity, community unevenly coexist or combine. In contemporary culture, one could conceptualize hybridity in relation to the emergence of a 'third space', a space of transgression and subversion, the place whence 'newness enters the world'. Hybridity in this sense participates in a counter-hegemonic move.

There is another sense of hybridity that I would like to signal here without discussing it; the rest of my chapter will retroactively give it its proper inflection. I would like to picture hybridity as a transitional concept, in the sense implied in the notion of the transitional object in psychoanalytic discourse, that is, of a passage from one state to another, an in-between object, a comfort for insecurity that becomes lodged in memory as a monument to the secret wanderings of desire. One could argue that hybridity is not what the (postcolonial) subject truly wants, that is, not the in-betweenness itself. For this subject at first wants to belong to neither one nor the other, neither the 'West' nor the 'non-West' but to both. Hybridity is unhomely, an uncanny place which holds the promise of a different place of belonging. Hybridity, as '*mélange*', as wild combination, is an indefinite state, a temporary state, indeed, a temporization, waiting to come into its own in its own space and time. This new home is a place beyond the spaces that border hybridity. Yet it is not the domain of the global either, for one sense of the global is the set of all sets, which has no content of its own. From the point of view of belonging, it is difficult to imagine a life-world which is the set of all other life-worlds. The human being must root itself inside a particular life-world commensurate with the existential and intersubjective dimensions of being, even if its desire reaches for the excessive, especially when it lives in the moment of the loss. In trying to describe this state of undecidable belonging, Gilroy refers to the 'rhizomorphic, fractal structure of the transcultural' (Gilroy, 1993a: 4), noting too the vitality of this restless state for cultural production. What, then, is the beyond of hybridity or syncretism? What being do we await? What new identities? They are questions that resist neat resolutions, not least because they refuse to consider the problem of subjectivity to be a simple black and white issue and resist the normalization and re-appropriations to which are prone the machinery of otherness.

The point to bear in mind is that new identities are political and contestatory in character, appearing in specific moments (for instance, the postcolonial) in response to specific relations of power (for instance, racist ideologies and practices). They are thus strategic and positional, their effects being in consequence mobile and conjunctural, for example, the current emphasis on border and translational identities bound up with the fact of diasporas, refugee and transitional existences which are the effects of globalization – a venerable process from the standpoint of the colonized – and the human fallout of ongoing military and economic conflicts.

I think we can take the proliferation of stories of the marginalized to constitute the already-said of an interrogation that has arrived at a point where it must rewrite *its* modernity. This is not to say that all spaces must be seen as varieties of the modern, for, clearly, modernity has not colonized every cultural space. But today we can hardly find a community or a subculture that has not in some significant way been touched by the hold of modernity, either directly – for example, regarding law, employment, technology – or, at the very least, because of the limiting effects of modernity, namely, in the way that modernity itself functions as limit and in the way that the existence of the modern world limits the possibilities of change or even of the survival of 'non-modern' spaces. So, while recognizing the stories of difference and their challenges to existing power relations, I would like to pursue a different itinerary in my exploration of the moment of the post of postcolonial and postmodern times. My interest here is two-fold. On the one hand, I want to try to move outside the oppositions of traditional/modern, Western/non-Western, and so on, by starting with the view, already proposed by a number of writers, that these new stories and accounts are not just narratives of difference but different narratives of modernity. On the other hand, the refusals and the kind of 'postcolonial' questioning to which I have referred indicate the extent to which the theoretical debate is ready to engage with fundamental issues of epistemology and ontology that have a universal bearing, yet avoids the Eurocentrism of the old humanisms. This suggests that, to begin with, we need to disaggregate the discourse of modernity, recognizing the plural character of the lived experience of modernity. Then we could begin to repose the question of being and of transfiguration.

Pluralizing Modernity

One starting point is the recognition of the ambivalent character and the fractures of modernity and its effects, for example in the notion of a counter-modernity or contramodernity, pointing to the narratives of a 'counterculture of modernity' (Bauman, 1992: 221) that valorizes its emancipatory and ethical project. These narratives are grounded in resistance to a disciplinary and subjugating modernity and in a critical, self-reflexive reason, open to the undecidable becoming of being. Two main themes run through our judgement of modernity. On the one hand, there has emerged the critique which recognizes the failure of the project of modernity, for example because of its terroristic impulse from the point of view of the violences that the grand narratives of modernity, and the performative requirements of late modernity, do to competing language games and legitimizing conceptual structures. This judgement is allied to poststructuralist and deconstructivist critiques of the notion of the unitary, rational, solipsistic subject that have demonstrated its logocentric, phallocentric and eurocentric privilege.

On the other hand, there is the recognition that some of the defining concepts of modernity, like freedom, liberty, human rights, autonomy, have played a significant part both in the struggles for decolonization and in contesting forms of oppression founded on differences of gender, class or race. My argument is that the recognition of ambivalences and aporias should be seen as a starting point for transfiguration, though there is no point in wishing to abolish them in some alternative totalizing scheme, and thus repeat other forms of terror, as Rose (1992) has argued. By pluralizing the discourse of modernity, we can understand some aspects of ambivalence to be bound up with the different filiations and affiliations that the thematics of modernity have established with capitalism and with colonialism. If we try to systematize these relations, we could imagine a tripartite series of relations between colonialism, capitalism and modernity. There would be no necessary relations between the three, but genealogical ones and relations of overdetermination and articulation. The point I want to draw from this approach is that the history of any one of the three is not separable from that of the other two, since each provide particular conditions and contingencies without which their separate histories would have been markedly different. The upshot of my point is that we must consider colonialism to have been intrinsic to the history of modernity, and that, by the same token, we cannot allow ourselves to forget, in narrating postcoloniality, that it is still bound up with both the late/postmodern and late/global capitalism. Rewriting modernity and settling accounts with its history means retrieving from the forgetfulness, to which it is too often consigned, the disturbing reality of these relations.

The claim that rational capitalism and European colonialism share a totalizing ambition is, I think, uncontentious from the point of view of history. Equally uncontentious is the claim that the logic of capitalism drives it towards the global extension of its control over the factors – of labour, resources, capital, technology – that enter the calculations of risk and of return on investments. In this sense, globalization and universalization are strategic moves that worked for capitalism. We could add to this the argument that the discourse of modernity, when it is grounded in the notion of the logocentric subject, is also driven by a totalizing vision. So, the particular discourse of modernity that founds its authority on the notion of a universal reason and a subject defined in terms of such a conceptualization of reason, not only erases cultural and cognitive differences – or, more accurately, reduces difference to pathology and error – it is complicit with systems of exploitation and the subjugating enterprise of imperialism. In other words, one can distinguish what one could call a positivist or technocratic discourse of modernity which is affiliated with that of rational capitalism through the privilege of instrumental reason and the notion of a logocentric subject that functions as a nodal or relay point. The co-articulation of logocentric reason, technocratic modernity, and imperialism by way of an egocentric ontology of being is what I would call occidentalism; it circumscribes the discursive space and the conceptual framework that legitimizes the privilege of a particular subjective project and the privilege of Europe in the idea of the West as the superior centre of world historical development.

One of the consequences of the formulation of logocentrism and cartesianism is the displacement of ontological and aesthetics questions on to the terrain of the humanities. From the point of view of legitimization and authority, a narrative of modernity is constructed which separates out and privileges rationality and scientific procedures, a narrative which, therefore, privileges epistemology as the ground for founding the grand narratives of modernity. This produces the ambivalences and aporias that, for example, Kant, Hegel, Marx differently attempt to resolve in their different configurations of liberty, emancipation, autonomy, progress in relation to a process of enlightenment. It can be argued that the fact of the tripartite system has the historical effect of emphasizing the positivist themes in the discourse of modernity, one consequence of which has been to lend to the notion of a unitary rational subject a performative credibility. The subject of imperialism and economic expansion retroactively, specularly, appears to confirm its discursive designation as agency and as the originary centre of world historical development. Within the same conceptual framework, the idea of the progress of humanity comes to be aligned with that of the progress of reason, which is linked in turn with the theme of the spread of civilization through the colonial enterprise, while the two are tied up with the idea of economic growth and development through the systematic application of instrumental reason. The three together establish a technology of becoming, a modern *techne* that enframes the history of modernity.

Yet, the diremptions do not disappear, neither in the discourse of philosophy nor by reference to political economy. In the period of the emergence of these ideas, the same narrative that locked women in a subaltern position also informed the arguments for the equality of women (as in Wollstonecraft), and, in another arena, sustained the struggles against slavery and colonial oppression (as with Toussaint L'Ouverture in Haiti) and, later, the decolonizing process. Also, the experience of modernity had never ceased to be the object of ambivalent critiques, for example, in Romanticism, or in the work of Baudelaire, and, classically, in Nietzsche. It is worth noting that if we look at who produce the critical or counter-discourse of modernity, we note the predominance of the marginalized: exiles, Jews, homosexuals, colonized and slaves, women, whoever for some reason or other does not quite fit the norm of the rational, unitary, masculine, white subject. The question that arises from my arguments so far is: how does one theorize differently the new understanding of modernity I am trying to signal, whereby (post)colonial experience is seen as an experience that belongs to the history of modernity?

Technology, *Techne*, and the Life-world

A problem which has intrigued me for some time about the conditions of (post)coloniality concerns the effects of technology in determining the limits of what it is possible for one to achieve or even to imagine. Some aspects of the standpoint are obvious enough and are well established, even if many analyses of culture tend to neglect them. For instance, we know the extent to which technology provides a leverage in settling the international distribution of economic and military power, operating through mechanisms like the licensing of products and systems, the flows of expertise, the sale of military hardware, the systematic use of a technology of terror to force the recalcitrant into submission, or the fact that the location of prestigious scientific and technological research and development remains largely centred in the 'West'. In these days of the multiplication of centres of economic and technological power and of globalization, say with Japan, Southeast Asia, it has been possible for some people to speak of multiple and radically different modernities. But, is this a hasty inference? For one thing, it is clear that these mechanisms and practices all inscribe already established inequalities of wealth and power and know-how, both within specific countries and internationally.

There is, however, a deeper and less visible feature of technology that I wish to signal. My analysis draws from two sources: Foucault's notion of technologies of the social and of governmentality and Heidegger's theorization of technology in relation to culture and to modernity. The questions to explore arise from, on the one hand, the view that modernity is instituted by means of specific apparatuses that constitute the domain of the social according to particular discursively constructed norms, and, on the other hand, from the thought that something like a modern *techne* animates the development of modernity and frames the conceptual limits that bound it.

The usefulness of Foucault in analysing the mechanisms of colonialism and imperialism has been amply demonstrated in the work around colonial discourse and its functioning in the exercise of colonial power, for example in the production of the discourse of Orientalism as described by Said (1978) or in what was at stake in the introduction of English in India and Africa as part of putting into place an apparatus of subjectification. Homi Bhabha (1994) has noted the complex relations of coordination and articulation between the schoolroom, the barracks, the church and the administrative quarters whereby the effectivity of colonial power was ensured. It can be argued that these apparatuses and sites constitute what I would call, extending Foucault's analysis, a colonial or imperial governmentality. Colonial rule was systematized and normalized through the implantation of an imperial governmentality. The elements of this complex apparatus are obvious enough, constituting a massive archive that has been interrogated by, among others, JanMohamed (1983), Viswanathan (1989), Suleri (1992), Hall (1992), the Subaltern Studies Group.

My interest concerns the effects of governmentality for the formation of subjects, through technologies of the social, many initially developed in the imperial context, that instituted practices for the disciplining and regulation of capacities and aptitudes, attitudes and orientations so that targeted groups ended up behaving within the limits indicated by normalizing discourses. The analysis of these mechanisms highlight, for instance, the 'ideological' level of their functioning, that is to say, they point to the problematic of how particular norms, values, attitudes become authoritative in the process of identification and self-regulation. They draw attention to the point of view of the establishment of hegemonic rule and thus to questions of the 'interpellation' and positioning of both colonized and colonizers. JanMohamed's (1983) examination of the politics of the literature curriculum in Africa proposes the functioning of a Manichean grid, constructed in terms of a series of polarities: of black/white, savage/civilized, evil/good, and so on, that operated as a cognitive and normative framework in authorizing what I am calling colonial governmentality. Things, of course, were never as uncomplicated or smooth-running as our reconstructions might lead one to believe. For the reality was one of constant conflict and contestation. Indeed, one cannot imagine the various apparatuses and mechanisms appearing without the assumption of an agonistic field that motivated and modulated their development. The process was even more fraught because of fundamental ambivalences in the mode of address of colonial authority such that it was doubly undermined, namely, from within the very discourse of modern subjectivity and, also, by forms of subversion such as the camouflage of mimicry, as Bhabha (1994) has argued.

This governmentality is still largely in place, operating in and through pedagogy and the curriculum, the legal and juridical apparatuses, the organization of administration, in systems for the management of public and private spaces and so on. It is invested in countless daily routines, ways of doing and behaving concerning things like health, the bringing up of children, the furnishing of private places, conduct in offices and the classroom, the driving code: so much of the mundane material and symbolic dimensions of the life-world which is taken for granted. Thus, a good deal of the mechanisms, as well as the norms of regulation, formation, normalization, disciplining and punishment in postcoloniality are those that were developed in the period of the systematic institution of modernity globally. Clearly, they are not the same everywhere, obvious distinctions and differences existing between, say, India and Brazil. The tenacity of indigenous cultures and different conditions have produced heterogeneous zones across the globe. Nevertheless, imperial governmentality has ensured that the authority of a mode and direction of economic and social transformation has become inscribed in the process called modernization, touching every part of the world, particularly in urban areas where already the spatial and temporal coordinates of social relations are anchored in the geography, the architecture, the various 'scapes' that embody the materialized transformations wrought by colonialism and imperialism. Modernity is made present and operative in and through these spatial and temporal features of the life-world. I wonder if we may regard them as the 'standing reserve' of colonial modernity?

Let me try to clarify this question. I shall do this by linking up several themes in Heidegger (1993), reading 'The question concerning technology' and 'The origin of the work of art' side by side, informed also by some remarks of Lacoue-Labarthe (1990) is his theses on Heidegger. Heidegger understands by technology not mere instrumentality but 'a way of revealing' (1993: 318). It is not the revelation of something already there but hidden, but a way of 'unlocking, transforming, storing, distributing, and switching about' (1993: 322) that have to do with 'unconcealment', a 'bringing-forth' which reveals the 'truth'. It is both *poiesis* and *physis*, that is to say, an irruption that brings forth out of itself the presencing of what waited in the shadows for the work of *physis* to open up and make appear: '*Physis* is indeed *poiesis* in the highest sense' (1993: 317). Heidegger uses the word '*Gestell*' to gather together in one term the meaning of producing, presencing, instituting and constituting which bringing forth out of unconcealment means (1993: 184ff.). *Techne* is the setting to work which accomplishes this unconcealment; it suggests the work of invention. However, *techne* is not to be thought of as craft or technique, for it is 'a mode of knowing' (1993: 184), at once knowledge and art, which brings into being, by setting to work, the being 'enframed' (1993: 325) by the modern episteme.

Heidegger's move away from the 'merely instrumental, merely anthropological definition of technology' (1993: 326) opens up the question of the being who is at work and at stake in the life-world which has been put into place with modernity. It is a more fundamental question than one concerning efficiency and rationality, since it suggests a 'critical ontology of ourselves' in the sense that Foucault understands the concept in his essay on the Enlightenment (Foucault, 1991) and which I want to examine in the context of the postcolonial. If we envisage postcoloniality to implicate a decolonization of mind, that is, a disruption of the system of authority inscribed in colonial discourse and a disengagement from the life-world instituted by imperial governmentality, what is the work that critique and testimony must do in the process of dis-identification and disaffiliation? What limits are there to the modifications of the spatial and temporal features of the world we have inherited and inhabit as inscribed subjectivities? What affiliations are there between the different narratives of self and of the community and the refigurations of the history of modernity that a postcolonial critical ontology suggests? One conclusion from my (condensed) account of Heidegger's questioning concerning technology indicates that in thinking about the legacy of colonialism/imperialism and the presence of modernity in what used to be called the 'Third World', we need to interrogate not only the material life-world and the limits and limitations that it conceals, but, just as crucially, the form of being which is enframed in that world and the narratives that give meaning to its existence.

Narrative and Identity

My starting point is the understanding of being as the entity that questions itself as to its way of being, that interrogates itself *as* being. A crucial dimension of this understanding is the proposition that claims temporality to be a fundamental dimension of being. One aspect of our being in time is the consciousness of our finitude and the anxiety bound up with this consciousness and with the 'spacing' of our experiences across the gap which the passage of time opens up for self-consciousness. The gap discloses the work of *différance*, if we understand *différance* to refer to the displacement of the problem of meaning – and of being – on to the plane of temporality, operating according to the process of deferral that works through trace and spacing. Trace is the illegible mark of the passage of time; it is disseminated in an infinite temporality that narration brings within the order of the intelligible through devices such as myth, as Lévi-Strauss long ago perceived. The discourse of logocentrism, breaking with the metaphysical and ontological comforts of religious foundation, attempts to fix and master the dispersed and elusive process of signification through the subterfuge of self-presence, for instance, as voice or as the originative consciousness of the unitary self-centred subject.

My next proposition, following from this, is that temporality cannot be expressed in the 'direct discourse of phenomenology but requires the mediation of the indirect discourse of narration' (Ricœur, 1988: 241). As Ricœur says: 'narrative is the guardian of time' (1988: 241). Narration, then, is the form in which we attempt to grasp our self as temporal beings. But, who narrates? And what relation is there between the 'who' of agency and action and the 'who' inscribed in narration?

Ricœur develops the question through a series of propositions, starting with the problem of the permanence in time of a particular 'self' which is implicated in our sense of a particular person remaining the same person over time. There are quite different approaches to the problem, for example, Husserl's problematic claim of the unity of consciousness as grounds for the identity of selves. The usefulness of Ricœur is that he makes the distinction between identity as sameness and identity as selfhood, or *idem* and *ipse*, in order to point out that the notion of self relies on narrative identity and not on the formal identity of an unchanging thing, a view which for him is consistent with the Heideggerian notion that Being is the entity that can 'relate itself to itself qua being' (Ricœur, 1991: 191). The way I would put it is that identity is not the sameness of a permanent unchanging entity but the mode of relating to being that can be characterized as selfhood; self is not a fact, it is not something that can be reduced to the facticity of the body or the mental apparatus. It knows itself 'only indirectly by the detour of the cultural signs of all sorts which are articulated on the symbolic mediations which always already articulate action and, among them, the narratives of everyday life' (Ricœur, 1991: 198).

In modern culture, although 'narrative constructs the durable properties of a character' (Ricœur, 1991: 195), the mediations and articulations are mobile, so that the self is not a fixed entity but is constantly refigured by the application of narrative, through a series of emplotments and the emergence of different discourses that provide the scripts for staging particular selves. Narrative has a recognition effect, since subjects recognize themselves in the stories they tell about themselves. Furthermore, each narrative identity is entangled with those of others, since the story of a person's life is a 'segment' of other people's life stories. Our life is in a sense a point at the 'intersections between numerous stories' (Ricœur, 1996: 6), its meaning bound up with an intersubjective domain constituted in the form of a narrated memory. The sense of a constant self itself 'refers to a self instructed by the works of a culture that it has applied to itself' (Ricœur, 1988: 247). Thus, we can say with Ricœur that 'life itself is a cloth woven of stories told' (1988: 246).

It is interesting that, for Ricœur, the idea of narrative identity can be applied to both a community and to particular persons: 'Individuals and community are constituted in their identity by taking up narratives that become for them their actual history' (Ricœur, 1988: 247). It is possible, therefore, to use Ricœur to re-examine the mechanisms whereby history and biography are intertwined, that is to say, how narratives about the collective or the community are co-articulated with the stories we tell and are told about us. One obvious mechanism refers to the functioning of particular narratives of race, nation, class, gender and so on, in stitching the one into the other, acting as ideological 'points de capiton' in this process. I shall examine an example of this later on. It should be clear from what I have said so far that one consequence is that variations in historical narration as well as different emplotments of individual lives have the effect of destabilizing narrative identity and leaving it open to refigurations in the light of different imaginary reconstitutions of memory and of history.

For that reason, the different devices that marginalized or subordinate groups have invented or preserved for keeping alive memories of their past are crucial in sustaining the 'identity' of the community and in informing resistance. Such devices may take the form of music, rituals, traditional stories, songs, ceremonies, the names of people or places, and so on, enacted, performed, or told as ways of constructing solidarity and belongingness. They participate in the process of subjectification, crossing or meeting other devices and techniques that may be in conflict with, or threatening for, the coherence and authority of an indigenous group's initial culture and tradition. The history of colonialism and imperialism abounds in such conflictual juxtapositions and in strategies for coping with or managing or accommodating what in effect constitute new technologies of formation. The Christianizing work of the missions, the introduction of English in India in the nineteenth century, the schooling of native American children in the reservations, the seasoning of slaves in the Americas are some of the cases in which the subjugated had to invent ways of safeguarding a memory of their culture and of reconstituting identities befitting the changed circumstances. These changes were not without costs.

We can pursue this by turning to another dimension in Ricœur's analysis of the relation of time and narrative that brings to our attention the psychic level of the relation between history, identity and narrative. He regards the process of the 'cure' in psychoanalysis to constitute a laboratory for 'a properly philosophical enquiry into the notion of narrative identity' (Ricœur, 1988: 247). My argument is that the work of 'working through' in psychoanalysis leads to a series of refigurations applied to previous narratives or figurations of the self; the new narratives have a cathartic effect for the subject. It can be seen from this that refiguration is the product of two related things; on the one hand, there is the difficult work we do upon ourselves in 'working through' traumas and the pain and anxiety associated with our existence as temporal beings, and, on the other hand, there are the effects for the process of identification of the new emplotments and scripts that are staged in the analytic experience. Something similar takes place in what is called 'consciousness raising' practices, in which historicization, biography and critique all come into play in a collective form of 'working through'.

A significant aspect in Ricœur's analysis is that he does not regard the process of refiguration and 'working through' to be ethically neutral. There is a phase in the process of self-formation and self-transformation that implicates a commitment to a position with implicit ethical values, expressed in the 'decision whereby a person says: here I stand' (1988: 249). In any case, 'narrativity is not denuded of every normative, evaluative, or prescriptive dimension', indeed, 'narrative already belongs to the ethical field in virtue of its claim . . . to ethical justice' (1988: 249). This point cannot be properly established without a detour through a deeper interrogation of the question of temporality than I am able to do here. I signal the point of view of ethics because I want to propose that the rewriting of history, in the sense in which I discussed it earlier, whether of oneself or of the community, is a profoundly ethical matter.

I do not mean by this that it is a matter of morality, that is to say, a matter of conformity or a return to norms within the frame of normalization. Lacan's discussion of the ethics of psychoanalysis, in linking the cathartic experience of analysis to the judgement of our action, rephrases the question of ethics by way of the economy of desire and thereby binds ethics to the finitude of being, which, in an overly Heideggerian gesture, he paraphrases on the side of 'being-for-death' (Lacan, 1992: 313). Ethics, in that sense, has a cost, weighed in jouissance, and kept in a 'space where accounts are kept' (Lacan, 1992: 317). I am suggesting that the settling of accounts – with the history of modernity – and the keeping of its and our accounts engage with both the process of memory and that of the judgement of ourself as particular beings, that is, they engage with our 'presentness'. It is a profoundly distressing engagement in that in it we measure ourselves against an infinite measure – the scale of jouissance, or of being-towards-death – and try to preserve the 'having been' both of our own existence and of something that goes beyond individual subjects.

I must amplify this before returning to the issue of postcolonial 'identity' because it concerns the question of historicization implicated in the notion of narrative identity. The problem of the relationship between history and the temporality of being hangs on rephrasing the question in terms of the relationship between the 'three dimensions of expectation, tradition and the force of the present' (Ricœur, 1988: 256), the dimensions which, for Ricœur, refigure on the existential terrain of human activity the 'discordant concordance' between the Heideggerian three moments of temporalization, namely, the 'having been', the 'making present', and the 'coming towards' which are involved in the temporal structure of Care. There is much to explain here, both in the way that Ricœur is putting the discourse of Heidegger to work and in an explication of the relevant passages from Heidegger. I shall have to be content with noting that the issue is central to an understanding of what our existence as beings in time means from the point of view of how we are to conduct ourselves. Ricœur's analysis is, I think, an attempt to shift the focus towards a more phenomenologically grounded approach, in contrast with the focus on ontology in Heidegger – though Heidegger does not quite neglect the ontic dimension, as the discussion of the relation of Care and selfhood makes clear. This passage of Heidegger gives a flavour of the connection I am trying to put on the agenda:

> The character of 'having been' arises from the future, and in such a way that the future which 'has been' (or better, which 'is in the process of having been') releases from itself the Present. This phenomenon has the unity of a future which makes present in the process of having been; we designate it as *'temporality'*. . . . *Temporality reveals itself as the authentic care.* (Heidegger, 1982: 274, original emphasis)

Heidegger's formulation, while underlining the relation of past, present and future as processes in cashing out the temporality of being, over-totalizes the relationship in the notion of unity. Existentially, after all, the future is projection or expectation, and only partially and retroactively can be construed to construct a unity of temporality. Unless, of course, it is posited as what brings into being a phantasized promise, made in the past of an ideal originary moment: it shall be in a time to come as it was in the purity of the beginning. This is indeed the road that Heidegger trod in supporting National Socialism, whereas the future must remain undecidable if we are to avoid the historical closure of the end of history or the myth of the future recovery or realization of a pure origin. The questions that arise are: how do we relate the notion that we have of ourselves in the present to history and to identity? And, how are we to judge ourselves in the present?

I will use Foucault's notion of presentness in order to indicate the link between the two questions. In his interrogation of the Enlightenment, Foucault (1991) uses the term presentness to refer to the problem of 'who we are in the present', a question which for him is at once a genealogical and an ontological one, requiring us to examine the conditions and the means whereby we have come to be who we are today and, at the same time, to judge ourselves in relation to a project of becoming, implicating our constant transformation in the light of the critical attitude central to the Enlightenment ethos. This 'critical ontology' indicates 'a philosophical life in which the critique of what we are is at one and the same time the historical analysis of the limits that are imposed on us and an experiment with the possibility of going beyond them' (Foucault, 1991: 50). Foucault's engagement with the legacy of modernity in his questioning of the Enlightenment brings together nicely the problem of being which I have laid out through Heidegger and Ricœur, and the problems of history and of 'identity'. Foucault's answer was to suggest a process of self-making that would be aesthetic and ethical in orientation, but with him this is given over to a solipsistic will acting in a world with no clear ethical grounds. The notion of narrative identity, on the other hand, enables us to rework the problem as one that involves the collective as well as the individual levels. The proposition that history and memory are entwined in the process of narrative allows one to argue for a basic link between historical consciousness and the projects we make for ourselves, and between the intersubjective or community level of narrative and the individual or subjective level. My juxtapositions transform the problems I originally started with and bring to light the following questions: what are the ethical implications of the temporality of being and our presentness in relation to the having-been and the coming-towards? What is the meaning of 'working through' in the context of the rememoration of history? And, finally, what meaning do we give to the post of postmodernity and postcoloniality in relation to the having-been of modernity?

In his discussion of expectation or the 'coming towards', Ricœur locates it in relation to the 'imperfect mediation . . . between the horizon of expectation, traditionality, and the historical present' (Ricœur, 1988: 256); he adds that it must be conceptualized as a structure of practice. Human beings make their history through their own activity, and the projection we make in our expectation 'is open to the future of the historical community, and . . . to the undetermined future of humanity as a whole' (1988: 256). Traditionality in his sense is not quite the same concept as the Heideggerian having-been, though the concepts of trace, heritage and debt govern both analyses. Importantly, for Ricœur, 'traditionality includes the confession of a debt that is fundamentally contracted on behalf of another' (1988: 256).

The question of debt is vital; I will pursue it by first turning to Derrida's meditations in the opening sections of *Les Spectres de Marx*, an essay haunted by 'a work around mourning . . . and about the economy of debt and the gift' (Derrida, 1993: 24), and placed under the sign of 'responsibility and respect for justice on behalf of those who are not here, those who are no longer or not yet present and living' (1993: 16). It is the recognition of this justice, irreducible to the law and to rights, applying beyond the present moment, that allows us to speak about the future. It is a concept of 'justice as the incalculability of the gift and the singularity of the non-economical ex-position towards the other' (1993: 48). The references in Derrida's discussion are to the concept of justice, or rather of *Dike*, in Heidegger, and the notion of justice in the work of Levinas, understood as 'the relation to the other'; they lead him to conclude that it is a 'gift without restitution, without calculation, without account' (1993: 53).

In line with the thought I am developing, can we not think of justice alongside the notion of debt upon which Ricœur insists when he says that, with regard to the past, '[W]e are not only inheritors, we are equally debtors to a debt which in some way renders us insolvent' (Ricœur, 1991: 186)? It is significant that both Derrida and Ricœur, in developing the notion of historical narration, refer to the victims of oppression and violences of one kind or another, both refusing the fictionalizing – as in the view that takes too literally the figurative, tropological and textual form of the writing of history – or the forgetting of the 'having been' of history which must then return to haunt us. It is a different restitution that is implied in the notion of debt, for '[i]f we are unable to "fictionalize" the dead, we would have to return their "having been" to them. . . . The past is not just what is absent from history; the right of its "having been" also demands to be recognized. This is what the historian's debt consists in' (Ricœur, 1991: 186).

So, the answer to the first question I posed earlier is that the ethical issue that underlies the standpoint of temporality as a foundational dimension of 'identity' – and that underlies the view that the narrativization of existence is the form in which we live the temporality of being – brings to the fore the relation to the other, understood, in the Levinasian sense, as responsibility for the being of the other. This responsibility, minimally, demands that we tell our story, the story of our presentness, in a way that preserves and respects the 'having been' of the other, and, therefore, by extension, that respects our own 'having been'.

Furthermore, such a narrative takes place on the terrain of 'working through', so that rememoration refigures, or can refigure, as part of the same work, both collective and individual history: it is not the space of 'forgetting'. With regard to modernity, we cannot rewrite it on the basis of forgetting either the violences that have been intrinsic to the particular discourse of modernity that I have called occidentalism, or of the debt we owe to those whose 'having been' is the conditional or future anterior of the present.

A desire to change is implicated in this work we do on ourselves, to change both ourselves and the conditions of existence so that the future may hold 'the promise of joy' or the promise of an end to oppression consistent with the notion of justice that I have been exploring. The transactions between memory and anticipation that constantly modulate the temporality of our being are central to this working through, for, '[W]ithout memory . . . there is no principle of hope' (Ricœur, 1988: 258).

Finally, let us look at the implications for the meaning of the post of the postmodern and the postcolonial. Modernity has witnessed the birth of the idea of history as a 'collective singular' giving expression to the supposition of the oneness of time. This idea, as we know, is at work throughout modern Western thought, underlying the yearning for the possibility of absolute knowledge and the possibility of writing the history of humanity as the epic history of what Ricœur has described as the 'equivalence between three ideas: one time, one humanity, and one history' (Ricœur, 1988: 258). Against this excessive demand of logocentrism – a demand the excessiveness of which signals the problematic of jouisance and of phantasized plenitude: the desire to recover the unnamable loss or to possess the secret which defeats the finitude of being – I have pointed to the disjunctions and aporias that condemn this project to failure. In relation to meaning or the search for the 'truth' of history, the problem is that there is always more than one possible narrativization of an event; there is, as Ricœur puts it, 'no plot of all plots capable of equating the idea of one humanity and one history' (1988: 259). Equally, from the point of view of the disjunctive modalities of temporality, we can turn to Derrida's point that we only now perceive more clearly the radical heterogeneity of historical accounts because of the ending of a *particular* concept of history' (1993: 38, original emphasis). It is the concept that had 'forgotten' the traces of what and who has come before, traces that have to be acknowledged when we recognize the multiplicity of existences that forces us to settle account with our present. Once again, the critique of modernity located in the moment of the post takes as target the philosophy of identity as sameness and its indifference to or hatred of difference. Indifference, because difference is conceptualized as deviation from the norm, that is, as error, rather than as an other valid existential, and hatred because the truly different fractures the oneness of identity and must be subordinated or annihilated.

Lacoue-Labarthe's engagement with/against Heidegger makes a number of points that connect my discussion so far with what I want to say about the postcolonial. He places his critique in the shadow of 'the exhaustion of the modern project in which the catastrophic Being of that project stands revealed' (Lacoue-Labarthe, 1990: 20). Heidegger's option in supporting National Socialism in 1933 was not an error but was in line with the historical 'destiny of the West' (1990: 22). It is the destiny that Auschwitz unveiled, for,

> In the Auschwitz apocalypse, it was nothing less than the West, in its essence, that revealed itself – and that continues, ever since to reveal itself. And it is thinking that event that Heidegger failed to do. (Lacoue-Labarthe, 1990: 33)

For Lacoue-Labarthe, the argument is anchored in two central themes: the discourse of Being that belongs to the West and the idea of the possibility of the accomplishment of the community as an organic polity. Condensing his elaboration to the barest of sketches, I would say that the steps connecting the two pass through three propositions: the notion of art conceived 'as harbouring within it the capacity of opening up a possibility of historical Dasein' (1990: 56); the aestheticization of politics coupled with the view of the artwork as 'a celebration of the national community' (1990:

68); and, thirdly, the realization of the community by a *techne* which has 'forgotten' *physis* to become a lethal machinery for 'bringing about . . . the unthinkable' (1990: 69).

The unthinkable here is the rational calculation of genocide involved in the Holocaust, but, can one not extend it to include the epistemic, onto-logical and psychic violences and the regimes of terror which accompanied colonialism and imperialism (and remain in place today), and, indeed, any system that institutionalizes oppression and exploitation? If one accepts this, my intention in drawing attention to the problem of the being of modernity and the life-world constituted with the modern *techne* becomes clearer, for it provokes us to interrogate that being from the standpoint of what has remained unthought in the discourse of the subject because of the success of the particular (occidentalist) project that had enframed its historical becoming. That project, while it lasted, had obscured funda-mental questions about our beingness that modernity itself had ironically opened up to a *secular* mediation.

Perhaps it is a little clearer, too, why I have proceeded by detours and suggestions in order to approach the place of the unthinkable and the 'forgotten', for the question of the refiguration and transfiguration of subjectivity that interests me could not be posed directly on the already invested territories of postcoloniality and postmodernity without the risk of repeating the presuppositions that support the catastrophic being of occidentalism. At the same time there are debts and memories, narratives of what has been and projections of the future that remain to be worked through and worked out, and that seem to demand the suspension of some of the narratives upon which we have come to rely to make sense of our presentness.

Towards Transfiguration

It is remarkable that the themes I have been trying to gather and regroup in my discussion are expressed in their immediacy and poignancy in the work of a Black American woman. Speaking about her novel, *Beloved*, Toni Morrison says: 'The book is not a historical novel . . . but it deals directly with the power of history, the necessity of historical memory, the desire to forget the terrors of slavery and the impossibility of forgetting' (Morrison, 1993a:179). Black American writers turn to history because 'we live in a land where the past is always erased and America is the innocent future in which immigrants can come and start over, where the slate is clean. The past is absent or it's romanticized . . . [yet, the vital thing is] . . . to come to terms with the truth about the past' (Morrison, 1993a: 179). Later she says: 'Black Americans were sustained and healed and nurtured by the translation of their experience into art, above all in the music' (1993a: 181). It is this music, what dwells in it, that she tries to reactivate in her writing.

Beloved, described as a 'magic realist' novel, a description Morrison spurns because it assumes that she 'has no culture to write out of' (Morrison, 1993a: 181), deals with the ghosts locked up at the heart of Black American history, yearning to be born again in the midst of the present. It is a story of an escaped slave woman, Sethe, who, at the point of losing her children to the slave agent, kills her daughter, Beloved, because she could not bear to let white men do to her children what they had done to her: 'dirty you so bad you forgot who you were and couldn't think it up . . . [they must not dirty] her best thing, her beautiful, magical best thing – the part of her that was clean' (Morrison, 1987: 251). The result is amnesia for those closely involved, until, years later, Beloved returns, the 'becoming-body' of the spectre (Derrida, 1993: 25), as a young woman, to 'join' with her mother in response to the latter's desolate yearning and pain. It is a story of how the out-of-jointness of time as lived by those subjected to an excessive oppression freezes the familiar events of existence: traumas and loss, birth and death, into an uncanny dreamtime that only cathartic violence or healing can reassemble. Violence binds both perpetrators and victims in the return of the past as the uncanny figure to whom justice must be rendered. In *Beloved*, the repressed and the unmourned return for real, demanding the recognition of their 'having been', a recognition that the whole community must share in order for the refiguration of the living to take place. The last part of the story unfolds as a collective process of 'rememory' and of rescue which counters the literal fading of Sethe as she gives herself to, and is possessed by, the object of loss, itself symbolic of unbearable other losses. A significant moment of healing comes when Beloved's sister calls for help from the women of the neighbourhood. They gather outside Sethe's house and sing, searching for the sound at the beginning when there were no words: 'the voices of women searched for the right combination, the key, the code, the sound that broke the back of words' (Morrison, 1987: 261). The uncanny force of the music and the communal host sets to right the disjunctions of time that injustice had wrought. Its work belongs to the economy of the gift, freely given, expecting no restitution and responding to an immemorial ethical imperative.

There are many other instantiations of the sublime in the book, often in the form of music – Sixo singing while being burnt to death by the slave agents, the chanting and dancing of slaves gathering in the 'Clearing' to get back in touch with the thing that humiliations and routine torture tried to beat out of them, the thing that puts back together the pieces of their humanity. *Beloved* is more than a story of the everyday distress of slaves retold as vernacular history; it is about the bodily and collective re-enactment of the unpresentable, it is about the phenomenal world that circumscribes our existence and the liminal spaces in it where something beyond the bits and pieces of daily living are assembled in an interiority, and it is about modernity as lived by those once considered outside the modern. Morrison is clear that in making present the 'having been' of

Black American history, in particular the terror that was slavery, she is giving voice to an experience of modernity in two senses. She argues that 'modern life begins with slavery . . . black women had to deal with "post-modern" problems in the nineteenth century and earlier. Certain kinds of dissolution, the loss of and the need to reconstruct certain kinds of stability. . . . These strategies for survival made the truly modern person' (Morrison, 1993a: 178). But the counterpart of the terror of slavery was another terror, nourished by the fears experienced in the Old World – of oppression, limitations to freedom, poverty, unfulfillable dreams because of the iniquitous conditions in Europe. These were transmuted on the clean slate of the New World into the 'American Dream' that would 'replace the powerlessness felt before the gates of class, caste and cunning persecution' (Morrison, 1993b: 79) into the fantasies of wealth and freedom, power over nature and destiny. Morrison considers romance to be the form in which this drama was replayed for the literary imagination. For Americans, romance provided the register in which could be inscribed the anxieties imported from Europe as well as the fears of newness and boundaryless-ness in the New World which harboured the greatest fear: 'The terror of human freedom – the thing they coveted most of all – . . . and the terror's most significant, overweening ingredient: darkness, with all the connotative value it awakened' (Morrison, 1993b: 37). American society and artists assumed that the black slave population was 'available for meditations on terror . . . [it] offered itself up for reflections on human freedom in terms other than the abstractions of human potential and the rights of man . . . [they] transferred internal conflicts to a 'blank darkness', to conveniently bound and violently silenced black bodies' (1993b: 37, 38).

The stories that Morrison tells and the reasons she gives for telling them lend substance to the rather abstract issues that I have been trying to make visible. The themes I have picked out – of rememoration, in the sense of the reworking of memory and history that refigures our selfhood/identity, the recognition of the impossibility of forgetting and the need to come to terms with traumas and with the repressed and the displaced, the aporias of a critical ontology that uncovers the questions of debt and justice – they are all the themes buried at the heart of the two series of the refiguration of modernity with which I have been concerned, namely, the postmodern philosophical critique of our presentness and postcolonial interrogations. While they signal the ending of a particular history, my line of argument has been to point to unfinished business at the discursive level and at the level of the material life-world. I am arguing that the work that is left to be done must involve at the same time the questioning of being in its most fundamental aspects, and the transformation of the late-modern life-world.

This task has its method, its strategies and its stakes. At the level of method, one can point to the work of an ex-centred, nomadic critique that cannot but draw from the interrogations of modernity and of being from within Western thought, yet locate itself in relation to the domain-in-process of the postcolonial and the postmodern. Furthermore, the goals of settling accounts with history, without forgetting its investments in our identity and the everyday world, means that we need to turn to an investigation of the interiority of the 'self', going beyond the limits of psychoanalytic theory. I have in mind here the historicization of the 'interiority' of the psyche, reworking some themes from the later work of Merleau-Ponty and from Deleuze and Guattari. It includes the recognition of the effects of the embodied and polysemic situatedness of selves, while making a place for the desire for something that transcends this condition. A domain already exists where the sublime and liminal features of our beingness find expression, it is that of 'art', for instance, the case of music as understood by Morrison. I think it is important that critique recognizes what it can learn from that domain and borrows from the insights and the signifying practices there.

Concerning strategy, we need to bear in mind that the instrumentalization of the life-world and of forms of the administration of things and people has gone on undiminished, still today referred to as modernization: of political parties, of means of communication, of the apparatuses of education and health, and so on. This new, but not so new, governance, overdetermined by the modern '*techne*', is affiliated to mutations of capitalism – transnational, corporate, bandit – the combined effects of which bring about or perpetuate the unthinkable in the name of efficiency.

This last point brings up the question of the stakes of transfiguration, namely, the ethical commitment implicated in a (Levinasian) recognition of the primacy of the relation to the other, and the reality of that relation inscribed and historically sedimented in the material and symbolic world that gives meaning to each of us. There are implications here concerning justice and the standpoint of responsibility for the other regarding the ethical determinants of action. They have a bearing for the question of strategy, since one may well ask: how can there be any possible reconciliation between such an ethics and any form of exploitation, in other words, with any form of social relation that does not respect the being and the time of the other?

I take the narration of the postcolonial to implicate having to address all these problems, without the comfort of thinking they can be resolved simply by subtracting or eliminating the 'bad' aspects of either modernity or traditional cultures, leaving us with the good or acceptable side of contemporary times. Transfiguration takes us to places we have never been before.

References

Appiah, Kwame Anthony (1992) *In My Father's House*. New York: Methuen.
Bauman, Zygmunt (1992) *Intimations of Postmodernity*. London: Routledge.
Bhabha, Homi (1994) *The Location of Culture*. London: Routledge.
Butler, Judith (1993) *Bodies that Matter*. London: Routledge.
Derrida, Jacques (1982) *Margins of Philosophy*. Brighton: Harvester Wheatsheaf.

Derrida, Jacques (1993) *Les Spectres de Marx*. Paris: Galilee.

Elliott, Anthony (1996) *Subject to Ourselves: Social Theory, Psychoanalysis and Postmodernity*. Cambridge: Polity Press.

Fanon, Frantz (1970) *Black Skin White Masks*. London: Paladin.

Foucault, Michel (1991) 'What is Enlightenment', in Paul Rabinow (ed.), *The Foucault Reader*. Harmondsworth: Penguin.

Gilroy, Paul (1993a) *The Black Atlantic: Modernity and Double Consciousness*. London: Verso.

Gilroy, Paul (1993b) *Small Acts*. London: Serpent's Tail.

Habermas, Jürgen (1987) *The Philosophical Discourse of Modernity*. Cambridge: Polity Press.

Hall, Catherine (1992) *White, Male and Middle Class: Explorations in Feminism and History*. Cambridge: Polity Press.

Heidegger, Martin (1982) *Being and Time*. Oxford: Basil Blackwell.

Heidegger, Martin (1993) *Basic Writings* (ed. David F. Krell). London: Routledge.

hooks, bell (1992) *Black Looks*. London: Turnaround.

JanMohamed, Abdul R. (1983) *Manichean Aesthetics: The Politics of Literature in Colonial Africa*. Amherst, MA: University of Massachusetts Press.

Lacan, Jacques (1992) *The Ethics of Psychoanalysis*. London: Routledge.

Lacoue-Labarthe, Philippe (1990) *Heidegger, Art and Politics*. Oxford: Blackwell.

Lyotard, Jean-François (1988) 'Reécrire la modernité', in *Les Cahiers de Philosophie*, 5: 193–303.

Lyotard, Jean-François (1994) *Lessons on the Analytique of the Sublime*. Stanford, CA: Stanford University Press.

Mercer, Kobena (1993) *Welcome to the Jungle*. London: Routledge.

Minh-ha, Trinh (1989) *Woman, Native, Other: Writing Postcoloniality and Feminism*. Bloomington, IN: Indiana University Press.

Morrison, Toni (1987) *Beloved*. London: Chatto & Windus.

Morrison, Toni (1993a) 'Living memory, a meeting with Toni Morrison', in Paul Gilroy, *Small Acts*. London: Serpent's Tail.

Morrison, Toni (1993b) *Playing in the Dark*. New York: Vintage Books.

Nancy, Jean-Luc (1993) *The Birth to Presence*. Stanford, CA: Stanford University Press.

Ricœur, Paul (1988) *Time and Narrative* (vol. 3). Chicago: Chicago University Press.

Ricœur, Paul (1991) 'Narrative identity', in David Wood (ed.), *On Paul Ricœur*. London: Routledge. pp. 179–99.

Ricœur, Paul (1996) *The Hermeneutics of Action* (ed. R. Kearney). London: Sage.

Rose, Gillian (1992) *The Broken Middle*. Oxford: Blackwell.

Said, Edward (1978) *Orientalism*. London: Routledge.

Said, Edward (1993) *Culture and Imperialism*. London: Chatto & Windus.

Spivak, Gayatri C. (1988) *In Other Worlds*. New York and London: Routledge.

Suleri, Sara (1992) *The Rhetoric of English India*. Chicago: University of Chicago Press.

Viswanathan, Gauri (1989) *Masks of Conquest: Literary Study and British Rule in India*. New York: Columbia University Press.

West, Cornel (1993) *Race Matters*. New York: Vintage Books.

INDEX

Note: The letter n following a page number indicates a reference in the notes.

Printed in the United States
22450LVS00001B/15